WILLIAM FAULKNER

David Minter is professor of English at Emory University and dean of Emory College. He is the author of *The Interpreted Design as a Structural Principle in American Prose* and editor of *Twentieth-Century Interpretations of* Light in August.

WILLIAM FAULKNER
HIS LIFE AND WORK

DAVID MINTER

THE JOHNS HOPKINS UNIVERSITY PRESS
BALTIMORE AND LONDON

The Johns Hopkins University Press, Baltimore, Maryland 21218
The Johns Hopkins Press Ltd., London

Originally published, 1980
Second printing, 1981
Third printing, 1981
Johns Hopkins Paperbacks edition, 1982

Library of Congress Cataloging in Publication Data

Minter, David L.
    William Faulkner, his life and work.

    Bibliography: p. 261
    Includes index.
    1. Faulkner, William, 1897–1962. 2. Novelists,
American—20th century—Biography. I. Title.
PS3511.A86Z913   813'.52 [B]   80-13089
ISBN 0-8018-2347-1

FOR CAROLINE

remembering especially the Old Vicarage,
Grantchester, January-July 1976

CONTENTS

PREFACE

The Writing of a Life

MY FOCUS in this book is double. On one side, I recount Faulkner's life and try to convey the sense of it; on the other, I discuss his published and unpublished writings and try to illuminate them. Yet I do not present this book either as a compilation of new data on Faulkner's life or as a series of new readings of his novels. In relating his life, I draw on scores of essays, monographs, and books, particularly Joseph Blotner's *Faulkner* (1974), which is a storehouse of facts. Throughout I try to subordinate critical discussions of Faulkner's writings to the task of sketching the "mysterious armature" (to borrow Mallarmé's phrase) that binds Faulkner's life and art together.[1] My claim to the reader's attention is specific, then; and it stems from the story I try to tell—of deep reciprocities, of relations and revisions, between Faulkner's flawed life and his great art. Faulkner could be cold and careless as well as charming, cruel and ruthless as well as sensitive; there were profoundly destructive as well as profoundly creative forces at work within him. But his is not merely the story of a flawed life that yielded great art; it is the story of flaws and achievements that had reciprocal causes and reciprocal effects. I try, therefore, to present his life as a life of writing and his art as a writing or reconstituting of his life.

By now we know that Faulkner's artistic achievement was great and that his life was more varied than we had long supposed. In addition, we know that the relations between his life and his work were unusually complex, not only because he was never in any ordinary sense an autobiographical novelist, but also because his own judgment on the issue was divided. Early in his career, at about the time he discovered the imaginative kingdom that he named Yoknapatawpha and made his signature, Faulkner decided to make his art "a touchstone." Nothing would suffice, he felt, except the effort "to recreate between the covers of a book the world" he was already preparing to lose and mourn. So, hoping to capture his "world and the feeling of it," he began to write, only to discover that to be truly evocative, art "must be personal."[2] Near the end of his career, however, as he looked back, hoping to gain some perspective on his achievement, he seemed to see some strange figure performing incredible feats. He was amazed, he reported, not by the relations he saw, but by "what little connection" there seemed to be between the work he had done and the life he had lived.[3]

In an effort to disclose the ways in which Faulkner's evocations were personal, I work simultaneously with his art and his life, bringing the two into many different juxtapositions and conjunctions. Throughout I assume one thing that is obvious and one that is at least plausible: first, that Faulkner explored a historical space to which he brought talent, even as he created an imaginative space to which he brought genius; and second, that his talent provides ways of getting at his genius, just as his genius provides ways of getting at his talent. By examining the space he explored and the life he lived, I try to illuminate the world he imagined and the selves he created; by examining the world he imagined and the selves he created, I try to illuminate the space he explored and the life he lived. In the process, I recount some things that are familiar and emphasize some that are not. Among many moments, I try to locate initiatory and shaping experiences; among many guises, I try to discern deeper faces. Even if we believe, as Faulkner probably did, that a book is in some sense a "writer's secret life, the dark twin of a man," we know that all relations between a life lived and words written are problematic.[4] In Faulkner's case, they are particularly complicated—in part because his writings are diverse and uneven as well as frequently magnificent, and in part because he was never an easy person to know. All of his life, at least all of it that is recoverable, Faulkner was driven by conflicting urges: the urge to avoid life and the urge to explore it; the urge to disguise his thoughts and feelings in a thousand ways and the urge to disclose them in a single sentence. Out of this conflict, he fashioned a life of more than usual interest and an art of the rarest power.

Before he began to write and long before he became famous, Faulkner learned to protect his privacy. He often sought adventures, and he persistently forced himself to take great chances: he wanted to be "man in his sorry clay braving chance and circumstance." But he remained divided and elusive. In some moods he simply enjoyed being outrageous; in others he tended to be evasive and deceptive; in still others he became deliberately misleading. Almost as deep as the shyness he felt toward strangers lay an aristocratic distaste for public exposure except on his own terms. Although he had committed no major crimes, nor even many acts he thought shameful, he still did not like people prying into his life. But he was cautious not only with rivals and strangers but also with members of his own family and with people he thought of as friends—which suggests that the sources of his wariness go back to the beginning. Our earliest accounts of him vary remarkably, and what they imply, later recollections confirm: that he developed early both a need and a capacity for establishing a wide variety of carefully delimited relationships with the people around him.[5]

Since the implications of Faulkner's kind of cautious variety are subtle and diverse, we must come to them slowly, but both his need and his capacity for such variety can be located. During his earliest years he experienced an unusually strong sense of holistic unity with his family, and especially with his mother. From these years, he gathered a sense of his world as blessed and of himself as virtually omnipotent. Although he suffered no great trauma, he lost this double sense of well-being at an early age, and he found the experience painful. Troubled in part by the loss itself and in part by the feeling that those who had bequeathed blessedness had also destroyed it, he emerged from childhood determined to control his relations to his world. In the small, seemingly limited towns in which he grew up, he met a variety of people both within and beyond his prominent, extended family, and he had easy access to all of them. Moving among them as a sensitive, curious boy, he tended to approach them on their own terms, and as he did, different sides of his character began to emerge. But since he was wary and determined as well as curious, he kept himself to himself, not so much by pulling back as by cultivating highly stylized relationships with acquaintances, friends, and relatives alike—a habit that lasted a lifetime.

In the stories he was reading as well as in the manners he was acquiring, he discovered a variety of guises, roles, and masks that enabled him to keep people at a distance. Eventually a sense of urgency reinforced his sense of caution. From the twenties into the forties, he was driven by the feeling that he had great work to do; and even after his powers had begun to fade, he was dogged by the feeling that he had to remain a "man working." Yet the work he did, he did alone. When he was with other people, he tended to play—sometimes for the purpose of resting and sometimes for the purpose of putting "things over on people," but always for the purpose of protecting himself.[6] Spurred by wariness and urgency, then by wariness and weariness, he insisted upon delimiting and stylizing his associations with people. As a result, many who saw him regularly, or at least repeatedly, saw him partially and yet took the discernible part for the evasive whole. The reports we have, then, are confused as well as confusing, not only because some people have inevitably claimed to know him better than they did, nor merely because some friends and relatives have tried to settle old grievances, but also because he was a shy and troubled boy who became a shy and troubled man. Throughout his life—from the years of apprenticeship through the years of great innovation and achievement to the years of painful decline—his manners tended to be formal, his statements formulaic, and his life ceremonial.[7]

Like his life, Faulkner's art serves the double purpose of deception and expression. Unlike his life, which shows much change and little development, his art shows great development as well as great change. The same man who insisted on establishing fixed, stylized relations with other people insisted on cultivating fluid and intimate relations with his fictions and his characters. During his career as a poet, when his voice remained rather directly his own, his art tended to reiterate his manners: it was primarily a way of controlling and delimiting his interaction with his world.[8] As he began writing prose, however, he began mastering techniques and strategies that permitted greater displacement and disguise. His art not only became more supple and subtle as it became more indirect; it also became more personal. Though it remained his way of insisting on unity and harmony, it became his way of confronting the radical variety, fluidity, and power both of his world and of his own consciousness. The separations and losses that enter his poetry primarily as borrowed emotions and borrowed phrases soon began to shape his fiction. In the years of his greatness, he permitted even the most familiar and essential demarcations—clear beginnings and endings—to become ghostly. Although he continued to seek a formal, ceremonial life, he experimented in art with the dissolution of everything: one part of the radically venturesome quality of his writing derives from his willingness to brave the loss of all familiar procedures and the disintegration of all familiar forms. His fictions are replete with false starts, hesitations, and regressions; and they insist upon giving us, not beginnings, harmonies, and endings, but the sense of beginnings, the sense of harmonies, the sense of endings. In his novels and stories, forms flow, alter, disintegrate, displacing and replacing one another without end. Yet, if one part of the richness of his art comes from all the things it resists, withholds, and disguises, another part comes from all the things it explores, discloses, and bequeaths.

In trying to deal with this large tangle, I have made use of all of the information I could find, including Faulkner's interviews, essays, and letters as well as his poems, stories, and novels. Yet even in my more speculative moments, I have tried to wonder in a disciplined, responsible way, without exaggerating the bases of my speculations; and I have tried throughout to enhance as well as illuminate the reciprocities between Faulkner's great art and his flawed life. Although Faulkner's flaws were many, they lay heavy upon him, and he did wonderful things with them. I hope, therefore, that the reader will feel in reading, as I have in writing, not only respect and gratitude but tenderness too.

ACKNOWLEDGMENTS

I AM INDEBTED to the American Council of Learned Societies and the National Endowment for the Humanities for research grants that helped me to begin this study, and to Rice University for research grants that helped me to complete it. I am also indebted to the following institutions for permitting me to examine their Faulkner collections: the Alderman Library, University of Virginia, Charlottesville; the Beinecke Rare Book and Manuscript Library, Yale University; the Humanities Research Center, University of Texas, Austin; the Howard-Tilton Memorial Library, Tulane University, New Orleans; the New York Public Library; and the University of Mississippi Library. Members of the staff of Fondren Library, Rice University, as well as members of the staffs of each of the institutions named above, helped me on many occasions, and I am grateful to them.

I owe a special debt of gratitude to Jill Faulkner Summers, executrix of the William Faulkner Estate, for permission to quote from unpublished manuscripts, manuscript fragments, and letters of her father.

To Max Apple, Roy Bird, Jane Butler, Sue Davis, Terry Doody, Rose

Graham, Alan Grob, Karen Hanson, Dennis Huston, Walter Isle, Valerie Lussenhop, Wesley Morris, Robert Patten, Monroe Spears, Pamela Thompson, V. W. Topazio, and Katharine Wallingford I am grateful for help, advice, and encouragement.

Jerome Charyn, Charles Feidelson, John Irwin, and R. W. B. Lewis were kind enough to read different versions of this work. I am grateful for the encouragement they offered and the suggestions they made. Both the students in my graduate and undergraduate courses and the members of Baker College, where I was Master, 1973–1979, showed interest in this book for what must have seemed to them a long time. I remember them with fondness as well as gratitude. A part of chapter 5 appeared in slightly different form as "Faulkner, Childhood, and the Making of *The Sound and the Fury*" in the November 1979 issue of *American Literature*. I am grateful to the editors of that journal for their receptiveness.

Two children, Christopher and Frances, gave up much pleasure to my unsteady progress in writing this book. "I'll tell you one thing," Christopher said, watching in frustration as I worked to improve my ragged prose: "You'll never get through if you keep changing words on every page." I am glad now to share with him and Frances the completion of my work, and I do so with gratitude for the wonder as well as the patience and understanding of their lives.

Every page in this book has benefited from the care and intelligence of my wife, Caroline, who has also shared its ups and downs with gallantry and love. In dedicating this book to her, I have been reminded again that our largest debts are those we can least hope to repay.

Note to paperback edition: I want to thank Morris Warman for the use of his splendid photograph of William Faulkner. In addition I am indebted to a number of people who have written and talked to me about my book in an effort to encourage me and help me improve it, especially Victoria Fielden Black, Richard Brodhead, J. Douglas Canfield, John Graves, Donald Kartiganer, Richard H. King, Hubert McAlexander, Hal Morris, Carolyn Porter, Michael Rogin, Louis Rubin, Bernard Schilling, and Floyd Watkins. And I owe a special debt to Joan Williams for her kind response to my book as a whole and especially my use of her novel, *The Wintering*.

WILLIAM FAULKNER

The life of every man is a diary in which he means to write one story, and writes another. . . .

J. M. Barrie,
The Little Minister

A book is the writer's secret life, the dark twin of a man. . . .

William Faulkner,
Mosquitoes

There is no sun without shadow, and it is essential to know the night.

Albert Camus,
The Myth of Sisyphus

ONE 1897-1918

A Small Boy and a Giant in the Earth

William Faulkner was born in New Albany, Mississippi, on 25 September 1897, the first child of Maud and Murry Falkner.[1] Shortly after his first birthday, he and his parents moved to Ripley. A few days before he turned five, they moved to Oxford, where he spent the rest of his childhood, all of his youth, and most of his adult life. Near Oxford, in a sanatorium on a hill outside Byhalia, another small Mississippi town, he died in 1962, on July 6, the birthday of the first of the Mississippi Falkners—his great-grandfather, the Old Colonel, William Clark Falkner.

In addition to possessing a suggestive symmetry, these simple facts hold several pertinences. More than any other major American writer of our time, including Robert Frost, Faulkner is associated with a region. He is our great provincial. And although his life was considerably more expansive than the facts of its beginning and ending suggest—although he lived in Canada, New Orleans, Hollywood, and Virginia; although he lived briefly and visited frequently in New York; although he traveled through Europe in the twenties and around the world in the fifties—it was with a sense of place that he began.

The Falkners lived east of the Delta, amid the hills of north Mississippi. The flat, black land of the Delta was the richest in the state. But the soil of the hill country was also strong, and since floods seldom threatened it, its crops were more predictable. The glory of the region, Faulkner later remarked, was that God had done more for it than man had yet done to it. In 1842, when the Old Colonel first saw it, it was still frontier. In the early 1900s, when William was a boy, the last of its Indians moved to Oklahoma. Not far from New Albany, Ripley, and Oxford there were still places where the hills, trees, and rivers, the coon, fox, and deer, even large cats and bear seemed undisturbed.[2] Through most of his life, Faulkner studied his region with care. In books by Francis Parkman, he read about the broader conquest of a continent. But in addition to ten volumes of Parkman, his library contained scores of books on the exploration and history, the geography, vegetation, and wildlife of the land crossed by the Natchez Trace.[3] Long before he was grown, he was a skilled woodsman and hunter. The land he walked as a boy and studied as a man he also came to love in an inclusive, unequivocal way. To its beauties and perils, even to its dust and heat, he extended the process of naming that became his art.

In addition to being strongly regional, the consciousness that dominates Faulkner's fiction is strongly historical. In 1900, less than a century separated Mississippi from its prehistory. Yet history, particularly the immediate past, was already a major preoccupation there, in part because the southern dream of transplanting the life of the English squire and landed gentleman possessed a historical bias, and in part because much "blood hot and strong for living, pleasuring" had already soaked back into Mississippi's soil,[4] but primarily because the Civil War had inflicted a double burden. In the North and West, people had emerged from battle ready to pursue progress and prosperity with redoubled vigor: what the power they had displayed made plausible, the righteousness they had served made appropriate. In the South, on the other hand, recovery came slowly—not only because the war had inflicted great damage and division, but also because recovery called for adjustments that betrayed the Old South's agrarian dream, giving rise to guilt even as it promised deliverance. Together the memory of failure and the sense of guilt undermined both confidence and hope. For what they implied was not large-scale progress and prosperity, but more failure and more punishment.[5]

Since William Faulkner grew up in small villages as a member of an extended and prominent family, personal and familial experiences intensified the lessons his region inculcated. "In a city," Ezra Pound

once remarked, "visual impressions succeed each other, overlap, over-
cross, they are 'cinematographic'"; in a village, he continued, people
possess a sense of sequence and shared knowledge. Because they know
who did what before, during, and after the Revolution, their life "is
narrative"[6] —which is what Faulkner's early life was. The small villages
in which his family lived encouraged excursions: it was easy to get out of
them into the big woods. But they also encouraged a feeling of involvement, even of intimacy. For Faulkner as for Nathaniel Hawthorne, the
story of region was inseparable from the story of family. The sense of
being entangled in a great web of persons and events, centering on family
but extending beyond it, is everywhere present in Faulkner's fiction,
from the Sartorises to the Compsons to the McCaslins.

If most modern Americans feel related to no specific place, group,
or time, but "to everywhere, to everybody, and to always"; if as a result,
finding "in environment no confirmation of their identity," they feel
abstracted and disconnected; and if in this we see the perils of newness,
freedom, and mobility, we also see the opposite of what William Faulkner
experienced as a boy.[7] With the sense of place and family pressing on him
from all sides, it was other perils that he learned. Deeply exposed to the
play of associations with creatures living and dead, he became acutely
aware of the force of human heredity and the flow of human generations.
Some of his characters are so full of names and places, the dates of births,
deaths, victories, and defeats of relatives and neighbors, that they feel
themselves less individuals than commonwealths: almost without knowing
it they come to view their lives as one perpetual instant in which the life of
self, family, and region mingle. Others of his characters, feeling both responsible and helpless, are doubly discomforted. In some moments their ancestors appear as gigantic heroes, larger and more admirable than they have any
hope of becoming; in others they appear as sinister shadows associated with
injustice, violence, and lust, even with inhumanity, fratricide, and incest.

Named by his grandfather, J. W. T. Falkner, for his great-grandfather,
William Clark, and for his father, Murry Cuthbert, William Cuthbert
Faulkner came early to feel himself branded. He was not only "a Falkner
of Mississippi," nor merely the firstborn son of the firstborn son of the
firstborn son of the founder, himself a firstborn son; he was also the
chosen namesake of the founder, which is to say, of a giant. In his extended family were several people who had lived large lives, including
a great-uncle named John Wesley Thompson. A forceful and violent
as well as successful man, Thompson helped the Old Colonel make his
start and partly reared the Old Colonel's first son, J. W. T. Falkner.
But it was William Clark Falkner who dominated the family's imagination. Telling stories about him was more than a pastime; presided over
by the unvanquished aunts whom Faulkner later immortalized, it was

a ritual in which everyone participated. For surviving members of the Partisan Rangers, the second of the Old Colonel's two Civil War regiments, the family still sponsored reunions where tales of his exploits were told and retold. Several family servants regularly recounted his adventures. At least one, "Uncle Ned" Barnett, wore frock coats, broadcloth suits, and high-crowned hats, as though to evoke the Old Colonel's sartorial splendor. To the servants who had known him, W. C. Falkner remained "Old Master" long after he was dead. Like the family and their neighbors, the servants called J. W. T. Falkner "the Young Colonel," or even "the Colonel," but they knew that he had fought in no wars, that his glory, like his title, was inherited.[8]

Planter, lawyer, soldier, writer, politician, and railroad entrepreneur, William Clark Falkner was in fact a man of many parts.[9] His life seems not so much to have touched as to have embraced the three major legends of the South: the Cavalier Legend, about family origins and personal style; the Plantation Legend, about "the golden age" before the war; and the Redeemers Legend, about the glorious unseating of the carpetbaggers. There was more than enough in his adventures to keep inventive descendants busy for years. Like the Sartorises of *Flags in the Dust*, the novel in which Faulkner first drew directly on the Old Colonel's exploits, the Falkners told and retold the story of their founder, letting it grow "richer and richer."[10]

That story began with a boy of seventeen arriving in Mississippi in 1842, following a solitary journey from Missouri through Tennessee. Accounts of the motives behind the journey vary. In one family story, the pattern comes from the Bible—having seriously injured a younger brother in a fight, the boy flees as an outcast. In another, the pattern comes from the nineteenth century—young, ambitious, and fatherless, the boy fearlessly sets out to make his fortune.[11] Given the man the boy became, the life he lived, both patterns are useful. For the Old Colonel was a violent man; and though he seems genuinely to have tired of it, violence pursued him as persistently and successfully as he pursued fame and fortune. Sooner or later, everything he touched—law and politics, railroads and land, pamphlets and novels—brought him fame, made him money, and surrounded him in controversy.

From the Civil War he emerged a decorated hero. Dubbed "The Knight of the Black Plume," he won praise from several of the most famed southern Cavaliers, including General P. G. T. Beauregard, General J. E. Johnston, and Colonel J. E. B. Stuart. But even in heroism he was controversial. After he led them to glory at Manassas, the men of his first regiment, the Magnolia Rifles, turned on him by choosing John M. Stone their commander. The Old Colonel, it seems, was too harsh, too ruthless, too reckless. Recouping, he formed a second regiment, the

Partisan Rangers, and continued to fight. Though frustrated in his efforts to regain his early glory, he managed during the last years of the war to make money, apparently as a blockade runner. Emerging from the war fairly prosperous as well as controversial, he built a railroad, wrote novels, enlarged his fame, and won election to the legislature, only to be shot down in the streets of Ripley by a former business partner named Richard Thurmond.[12]

With their move to Ripley in 1898, the Murry Falkners returned to the family's first Mississippi center. Before the Old Colonel's death in 1889, J. W. T. Falkner had moved his family to Oxford. But the family's founder had lived in Ripley from the 1840s until his death, and it still bore his mark. There his ornate mansion still stood; there an eight-foot likeness sculpted in Carrara marble towered above his grave; there his railroad was still *the* railroad. For several decades Ripley had provided him a nearly perfect scene; for several years, it did almost as much for his grandson, primarily because of the railroad. Of the family's several business interests, only the Gulf & Chicago appealed to Murry. Although most buildings, particularly schools and churches, seemed to him confining, he liked railroad stations, where women came and went while men sat and talked. As a boy, he had enjoyed watching trains and listening to their whistles; as a man, he enjoyed swapping tales about hunting and fishing or about the distant places that trains brought to mind.[13] After two unhappy years at the University of Mississippi, he left school to become a fireman on the railroad; later he worked as an engineer and conductor. Moving to New Albany, he supervised the line's passenger service; with the move to Ripley, he became its treasurer.

A large, active man, Murry found both self-expression and close relationships difficult. So long as conversation remained casual, staying within familiar bounds, he remained composed and polite. But disputes, even free-flowing discussions, made him feel awkward and inadequate. At home he established a rule against conversing during meals.[14] With his father, too, he was uncomfortable, perhaps because he sensed, as others did, that his talents and ambitions fell short of his father's expectations—that he was at once too restless and too easily satisfied. At least one reminder, his younger brother, was close at hand. A successful student all the way through the University of Mississippi, J. W. T. Falkner, Jr., would soon follow his father into law, banking, and politics. Hoping to outdo his brother and please his father, Murry tried to curb his restlessness and to show more ambition. After his marriage in 1896, he began accepting larger responsibilities and planning for the future. With the railroad showing a good profit, he began investing his money. Soon he was able to buy part of a drugstore in Ripley and all of a farm west of it. Both his father and his wife, who also harbored large ambitions, seemed pleased with his

performance. For himself, he retained the habit of getting away—out to
the farm or off into the woods. Pinned down and crowded, he became
violent; in one fight, he very nearly lost his life. Free to roam familiar
woods or unexplored river bottoms, his energies found tasks of their own.
Riding horses and training dogs, fishing and hunting were things he felt
easy doing. For a time he thought that he had found in Ripley a happy
ground where he could meet the expectations shared by his father and his
wife without giving up the excursions he needed.

For Murry and his family, then, the years in Ripley seemed almost
ideal. A small, gifted woman, Maud Butler Falkner preferred reading,
painting, and going to church to hiking, riding, and hunting. And since
she was opinionated and outspoken as well as pious, she tended to be
blunt. Murry knew that she had agreed to marry him only a month
after his first big promotion with the Gulf & Chicago; and he knew that
she expected large success. Her refinement, her talk of books, art, and
prayer, might vex him, just as his crudity, particularly the profanity
and whiskey that went with hunting, might offend her. But the tension
between them was not severe, and it was too familiar in the life around
them to be disturbing. During the early years of their marriage, when his
name was making them prominent and his position was making them
prosperous, they accepted life together with ease. Following their marriage
in November 1896, their first son, William, was born in September 1897;
their second, Murry, Jr., called Jack, in June 1899; their third, J. W. T.
III, called Johncy, in September 1901. After Murry's appointment as
treasurer, they began to share the expectation that he would soon replace
his father as president of the railroad.

As it turned out, J. W. T. Falkner, the family's patriarch, had plans
of his own, and they did not call for being replaced by anyone, particularly his eldest son. After his own father's death, he had moved the
family's center to Oxford and turned its attention toward banks, land,
and politics. For him the railroad was more a bother than a passion.
Tired of running it himself, he had no intention of turning it over to
Murry, in part because he had limited confidence in Murry's abilities,
and in part because he wanted capital to support other ventures. In 1902,
four years after Murry's move to Ripley, J. W. T. Falkner announced his
intention to sell the Gulf & Chicago Railroad Company for $75,000. He
had given Murry his start, and he would continue sponsoring him; in
many ways, he was a generous father. But he kept his own counsel, and
he assumed that a son should do what his father's interests required.
Regarding those interests as shared, he seems scarcely to have noticed the
privileges he claimed for himself. All of his life, Murry had been dutiful,
subordinate, uncomplaining. For as long as his father lived (until 1922),
he remained just that, making imposition easy. At home, where Murry

decried his loss, his sons learned early that the railroad had been his "first and lasting love." But to his father, Murry did not complain.[15]

Finding their life disrupted, Murry and Maud prepared to make a new start. Murry's father thought they should move to Oxford, where he had a law practice, several businesses, and a bank, and where he and his wife, Sallie Murry, had just built a fine home called "The Big Place." Murry and his family were welcome to the house his parents had vacated, and in Oxford he was sure to find work. At first, resisting his father's suggestion, Murry played with the idea of borrowing money and buying the railroad himself, a plan Maud may have favored.[16] As difficulties arose, however, Murry's resolve began to waver. Soon his thoughts turned toward Texas. Preceding the Old Colonel lay a string of restless men who had moved on to make new starts—one had journeyed from Scotland to South Carolina; another from South Carolina to North Carolina; another from North Carolina across Tennessee to Missouri. The Old Colonel himself had come to Mississippi hungry and penniless. Recalling novels about cowboys, the only books he had ever enjoyed reading, Murry decided to move to Texas and become a rancher.[17]

Dreading the move and doubting its outcome, Maud Falkner vetoed Murry's plan. Her early life had become a struggle when her father deserted her and her mother, leaving them penniless to make their own start. Working hard, Maud had managed to graduate from a small state college and make a promising marriage. She had no intention of moving hundreds of miles to begin again among strangers. If she and Murry stayed where the Falkners were prominent, he could get plenty of help. Despite her small size—she was barely five feet tall— and her fine features, Maud possessed more energy and far more determination than her large husband. Outliving him by twenty years, she retained to the end her erect posture and her sharp opinions. On her deathbed she talked with her eldest son of a heaven where she would not have to see the husband she said she had never liked.[18] In 1902 she was only a little less blunt.

Feeling betrayed by his father and his wife, Murry Falkner toyed with the idea of forcing a crisis, only to have his will fail. Sending his family by train, he loaded their possessions in a wagon and drove alone toward Oxford. Both his wife and his father had now assumed major roles in the great disappointment of his life. As time passed without his finding any way to redirect his life or avenge his losses, his bitterness deepened. In the scattered rages of which his father knew little, his wife and sons much, he recalled not only the railroad he had lost but the ranch he had never possessed. He and Maud had had three children between September 1897 and September 1901, but their fourth and last son, Dean, was not born until 1907, by which time their mutual resentment and mistrust were deep, frozen, and familiar.

To the rest of the family, the move to Oxford seemed all gain. Arriving after dark, on a September evening in 1902, near William's fifth birthday, they moved into a comfortable house near "The Big Place," the center of family activities. A town of nearly two thousand, Oxford was several times larger and considerably more varied than Ripley. It was the county seat of Lafayette County and the home of the University of Mississippi. Race and class influenced one's language, manners, food, and clothing, as well as one's freedom and opportunity. Yet, despite the lines that separated and defined them, the people of Oxford found interaction easy. All of the Falkners thought themselves aristocrats; they could be stiff, proud, overbearing. But they were not snobs, and they enjoyed much casual intercourse with every segment of Mississippi society. A few blocks north of the family home, the courthouse stood in the middle of the town square, surrounded by stores that sported new boardwalks. On Saturdays the square was the scene of horse auctions and other free-wheeling transactions. A few blocks south and west of the house, there were woods where the Falkner boys liked to play. Ten or fifteen miles north, at a point where the Tippah River joined the Tallahatchie, the Falkners owned a large two-room cabin, called the "Club House," where they hunted coons, squirrels, fox, and deer. Thirty miles west was the storied and game-rich Delta where another prominent family, the Stones, had a hunting cabin. A few miles south was a river called Yocona in Oxford and named Yoconapatafa on older maps.[19]

For William and his brothers, Oxford was an almost perfect world: it provided adventures yet permitted easy mastery and easy escape. To their father, on the other hand, it brought hardship and bitterness. With help, Murry always managed to find work and so was saved the indignity of failing to support his family. But the relative independence he had known in Ripley, and the hope, died quickly. At first he directed the grading of North Street. Later he ran several businesses, including a hardware store and a livery stable. But few of his jobs held any intrinsic interest for him; even the best of them, the livery stable, failed to match the magic of the railroad. Although his family's status guaranteed him work and so helped to make his life more bearable, it also made his failure conspicuous. As he moved from job to job, finding no place of his own, he became widely regarded as the failed descendant of a lengendary grandfather and a successful father. Soon even his younger brother was outshining him. After fifteen years of shifting around, trying one thing and then another, Murry accepted appointment as secretary and business manager of the University of Mississippi. In this, the last of several positions arranged by his father, he served dutifully for ten years, only to be dismissed in a political shuffle. By then, even the hills and woods had lost most of their shimmer. Much of his time he spent alone, sitting in silence, as though he had simply "got tired of living." In 1932 he "just gave up" and died.[20]

Occasional eruptions excepted, Murry Falkner kept most of his bitterness to himself, even when he was still young. Although it was quick to sour him, his reversal of fortune was slow to diminish his love of horses, dogs, and excursions. He enjoyed taking his sons down to the livery stable and out into the woods. Before entrusting them to the public schools, he taught each of them the things he knew best—how to ride, track, hunt, and fish. At night at the Club House, away from his wife and his father, with whiskey to drink, some of his wariness faded. Surrounded by his sons, he told tales of the wolves and panthers he had hunted and the railroad he had loved. Yet even on these occasions, his sons remained uncertain of his affection. More than his bitterness, it was his need and capacity for love that he kept to himself. None of his sons remembered him as "an easy man to know" or an easy man to love. With them, as with others, he remained distant and cautious. Looking back, they thought of him as a cold man whose "capacity for affection was limited."[21]

Since he knew the woods best, Murry Falkner talked of them most. But he liked sports, which he also thought of as manly; and he took pride in his sons' exploits. In his second attempt at the eleventh grade, then the final year of high school, William started as quarterback on the football team. In the summers, baseball was his game, pitcher or shortstop his position. According to one of his playmates, he was "by far the best player among the boys who played together those summers."[22] Later he turned to tennis, golf, and sailing. Yet he began early to feel disadvantaged, particularly in his father's eyes, and primarily because of his size. He was always small for his age. Soon even his younger brothers, who were built more like their father, were taller and heavier than he. William's height and small frame, the shape of his head, the color of his eyes, all owed more to his mother than to his father, a fact clear to his family even when he was still young. As tension between his father and mother increased, his father came more and more to regard him as his mother's son. Sometimes in rough teasing, his father called him "Snake-Lips."[23]

More than fine features, however, it was lack of size and strength, and specifically lack of ability to fight, that preoccupied William, early and late. In 1953 he suggested that Sherwood Anderson had always wished that he was "more imposing-looking." It was, he suggested, because Anderson was "a short man that probably all of his boyhood had wished he were bigger so he could fight better, defend himself," that he made his characters tall.[24] In the early 1930s, when one of his brothers complimented him on his recent success in writing books and in rebuilding Rowan Oak, he tied his large achievements to his small size: "Well," he replied, "as big as you are, you can march anywhere you want, but when you're little you have to push."[25] Unable simply to march, yet feeling tested and driven, William pushed, even when he was very young. Brothers and friends alike remember him as instigating, directing, leading. It was characteristic of him that he wanted to be the quarterback in football, the pitcher or shortstop in baseball.

In several notable respects, however, all of the Falkner boys were children of their mother. Phil Stone, who knew the family well, particularly William, thought that all of the boys felt their mother's strong domination and that all of them feared and resented it.[26] Maud was a pretty woman with fine, distinct features. In contrast to the light blue of the Falkners', her eyes were so dark that their pupils and irises seemed to merge. As it came down from her forehead and up from her small chin and mouth, her face seemed to converge on her eyes, stressing their beauty. Sometimes laughing, always penetrating, they were clear, bright, intense, determined. Despite the difficult years following her father's desertion of her mother, she had persisted in her ambition to graduate from college. From that experience she emerged valuing education and admiring the determination that had got her what she wanted.

An avid reader as well as a gifted painter, Maud taught all of her sons to read before sending them to the public schools. Systematic in her approach, she moved them from early primers through *Grimm's Fairy Tales* to the classics, including Dickens, keeping them well ahead of their classmates. In the process she conveyed, as one of them later put it, "an abiding love for literature" and a sense of its power to move readers to tears or "unabashed delight." In addition, she conveyed a clear set of expectations: that they learn quickly and well; that they absorb the conventional pieties; they they live with stoic resolve; and that they give her their devotion. Although warmer and more affectionate than her taciturn husband, she practiced restraint, and she was capable of severe sternness. As the years passed and her husband began to make less money and drink more whiskey, she held fast to her convictions. "Don't Complain—Don't Explain" was the message she hung in red above the kitchen stove.[27]

Although he learned games quickly, William took greater pleasure in activities that rewarded imagination more than size and strength. In nearby woods, such as those behind the old Shegog Place, which he later bought, he devised new versions of old games by revising rules and redefining boundaries. Together he, his brothers, his cousins, and their playmates tracked small animals or each other; searched for the rare blue egg of the China bird; or played some variety of war or hide-and-seek.[28] Other pleasures he associated with attics, porches, and rainy days, and with his maternal grandmother, Leila Butler, whom he called Damuddy. Never more than marginally interested in the Old Colonel,

Damuddy shared her daughter's hatred of the foul language and the drinking that went with hunting and fishing. Deeply pietistic, she seems in fact to have had little use for men in general, perhaps in part because one of them deserted her, forcing her to relinquish a scholarship for studying sculpture in Rome. But she knew how to draw and paint as well as sculpt, and what she knew, she loved.

A frequent visitor in her daughter's home, she moved in to stay in 1902, bringing her easel with her. Although her presence probably did nothing to ease tension between Murry and Maud, it did much to enrich the experience of their children. In William, the small boy who resembled his mother, she took special interest. For him she carved a nine-inch doll that she dressed in a policeman's uniform, complete with brass buttons. Giving it an Irish name, Patrick O'Leary, William took it to the family attic, where he spent rainy days creating stories about it. Aided by Damuddy's instruction and his own quickness, he soon learned to draw well. Sometimes in the years just before her death on 1 June 1907, Damuddy helped him direct his friends in building miniature villages in the family's front yard. One participant reports that, using sticks, grass, stones, and glass, "they built walks, streets, churches, and stores. Both William and his grandmother were good at improvising and using materials at hand. . . . William was the leader in these little projects. He had his grandmother's artistic talents for making things, and his imagination was obvious even then."[29]

If, in the small boy who liked to draw pictures and build villages, we see the figure of much that was to be, in the boy who was becoming restless in school, we see signs of things more immediate. William began the first grade in 1905, on his eighth birthday, skipped the second, and remained an excellent student through the third and fourth grades. Although he showed special interest in drawing, painting, and reading, he received good marks in all subjects, including deportment. At home, he performed his assigned chores with no more·than ordinary prompting. In the fourth grade, however, when he was ten, his manner began to change. He did what he had to do to make the honor roll at school and to avoid trouble at home, but he became more recalcitrant and more silent.[30]

Never challenged or in any real sense educated by Oxford's public schools, William appears, even during his early, exemplary years, to have been the willing victim of a situation that left him free to learn from his father and mother, or from Damuddy and other tellers of tales. What changed slightly in the fourth grade and emphatically in the fifth was not so much the scenes and sources of his education as his desire to please his parents. He ceased to care. Sometimes he simply played hooky; even when he attended school, he was quiet, withdrawn, inattentive. Sitting at his desk, ignoring what was going on around him, he read, drew, or wrote what he pleased. Standing on the playground, he seemed to live wholly within himself. He was "a little fellow," one classmate remarked. "On the school ground he stood around a great deal," listening rather than talking, watching rather than playing.[31]

William's move from compliance and participation toward silence and stillness was partial. Even later, when he began dramatizing the role of the observer, he continued to move back and forth between participation and withdrawal. Sometimes he was active and forthcoming, playing several sports and engaging in varied experiments. Three of his projects—one involving wings made of corn shucks and two involving gun powder, which he used to produce a flash for a picture and to fire an old Confederate pistol found in the woods—very nearly cost him and his brothers dearly. Still, the change in him was definite and, as it turned out, lasting. The decline that began during his third year in school persisted through two rounds with the eleventh grade. He never graduated. Toward the end he continued only in order to play football in the fall and baseball in the spring.[32]

Given his father's indifference to education, the burden of William's truancy and inattention fell largely on his mother. She did what she could, encouraging, cajoling, threatening. William, a brother reports, stood quietly, seeming to listen, then went his own way without trying to explain or defend his behavior. About the time his truancy began to distress his mother, his mounting aversion to work began to disturb his father. A few of his schemes for avoiding chores must have seemed amusing even at the time and even to his father. During the winter of 1910 he enticed Fritz McElroy to carry coal for him by concocting a continuing story, released serially, as it were—which he terminated each day at a point calculated to bring his larger, stronger friend back for more. Not all his schemes were clever, however, and several were annoying, particularly when he put his inventiveness to concocting lies rather than fanciful tales. "It got so when Billy told you something," a cousin recalls, "you never knew if it was the truth or just something he'd made up."[33]

In other senses, as well, stories began filling his days. At home he spent much of his time reading. By age ten, when his resistance to school commenced, he was reading Shakespeare, Dickens, Balzac, and Conrad. At the stove in his father's office he watched and listened as his father's friends drank whiskey and swapped tales. At the courthouse he listened to old men tell stories about the War. At the fireplace in Mammy Caroline Barr's cabin he found another place to listen. Born into slavery in 1840, Mammy Callie, as the Falkner boys called her, was more than sixty years old when the Murry Falkners moved to Oxford. Small like Maud Falkner, Mammy Callie could be stern and formidable. But her capacity for feeling and expressing love lasted her a century, surviving great hardship, and it enabled her to give William tenderness and affection as well as entertainment. Unable to read or write, she remembered scores of stories about the old days and the old people: about slavery, the War, the Klan, and the Falkners. Years later, amid the malaise of Hollywood, Faulkner repeated some of her stories about the lives and habits of small animals, and so shared with others the wonder and delight she had shared with him.[34] Earlier, secure in her presence, he crossed from listening to speaking, and so began telling tales of his own—versions, one judges, of those he was hearing at his father's livery stable, at the courthouse, or on the porch of "The Big Place," his other regular stop. There he played with Sallie Murry, a cousin who seemed almost like a sister to him, and there he listened, while his grandfather told stories about the Old Colonel. Now and then, having listened quietly, he was permitted to handle the Old Colonel's cane, books, and watch, even the broken pipe that had fallen from his lips on the day he was shot. As mementoes of these occasions, which clearly meant much to both of them, his grandfather gave him replicas of one of his handsome vests and of his watch fob, making him, William said later, "the proudest boy that ever breathed." Soon he began smoking a pipe of his own, a habit that lasted a lifetime.[35]

William may at times have felt, as Quentin Compson does in *Absalom, Absalom!*, that "his very body was an empty hall echoing with sonorous" names, that he was "a barracks filled with stubborn back-looking ghosts." Perhaps no boy could have heard so much so often without occasionally asking, "Why tell me about it? What is it to me?" But in fact he seems to have sought more than to have endured the stories. An acquaintance who knew him for many years once remarked that he had obviously heard every version of every story and had obviously remembered all of them. This remarkable retentiveness, for scenes, events, characters, even words and nuances, became one of his defining qualities.[36] In the seventh grade he began studying Mississippi history, particularly that part pertaining to the Civil War. Years later his library included the works of Douglas Southall Freeman and Bruce Catton on the Civil War, Calvin Brown on the *Archeology of Mississippi*, even the *Mississippi Provincial Archives*. In 1932, following the death of his father, he became the head of his clan and so inherited the massive family Bible, in which having made all the obligatory entries, he also recorded as much of his family's genealogy as he could discover. But most of what he knew about his region and its past, certainly about his family and its past, he learned from "old tales and talking"[37]—a fact that helps to account not only for the conversational form of a novel like *Absalom, Absalom!*, but also for the remarkable fluidity, the fundamental seamlessness, of time as we experience it in his fiction, where history always includes present and future as well as past.[38]

As the months drifted by and William continued moving into and out of stillness and silence, resisting the pressures put on him to comply, the change became conspicuous. Observing the observer, people termed him lazy, "almost inert." Sometimes he joined the old men of Oxford on the town square, complete, after 1907, with a monument to the county's Civil War heroes. There he sat or stood motionless, quiet, as though held fast by some inner scene or some inner sense of himself. Seeing him alone, still and silent on the playground or the square, people began to think him "quair," a judgment his family, and particularly his father, came increasingly to share. Murry Falkner could understand almost any kind of aversion to school, and he liked a good story as well as the next man. But he was confounded by the way William practiced stillness and silence and evaded chores and tasks; by the way he read as well as listened to stories and wrote as well as read poetry. As the seasons came and went Murry's consternation deepened, particularly when he heard that William had begun to stand silently watching while other boys danced with his girlfriend, Estelle Oldham, to the music of W. C. Handy.[39]

By 1916, when it became clear that William's second attempt at eleventh grade was going the way of his first, worry spread from father to grandfather. What could one do with a boy who acted like some kind of intellectual and yet declined to graduate from high school? Phil Stone, another local intellectual, had at least made himself an honors student. Determined to turn things around, the Young Colonel made his grandson a bookkeeper in his bank. What better place to teach him the value of exacting work and hard-earned money? In apparent compliance, William spent several hours each day cooped up in the bank. Later he joked about these months: "Quit school and went to work in grandfather's bank. Learned the medicinal value of his liquor. Grandfather thought it was the janitor. Hard on the janitor."[40] Still, although it gave him experience that he could later turn over to a letter-writer named Byron, his time at the bank did nothing to settle him down. At no point did he apply himself, even reluctantly, to his job. Working for money, he decided, was contemptible. As he began consorting with known drinkers, even the "town drunks," his mother's anxiety mounted; she knew as much as she wished to know about people who sought release from difficult or unpleasant situations by drinking whiskey. When William began spending less time at the bank and more in activities emanating from the University of Mississippi, she and the rest of the family silently acquiesced.[41]

Earlier, not long after her eldest son began his struggle against school and work, Maud Falkner had noticed a slight stoop in his shoulders. Determined to teach him to walk as his great-grandfather was said to have walked, with his head high and his back rod-straight, she began each day by lacing him into a canvas vest that straightened his shoulders. His cousin, Sallie Murry, found a similar brace so uncomfortable and restrictive that she regularly looked for someone willing to loosen the laces across her back. William wore his for nearly two years with scarcely a murmur. Later he resumed the games—baseball, football, tennis—that the shoulder brace had precluded.[42] In the meantime, it fit, even reinforced, his experiments with stillness and silence, in which his need for self-denial and self-punishment as well as self-dramatization found expression. One problem that clearly troubled William had to do with size. As his friends grew, he felt more and more disadvantaged, and as he felt more disadvantaged, he experimented more concertedly with withdrawal. At one time or another, he practiced denying himself almost everything—not only baseball and football but hunting and dancing as well. As though to accentuate the fate of being small, he began wearing tight clothes and limiting his breakfast to toast and black coffee.[43] But it was more than being small that troubled him; it was shame and guilt born of witnessing conflicts between his parents to which he could find no acceptable response.

As the decline triggered by the family's move to Oxford deepened, Murry Falkner became widely regarded not only as a failure but also as a drinker. Occasional drunkenness was a familiar part of being male and Falkner, just as bearing it was a familiar part of being female and Falkner. But as Murry's sense of failure and resentment deepened, he drank more, and as he did, Miss Maud's resistance hardened. She genuinely abhorred drinking. At times, particularly when Murry became loud and abusive, she may well have felt that he drank not so much to get away as to punish her. In any case, as he extended his role by drinking more, she extended hers by dramatizing his failure, his weakness, his guilt. Other Falkners, including the Young Colonel, had made taking "the cure" at the Keeley Institute near Memphis another family tradition. In its established mode, "the cure" resembled a short vacation. Under Miss Maud's supervision, it became a rite of punishment and expiation. She not only accompanied her husband, she took her sons with her as witnesses. While their wayward father dried out, William and his brothers waited with their mother in facilities provided by the Institute. When, following several days' treatment, Murry emerged pale, debilitated, and humbled, the family returned to Oxford together by train.[44]

Like most children, William had experienced nights "of loneliness and nameless sorrow," when temporary separation from his parents made him feel permanently lost and forsaken.[45] But the conflicts epitomized by the journeys to the Keeley Institute almost certainly aroused anxiety that ran deep. In years to come he avoided referring to these scenes yet persisted in repeating them. Like his father, he learned most of what there was to know about drinking whiskey and taking "the cure." Unlike his father, who eventually managed to control his drinking and avoid the Keeley Institute, William never managed to quit. Despite many periods of control and a few of sustained abstinence, he went on drinking. At times he associated heavy drinking with triumph and release—with feeling "bigger, wiser, taller." At others, he associated it with clairvoyant, visionary states; with deliberate pursuit of suffering; or with some interface between consciousness and oblivion, life and death.[46] But he always associated withdrawal with pain and humiliation, and, more tellingly, with the need for gentle affection that he otherwise found almost impossible to express. Many years later, in one of the darkest periods of his life, he submitted to a series of shock treatments, after which his doctor found him almost childlike in his longing for tenderness.[47]

His more immediate response to the scenes that surrounded his father's drinking was to move away from his father and toward his mother. In his fiction, he characteristically mingles compassion with judgment. Even his most terrible villains, Popeye in *Sanctuary*, Percy Grimm in *Light in August*, he treats with considerable sympathy. Toward almost defeated humanity, he shows particular tenderness. During his youth and early manhood, however, he reserved most of his sympathy for his mother, most of his judgment for his father. Addressing his father as "Sir," he remained outwardly respectful, but he thought of him as an embarrassing failure and a dull man.[48] Sensing judgment and rejection in terms like "Snake-Lips," knowing that his father thought him not only lazy but odd—too obviously like his mother and too caught up in poetry— he found ways of expressing the judgment he usually hid. Sitting on the porch one evening, he responded to one of his father's last overtures with contempt. Having heard that his son now smoked a pipe, as his great-grandfather had, Murry Falkner offered him "a good smoke"—a cigar. "Thank you, sir," William replied, accepting the cigar. Then reaching into his pocket for a pipe, he tore the cigar in half, stuffed one piece in his pipe, and lit it. After watching him and saying nothing, his father turned and walked away. "He never gave me another cigar," his son recalled.[49] To the end of his life, Murry Falkner also denied reading anything his son wrote, perhaps in part because he knew what he would find there. In *Flags in the Dust*, the first novel in which he drew directly on family legends, William Faulkner not only made family decline his theme, he also assigned to the father of the Sartoris twins a totally inconsequential life. The second John Sartoris, whose name we scarcely hear, lives "for the simple continuity of the family," and dies in 1901, a year before Murry Falkner's move from Ripley to Oxford.[50]

With his mother, William was far less direct. In several ways—by ignoring his chores, neglecting his lessons, and fooling around with whiskey—he expressed resentment. But for the most part he remained an obedient, admiring son for as long as his mother lived (until 1960). When he was away from home, he wrote to her faithfully, often without mentioning his father. When he was in Oxford, he visited her daily. After his marriage in 1929, when Miss Maud made clear how little pleasure she took in his wife's presence, he left his wife at home, giving his mother what she expected, a part of most of his days to herself. Toward her he remained not only dutiful but approving. Repeating the last statement she made about his father—"I never did like him"—he accompanied it with a soft laugh.[51]

What Faulkner admired in his mother—fierce will and enduring pride—entered his fiction in several obvious ways. Like Aunt Bama, the Old Colonel's youngest child, and Auntee Holland, the Young Colonel's only daughter, Miss Maud was for him one of the unvanquished. His father's conspicuous inadequacies and narrow judgments, which he despised and resented, also entered his fiction. Between the strength of one and the weakness of the other, he preferred the strength. But there are signs that he found choosing between them painful; that he feared the consequences of choice; and that he resented his mother's insistence that he choose. For what is striking about the clear pattern he established in dealing with his parents, beyond the direct ways in which it entered his fiction, are the reversals he worked on it. In his fiction, mothers generally fare no better than fathers, and women perhaps less well than men. We encounter many flawed, failed parents in his fiction, but we also sense a deep, varied dis-ease with women, or at least what his stepdaughter later termed a "rather strong distrust" of them. Furthermore, when he came to create an ideal community, in "The Bear," he recalled the world his father had shared with him at the Club House. The big woods of "The Bear" provide a world of slow time, where the hunters and the prey are bigger, braver, and wiser. It is a world where deep wounds heal, and it is a world without women. Faulkner was suspicious of this ideal, as he was of Ike McCaslin's heroism and martyrdom, but he was also drawn to it. The deep nostalgia that informs so much of his fiction is often associated both with loss of the big woods and with loss of childhood—that is, a world prior to disappointment, division, bitterness, a world not yet in need of face-lifting.[52]

Faulkner's fiction thus reveals what much of his life disguises: that he associated the onset of division and bitterness not simply with the flow of time but with the conduct of his warring parents. In the father whose failures were many and repeated, he saw weakness that was too conspicuous. In the mother who made him perfectly aware of his father's weakness and then forced him to choose between that weakness and her strength, he saw fierceness that went too far. Beyond this his fiction reveals the deeper direction of his sympathy, which was toward children.

Caught between the death of her mother and the life of her father, Miss Rosa Coldfield in *Absalom, Absalom!* discovers that her childhood was lost before it was possessed. In *The Sound and the Fury*, Quentin Compson is a boy without an adequate father and, like Darl in *As I Lay Dying*, a boy who in some fundamental sense "never had a mother." In *Absalom, Absalom!*, Charles Bon not only finds himself deprived of a visible father and burdened with "too many brothers"; he also finds himself the instrument of his mother's revenge and the victim of his father's retaliation. Discerning the pain of his predicament, Charles discovers that he is younger than he thought he was, and more vulnerable. Desolated by his sense of himself as part orphan, part unwilling competitor, part manipulated instrument, and part victim, he begins "feeling that same despair and shame like when you have to watch your father fail in physical courage, thinking, *It should have been me that failed.*"[53]

What these betrayed children suggest, other Faulkner characters confirm. Burdened with families that are so large and inbred as to seem suffocating, the Compsons, Sartorises, and McCaslins feel caught and held. Like Nathaniel Hawthorne's Pyncheons, they suffer a malady that resembles catatonia: they find stillness and repetition easy, motion and innovation almost impossible. At the same time, they recall the deserted and deprived children of Charles Dickens, primarily because their parents are inaccessible, inadequate, or, as in the case of the Sartoris twins, too soon dead. Left without parental tenderness and love, Benjy, Quentin, and Caddy turn to Dilsey and to each other. Left without an adequate model and sponsor, Thomas Sutpen chooses a surrogate father. Resenting their parents, some of these characters avoid parenthood altogether.[54] Those who do not avoid it find repetition almost inevitable. Miss Quentin, the only grandchild of the Compsons, never knows her parents and certainly never feels their love. In *The Sound and the Fury*, moreover, as in so many of his stories, Faulkner makes repetition not only a theme but a structural principle. What is for his characters a fated limitation becomes for him, as we shall see, a form of innovation, a means to imaginative mastery.

About the time his break with his father began, William started thinking of himself as the child of his great-grandfather. Cuthbert, the name he had from his father, he rejected as a sissy name; William, the name he had from the family's giant, he took as his own. At age nine, shortly before his resistance to school and chores began, he began saying, "I want to be a writer like my great-granddaddy"—a statement he repeated until it became almost formulaic.[55] Years later, for his first published book, which he dedicated to his mother, he wrote a sketch introducing himself simply as the "Great-grandson of Col. W. C. Faulkner, C. S. A., author of 'The White Rose of Memphis,' 'Rapid Ramblings in Europe,' etc."[56]

Having thus made himself his great progenitor's representative, he went on to exercise subtle authority, even a kind of dominance, by adding to the Old Colonel's surname the *u* he had already added to his own. Later, with his sense of self firmer, he made even clearer the authority he sought. The *u* that his parents regarded as a general declaration of independence, he associated specifically with the Old Colonel: he was replacing a letter that he claimed his great-grandfather had deleted.[57] But the prior and deeper act was the act of identification. As his brother Jack later noted, his early statement of intention matched "his character and his dreams"; from boyhood on, Jack said, William "patterned his life after the Old Colonel's."[58]

Sometime around 1910, William began writing poetry as well as reading it. In part a way of exploring what it might mean to be a writer like his great-grandfather, writing was also a way of exploring what he could do as an observer whose faculty for application centered more and more in his sensibility and imagination. Years later he began writing stories like those he was listening to and occasionally telling, but even then he continued to describe himself as "a failed poet," as though to recall his earliest self-conception. Poetry contributed, he said later, to his "youthful gesture" of "being 'different' "—a gesture to which he devoted considerable effort for a long time. [59] Aided by his grandfather's generosity, he continued the family tradition of sartorial display by wearing high collars, silk ties, and expensive suits. To accentuate his smallness, he had his mother alter his clothes until they were skin tight. Aided by memories of his mother's canvas harness, he walked slowly about or stood motionless as a statue, his back rigid, his head high, his eyes stark and imperious, hoping that some passerby would mistake him for a mannequin. Before long, people were calling him "Count" as well as "quair."[60]

Although he tried to ignore such insults, there were times when self-doubt seemed almost to possess him. There were few people in whom he could confide, and since he knew no one interested in using his talents as he was trying to use his, there was no one with whom he could compare himself. Most of the people around him saw nothing more than pretense or perversion in his affectation and eccentricities. He would be a long time finding people of consequence convinced of his talent. His long-standing loyalty and continuing dependence on his mother had several sources and several consequences and so must be viewed in different ways, but they derived in part from his early awareness that she believed in him deeply. By repeated testing, he knew that her devotion to him had overcome her commitment to propriety and had survived her hatred of whiskey. Needing as he did to match moments of doubt with moments of confidence, such knowledge was crucial. "A man who has been the indisputable favorite of his mother keeps for life," Freud said, "the feeling of a conquerer, that confidence of success that often induces real success."[61] For William nothing was simple; his moods were almost always under siege. But he knew that he was the favorite of his mother, as he had been of his grandmother, and though his privileged status imposed expectations, it also provided assurance that enabled him to explore rather than merely resist estrangement.

In the aesthete and the dandy, he found ways of expressing his sense of himself as observer, thinker, poet, and, by implication, his sense of his world, perhaps especially of his large, hapless father, as *other*. In the poetry he was reading, particularly that of Swinburne, he discovered what T. S. Eliot had discovered: a word-oriented world that promised purity, holiness, redemption, precisely because its thrilled effect depended on words written rather than objects evoked.[62] His taste in poetry ran to Romantic, late-Romantic and even specifically Decadent verse. In his early poetry he drew, not on his knowledge of the hills, birds, and inhabitants of Mississippi, but on his knowledge of English poetry of the nineteenth century. It is "filled with copses and glades and brakes . . . wolds, leas, and downs," which means, as Cleanth Brooks has noted, that it is "disconcertingly literary."[63] Yet this quality, which clearly damaged it as poetry, increased its usefulness to the young Faulkner. As he read and wrote, he continued to seek different ways of responding to life, in part because he needed to feel that he was a man of action; and he continued to seek different ways of testing his tolerance of danger, in part because he needed to feel that he possessed great physical courage. The thrill of hunting lasted a lifetime. Later, golf, tennis, sailing, flying, and riding supplied some of the satisfactions he found early in baseball and football: they tested skills and resolve, proving again and again that he was not afraid to be "man in his sorry clay braving chance and circumstance."[64] Still, his commitment to art, like his need of it, was incurable. There was a part of him, he said, that could not do anything except write. Furthermore, as he read, reread, and began to imitate the word-oriented world of Swinburne, he continued, apparently without quite knowing why, to seek out stories about the world of his own experience.

Although it took him some time to discover the significance of this double commitment, the pattern was there even when he was reading poetry more than he was writing it. And the pattern was oscillation. Years later, when he finally discovered his imaginative home, it was, as we shall see, a place born neither of Mississippi life nor of English poetry, neither of actual earth nor of imaginative heaven, but of tensions between them. In this regard, the beginning of *Light in August* is particularly instructive. For the power of that beginning depends, not upon its evocation of the hot, dusty roads of Mississippi, nor upon its allusions to Keats's urn, but upon the rhetorical skills of a writer who commits himself to evocation and allusion simultaneously. There are moments, to be sure, when Faulkner's fiction seems wholly committed to the triumph of art; in such moments, it moves back toward his early conception and practice of poetry—toward the late Romantics and Decadents. Faulkner knew much about the disappointments of reality, and he felt a desire to master and escape them with transforming words. His fictions enact as well as depend upon a process of mythification whereby events that once happened grow richer and richer and people who once lived grow bigger and bigger. Still, the remarkable fecundity to which he broke through, beginning with *Flags in the Dust*, was inspired, not by the world of fact and dialect as given by perception to reason, nor by the world of dream and desire as given by imagination to aesthetic contemplation, but by play between them. What discontent did to reality, which was to mitigate against it, suspicion did for art; and what delight did for reality, which was to commit him to it, it also did for art. In terms of what amused and moved him as well as what threatened and repulsed him, he was so deeply divided that his genius found expression neither in modern aestheticism's commitment to the triumph of art nor in modern realism's commitment to the triumph of reality, but in both.[65]

That his early poetry bespeaks deep ambivalence toward the role of the observer and the fate it implies—that the persona of *The Marble Faun*, for example, describes itself as "mute and impotent"—suggests something of the suspicion, division, fear, and pain of Faulkner's earliest years as a writer. In theme as well as technique, his early poetry is frequently imitative, particularly in its world-weariness, its unrequited love, its melancholy. But intertwined in Faulkner's familiar affectations are two kinds of morbidity. In "A Diana" we meet one who, like Milly Theale, "turns to night, and weeps, and longs to die"; in other works we find a perspective, like Emily Dickinson's in "Because I Could Not Stop for Death," that is distinctly post-mortem. The isolation, silence, and stillness Faulkner was practicing in life and rendering in poetry is thus associated not only with muteness and impotence but also with the threat of extinction.[66]

Later Faulkner created characters who respond to some traumatic event by engaging in elaborate acts of reseeing. Rebuffed at the plantation owner's door, the young Thomas Sutpen flees to a cave, where he reviews the whole of his life. It was "like when you pass through a room fast and look at all the objects in it and you turn and go back through the room again and look at all the objects from the other side and you find out you had never seen them before."[67] In part a version of what almost every child goes through on discovering "the facts of life," what Faulkner describes here is also a familiar part of every great revelation and of every true conversion.[68] For Faulkner, writing *The Sound and the Fury*

seems to have been such an experience: "Without heeding to open another
book and in a series of delayed repercussions like summer thunder I discovered the Flauberts and Dostoevskys and Conrads whose books I had
read ten years ago."[69] Furthermore, in this book, in which writing became his way of rereading and reseeing, he began forcing his readers to
practice reseeing and rereading. No major writer of our time has done
more to make us see and resee inexplicably forbidden scenes, now with
this bit added or that taken away, now from this angle, later from another.

Whereas many of Faulkner's characters wrestle endlessly with the
events of their lives, unable to do anything, the young Thomas Sutpen
discovers what he takes to be the logic of his. Sitting alone, still and silent
in his cave, he sees as though for the first time the hopelessness that
shapes his sisters' faces, the failure and defeat that define his parents'
lives. Knowing that he must "do something" if he is "to live with himself for the rest of his life," he takes the owner of a great plantation, the
epitome of ease and success, as his model; the "design" he pursues is for
the most part an elaborate imitation. His story comes to us as a series of
recalled conversations about events, some remembered, some imagined.
As his tellers and listeners change roles, we begin to recognize mixed
motives and deep ambivalences. In the novel's opening pages Miss Rosa
Coldfield's remembered voice evokes the figure of Sutpen, long since
dead. Lost before it was possessed, Miss Rosa's childhood is associated
with "the very damp and velvet silence of the womb," while her life is
associated with prolonged and "furious immobility." In her voice as in
the motions of her mind, contrary impulses, the urge to create and the
urge to destroy, combine in remarkably undisguised ways. As she evokes
and celebrates, she also judges and dismembers.[70]

Some such doubleness began early to inform Faulkner's address to
his experience and to the past, as we see both in the games he played with
his parents' lives and in his evocation and incorporation—his assimilation—
of his great-grandfather. Through an act of imagination and a strategy
of imitation, he began to absorb his great progenitor. Years later, after
he had refined his parents' generation almost out of existence in *Flags
in the Dust*, he created a character named Gail Hightower, whose life
revolves around moments out of his family's past. As a child, Hightower
has sat for hours "with rapt, wide, half dread and half delight," listening
to an old servant tell stories out of the past. As a man, he recalls stories
about his grandfather with such regularity and intensity that his grandfather becomes the great figure in his life. Precisely because he is a ghost,
an abstraction "never seen in the flesh," Hightower's grandfather can
become "heroic, simple, warm." As Hightower recovers one generation,
however, he dismisses another: as the ghost of his grandfather becomes

real, the figure of the father "he knew and feared" fades until it becomes "a phantom." "So it's no wonder," he thinks in a moment of remarkable illumination, "that I skipped a generation. It's no wonder that I had no father."[71]

If a part of what the young William Faulkner was trying to see and resee as he sat or stood in self-imposed stillness and silence was the significance of his father's failure and his mother's fierce pride and possessiveness, surely a part of what he was seeking in the stories he listened to was other models. While still young, at about the time he began exploring the loneliness and isolation that he felt, he also began exploring the model he had chosen, or been given, since in the end it came to the same thing, his namesake and great-grandfather. In this exploration as in his exploration of loneliness, he displayed what Ben Wasson described as "a rare ability to dramatize himself interestingly."[72] In addition, he disclosed a talent for convenient definition, as we see most clearly in the simplification with which he began. The Old Colonel had been a writer—of a narrative poem called *The Siege of Monterrey*, a play called *The Lost Diamond*, and several novels, including one, *The White Rose of Memphis*, that substantially increased his fame. But he had been a writer after many things and in addition to others. During the last months of his life, sitting for a photographic portrait in New York, he ordered a larger-than-life statue of himself. Placed by his family on a fourteen-foot pediment, the eight-foot statue still towers above his grave, reminding us that in his own eyes as well as in those of his descendants, he was a giant. So far as we know, only one great-grandson ever described him simply as a writer.

To a boy who was burdened with a father he could not accept, however, and who was thus in need of a model that promised success as well as independence, some such revision was necessary. William knew that his great-grandfather had ridden through his "country like a living force."[73] To refer to the Old Colonel as a writer was to distort him almost beyond recognition. Still, if remoteness in time could accommodate the kind of elaboration his family practiced, surely it could accommodate the kind of distillation he required. For a small boy looking at a giant and needing total mastery, allowances had to be made. Too many things open to founders were closed to descendants; whatever else it might teach, his family's history almost shouted that lesson. His father's failure was extreme, but even his grandfather, who at times recalled the original, was but a miniature. What he represented, almost as much as the other descendants, was a process of declension. That the one who had done the most had done so little could scarcely encourage a small boy. Yet, perhaps in the role to which he had come, as a reader of books, an observer of life, a hearer of tales, a writer of poems, he could make himself a creature of force if, in the first step toward appropriating his heritage, he could redefine the giant.

TWO 1918-1924

The Great War and Beyond

Uneasy with the role of the observer and the restrictions it imposed, Faulkner continued moving in and out of it. Having shed his harness in the ninth grade, he began playing baseball and football. Two years later, in the fall of 1915, he resumed hunting. Although he still listened more than he talked, he learned again to enjoy the drinking and tale-swapping of the hunts. Other activities he learned to go without. About the time he returned to football, he gave up dancing. Sitting or standing on the sidelines, still and silent, he watched while others, including Estelle, danced. Determined in his independence, he steeled himself against ridicule—"Snake-Lips," "Count," "Quair." Having quit high school and drifted away from the bank, he spent more time around the University of Mississippi, where he found a few activities and several students that he liked. In the fall of 1916 he began a long friendship with Ben Wasson. The next spring *Ole Miss*, the student yearbook, included one of his drawings, his first published work.

But such things belonged to the edges of his life. When he grew tired of reading and writing poems, of listening to stories and drawing pictures, he liked to walk with and listen to Phil Stone or walk and talk with Estelle Oldham. Despite the distances he sought and the careful indifference he cultivated, he recognized the threat isolation posed. Having made stillness and silence principles of his existence, he found in listening one bridge, in making poems and drawings others, and in talking yet another. Earlier, in the security of Mammy Callie's hearth, or in scattered moments with friends like Myrtle Ramey, Dewey Linder, and Sallie Murry, he had talked as well as listened. But more and more it was to Phil and to Estelle that he turned.

Professional rivals, the Stones and Falkners were social allies. They represented tradition, and they shared interests—the women in the Methodist Church, the men in drinking and hunting as well as making money. But since Phil was four years older than William and was also academically ambitious, he took little note of William until the summer of 1914. Having returned from Yale with a B.A. cum laude (he had taken the same degree with the same honors at the University of Mississippi a year earlier), Phil heard that William was writing poetry. Although he planned to enter law school at the University of Mississippi, to take another degree he would then repeat at Yale, and though he intended to join his father and brothers in the family law firm, Phil loved literature, particularly poetry. Given the improbable news about William, he went to the Falkner home. Hearing why Phil had come, saying almost nothing, William gave him the poems he had been accumulating, and watched as they were read.

Phil Stone seems, on the spot, to have sensed at least a part of what the poetry promised: "Anybody could have seen that he had a real talent," he said later. "It was perfectly obvious."[1] Almost alone in seeing what he thought of as obvious (William's mother, too, believed her son had talent, even suspected that he was a "genius"), Phil Stone adopted William as a protegé. Years later, their friendship strained almost to breaking. Being a frustrated teacher and knowing that he would have only one student, Phil could never decide whether he wanted William to attain greatness or remain an admiring follower. When it finally came, the fame he had prophesied and promoted seemed a mixed blessing. Exaggerating his own role, he decided that too much glory was going to the maker of the poems, too little to the maker of the poet. But during the long period in which his younger friend remained merely promising, in need of tutoring and touting, Phil remained a loyal friend. Seeing in William a worthy project, he set out to fill the several vacancies he saw in William's life by being his friend, tutor, and sponsor.

A part of what William needed was personal and informal. Despite differences in age, experience, and manner, Phil and William shared more than an interest in literature. Phil knew something of what it meant to be different in Oxford, and even more of what it meant for a Mississippi boy to resemble his mother more than his father. Like William, Phil had been taught that art "was really no manly business."[2] Bearing the honorary title of general, James Stone was aggressively "masculine": he drank hard, gambled big, and hunted bear. Eventually Phil followed his rugged father into each of these habits, as well as into law. But he had been sickly as a child, and, even as an adult, he resembled his introspective, unwell mother, Miss Rosa, both physically and temperamentally.[3] In a series of schools, he found what he needed: places where he could turn his differences to his advantage. Working hard, he won honors in which both of his parents took pride. Having completed school, he would never again be either so happy or so successful. Yet even in his success, he had suffered enough to appreciate William's deeper estrangement. "There was no one but me," he later wrote, "with whom William Faulkner could discuss his literary plans and hopes and his technical trials and aspirations."[4]

From the summer of 1914, when he came home with his first Yale degree, until the fall of 1916, when he went back to take a second, Phil encouraged William in his pursuits and ambitions, occasionally listening as William described them. But since William needed instruction as well as encouragement, and since Phil was as devoted to talking as William was to listening, Phil listened little and talked much. Earlier William had accepted and by now he was deliberately seeking a situation that left him free to educate himself with books and stories. But he had not done so without paying a price. His mother's interests included many of the classics of literature and philosophy; beginning with the Bible, Plato, and Aristotle, they reached to Conrad.[5] But there were large gaps, and there was no one to fill them: no one who read as William read, nor anyone who tried to write.

Fresh from college courses and conversations, Phil knew interesting things; most of all, he loved to talk, endlessly, it seems, about everything he knew. As he began to direct William's reading, their relationship assumed the pattern it retained. A master of extemporaneous lectures, Phil talked while William, a master of nothing if not listening, sat or walked silently, attending what he wanted, ignoring the rest. Absorbed in what he was saying, Phil developed a faulty sense of what his younger friend was doing. Later he believed there was almost nothing he had not taught William: all the literature, philosophy, and history, everything from commas to the more "obvious truths" of moral philosophy.[6] Yet, since William seems to have learned early and easily as much as he ever cared to know about commas, if not about obvious truths, it is likely that Phil, taking silence to signify attention, understood only part of what was going on. As the years passed, leaving him little of his friend except old manuscripts and memories, he tended to exaggerate how untutored was the genius he

had discovered, how great the labor he had performed. Long before Phil
became his friend, William had shown that he was capable of choosing the
books he would read, the classes he would attend, the words he would
hear. Still, Phil taught William much. He knew Greek and Latin and was
well read in the literature of both languages. His knowledge of southern
history, particularly the Civil War, was detailed and exact. In later years
he felt especially proprietary toward Faulkner's Snopes stories as well as
his poetry. And that feeling had this basis at least: he did as much as anyone else, including the Young Colonel and Uncle John Falkner, both of
whom were deeply involved in county and state politics, to focus William's attention on "the rise of the redneck" and the changes it was making in the life of Mississippi, and he did more than anyone else to direct
Faulkner's study of poetry. In particular, he turned William, first, toward
the more familiar poets of the nineteenth century, and then, toward the
Symbolists, who comprised one of the most sophisticated movements in
literary history. He bought scores of books from the famed Brick Row
Book Store of New Haven and he prided himself on knowing both the
background of the Modernist movement and the works of Yeats, Pound,
Eliot, and Joyce.

If it was more and more to Phil that William listened, it was more and
more to Estelle Oldham that he talked: "With her listening," a brother
later wrote, "Bill found he could talk. From then on he spent more and
more time down at her house, being with her and talking to her and listening to her play."[7] So prominent and prosperous that not even being Re-
publicans robbed them of respectability, the Oldhams moved to Oxford
in the fall of 1903, less than a year after the Murry Falkners moved from
Ripley. From boyhood on, William regarded the Oldham home as a haven
where people enjoyed music and conversation. The Oldhams had no rules
or mottoes to discourage talk, even about books. With Estelle away at
Mary Baldwin College, William continued to visit her family. Years later
he presented the Oldhams one of the first copies of his first book.[8] But he
went primarily to visit Estelle—to hear her play the piano, to talk about
his hopes and plans, to read his poems, to display his drawings. Only with
her did he talk as much as he listened.

Early, still children, Estelle and William became "sweethearts," and
for several years their relationship followed a familiar pattern. They
played and talked, went to parties, learned to dance. But as the change in
William became more pronounced, as his moodiness increased and his
aversion to school and work mounted, their relationship changed. William
still came to call; he still talked to Estelle, sharing his life with her; he still
counted on her to listen. But to all appearances, he became more a devoted friend than a suitor, or if a suitor, one among many, and one who
recognized that, as the ne'er-do-well son of a failed father, he was

unacceptable. Receiving the court and enjoying the attention of many, Estelle led an almost independent social life, the sense of which William's first published drawing (and many of his early poems) suggests. Depicting a very tall, almost elongated, couple dancing, the drawing's austerity and stylization distance its subject. An "excellent dancer," once "much in demand by the girls," William had renounced dancing. Painfully conscious of his height, more comfortable watching, he went to many dances but rarely danced. Vivacious and attractive, light, graceful, and tireless, Estelle went to parties with her suitors, and with them, she danced the dances. When William danced it was with Estelle, and when she watched, it was with William. But for the most part she danced while he watched, sometimes well into the morning.[9]

What reconciled William to such a role, in addition to the way it corresponded to his self-conception, was the secret understanding he had with Estelle: that she would receive other suitors, accepting occasional gifts and exchanging casual pledges, but that she would always be his. The obvious facts about Estelle—her popularity, her eminent social position, her orthodox ambitions and delights—had become immensely important to him. Among the few to whom he talked, she was the only one to whom he talked easily, yet she was not only preeminent; she also believed in him so deeply that, pursued by many, she had committed herself to him.[10]

Much of this pattern fit Faulkner's deepest sense of his relationship to Estelle, which was a highly romantic version of a great and star-crossed yet compelling love. The oblique eroticism of his early poetry, in addition to reflecting his fondness for Swinburne, suggests that direct expression remained so difficult as to be almost impossible. In his poetry as in his drawings, sexual union is clearly associated with dancing—the activity that he had renounced and Estelle had embraced. In *The Marble Faun* the central figure cannot break his marble bonds. The activities he observes, such as the freedom of the "quick keen snake," he cannot directly experience. Haunted by the things he knows "yet cannot know," he longs to be free— to abandon stillness and silence, together with the impotence they imply, and so dance "the immortal dance" to Pan's shrill pipes.[11] Although his deliverance is deferred, his languishing and longing make his need of eventual deliverance clear, and also his need of its assurance. Meanwhile Estelle's secret pledge affirmed that William possessed talents others failed to see, including the power to stir women.[12]

As weeks stretched into months, Estelle found it difficult to keep her promises. Light-hearted and gay, she drifted in and out of several pledges before exchanging one with the more persistent and acceptable Cornell Franklin. Finding herself doubly pressured, by suitor and family, she sought to extricate herself by suggesting to William that they elope. What William must have known, Estelle's suggestion clearly implied: that they could not get parental approval. Regarding him as unsettled and without prospects, even his own family felt that he had no business talking of marriage. Still he insisted on waiting for their parents' good wishes.

In this determination, William appears almost to have desired his fate— to have decided to know for himself the unrequited love of which he had been making poetry. Certainly his scruples did as much as Estelle's carelessness to end their improbable arrangement. But he found no relief in any sensed complicity. Although he had practiced denying himself many things, he was not prepared to give up Estelle's commitment. Rejected by two sets of parents, betrayed by his love, he sank into bitterness. In the weeks after the announcement of Estelle's engagement, he learned how much he had counted on her belief in his dream and his powers. If his refusal to elope suggests that he continued to fear deliverance, his unhappiness shows that he continued to need assurance. Estelle might, as she insisted, still believe in and love him, but surely her willingness to marry someone else meant that she was neither convinced nor stirred enough. For a time William stayed on, hoping something would happen; and while he waited, he continued to give Estelle poems and drawings. The poems spoke of rejected, enduring love. One of the last drawings depicted a small, Mephistophelian creature looking down to see a beautiful nymph bewitched by the music of a satyr. But as the day of the wedding, 18 April 1918, drew near, self-doubt, pain, and bitterness made talking to Estelle more and more difficult. The hours he had spent watching her dance with other suitors did nothing to prepare him for the coupling he now contemplated. Without her commitment to validate it, the role he had created for himself seemed to him impossible to sustain. As his brother John later remarked, "His world went to pieces."[13]

With his own world collapsing, Faulkner sought relief in a larger chaos. Almost exactly a year earlier, 6 April 1917, his country had admitted what Europe had known for several years: that the peace, prosperity, and progress that had dominated the West for nearly a century had come to an end. Perhaps in a larger collapse he could find action to divert him. As a boy, flying had fascinated him. Having first built wings of corn shucks, he later built, and for a few moments flew, a plane made of beanpoles and paper. Over the last months, as news of the war increased, he had read so much about the war over France that his mind was filled with the names of pilots. Perhaps, like them, he "could get to France and become glorious and beribboned."[14] If wholesale slaughter and destruction were what the nineteenth century had led to, he wanted to know them for himself.[15] With courage and luck, he might find in the war that was changing the West what the Old Colonel had found in the war that had changed the South: an occasion for heroism. Having fought, the Old Colonel returned to build a railroad and write a popular novel. Later William might return

and resume life, but in the meantime, he would seek glory and release in
what Yeats called the "delirium of the brave."[16]

Determined to be a pilot, he presented himself at the recruiting station, only to be rejected. He was too small, they told him, too short and
too frail. With his dramatic exit blocked, he found remaining in Oxford
all the more impossible. News of the war filled the air; reminders of Estelle's marriage were everywhere. With March almost gone, he decided to
go to New Haven, where Phil Stone was studying for his second law degree. Perhaps there he would find, if not a grand diversion, at least a few
distractions. Such distractions as came, however, served mainly to remind
him of the war he was missing. Needing money, he took a job as a clerk at
the Winchester Repeating Arms Company, where people talked mainly
about how the Allied forces might counter the spring advances of the Ger-
mans. Ignoring the war, Phil Stone tried to keep William's mind on poetry;
he introduced him to writers like Stephen Vincent Benét, a publishing
poet at the age of seventeen, and to friends who liked to discuss aesthetics
and to quote Browning and Yeats. But among the people Stone knew,
the ones who interested William most were those who liked to talk of
war as well as poetry; and among new acquaintances, the ones he listened to most were officers attached to an R.O.T.C. unit at Yale, some
of whom had fought and been wounded as members of the Royal Air
Force.[17]

With May approaching, William determined to find another way of
entering the war. Rejected by lover, parents, and local recruiting station,
he had left Oxford for New Haven. But such relief as he found there did
not last long. A century earlier, another burdened and restive son had
changed his name from Hathorne to Hawthorne. Like Hawthorne, William
had learned early to regard family, region, and past both as burden and as
field of play; like Hawthorne, he had learned to associate his ancestors
with crime as well as glory; and like Hawthorne, he was learning to swing
to and fro between a desire to evoke and celebrate shadows and a desire
to escape them. Soon he, too, was busy creating a persona. With the help
of the R.A.F. officers, he began acquiring a British accent and creating a
British identity. If as William Falkner of Oxford, Mississippi, he was unfit
to serve, perhaps as William Faulkner of England he would be acceptable.

On 14 June, armed with his revised name, an imperfect accent, and a
borrowed London address, he made the trip from New Haven to a British
recruiting office in New York. With him he carried several improbable
documents: letters written by the officers he had met in New Haven stat-
ing that he was an English student who wanted to enlist in the R.A.F.;
forged papers attesting that he was William Faulkner, born 25 May 1898,
in the village of Finchley, county of Middlesex; and a letter from an
imaginary vicar, the Reverend Mr. Edward Twimberly-Thorndyke, praising

his honesty and integrity as a young Christian gentleman. Whether be-
mused, fooled, or desperate for recruits, England's representatives accepted her adoptive son, whereupon he promptly enlisted for pilot training
in the R.A.F. Ordered to report for duty in Toronto on 9 July, he returned to New Haven, then left for Oxford.[18] Now at least the bitterness
that had become so large a part of his life was mixed with a sense of great
expectation. Estelle might be married to a major, his brother Jack might
already be in training, but he had begun a journey that would take him to
France and to glory.

When his great adventure came, it was another opportunity lost,
another dream missed. For five months he performed calisthenics, practiced
marching, and studied principles of navigation and flight. When the war
ended, on 11 November 1918, Cadet Faulkner was stationed at the School
of Military Aeronautics in Toronto, in the third and final phase of pre-
flight training, almost within reach of an airplane. Though he had seen
many planes and heard many stories, though it is possible that he had
flown, it is certain that he had seen nothing of the skies over France. His
only clear gain, aside from what he had seen and heard, was in weight; he
no longer seemed quite so frail.[19] But he had suffered no wounds his record would show, nor had he received any decorations or commendations.
In early December he returned to Oxford; by early January he was officially demobilized. Two years later, in November 1920, he received a
scroll making him an honorary second lieutenant, R.A.F.

A rejected lover descended from heroes, Faulkner found both his
cadet's uniform and his fate offensive. That he had been stuck in school
studying and watching airplanes while others were flying was worse than
disappointing. Even a younger brother, having actually fought and bled in
the Argonne Forest, would return beribboned. Several years later, Faulkner's bitterness shaped the first page of his first novel, where Cadet Julian
Lowe, suffering a jaundice shared by all those on whom "they had stopped the war," sits regarding his "world with a yellow and disgruntled
eye." Smoldering in "disgusted sorrow," "knowing all the despair of abortive endeavor," Cadet Lowe not only hates "the sorry jade, Circumstance"
for robbing him of his chance at glory, he also envies all heroes, even those
dreadfully scarred.[20] Earlier, in the weeks just after armistice, Faulkner's
disappointment found expression in improvisation that was imaginative
without being literary. Having created a persona with which to enter the
war, he created one with which to leave it.

Before his return to Oxford, his letters began reporting as actual a
series of adventures that were only imagined. In August he described for
his family improbable "joy rides" hitched with friends. In mid-November,
though operations had in fact been curtailed, he described both flight
training and solo flights. In December he returned home dressed as a hero.

When he got off the train, his brother John reports, he appeared, not in the mundane issue of a cadet on whom they had stopped the war, but in a British officer's uniform complete with a Sam Browne belt, a tunic adorned with wings, and an overseas cap. Carrying a swagger stick, he was also limping—from an injury, he reported, incurred in a crash during training.[21]

Accounts of his flights and injuries varied from time to time. In some versions the training mishap became an unauthorized solo flight of a half-drunk cadet celebrating the armistice. Always involving either his legs or a hip, his injuries sometimes included a skull fracture that had left him with a silver plate and lingering pain. A few people got the impression that the crash and injuries resulted from combat in the skies over France. Clearly compensatory, the persona of the injured pilot or, more impressively, the wounded hero brought the young cadet a taste of the glory and recognition he needed. But years later, after fame had come, Faulkner continued playing with the facts of his life; and even after some of his fabrications had worked their way into biographical notes, creating embarrassing moments for him, he resisted disowning them.

What this devotion suggests is that Faulkner's fabrications were for him more than compensatory. "Anyone who writes," his brother John later noted, "spends a lot of his time in an imaginary world. . . . It's easy enough for him to become someone he is not. Bill was about the best at it I ever saw."[22] Related to his "rare ability to dramatize himself interestingly," fabrication was for Faulkner a mode of imaginative appropriation. Like the stories he later wrote, both the stories he told and the roles he projected possessed authority. Far from simply borrowing them, he appropriated and transmuted them.

In the months after the war, as hope began merging with disillusionment, the event he had missed became all the more important. Yet his only recourse was to experience it indirectly—through what he had heard and could read, through what he could feel, project, and express. He knew that many men had gone into the Great War full of expectation—thinking that they "knew what Glory was, and what Honor meant" and believing that they would experience them—only to emerge disgusted and disillusioned. For others the sense of the war as whimsical, accidental, arbitrary, had been acquired in trenches, gunboats, or cockpits. But he saw in the meager things that he had experienced entry into grand things that he had missed. For him, too, the war had become a world wholly unacceptable to desire, which meant that there was expression as well as deception in the costume he wore and the limp he affected. In the persona he created as in the stories he would write, he borrowed much. But what he borrowed he made his own. Later he began to transmute the experiences of others—tales heard, stories read, things imagined—into poems like "The Lilacs," "The Ace," and "November 11," or stories like "Victory," "All the Dead

Pilots," and "Honor." The creation of a persona was, among other things, an imaginative rehearsal.[23]

Soon after his return, the persona of the injured pilot began to blend with others. At "home again in Oxford, Mississippi, yet at the same time . . . not at home," he moved back into civilian life tentatively, almost as if, like the war, it were somehow temporary.[24] Having worn his uniform at home, down to the square, out to parties, having posed for photographs, he gradually put it aside. With "the co-ordinated chaos of war" gone, there was before him the question of how to continue.[25] The loss of Estelle, the frustration of the war, his months in Connecticut and Canada, had changed him. People who met him now for the first time thought him not only silent and watchful but vaguely "foreign."[26] Yet he responded to the necessity of continuing his life by resuming his role as a dependent son.

In 1917 Murry Falkner had accepted appointment as assistant secretary of the University of Mississippi. Another position arranged by his father, this one was smaller but more stable than some he had held earlier. In return for a small salary and a house on campus, he performed simple tasks. Working steadily, he was later named secretary and business manager of the university. Having given up hope of large success, he seemed more content now; with most people around him, including Miss Maud, his relations had eased. Toward William, however, he remained cool. Of the letters William wrote from New Haven and Canada, one fragment has been published. Like several letters he later wrote from Paris, it is written specifically to his mother.[27]

To the problem of living with the father he could never accept and the mother he could never reject, William's solution was to compromise. Working occasionally and studying sporadically, he tried at times to conform to their expectations, particularly those of his mother, who persisted in thinking of him as one of destiny's children. But for the most part he went his own way, without waiting to hear complaints or offer explanations. Much of his reading and writing he did alone in his room, where he also made a point of keeping whiskey. He enjoyed seeing the Oldhams, with whom he talked, and the Stones, with whom he hunted and played golf as well as talked. Although Phil lived in Charleston now, he and William managed to see each other frequently. Together they made trips to Memphis, New Orleans, or Clarksdale, where they became friendly with several shady characters, including Dot Wilcox and Reno DeVaux.[28] When, as happened occasionally, Faulkner felt that he simply had to get out of Oxford, almost any excuse or destination would do. Sometimes he chauffered his uncle John, who was campaigning for a judgeship. Visiting small towns and listening to the stories told around boardinghouses, in town squares, or at political rallies, he found entertainment as well as release.

Within weeks of his return he had established a pattern that lasted several years. Moving in and out of Oxford, he also moved in and out of roles. Sometimes he presented himself as the ne'er-do-well relative of his prominent grandfather or uncle, sometimes as the immaculate dandy, sometimes as the ill-kempt bohemian, but almost always as "the poet" and almost always as a drinker. While few people saw him drunk, almost everyone noticed how much he seemed to drink. By attributing his drinking to grief inflicted by a lost love or to wounds suffered in the Great War, he made it more a sign of what he was than merely a thing he did. Like his moustache, it suggested that, though once a boy and still small, he was a man; but even more, it suggested some terrible, slightly mysterious ordeal that he was not yet wholly beyond.[29]

Bearing the title "poet," which Stone helped spread about, Faulkner resumed reading and listening, drawing and writing. Writing had not yet become, as it would, a sustaining purpose, an activity so compelling as to deliver him from morbidity and fear by giving him, from day to day, "something to get up to do." But it was becoming both the major form of his groping and a new stage in his prolonged self-education. Later he described all of his fiction as self-involved: "I am telling the same story over and over, which is myself and the world."[30] In the years just after the Great War, it was through poetry that he expressed this involvement of self and world. Encouraged by Phil Stone, he was reading not only Yeats and other Modernists, but French poetry of the late nineteenth and early twentieth centuries. As he read, he began to adapt, to translate, to write. During the spring and early summer of 1919, with a visit from Estelle approaching, he wrote more and more. From these months came versions of a long poem written in octosyllabic couplets; called *The Marble Faun*, it became his first book, although it would not be published until December 1924. From these months, too, came his first published poem, "L'Après-Midi d'un Faune," which appeared in the *New Republic* on 6 August 1919.

As it turned out, Estelle was there to share his triumph. Having arrived in June, she stayed until September, visiting her family and showing off her first child, a daughter named Victoria. Since her husband had remained at their home in Honolulu, Estelle was free to spend long hours with Faulkner, who, despite his lingering bitterness, still wrote primarily for her. His first period of striking poetic production coincided with her first visit, in 1919; and his second, when he wrote the poems he initially called "Vision in Spring," coincided with her second visit, in the spring of 1921. At the end of her first visit he gave her a volume of Swinburne that he had been reading, complete with an inscription so passionate she had to tear it out before taking the book to Honolulu;[31] at the end of her second he gave her a book he had made of the poems he had been writing.

Years later, after Faulkner had turned to fiction, Phil Stone doubted "if it was his early ambition to be a poet as much as it was my ambition for him to be one."[32] Certainly it was the poet in Faulkner that Stone most admired and influenced, and Stone may well have prolonged Faulkner's commitment to poetry. His move toward prose would be, among other things, a move away from Stone. But it was Faulkner's conception of his relation to Estelle, more than Stone's promptings, that kept him a poet. For as long as he lived he tended to think of himself as a man writing to or for some woman. In April 1925, when he was completing his move toward fiction, he published an essay in the *Double Dealer* in which he claimed to have taken up poetry " for the purpose of furthering various philanderings," suggesting that women are vulnerable to such a tactic because they are interested, not in "art for art's sake," but in "art for the artist's sake."[33] Of limited value as an account of Faulkner's early career, "Verse Old and Nascent: A Pilgrimage" has at least one merit: it suggests that Faulkner's conception of his relation to Estelle had become highly stylized. In the poetry of 1919 this process was already well under way. In "L'Apres-Midi d'un Faune," the poet follows his beloved through "singing trees," praising her "lascivious . . . knees," watching as "She whirls and dances," until finally they walk "hand in hand." Although he feels "a nameless wish to go/To some far silent mid-night noon," it is not until his nameless wish has faded that, suddenly, "A sound like some great deep bell stroke/Falls, and they dance."[34] In *The Marble Faun* the poet's dissatisfaction runs deeper. A "prisoner to dream," he sings, straining against the bonds that are his fate. In desire he is part romantic lover and part would-be follower of Pan; in actuality he is one for whom release is deferred. Sentenced to sitting and peering, to brooding and yearning, doomed to "sigh/For things" he knows yet cannot "know," he is sad beyond measure, not only for things dreamed and missed, but also because he cannot understand the forces that constrain him. Despite his "questing," he cannot "reason why."[35]

If in one of its aspects the poetry of 1919 bespeaks Faulkner's continuing preoccupation with his unfinished first love, in another it bespeaks his continued wrestling with the implications of his vocation. Shortly before Estelle's departure in late September, Faulkner decided to take advantage of a new policy at the University of Mississippi, that waived entrance requirements for veterans. As a special student, exempt from all requirements, he registered for French, Spanish, and English. Intent and steady in the beginning, he worked hard on each of his courses. To his mother he seemed more disciplined than ever before. But he soon let his interests guide him, and they promptly took him toward French literature, which was where his reading had been heading for several months. In the first semester he very nearly failed English; in the second, he dropped it. Although he was still reading Swinburne, Keats, Housman, and Wilde, and was now echoing T. S. Eliot, finding Prufrock's diminished life particularly haunting, he was also reading the French, and especially the French Symbolists.[36] From Mallarmé he took the title of his first published poem; from Verlaine's "Le Faune" he took the central device of *The Marble Faun*. Given some impetus and direction by Stone, he was working his way through every major and several minor figures, French and English, of the late nineteenth and early twentieth centuries.

In several scattered lines, *The Marble Faun* shows talent; in a few lines, it shows genuine strength. Finally, however, its primary interests derive less from its scattered moments of force than from its crippling weaknesses. Because it is so imitative and so literary, it points clearly to the period that now held Faulkner's attention. It both evokes and participates in the tone and the mood, the aestheticism and the decadence, of the late nineteenth century.[37] In addition, it indicates why Faulkner found poetry so restrictive and constraining, for it is a work in which felt presences overwhelm persona and echoes drown out voice. What we discern, therefore, is not the source of Faulkner's originality but the direction of his self-education. From dramatists like Oscar Wilde, from novelists like Joseph Conrad, and from several poets, French and English, he was absorbing techniques and preoccupations that would enable him to participate in the flowering of the 1920s. In addition to defining the generic and historical focus of his self-education, *The Marble Faun* helps to define the mode of that education. Years later Faulkner said that he wrote *The Sound and the Fury* "and learned to read," suggesting that writing was his way of assimilating what he had read.[38] *The Marble Faun* suggests that by 1919 writing had already become the last phase in an educational process so acquisitive as to seem imperial. It was as though nothing he read truly belonged to him until he had echoed, imitated, or adapted it.

In one respect, however, there is crucial distance between the poets Faulkner was reading and the poetry he was writing. *The Marble Faun* brings pastoral art and modern aestheticism into a conjunction that not only exposes the weaknesses of pastoral poetry, particularly its artificiality, but also establishes the pertinence of those weaknesses to our understanding of modern aestheticism. *The Marble Faun* constitutes less a celebration of art's power than an encounter with art's limitations. Faulkner's faun stands fixed, as Lewis Simpson has noted, "in a dispossessed garden"; cognizant of his weaknesses and limitations, he remains powerless to overcome them. As a result, we observe not only Faulkner's discontent with restrictions he had helped to impose on himself, nor merely his version of modernity's "rejection of pastoral," but his recognition that the weaknesses of the pastoral infect modern art.[39] The faun knows that he epitomizes form and assumes that he can never die. Yet he finds this the opposite of consoling precisely because it means that he will never live. The immutability of the "cold pastoral," which Faulkner associated with Keats's urn and considered the epitome of form, becomes undesirable the moment its price, the foregoing of "wild ecstasy," is named. Years later Faulkner gave Judith Sutpen words to express what he was beginning in the early 1920s to suspect: that things that endure are limited precisely because they "cant ever die or perish."[40] Between *The Marble Faun* and *Absalom, Absalom!*, he gave characters words to remind us of the emptiness of words and the emptiness of form. In a related strategy, he began stressing, often in mystifying contexts, that his own best novels were incomplete, unfinished, his own fictional kingdom living and changing. This emphasis upon his work's mutability was matched, of course, by insistence upon its immortality. Sometimes, as though to acknowledge the contradiction we customarily sense between these stresses, he spoke as though his novels were finished forms, his kingdom evolving, changing. But as often as not, he assumed that to live forever his work must first live, and so he treated as complementary categories we customarily view as contradictory.

Since it was a national reputation, and a large one, that Faulkner sought (his problem "as a poet," he once remarked, was "that he had one eye on the ball and the other eye on Babe Ruth"),[41] he tried to follow his *New Republic* triumph with others. In this endeavor, Phil Stone again proved helpful. Assisted by his secretary, he handled much of Faulkner's typing and most of his correspondence. Despite Phil's help, three years and many rejections separated Faulkner's first appearance in a national journal, in August 1919, from his second, in the *Double Dealer*, in June 1922. In the meantime, before and after his year as a student at the University of Mississippi, he worked steadily to expand his local reputation. By 1925, three university publications, the yearbook (*Ole Miss*), the newspaper (the *Mississippian*), and the humor magazine (*Scream*), had published at least forty-one of his works—seventeen drawings, sixteen poems, six reviews, one short story, and one prose sketch.[42]

Combined with his "foreign" manner, his drawings and writings made him a conspicuous figure. Since he was still "almost painfully shy," he often seemed to other students distant and arrogant.[43] Recalling the early 1920s, Phil Stone said:

He had an aristocratic, superior appearance—which most people considered an affectation—and an aloof reserve and an arrogant snappishness when someone tried to get familiar. So he was considered affected, peculiar, a crank, or a harmless ne'er-do-well. And thus he became "Count No Count."

The old families of Oxford tolerated him because, after all, he was a member of the Faulkner family. . . . But they did not invite him to their houses, as a rule, and my frequent statements that he was a writer of ability and would one day be more famous than Stark Young [another native son] . . . provoked guffaws from the general public and polite, derisive smiles from the old families.[44]

Slightly confused by his guises, never quite sure whether to treat him as an elegant "foreigner" or a literary bum, Faulkner's fellow students settled for thinking of him as both affected and decadent. Describing him as the "beau-u-tiful man with cane," the "peculiar person who calls himself William Falkner," they greeted him with ridicule.[45] Practicing stoicism that he associated with A. E. Housman, Faulkner responded to a few of the attacks as though bored and ignored the rest. Whatever pain he felt he kept to himself, even when his detractors used his size and boyish appearance to cast aspersions on his masculinity.

With a few students, particularly Ben Wasson, whom Faulkner had met before the war and now saw regularly, he was more at ease. And he enjoyed one or two members of the faculty, especially Calvin Brown, a sensitive and intelligent man whose wife, Ida, was a historian as well as a great raconteur. Sometimes, feeling that he had to get away from the university, he returned to the square to sit alone, silent and motionless, with the town's old men. At the university, as one acquaintance remembered, he possessed an "ability to lose himself in his own private world."[46] Walking across the campus or down a sidewalk, he was often oblivious of people he passed, acquaintances who spoke. On other occasions, feeling a need to get out of Oxford as well as away from Ole Miss, he simply disappeared without telling anyone where he was going. His trips to see Phil, their jaunts to nearby towns, were, among other things, means of getting away. In his parents' home on the campus, where his father now worked, he kept whiskey in his room. In Clarksdale, Memphis, and New Orleans, he made a point of drinking conspicuously.

During what Malcolm Cowley has called "the long adventure of the 1920s,"[47] many writers experimented with retreat or flight. Some, recalling the American Transcendentalists, withdrew to live a simplified life; in small enclaves or communities of artists, they tried to reduce externals to the essentials, their avowed purpose being to foster internal growth and permit new worlds to open within. Others, following the example of Henry James, withdrew for the purpose of complicating life. Absorbing foreign manners and customs, new rituals and artifices, they sought to enlarge their experience and enrich their lives. In these two forms, exile became the dominant pattern of a generation. During the 1920s Faulkner lived in two of the enclaves and made a journey through Europe. But even in Mississippi he experimented with departures and returns, withdrawals and reintegrations. One such experiment is of special interest, though it seems at first pure regression.

Soon after his return to Oxford, Faulkner began playing with his youngest brother, Dean, and the two sons of Calvin and Ida Brown. Going back to Bailey's Woods, he taught his followers skills he had acquired and games he had devised as a boy. They hunted, stalked, and chased one another; around campfires he told stories, "the tone" of which, one of the boys remembers, was "of supernatural horror" relieved by "humor, fantasy, or irony." Later, particularly in 1923 and 1924, he combined the same interests—love and knowledge of the woods, delight in play and in stories—by working with the local boy scout troop, for a time officially, as its scoutmaster. To many people in Oxford and many students at Ole Miss, he seemed the epitome of affectation. Off in the woods, away from wearying considerations and disdain, surrounded by young boys, his reserve faded: "I have never known a man less capable of sham," one of his followers reports.[48] Later, particularly in *The Sound and the Fury*, Faulkner wrote stories of the passing of a world that were also stories of the passing of childhood. In the years just after the Great War he sought not so much to recover a lost world as to acquire a deeper sense of what its loss entailed. And he did so not merely by recreating scenes he had known as a boy but by experimenting with a role he had seen his father play.

In May 1920, having completed one year as a special student, Faulkner won a prize for poetry and ended his formal education. Early the next semester he officially withdrew from the university without bothering to register for any courses. With no classes to punctuate his days, he had more time to himself. When money ran short, he took odd jobs. Between jobs he rode around rural Mississippi with Phil Stone, sometimes going as far as Memphis, where violence, gambling, and prostitution lent excitement to life. Still living on campus, he continued to see students and write for student publications. But shortly after he dropped out of school he began spending most of his time with a drama group that Ben Wasson had organized and named the Marionettes.[49]

After several months' work with this group, Faulkner completed a one-act play called *The Marionettes*, which he conceived primarily as a tribute to several people he had come to like, particularly Ben and Mary Helen Wasson, Lucy and Ellen Somerville. One of several "books" that he made as well as wrote, *The Marionettes* consists of a finely lettered "pen-printed" text and ten delicately lined pen-and-ink drawings. Although it is written primarily in prose, it includes several songs written in tetrameter couplets that resemble those of *The Marble Faun*. Its prose, too, is strongly reminiscent of Faulkner's poetry. The action of the play is static, its language cadenced and self-conscious. Like the prose and poetry of the play, the drawings are heavily mannered. Taken as a whole, the book owes much to the edition of Oscar Wilde's *Salomé* illustrated by Aubrey Beardsley. More generally, it evokes an era. Like *The Marble Faun*, it echoes so many late nineteenth-century poets, French and English, that it becomes, as Noel Polk has noted, not only "a remarkable synthesis" but "a very self-conscious display" of Faulkner's reading in fin de siècle aestheticism.[50]

As his roaming and drinking had increased, Faulkner had begun playing the elegant aesthete less, the careless bohemian more. Still, in both appearance and content, *The Marionettes* belongs to his life as aesthete; it is an extraordinarily self-conscious performance. For every aspect of its physical appearance, Faulkner showed the kind of excruciating care that he occasionally gave to his wardrobe and always gave to his handwriting. Initially open, flowing, familiar, his script had moved steadily toward printing that was so small and tight as to seem neat yet very private. More than self-conscious, *The Marionettes* is self-involved in ways that locating influences fails to suggest. Since Faulkner follows Verlaine in using traditional pantomime figures, Verlaine's presence is particularly pervasive. But in this case Verlaine's presence as poet blends with Faulkner's as translator. Early in 1920 Faulkner had published four adaptations of Verlaine. In *The Marionettes*, he echoes at least two of these, "Fantouches" and "Clair de Lune"; in addition, he echoes *The Marble Faun*. Earlier he had used his writing to display his reading; now he was using it to recast his earlier writing. In the process, he returned to preoccupations that went back to his youth.

Strewn with erotic images that revolve around the dance as a metaphor of sexual union ("And I must never learn to dance./O please don't make me want to try!" Marietta says to Pierrot),[51] *The Marionettes* may well suggest meanings beyond any Faulkner could have intended. But he clearly intended one thing that allies the play with his move from the tight aesthete toward the loose bohemian: namely, a direct contrast between "the impotent faun-like Pierrot" of the poems of 1919 and "the Jurgen-Don Juan-like Pierrot" of *The Marionettes*. Whether or not Faulkner's "various philanderings" had taken a new turn, there are signs, beyond his writings as well as within, that his attitude had changed; that he was tired of silence and stillness; that he wanted deliverance. Among other creations of the years to follow were several stories suggesting that he had fathered illegitimate children.[52]

Centering on the contrast between Pierrot's disorder and the garden's formality, *The Marionettes* suggests the issue to which, more and more, Faulkner's reading and writing were taking him. Despairing of the garden's artificiality, Pierrot becomes a disciple of disorder. Like Marietta's mechanical gestures and stylized speeches, her reluctance to dance seems to Pierrot to reflect both the warnings of her aunts and her own fears. To him she represents capitulation to the little life of the formal garden. But if in one of its aspects the formal garden represents civilization, and the restrained, diminished life it requires, in another it represents art. Far from being some grand metaphysical supplement raised up beside life in order to overcome it, art is seen as continuous with the revisionary impulse that, turning nature into a garden, has ordered life only by diminishing it. Which is to say that for Faulkner the sublime faith of fin de siècle aestheticism, its belief that art ("all discrimination and selection") was superior to natural and historical existence (the "stupid work" of "clumsy Life"), was proving less and less tenable.[53]

We thus see in *The Marionettes* something of why poetry was already becoming a dead end for Faulkner. And the problem turned mainly on voice. Although they had external corollaries, the pressures Faulkner felt came mainly from within. Too many avenues seemed closed, restricted. Occasionally during these years he dressed in baggy clothes and played the role of the drunken clown, even on the local golf course. It was freedom that he required, not the skin-tight trousers of his youth, or the studied uniform of the wounded veteran, or the careful costume of the dandy, but the baggy pants of the clown or at least the bohemian. Poetry seemed to him—and as he practiced it, it was—all order and restraint. In it, will and conscious intent counted for almost everything. His handwriting was becoming more and more constricted, so private that sometimes even he had difficulty reading it a day or two after producing it. But he needed to find a literary mode less haunted by giants and less bound by conventions. Only then could he hope to discover voices that would encourage him to use not simply the books that he had read and the emotions that troubled him but the world he had observed and the old tales and talking that he had heard.

During the spring and early summer of 1921 Faulkner "pen printed" another book, which he called "Vision in Spring." With Estelle back for a second visit, he wanted poems to read as they walked and a book to give her when she left. The writing went well enough, but as the summer faded his restlessness and discontent deepened. Both life and poetry seemed stale now. Earlier Stark Young had offered to help him find work in New York. By fall he was living in Greenwich Village and working on the corner of Fifth Avenue and 43rd Street in the Doubleday Doran Bookstore that Elizabeth Prall managed. Though he soon tired of it, he enjoyed selling books and did it well. He also enjoyed telling "lurid tales about his life." Using a cane, he walked with a distinct limp. Several acquaintances got the impression that he drank heavily and that he had suffered severe injuries to his head as well as to a leg and hip in the Great War. Others had a vaguer sense of the trauma he had endured, though they gathered that he was not yet wholly beyond it. Most of the time, however, he kept to himself. Surrounded by painters and writers, he enjoyed both the sense of their presence and the sense of his own anonymity and solitude. Left alone, he began writing fewer poems and more fiction. Soon, however, he found himself stymied again. Though poetry was no longer working as it had, fiction was not yet working as it would. Within a few months, his restlessness had taken him back to Oxford and the most improbable job he would ever hold.[54]

In part it was Stone's doing. Uneasy with his protegé so far away, coming under strange influences and doing who knew what, Stone arranged to have Faulkner appointed postmaster of the university post office, and then urged him to accept the position. "I forced Bill to take the job," he later remarked, "over his own declination and refusal. He made the damndest postmaster the world has ever seen." If the reasons for Stone's urging were apparent, the reasons for Faulkner's acquiescence were not. "It never ceased to amaze us all," his brother Murry said; "Here was a man so little attracted to mail that he never read his own being solemnly appointed as, one might say, the custodian of that belonging to others."[55] But Faulkner was twenty-four now, and though his relations with his father had eased, he felt the awkwardness of continuing dependence. During the three years since his return from the war, nothing had happened to suggest that he could support himself by writing, and he was tired of making do with odd jobs. With a small post office to run, he could support himself and still be free to set his own hours.

Given his approach to it, the job was in fact only a minor inconvenience. When he felt restless, he simply closed the office and went out into the woods or over to the golf course. On hot or rainy days, he stayed on the job, reading or playing cards with friends, one or two of whom he hired as part-time clerks. Mail he thought important, he handled with some regularity; mail he deemed insignificant, such as university bulletins and catalogs, he accumulated in large carts, dispatching or delivering it when the mood struck him; mail he regarded as junk, he simply discarded. The more interesting periodicals he kept several days in the back of the post office, where he had established a reading room for the enjoyment of the postmaster and his friends.[56]

Although mail presented a small problem, patrons gradually became a big one. Irregular hours, mysterious delays, and strange losses gave rise to complaints, as did the manners of the public servant. Accommodating to friends and polite to acquaintances, Faulkner could be rude to pushy strangers. For a while most of the complaints were unofficial and good-natured: one student publication suggested that the postmaster's motto was "Never put the mail up on time" and that his hours were 11:20–12:20 every Wednesday.[57] Eventually dissatisfaction overcame both public restraint and official indifference, forcing an investigation. But in the meantime, which turned out to be three years, Faulkner enjoyed having a little more money. Soon he was able to buy a car, which made excursions with Phil and private rides with women easier to arrange.

During the three years following his return from New York, Faulkner continued to publish in student publications—a few drawings, an impressionistic sketch called "The Hill," and several reviews. In June 1922 he published a poem called "Portrait" in the *Double Dealer*, a "little magazine" with a growing reputation. But as aestheticism's appeal faded, his writing began to change. Soon he was revising poems more, writing them less. Although his second volume of poems, *A Green Bough*, would not be published until 1933, many of the poems in it date from the early 1920s, and none can definitely be dated after 1926.[58] As his production of poetry slowed, his production of reviews—of poets like W. A. Percy and Conrad Aiken, dramatists like Eugene O'Neill, and novelists like Joseph Hergesheimer—picked up. Unlike the poems and drawings of these years, which show little development, the reviews engage problems that continued to concern him for years.

In one review he quoted lines from Sean O'Casey describing mitered bishops who strain at the bars of paradise, hoping to see the lady Helen walking in her golden shawl—lines that he later adapted for use, first in poem III of *A Green Bough*, and then in *The Hamlet* and *The Mansion*. In another review he wondered whether the region and dialects that he directly knew could be put to literary use, and whether "a man of real ability" does not find "sufficient what he has to hand."[59] In yet another, he articulated the doubts about aestheticism that were already changing his conception of himself as a writer. Having tied Joseph Hergesheimer's novels to an attenuation of life—to fear "of living, of [being] man in his sorry clay braving chance and circumstance"—and even specifically to "sex crucifixion," he went on to associate Hergesheimer's works with a slightly disguised version of an image familiar to every reader of Keats and every reader of Faulkner. *Linda Condon*, he wrote, "is not a novel. It is more like a lovely frieze: a few unforgettable figures in silent arrested motion, forever beyond the reach of time." Rather than creating life around them, Faulkner continued, Hergesheimer's characters "are like puppets assuming graceful but meaningless postures in answer to the author's compulsions."[60]

Published 15 December 1922, Faulkner's review of Hergesheimer's fiction is remarkable in several respects, including its evocation both of the still garden of *The Marble Faun* and of the pantomime figures of *The Marionettes*. In the tone of this evocation, however, judgment mingles with sympathy, suggesting that Faulkner was discovering in self-involvement a potential for self-criticism. In one telling statement—"One can imagine Hergesheimer submerging himself in *Linda Condon* as in a still harbor where the age cannot hurt him and where rumor of the world reaches him only as a far faint sound of rain"—he looks forward even as he looks back. Hoping to escape the sounds and smells that disturb him, Quentin Compson submerges himself in "the secret shade" of the Charles River. Writing about *The Sound and the Fury* in 1933, several years after he finished it, Faulkner described it as a vase he had made so that he could escape into it—though "I suppose," he added, that "I knew all the time that I could not live forever inside of it." A year earlier, in 1932, he had depicted Gail Hightower seeking similar shelter within the church, within his vocation as minister, within the walls of the seminary: "When he believed that he had heard the call it seemed to him that he could see his future, his life, intact and on all sides complete and inviolable, like a classic and serene vase, where the spirit could be born anew sheltered from the harsh gale of living and die so, peacefully, with only the far sound of the circumvented wind."[61]

The impasse to which the Hergesheimer review points would also find expression in *Soldiers' Pay* (1926), in which Faulkner associates Margaret Powers with an indictment of Beardsley's drawings as mannered and decadent, filled with "meretricious trees and impossible marble fountains."[62] In the early 1920s, however, though he was already discovering how false and impossible poetry was for him, he was not yet in command of what would take its place. Only a slight story called "Landing in Luck" (1919) and a brief sketch called "The Hill" (1922) anticipate the experimental prose he began writing in New Orleans in January 1925. In the meantime, he had to rely on poetry. In June 1923 he sent the Four Seas Company of Boston a revised version of "Vision in Spring," retitled "Orpheus, and Other Poems." Unwilling to publish the poems without a subsidy, which Faulkner could not afford, Four Seas returned the manuscript. Frustrated and angry, Faulkner said: "If they want a book to remember, by God I'll write it."[63] But in fact, reading novels and revising poems, he published nothing at all in 1923. With the coming of spring, urged on by Stone, he submitted *The Marble Faun*. Again Four Seas wanted a subsidy, but this time Faulkner agreed. In December 1924 his first book, dedicated to his mother, was published.

Since "general contempt for the ineffectual Count Faulkner" was spreading as the crisis over the post office mounted, publication of *The Marble Faun* proved fortuitous. In September Faulkner had received notice that official charges—neglect of duty, indifference to patrons, abuse of mail—had been filed against him. Knowing the charges to be true, hating the job and wanting out of it, he decided to await investigation. When an inspector arrived, he expressed relief. "You know, all my life I probably will be at the beck and call of somebody who's got money," he said. "Never again will I be at the beck and call of every son-of-a bitch who's got two cents to buy a stamp." Partly because he got on well with the inspector and partly because the Falkners were prominent, he was permitted to resign as postmaster. From his position as master of the local boy scout troop, he was simply dismissed, primarily because his reputation as a drinker had reached the ears of too many local ministers.[64]

There was little left in Oxford to hold him. With publication of *The Marble Faun*, he had brought his career as a poet to a kind of conclusion. In 1933, almost as an act of loyalty to the self-conception that informed his early years as a writer, he published another volume of poetry, *The Green Bough*, but it was mostly prose that he was writing now. Though Stone was pushing copies of *The Marble Faun*, its author needed to get away. Not even the presence of Estelle, just arrived for her third visit since his return from the war, could hold him. Earlier her arrivals had moved him to poetry, and it probably seemed strange to leave her now in the town she had never known without him. But he had a book to give her, and a need to be free. He was twenty-seven, and time seemed to him short. In Phil Stone he had found a tutor; in Estelle and a few friends, an audience; in writing poetry, a means of appropriation and expression. But he needed a change. He needed the presence and example of people who shared his interests and problems, who wouldn't laugh at what he was "trying to do . . . no matter how foolish it might sound."[65] Above all, he needed less specific instruction and a less limited audience.

THREE 1925-1926

Versions of the Artist

In the fall of 1924, while he was planning a trip to Europe, Faulkner wrote a brief sketch for Four Seas to use in publishing *The Marble Faun*. In most respects the sketch is not surprising. It lists various jobs Faulkner had held and notes that he had served "during the war in the British Royal Air Force." But it includes two statements that are curious. First, mentioning neither of his parents, it introduces him as the "Great-grandson of Col. W. C. Faulkner, C. S. A., author of 'The White Rose of Memphis,' 'Rapid Ramblings in Europe,' etc." Second, it describes Mississippi as the place of his birth and the scene of his "boyhood and youth," yet gives Oxford as his "present temporary address."[1]

In the first of these statements we see another phase in Faulkner's appropriation of his great-grandfather; in the second we see a deeper restlessness and a new intention. It is as though, feeling that he had formally become a writer, Faulkner had determined to claim the Old Colonel more completely for himself. Certainly he establishes a close correspondence. Making the names match, he introduces the Old Colonel in terms of three common denominators—military service, writing, and Mississippi. Even his projected journey to Europe he privately associates with the Old Colonel's European tour of 1883. When, after two false starts, he made that journey, the relation he saw became clearer. Having sailed with the intention of writing impressionistic sketches for regional newspapers, he promptly began writing letters that reminded his family of the Old Colonel's travel sketches.[2]

Faulkner's restlessness ran deeper, however, than any the Old Colonel had ever shown. Soon after mailing his sketch to Four Seas, he wrote Ben Wasson describing the relief he felt at being free of the post office and announcing his determination to avoid such traps in the future.[3] But his departure discloses a larger sense of entrapment. He wanted to keep in touch with Phil Stone, who remained his friend as well as his unofficial literary agent; and he wanted to go on seeing Estelle, who was spending more time with her parents now that her marriage was collapsing. But he also wanted to get away, to live and work in other places, especially Europe. Permanent exile probably struck him as nothing more than a remote possibility. Even the several years' stay that Stone was apparently urging—in the hope that fame missed in Oxford might be found in Paris— may well have seemed unlikely. But he was ready to reverse the pattern of living in Oxford and making excursions from it that he had worked out in the months immediately following the war.

Shortly after his arrival in New Orleans in early January 1925, Faulkner went to see Elizabeth Prall, a friend from his days in the bookstore in New York. Several months earlier he had visited her and met her husband, Sherwood Anderson, with whom he had felt immediate rapport. Although Anderson was gone on a several weeks' speaking tour, Elizabeth Prall Anderson invited Faulkner to stay in a spare room in the apartment she and her husband kept in the center of the Vieux Carré. Almost on the spot, Faulkner decided to delay his departure for Europe.[4]

Entry into the colony of writers and artists in New Orleans proved easy for Faulkner, in part because the group tended to be open and friendly; in part because he was thought of as a friend of the Andersons; and in part because the self-conception he brought with him, that of a bohemian poet, fit in nicely. Drinking conspicuously, he spiced his conversation with references to the illegitimate children he had left in and around Oxford and to the harrowing war experiences that had made him a poet. People who met him noticed that he limped, and many of them believed that he had made a brilliant record and been severely wounded while serving in the R.A.F. Internal dramas and adventures would never suffice: he always needed to exaggerate the dangers he had encountered, and "he loved to put things over on people."[5] Later he glamorized his months in New Orleans with stories about escapades as a bootlegger. In fact, however, his New Orleans adventures were of a different kind. The people who listened to his stories and noticed his limp also enjoyed his wry comments and his occasional tall tales. But what they appreciated most was his habit of listening intently to their talk about the writings of Conrad, Eliot, and Joyce, or the ideas of Freud, Frazer, and Bergson. Since he tended to be deeply competitive, his relations with Anderson and a few other New Orleans writers later became strained. He often felt more comfortable around painters and sculptors than other writers. Still, near the end of his active participation in the life of the Vieux Carré he characterized what he had found there with some irony, yet with feeling, too, as a "fellowship where no badges are worn and no sign of greeting is required." During his last years in Oxford, his relations with his world had become too strained to be creative. As tension with almost everything external to him had increased, even his inner self had become less energetic, more impoverished.[6] In New Orleans he discovered not only what his friend William Spratling called "a constant stimulation of ideas" but also a more intense version of what he had experienced with the Marionettes—a sense of shared interests and commitments.[7]

Soon he was writing with intensity deeper than any he had ever known. Burdened with no responsibilities, given ample freedom, he spent hours each day writing. During the next few months he published thousands of words. People who drank hard and talked big were easy to find. What set Faulkner apart was how early he began writing and how long he stayed with it. To those closest to him he seemed to be "boiling with ideas all the time." He remained shy, yet he found help at every turn from a few people introduced by Stone and many introduced by Elizabeth Anderson. William Spratling, John McClure, Julius Friend, Hamilton Basso, Lyle Saxon and Roark Bradford all befriended him. In the people associated with the *Double Dealer* he found writers and artists with whom he shared interests; and in their magazine he found a place to publish his articles, poems, and sketches.[8]

Although the *Double Dealer*'s circulation remained small, its reputation had grown and its editors felt adventuresome. They had published work by Hart Crane, Ezra Pound, Ernest Hemingway, and Sherwood Anderson; and they took satisfaction in juxtaposing established writers with unknown regional writers. Three years earlier they had published a poem by Faulkner called "Portrait." In the first issue after his arrival in New Orleans, they published another of his poems, one of his essays, and a long prose piece called "New Orleans." It was a sign of things to come. In the weeks and months that followed, Faulkner continued to publish in the *Double Dealer* and began publishing in the New Orleans *Times-Picayune*, where several writers associated with the "little magazine" worked as reporters or feature writers. From the newspaper he began to make a little money as a writer; from the magazine he began to understand what it meant to be a writer with readers.[9]

The big project he had in mind was a book of poems called "The Greening Bough." He still thought of himself as a poet; it was in fact Robert Frost's emergence in England that Stone hoped Faulkner might repeat by going to Europe. But while his *Double Dealer* reviews and poems showed little advance over those published at the University of Mississippi, his prose sketches showed clear development. Working out of the fundamental impulse of the Symbolist movement, he had been trying for years to find metaphoric patterns that captured the subtleties of consciousness. Writing poetry he had met with only scattered success; writing prose he began a period of dramatic growth.

Having finished a series of eleven impressionistic monologues called "New Orleans," which he published in the *Double Dealer*, he began a series of longer, more complex sketches for the *Times-Picayune*. In both series he experimented with themes, structures, and even characters that he later used in more sophisticated ways. It was almost as though he had begun yet another apprenticeship. Earlier he had made poems and reviews the final step in his appropriation of the books he was reading; now he was using his prose sketches for the same purpose. Ever a brash borrower, he took what he needed where he found it. From Julius Friend's tribute to Conrad, published in the October 1924 *Double Dealer*, he took the phrase "eternal verities"; from John McClure's review of *The Marble Faun*, he took the idea of noble failure; later, from a review of *Soldiers' Pay*, he took the idea of fiction as a compound of "imagination, observation, and experience." These and other borrowed ideas he used until they became wholly his. In the sketches he was writing, several presences reappear; at least one, Joseph Conrad's, is so prevalent as to suggest that Faulkner was rereading him. Conrad's "impressionistic" method was apparently "a topic of lively discussion" in New Orleans at the time. Certainly we sense Conrad's influence in Faulkner's use of scrambled chronology and withheld information, as well as in his preoccupation with stories having to do with failure of nerve or character. Soon Faulkner was using impressionistic techniques as Conrad had used them, for the purpose of reclaiming melodramatic plots for serious fiction. Several of Faulkner's sketches focus on acts of seeing, reseeing, or detecting; and several of them come to us through a narrator or observer who remains sympathetic yet more or less detached, near the action yet, like the reader, partially confused.[10] In these distancing devices, Faulkner discovered techniques that later allowed him to use actions that were horrendous or preposterous, sentimental or melodramatic, without committing himself to them unambiguously.

In many of the sketches, style is Faulkner's major concern. Although his language is basically colloquial, he achieves greater resonance by using traditional rhetorical devices, and greater richness by using dialect. Of several experiments of this sort, "The Longshoreman" is the most interesting. In it a black man's dialect evokes a rich religious heritage, preparing for the emergence of more traditional rhetoric: "White man gives me clo'se and shoes, but dat dont make no pavement love my feets. These cities are not my cities, but this dark is my dark, with all the old passions and fears and sorrows that my people have breathed into it."[11] Although the break in voice here is too abrupt, it accomplishes its purpose. For it allies the psyche's deeper perceptions and needs with more traditional syntax and diction, thus defining them as shared. Whereas the dialect seems accidental and public, the rhetoric seems at once private and universal. With practice, Faulkner became more skilled in mixing his modes and making his moves. But he remained insistent, even abrupt, in mingling the colloquial and the elevated, as the first chapter of *Light in August* clearly shows.

Late in February, Faulkner decided to spend a few days in Oxford. He wanted to see Estelle Franklin and talk with Phil Stone about his plans. Once again he was thinking of starting for Europe. Instead, he returned to New Orleans, moved to a spare room in William Spratling's apartment, and began two new adventures, one a friendship with Sherwood Anderson, the other a novel called *Soldiers' Pay*. Although Anderson and Faulkner were working hard, they saw each other regularly, sometimes in the afternoon, sometimes in the evening. Since the more loquacious Anderson was nearly twice Faulkner's age and was also famous, he easily assumed the role of master, leaving Faulkner the role of protégé. In the afternoons, Faulkner recalled, "We'd walk and he'd talk and I'd listen"; in the evenings, "We'd sit around till one or two o'clock drinking, and still me listening to him talking." The two men shared an interest in painting as well as writing, and both loved tall tales. From his acquaintance with Faulkner, Anderson got three things: an episode that he turned into a story called "A Meeting South"; many pleasurable hours; and, finally, an injury. From Anderson Faulkner got much more: decisive help in getting his first novel published; miscellaneous advice; memories on which he would base a character in *Mosquitoes*; and, most of all, a usable model.[12]

Drawing on their shared love of tall tales, Anderson and Faulkner collaborated in creating Al Jackson. Initially half horse and half alligator, Al Jackson became half man and half sheep, and then a sharklike creature who preyed on fat, blond, female swimmers. From this brief collaboration, Anderson emerged with a clear impression and a warning. "You've got too much talent," he said to Faulkner. "You can do it too easy, in too many different ways. If you're not careful, you'll never write any-thing."[13] More important than Anderson's advice, however, was the kind of model he provided. Since Anderson was short, he seemed to Faulkner physically unimposing. As a writer, he was accomplished enough to be impressive, yet flawed enough not to seem overwhelming—a combination that made him an almost perfect master. Faulkner genuinely admired *Winesburg, Ohio* and several of Anderson's stories, including "I'm a Fool." But he recognized limitations in Anderson's work, particularly its "fumbl-ing for exactitude." The first significant writer he had known, Anderson was a fictionist he could try to emulate and hope to surpass. Of Ander-son's fiction he could say, to paraphrase James Dickey's description of Carlos Williams's poetry, if this is fiction, then maybe I can write some too.[14]

This recognition was crucial to Faulkner. Some writers of talent or genius learn early "to trust themselves in an essential way, whatever moments of doubt they may have"; and some are "remarkably lucky, or wise, in finding a circle of friends" who believe in their powers before they have "given much evidence" of them. According to Lionel Trilling, this is what happened to John Keats—with the result that Keats found it easy to trust his own thoughts and emotions in propounding "the great questions" and attempting "the great answers." Faulkner occasionally announced—once to an astonished woman on a golf course—that he was a genius who would one day be famous, and in some moments he clearly believed that he was, even before he moved to New Orleans and met Anderson. But he was slow to trust himself in a fundamental way, and slow to find people who believed in him, particularly people whose talents he respected. Anderson was short, and he wrote awkward prose. Yet, combined with his age and achievement, these perceived limitations en-abled Anderson to help Faulkner as no other New Orleans writer could, by fostering in Faulkner the same belief and desire that Faulkner saw in him—the "belief, necessary to a writer, that his own emotions are im-portant," and "the desire to tell them to someone."[15]

Faulkner had of course been edging toward such belief and desire for years. But in the few months given him, Anderson helped Faulkner to a stronger sense of them, in part by speeding him toward fiction. Later, in 1926, Faulkner collaborated with William Spratling in writing *Sher-wood Anderson and Other Famous Creoles*. Coming as it did after Hem-ingway's condescending parody in *Torrents of Spring*, Faulkner's gentler play with Anderson's style injured a man who had befriended him. Even before what Faulkner later called "the unhappy caricature affair," rela-tions between them had become strained. Both men were deeply sensitive and deeply competitive. With one man's career near a remarkable begin-ning and the other's already in a slow, painful decline, the master-protégé relationship was impossible to sustain. The help Anderson gave Faulkner

and the advances it made possible left both men feeling uneasy with the
roles into which they had fallen. Years later, however, looking back,
Faulkner described Anderson as a giant and as "the father of all of my
generation" of writers—terms that exaggerate Anderson's achievement
even as they suggest the crucial role he played in Faulkner's development,
particularly during the months of 1925 when he was writing his first
novel.[16]

Following his return to New Orleans in March, Faulkner continued
to write sketches that reached a small audience and brought in small
fees. Although everything he had sent to popular magazines like the
Saturday Evening Post had been rejected, he still intended to master the
requirements of commercial fiction. Sometimes he felt uncomfortable
writing for money, as though he feared such abuse might destroy his
talent. But he wanted recognition and success, and he was incapable of
divorcing them from money. The middle way, bourgeois means and
manners, offended him. The poverty and obscurity in which he lived,
though he later wrote tenderly of them, offered no long-term alternative.
For, as Elizabeth Prall Anderson noted, he already possessed expensive
tastes to match his large ambition. Thus divided, committed to fame and
fortune as well as to art, he wanted to find some way of becoming famous
and making money without compromising or corrupting his work. As it
turned out, the solution he hit upon while writing *Soldiers' Pay* later
became one of the organizing principles of his life: though he gave scattered hours and considerable talent to commercial fiction, he tried to save
his genius for his art. In New Orleans, in March, April, and May 1925,
this strategy meant working long days, perfunctorily on the sketches and
intensely on his novel. In "the morning, in the afternoon and often late
at night," he was always at it.[17]

In writing *Soldiers' Pay*, which he first called "Mayday," Faulkner
followed a procedure that became his regular practice. He wrote by hand,
revised his manuscript, then made a typescript that he revised further,
sometimes shifting large sections. The care with which he outlined the
novel in advance suggests a clear sense of purpose. It also suggests continued development in his imaginative appropriation of the war. During the
writing he not only engaged in an extended and elaborate impersonation
of the wounded veteran; he also wrote a brief piece called "Literature and
War," which is his most direct assessment of the efforts of others "to
use the late war" for literary purposes.[18]

In *Soldiers' Pay* he borrowed from what he had written as well as
from what he heard, read, and projected. Having taken an epigraph—

> The hushed plaint of wind in stricken trees
>   Shivers the grass in path and lane

And Grief and Time are tideless golden seas—
  Hush, hush! He's home again.

—from one of his earlier poems, he began his novel with a contrast between two figures that had long engaged him: one a cadet on whom
"they had stopped the war," the other a dreadfully scarred R.A.F.
pilot who has returned home maimed and moribund. The first of these
figures resembles the young cadet and "barracks ace" of "Landing in
Luck," Faulkner's first piece of published fiction; the second resembles
a figure present in several of his poems, including "The Lilacs" and
"An Armistice Day Poem," from which he took the epigraph.[19] There is
another way of viewing these figures, however, and it is more suggestive
of what the novel represented in relation to Faulkner's own experience.
In Cadet Lowe we see an image of several things Faulkner had experienced
directly—the frustration, bitterness, and humiliation of proposals rejected
and adventures missed; in Lieutenant Donald Mahon we see an image of
horrors Faulkner knew only through hearing and reading, imagining and
projecting.

Later Faulkner used the war and its aftermath as the setting of several
stories and novels that are superior to *Soldiers' Pay*. However impressive
Soldiers' Pay may be as a first performance, to most present-day readers
it is little more than a museum-piece in which Faulkner tried to master
the war imaginatively and then enroll "himself among the wasteland-
ers."[20] But *Soldiers' Pay* also expressed Faulkner's determination to discover ties between his own experiences and those of his generation. For
years he had continued to feel and dramatize estrangement. Yet what
did believing in the significance of one's own emotions and experiences
entail if not conviction that in some sense they were shared? The evocation of Aubrey Beardsley, like the presence of nymphs and satyrs, or,
more tellingly, the garden—these and other elements in *Soldiers' Pay*
reflect Faulkner's need to stress continuities not only between his present
and past work, but also between his experience and the experience of
others, between his world and others' worlds. Donald Mahon's wounds,
which epitomize the psychic and physical injuries inflicted by the war,
not only represent more terrible versions of injuries Faulkner had feigned;
they also impose extreme versions of the limitations with which he had
been experimenting since boyhood.

Mahon is already sentenced to stillness when the novel opens; after
he loses his sight, he can only listen. At a dance to which he is taken, he
listens while other veterans stand awkwardly on the sidelines watching;
although he is aware of the distance that separates him from other veterans, they are aware of the distance that separates them from the boys
and girls who know little about war but much about dancing. What

wounds do emphatically for him, felt distance does effectively for them. Extreme versions of the wounds Faulkner had affected, Mahon's wounds imply many things, including both a reprieve from sexuality and a promise of premature death. The dance other veterans know by watching, remembering, and anticipating, Mahon knows only by hearing. Many of Faulkner's fabrications about his war experiences, including those about injuries to his hip and his head, were clearly self-enhancing. But he had learned early to let his hand express what he could not permit his body to do or his mouth to say. Remembering this habit, and remembering too that he had begun practicing stillness and silence as a boy, we should recognize his shadowy presence in *Soldiers' Pay*, poised between more and less terrible modes of truncation, more and less terrible versions of retirement. As he practiced it, poetry too had implied truncation: it had imposed severe restrictions on rhythm and diction, and it had controlled the way he echoed his ancestors and used his experience. Prose, on the other hand, was already taking him toward a sense of language as field of play without bounds, a sense of language as permitting almost anything, the dance of sex and the dance of death.

During the early stages of the writing of *Soldiers' Pay*, Sherwood Anderson read what Faulkner wrote, offering encouragement. In late May, when Faulkner finished it, Anderson agreed to recommend the book to his publisher, Boni and Liveright, on the condition that Faulkner not expect him to read it. The condition hurt Faulkner, but the offer was too good to turn down. Phil Stone could help him get the manuscript typed, but no one could help as much as Anderson in getting it published. Keeping his disappointment to himself, he took the address he needed, packed his manuscript, and left for Oxford.[21]

Although Estelle Franklin was still in Oxford, Helen Baird, a woman Faulkner had met in New Orleans, was in Pascagoula. Leaving Phil to supervise the typing and Estelle to care for her two children, Faulkner joined Helen in Pascagoula, where he could swim and sail as a guest of Phil's brother. Reciting Swinburne and Housman to Helen as they walked the beaches, he waited for Phil's secretary to finish his manuscript. Soon he was writing poems and making up stories for Helen. But no one found him winning. To Helen he seemed small and preoccupied. To her mother, who found his beachcomber costume and bohemian hygiene offensive, he seemed disreputable and presumptuous. Toward the end of June, Mrs. Baird took her daughter and left for Europe, adding her name to the list of disapproving parents. Waiting a few days, Faulkner returned to Oxford, where he mailed his manuscript and began thinking of Europe himself, this time more definitely.[22]

Without having met any of them, Phil Stone had apparently prepared letters introducing Faulkner to such luminaries as Pound, Eliot, and

Joyce. Although he probably knew he would never use them, Faulkner packed the letters along with a few clothes and left for New Orleans. For the third and last time, he was on his way to Europe. In New Orleans he found William Spratling preparing to leave for Italy. On July 7, six months and thousands of words after his first arrival in New Orleans en route, he sailed with Spratling for Genoa. During the four weeks' voyage, he wrote sketches for the *Times-Picayune* and threw some of his poems into the sea.[23] From Genoa he started toward Paris, prepared to walk most of the way. As he walked, he went out of his way to visit places that interested him. Later, on another walking tour, he saw the great cathedral in Rouen, visited Gallo-Roman ruins, and brooded over the battlefields between Compiègne and Amiens where nearly 500,000 men had died. During a brief stay in England, he visited coffee houses associated with writers from Marlowe to Dickens, and walked through the countryside of Kent, which he associated with Conrad. But he spent most of his time in Paris. There he vistied the tomb of Oscar Wilde, the bookstore Sylvia Beach called Shakespeare and Company, and the cafe James Joyce was known to frequent. Yet he made no effort to meet Joyce or even any of the Americans who had made expatriatism fashionable. During his weeks in Paris, he ate, drank, and talked with a few art students from Chicago and a few French people on whom he could practice his French. In Paris as in New York, he enjoyed both the presence of other artists and writers and his own privacy and anonymity. He lived in simple hotels and ate in restaurants patronized by workingmen; he visited the Louvre and Jeu de Paume and frequented the Luxembourg Gardens, where old men joined young boys in sailing toy boats and playing croquet. The few amenities he required, and all the entertainment, he found easily.[24]

Shortly after his arrival in Paris, he began growing a beard and writing. Poems and sketches soon gave way to sporadic work on "Mosquito," a novel about several writers and artists, one of whom mentions a poet named Faulkner. Later it became Faulkner's second novel. But in Paris he soon put it aside in order to work on a story about an artist named Elmer Hodge. Writing concertedly, Faulkner pushed "Elmer" almost to completion, only to abandon it. Later, he drew "characters, themes, and even patches of dialogue and imagery" from it for use in novels as different as *Mosquitoes, Sartoris,* and *The Wild Palms*. Yet, even a decade later, after he had published several masterpieces, he remained unable to complete it. In 1958 he suggested that he had failed because his story "was not funny enough." But the reasons for his failure, like the reasons for the failure of the story's humor, ran deeper: "too close to him in time," the novel remained "too nearly autobiographical."[25]

"Elmer" suggests that, having left home for Europe, Faulkner had begun a process of direct self-examination. Early in "Elmer" we are aware

of "the cold and restless monotony of the Atlantic." Throughout the
story we see Faulkner transpose his experiences and impressions into fictional form, a process he begins by deliberately distancing himself from
his protagonist. He writes in the third person, and his narrative voice,
often distinctly ironic, suggests a clear sense of superiority. But the means
he employs for distancing Elmer also suggest obvious ties. Elmer becomes
an observer who watches the other "boys playing their games," not because he is short and frail, but because he is tall, slow, and awkward.
The son of a restless, driven mother and a weak, failed father, Elmer seeks
fame, fortune, and a bride by becoming a painter rather than a writer.
He is a veteran who walks with a cane, and he is the father of an illegitimate child. When his story begins, he is either in France or nearing it.
Moved by the scenes around him, he enters dreamlike states of reverie;
staring either at the sea or a river, he resees and reconstitutes his life. The
result is a portrait of the artist presented as a kind of psychosexual history, the terms being so distinctly Freudian as to make it inconceivable
that Faulkner did not know exactly what he was doing.[26]

Having earlier drawn "smokestacks" and several other phallic objects,
Elmer now paints men and women. A familiar kind of romantic, he
associates the figures he paints with something "that he dreaded yet
longed for"; his purpose is to "make them conform to that vague shape
[s]omewhere back in his mind." The origins of that vague shape are in
turn clearly incestuous. His earliest memories are of his mother's body and
the thrilled effect of touching her breasts and heart. From this forbidden
love for "the dark woman. The dark mother," he has gone on to another
forbidden love—for a sister named Jo-Addie. This name, which is appro-
priately bisexual, is also particularly resonant. For it anticipates names
Faulkner later gave to a daughter named Compson and a mother named
Bundren, both of whom become involved in relations, the one with a
brother, the other with a son, that possess distinctly incestuous overtones.
Even more than the second, the first of these figures, Caddy Compson,
clearly occupied a special place in Faulkner's experience. Calling her his
"heart's darling," Faulkner associated her both with the sister he never
had and with the daughter he was fated to lose. He also associated her
with Keats's urn, which he in turn associated with life and with art—
with life because it depicted love that was dreamed yet denied, felt yet
deferred; and with art because it epitomized form.

As it turns out, Elmer is fated to lose the sister he has and fated to
find in the loss of that dark, conglomerate, possible yet forbidden object
of desire the experience that turns him into an artist. After Jo-Addie
has run away, leaving Elmer with a memory of one who had "accepted
him" and one whom he "had worshipped . . . quietly," she sends him a
gift, "a snug cardboard box containing eight colored wax crayons."

Forever after he associates painting with the memory of his sister. For him, she both embodies beauty and is distinctly bisexual: though there is "a marked indentation in the thigh above the hip-socket," her stomach is "poised and flat as an athlete's on her little wary hips." In late pre-adolescence and adolescence, Elmer's devotion to Jo-Addie tends to bi-furcate. Briefly in the fourth grade he is drawn to idealized versions of himself—in particular, to a boy who possesses "a sort of cruel beauty," which he admires from afar. In other moments he is drawn to "Diana-like" girls who combine fierceness with purity, great beauty with un-attainability. Later, in young manhood, he falls in love with Ethel, a girl—"fierce proud Dianalike . . . small and dark and impregnably virgin-al"—whom he persists in thinking of as approximating his ideal, even though, pregnant by him, she determines to marry someone more appro-priate.[27] Thus rejected and betrayed, he joins the army, only to encounter new indignities. Wounded by his own "awkward hands" in grenade practice, he returns "from his futile and abortive attempt at the war" determined to win the girl of his dreams. Soon, however, his love shifts to Myrtle (she is "like a star, clean and unattainable for all her . . . human-ness"). Finally, after Myrtle's mother has packed her off to Europe—in part to get her away from unsuitable Elmer—he goes to Europe, hoping to become a famous painter, to make a fortune, and to win his love.

In the tone of the "Elmer" manuscripts, in the comments he made about them, in the fate he projected for his protagonist—at every point it is clear that Faulkner felt deep irony for his artist. "Elmer is quite a boy," he wrote his mother. "He is tall and almost handsome and he wants to paint pictures. He gets everything a man could want—money, a Euro-pean title, marries the girl he wants—and she gives away his paint box. So Elmer never gets to paint at all."[28] Yet even as he represents the artist who fails because he sacrifices art to life, Elmer also suggests the terms in which Faulkner had come to view a commitment to art. He knew not only what art seemed to derive from but also what it seemed to mean going without: fortune, fame, and love. For him "Elmer" was in part a way of steeling himself against a failure of nerve and will. In a New Orleans sketch called "The Artist," he portrays the artist as one who sacrifices almost everything for "a dream and a fire" that he can never control. This sacrifice is made precisely in order to enter the world of creation: "But to create! Which among ye who have not this fire, can know this joy, let it be ever so fleet?" In a later sketch called "Out of Nazareth," he expresses both the need to create and the conviction that words were to be his life, his "meat and bread and drink." Viewed in this context, "Elmer" is a portrait of the artist Faulkner did *not* wish to become: the artist who reduces his gift to a flair for romantic living, and so surrenders his chance to live in and out of the world of creation.[29]

But "Elmer" is more than a depiction of tension between life and art, between "everything a man could want" and the mere painting of pictures; it is more even than an oblique recommitment to art. It is also an examination, essentially in psychological terms, of the sources of artistic impulses. Sex, religion, and art are inextricably entangled in "Elmer." Feeling his tubes of paint, Elmer thinks of them as "virgin," "immaculate," and "pregnant." Hovering "over them with a brooding maternity" he takes "up one at a time those portentous tubes in which was yet wombed his heart's desire, the world itself." To him they seem "thick-bodied and female and at the same time phallic: hermaphroditic." A part of what one senses here is definition of the artist's relation to his work as bisexual, the feminine-masculine work corresponding to the masculine-feminine self. Since the "vague shape [s]omewhere back in his mind" is forbidden yet necessary, Elmer both dreads and longs for it: it both can't and must be what he will know. As a result, all his efforts "to draw" figures of "men and women" so as "to make them conform to that vague shape" must proceed by indirection.

The view toward which Faulkner thus moves is striking, even radical, for the choice that Elmer faces is whether to accept himself and Myrtle as an approximation of the impossible and forbidden "vague shape" in his mind, or to persist in making paintings as approximations. As Faulkner presents them, both the real woman (Myrtle) and the paintings are substitutes for, signs of, the impossible and forbidden shape in Elmer's mind. If Elmer is to remain an artist, Myrtle must remain a secondary substitute of the vision for which his art is the primary substitute. "And if I see her not," Pound wrote of his artist-hero's quest for his Beatrice, "No sight is worth the beauty of my thought."[30] Accepting Myrtle as his true Beatrice, Elmer fails the test of the artist and so forfeits his vocation and loses his soul. "I want it to be hard," he says, "I want it to be cruel, taking something out of me each time. I want never to be completely satisfied with any of [my pictures], so that I shall always paint again."[31] Yet in the end, he is easily, even conventionally, satisfied. Far from continuing to view his love for Myrtle as a sign of his love for his art, making his art the finer sign of the deeper, impossible image, he accepts Myrtle and her millions as the real thing and stops painting.

As the story of Elmer neared its conclusion, Faulkner's control of it dissolved, perhaps because it was too close to him at a time when his sense of himself, his present, and his future remained too uncertain. During the weeks in which he worked most concertedly on "Elmer," he grew a beard and sketched several pen-and-ink portraits of himself, the largest and most careful "on a used sheet" of his manuscript.[32] He still wanted money and recognition, and he knew that by naming his vocation he could begin making a career. With the move toward fiction, he had begun discovering his own voice. Still, both the timing and the phrasing of his query and his answer seemed to him crucial. In much of its language, "Elmer" discloses curiosity about the impulse to become an artist; in its ironic tone, it reflects Faulkner's intention to avoid Elmer's failure of nerve. But Faulkner knew that the words he wrote, more than the gestures he made or the roles he played, tended to fix the features of his life, and so reluctance continued to dilute resolve. When he later had occasion to name his vocation, he sometimes mentioned the career he had abandoned ("failed poet") as well as the career he had chosen. In the meantime, "Elmer" engaged the issues it posed even as it distanced and disguised them. In Elmer's father we see a mode of failure Faulkner associated with Murry Falkner; in Elmer's mother, a mode of fierceness that he associated with Miss Maud. In Elmer we see familiar preoccupations and vacillations. In Jo-Addie we see a brave, caring, yet independent figure Faulkner had never directly known. Later, out of need deeper than any he had yet felt, he recreated this figure. Like Jo-Addie, Caddy Compson is gallant and tender; like her, she is loving and giving; and like her, she runs away.

With "Elmer" abandoned, Faulkner's own restlessness returned. In late September he left Paris to visit Rennes, Rouen, and Amiens, where he spent his twenty-eighth birthday. Back in Paris, he learned that Boni and Liveright had agreed to publish *Soldiers' Pay*. Still unable to work, he decided to visit England. Already his stay in Europe was nearing its end. The several years envisaged by Stone had shrunk to five months, and there had been no great discovery. He was a minor regional poet about to become a minor regional novelist. Closer now than before to a sense of vocation, not merely as a writer but as a writer of fiction, he remained uneasy and unsettled. The expansiveness he had felt in New Orleans had largely dissipated; it was much harder to feel big in Paris. Remaining there through November, he decided to have a series of photographs made.[33] Though extravagant for one who had lived frugally, the portraits seemed to him necessary; certainly they fit his work there—his portrait of Elmer and his sketches of himself.

Back in Oxford, a perfect figure of the bearded bohemian writer, he waited impatiently for the publication of *Soldiers' Pay*. Encouraged by Liveright's acceptance of the novel, he began working on stories he thought of as commercial. Finding them easier to begin than to finish, he became more and more restless. Soon he established a retreat in one of the dormitories of the university where he drank and told stories. Saying nothing to his parents, he sometimes disappeared for several days. By February 25, when *Soldiers' Pay* was released, he was in New Orleans. Its reception, falling far short of his expectations, was a sign of things to come. Although critics liked the novel well enough, few people bought it and everyone in Oxford was aghast: his mother thought it scandalous; without bothering to open a copy, his father declared it unfit to read; and the university, having refused to buy a copy, also declined to accept one as a gift. Later, as his fiction drew closer to home and it became clearer that he was raising personal dissatisfactions and regional problems to the level of grand observation, resistance deepened. For more than two decades, most Mississippians continued to pay him the rare tribute of trying to ignore or forget the painful problems he was raising, just as they continued to pay themselves the dubious tribute of refusing to believe that anyone who resembled them could be a great writer. But at first they merely declared themselves appalled.[34]

As summer approached, Faulkner decided to go back to Pascagoula. He was tired of New Orleans and uncomfortable in Oxford. Since his return, he had seen Estelle several times, but Helen Baird was in Pascagoula, and he still hoped to impress her. They swam and boated, walked and talked. Helen was young, lively, and gifted, and he liked reading poems and telling stories to her. Both of the gift books dating from this period, an allegory called *Mayday*, dated 27 January 1926, and a sonnet sequence called "Helen: A Courtship," dated "Oxford-Mississippi-June 1926," were made for Helen. Neatly hand-printed and bound by Faulkner, these two books establish what "Elmer" had only suggested: that Helen Baird had displaced Estelle as the great love of Faulkner's life. Their meeting had been a seemingly casual one in New Orleans sometime early in 1925, but Faulkner's feeling for Helen had deepened quickly.[35] Although "Helen" is dated June 1926, the dedication poem and the first seven sonnets in it are dated "Pascagoula-June-1925." Taken together the sonnets of 1925 and 1926 show that the courtship begun in New Orleans and resumed in Pascagoula had continued to preoccupy Faulkner during his stay in Europe. He felt the weight of Mrs. Baird's disapproval and knew that it began with his disreputable clothes and empty pockets. But he also knew that his second great love, unlike his first, was thwarted more by the indifference of his beloved than by the disapproval of her mother. In an undated letter that recalls his first memory of Helen, sitting on William Spratling's balcony in a linen dress, he pictures her "not thinking even a hell of a little bit of me," and adds that perhaps she had "already decided not to."[36] Helen's indifference stemmed in part from her endorsement of her mother's values. She enjoyed being around eccentric people, but when the time came to marry, she chose a promising young lawyer from New Orleans. In addition, Faulkner's size and appearance bothered her—he reminded her, she said, "of a fuzzy little animal." Even his literary gifts she judged negligible. Don't bother reading *Mosquitoes*, she told a friend after Faulkner had dedicated it to her, "It's no good." In addition, Faulkner's interest both in other people and in his own emotions struck her as secondary to his interest in writing. That he lived to write seemed to her to mean not only that his prospects were meager but that his life was peculiar: that he was an incurable observer and a tentative participant; that he characteristically stood "beside himself with a notebook in his hand always, putting down all the charming things that ever happened to him, killing them for the sake" of something he might or might not later write.[37]

In addition to the implications it held for the writing of "Elmer" and *Mosquitoes*, Faulkner's courtship of Helen Baird is striking in several ways that can be got at by examining its form. Almost from the beginning, Helen displayed indifference that not only matched but deepened Faulkner's ardor. Though she tolerated his declarations, she emphasized her unavailability. Even before the end of their first Pascagoula interlude, he could see what fate awaited him. Myrtle, he had written in "Elmer," was "like a star, clean and unattainable for all her . . . humanness."[38] But unattainability in fact fascinated him. In "Carcassonne," a piece published in 1931 but written earlier, probably in 1925, man's dream includes a place that is evermore about to be glimpsed and a deed, impossibly *"bold and tragical and austere*," that is evermore about to be performed.[39] In a piece called "Nympholepsy," which also seems to date from early 1925, a cloddish laborer glimpses a human body that he takes to be that of "a woman or a girl" and that he deems to be beautiful: "For a moment there was an old sharp beauty behind his eyes. Then his once-clean instincts become swinish got him into motion." In this curious piece, desire for "companionship" is associated with purity, and desire for "copulation" with filth. Later Faulkner's protagonist pursues a figure that is clearly female. Although he recognizes her purity and longs simply to approach her, he also admires her beauty and writhes "thinking of her body beneath his," an act he associates with "the dark wood." Caught between impulses that Faulkner clearly presents as contradictory, the man must make do with the thrilled memory of having touched her: "But I touched her! he repeated to himself, trying to build from this an incontrovertible consummation. Yes, her swift frightened thigh and the tip of her breast." Even this memory, however, the closest he comes to consummation, is mixed. For it includes not only the thrilled effect of touching her but the memory of seeing her frightened flight: "I wouldn't have hurt you, he moaned, I wouldn't have hurt you at all."[40]

Together, "Nympholepsy" and "Carcassonne" bring great art as well as great heroism and great love under the aspect of the unattainable. As Cleanth Brooks has noted, "Carcassonne" resembles in theme and style "Faulkner's romantic celebrations of the role of the imagination and his reflections on the plight of the artist."[41] Later Faulkner went out of his way to associate the writers and the novels he most admired with grand failure. But long before his statement contrasting Thomas Wolfe's courage with Ernest Hemingway's caution, he had learned to associate great art directly with grand failure and indirectly with impossible heroism and unattainable beauty. The implications of this pattern, and the way in which it takes us back to "Elmer" as well as forward toward *Mosquitoes*, become clearer in *Mayday*, the other gift-book Faulkner made for Helen Baird in 1926. *Mayday* is an allegory that owes much to Arthurian romances and even more to *Don Quixote* and James Branch Cabell's *Jurgen*, for it combines romantic questing with ironic distancing. Like the protagonists of Cervantes and Cabell, Faulkner's Galwyn gives up a meager, mundane life for bold, heroic adventure. He pursues as well as rescues maidens, and he longs to possess them. What he discovers, however, is the emptiness of possession. When no damsel matches the beauty of his thought, nor any satisfaction the depth of his desire, he faces a quandary. Which will he choose, the Lord of Sleep demands, endless questing or dreamless sleep? The one offers hunger, pain, and frustration suffered in exchange for glimpses of paradise and empty conquests; the other promises the sure peace of forgetfulness.[42]

Although Faulkner is clearly ironic in his treatment of Galwyn's predicament, he reserves most of his irony for the choice Galwyn makes, which is for death. Looking down into the river of forgetfulness, Galwyn sees for the last time the image he has pursued—that of a young girl with long, shining hair. With the image before him, he decides to die rather than go on seeking mere approximations. In this moment, death, whose promises are known to be attainable, is linked to "Little Sister Death"[43] — a phrase Faulkner had taken from St. Francis of Assisi; had used in one of his New Orleans sketches; and would use again in *The Sound and the Fury* in connection with the most important of all his failed knights. In Quentin Compson, despair derives from an unattainable love: like Galwyn's, Quentin's dissatisfaction is associated with inadequate substitutes, his weariness with repeated failure; and, like Galwyn, he drowns himself. But Quentin's beloved object is unattainable because she is his sister; his love is impossible because it is forbidden. And it is this confluence—of beloved object, sister, and death—that gives specificity to Faulkner's preoccupation with the familiar romantic association of both the beautiful and the heroic with the ineffable. The *"bold and tragical and austere"* act that Quentin contemplates yet fears is the act of killing his rivals so that he can possess his sister. Hoping to see the beautiful Iseult bathing in a river pool, Galwyn kills two men: one is a stout yeoman, the other a gallant knight; one is described as "a family man" with an eye for "the appearance of things," the other is named Sir Tristan. In immediate terms what Galwyn gains from such brashness is clear. For the fair Iseult, though she screams and delicately covers her eyes, neither covers her body nor flees his gaze nor resists his embrace. Only later, after the possession that has promised so much has yielded too little, does Galwyn discover the heavy price of possession.[44] In "Elmer" repeated clumsiness and failure lead to easy surrender. In *Mayday* repeated success leads to despair: Galwyn's fate is sealed the moment Iseult embraces him. By contrast, the protagonist of "Nympholepsy" is considerably more fortunate. For, unlike Iseult, his beloved runs away, having first given him all he needs—the thrilled memory of a touch on the basis of which he can try "to build . . . an incontrovertible consummation." What these three figures provide is not only another way of viewing Faulkner's courtship of Helen, but also a new way of viewing Quentin's fear and despair. For they suggest that Quentin is troubled as much by the incontrovertible fact of Caddy's being available as by the obvious fact of her being forbidden.

Behind all of these stories lay preoccupations that had already surfaced in "Elmer." Faulkner thought of Helen, as he did of Jo-Addie, in distinctly bisexual terms. In the dedicatory poem of "Helen," he describes "Her boy's breast and the plain flanks of a boy." In the fifth and sixth sonnets he specifically ties her to her mother. In the first of these he seeks to persuade the mother that he is a constant and proper suitor: "No: Madam, I love your daughter, I will say." In the second he tries to defend his health: "My health? My health's a fevered loud distress." And then he tries to reawaken in the mother some memory of the ardor and desire of her youth. In several of the sonnets, as in the dedication to *Mayday*, he views both the proposals he has made and the poems he has written to Helen as "a fumbling in darkness." In "Elmer" the figure that lay hidden in that darkness—"The vague shape [s]omewhere back in his [Elmer's] mind" that "he dreaded yet longed for"—was "the dark woman. The dark mother." From this dark figure evolved both Jo-Addie and Elmer, each of whom is bisexual. Remembering the sense of his mother's body, the thrilled effect of touching her breasts and heart, Elmer creates, out of his own bisexuality, first, images of smoke stacks and images of vague, dark places; and second, human figures that are sexually differentiated. Since the union he seeks is possible yet forbidden, he must rely on approximations. So long as the approximations that he seeks—such as union with the "impregnably virginal" Ethel—remain approximations, and so long as he is careful never to paint a picture with which he is "completely satisfied," he persists in courting women and painting pictures. When, on the other hand, he confuses what he possesses with what he desires, when he takes fortune, fame, and marriage as the real thing, the forces that drive him toward art dissipate. For he loses the need to hold "those portentous tubes" of paint, "thick-bodied and female and at the same time phallic: hermaphroditic"—that is, he loses the need to hover "over them with a brooding maternity" and so create figures of "men and women" that conform to the "vague shape" of his forbidden "heart's desire."⁴⁵

Although it would be foolish to confuse Faulkner with Elmer Hodge, it would also be foolish to ignore the pertinence of Elmer's preoccupations to understanding Faulkner and the novel he was about to write. Helen Baird seems almost to have recognized several things that most people missed—that Faulkner used stillness and silence as preludes to writing; that he stood outside the life he lived, jotting things down as he went along; that there was a doubleness in his emotional entanglements; that he deliberately cultivated emotions with the intention of transmuting them; and that he found her more compelling because he knew her to be unattainable. Yet, in one conclusion she seems to have drawn—namely, that Faulkner felt no authentic desire and suffered no lasting pain—she was clearly wrong. The poems he wrote show convincingly that he loved her and that he wanted to make love with her—to sleep with her and, in a moment almost beyond consciousness, to resolve "the dilemma of desire" not only by touching her soft breast but by gently breaking her "hushed virginity."⁴⁶ Later, in the aftermath of Helen's rejection, Faulkner wrote a letter that conveys not only genuine pain but a continuing need for tenderness. In *The Wild Palms*, written nearly ten years later, that pain and need surfaced again: Charlotte Rittenmeyer is among other things an evocation of Helen Baird.⁴⁷

Having earlier made clear that she found several men, including her brother Josh, more attractive than her fuzzy poet, Helen finally put Faulkner aside by announcing her intention to marry Guy Lyman. The announcement came sometime in the summer of 1926, the marriage in May 1927, about a week after *Mosquitoes* was published. "But people do not die of love," one of the characters in *Mosquitoes* remarks, ". . . you do not commit suicide when you are disappointed in love. You write a book." In this novel, which Faulkner felt Helen's rejection had hurt him into writing, both his sense of her and her sense of him found expression; in addition, other people in New Orleans and Pascagoula, including Sherwood Anderson, figure prominently in the novel's action. It is, then, part roman à clef as well as part *Kunstler-roman*, part novel of ideas, and part satire.⁴⁸ Like *Soldiers' Pay*, it attempts more than it achieves; and like *Soldiers' Pay*, it remains for most readers a kind of museum-piece. Still, for Faulkner it moved several things toward resolution. By distancing him from Helen and from New Orleans and its literary community, it started him back toward Mississippi and a major discovery. It also pushed farther the examination of his vocation that had dominated "Elmer." And since it was for him a way of resolving "the dilemma of desire," it further focused the problem of vocation on the problem of the relation of art to sex.⁴⁹

Drawing on several outings arranged by the Andersons, Faulkner focused *Mosquitoes* on a yachting expedition on Lake Pontchartrain.[50] Into this limited scene he brings a considerable array of artists, pseudo-artists, hangers-on, and patrons, and a considerable variety of sexual inclination and activity, masturbatory, incestuous, heterosexual, and lesbian. While in "Elmer" he had been limited to a single character and his history, in *Mosquitoes* he is able to work out several different relations between sex and art, and several versions of the artist, most of which he clearly hoped to avoid.

Almost aggressively self-involved, the novel is psychologically daring. Midway through it, Faulkner makes a direct appearance as a sunburned, shabby man, "not dangerous: just crazy," who has said "he was a liar by profession," and whose name his character can barely "remember— Faulkner, that was it." Later he attributes some of his own narcissistic verse to a lesbian poet.[51] Along the way he entertains the possibility that "all artists are kind of insane" and that all art is the product of "perversion." Years before, in an essay published in the *Mississippian*, he had described writers as people "pathetically torn between a desire to make a figure in the world and a morbid interest in their personal egos"—a "deadly" combination that he went on specifically to associate with Sigmund Freud. Both this desire and this interest figure prominently in *Mosquitoes*, as does Freud's presence.[52]

Mr. Talliaferro is a buyer of women's clothes. Timid and effete, he resembles J. Alfred Prufrock in several obvious ways. Impotent, he makes a habit of substituting words for actions. Talking constantly of sex and doing nothing, he epitomizes one of the novel's major themes, the sterility of mere talk: "Talk, talk, talk: the utter and heartbreaking stupidity of words." In addition to talking, he spends much of his time watching, yearning, hoping. Having suffered repeated failure as a lover, he wants to find some formula that will deliver him from impotence: "But it was unbearable to believe that he had never had the power to stir women, that he had been always a firearm unloaded and unaware of it. No, it's something I can do, or say, that I have not yet discovered." Another figure, Mark Frost, writes short, obscure poems that remind one "somehow of the function of evacuation excruciatingly and incompletely performed." He is at once a classic case of arrested development (he is so oblivious to women that he does not even recognize their attempts to seduce him) and a classic instance of the minor regional poet (he is, he announces, "the best poet in New Orleans").

Neither Talliaferro, the nonwriter, nor Frost, the constipated and stunted poet, does much to stimulate the curiosity of other characters on board the *Nausikaa*. But Eva Wiseman, another minor poet, provokes several interesting discussions of art. One of her friends, Dawson Fairchild, finds it difficult "to reconcile" her seemingly narcissistic verse with her life, an effort her brother Julius regards as doomed from the start. A book, Julius counters, is not a part of the writer's social self. It is "the writer's secret life" and "dark twin"; "you can't reconcile them," he concludes. And in fact, the narcissism of the poetry Faulkner attributes to Eva Wiseman fits what we see of her secret life: while Fairchild and her brother discuss her poetry, she sits silently "thinking of Jenny's soft body." Meanwhile, the two men edge toward a poetic theory—of art as "a kind of dark perversion"—that is compatible with her practice as a poet. "It's a kind of dark thing," Fairchild says. "It's kind of like somebody brings you to a dark door. Will you enter that room, or not?" A substitute for entering the dark door, art becomes an act of individual creation wherein the self, out of its own bisexuality, "can create without any assistance at all." For Eva Wiseman such creation is appealing because she is afraid even of dark rooms inhabited by nothing stranger than other versions of herself. For men, as Fairchild presents the case, art's appeal is double. It can substitute for approaching the forbidden figure in the dark room, and it can do more. Women, he says, get "into life" and become "a part of it . . . without art," by conceiving and bearing children. At such creation, a man "can [only] look." But "in art, a man can create without any assistance at all: what he does is his. A perversion, I grant you, but a perversion that builds Chartres and invents Lear."

From Dawson Fairchild, Faulkner's clear evocation of Sherwood Anderson, and a few other figures, particularly Julius Wiseman, come most of the novel's discussions of art. Fairchild, once creative, now fumbles and flounders; though he cannot admit it, his days as an active novelist lie behind him. Earlier he possessed the quality that Helen Baird sensed, and disliked, in Faulkner: "A kind of voraciousness that makes an artist stand beside himself with a notebook in his hand always," assimilating and analyzing "all the charming things that ever happen to him, killing them for the sake" of something he might or might not later write. Such an artist cares nothing even for "love, youth, sorrow and hope and despair," except what he might later make of them.[53] In a dedicated sculptor named Gordon, however, we see an artist still possessed of this voraciousness and still capable of compelling creation. Early and late he practices deliberate sublimation; in between he finds himself infatuated with Patricia Robyn, Faulkner's clear evocation of Helen Baird.[54]

When we first see him, Gordon is living contentedly with "the virginal breastless torso of a girl" he has sculpted; at once "motionless and passionately eternal," Gordon's work of art represents his "feminine ideal." Yet he soon finds himself drawn to Patricia's "taut, simple body, almost breastless and with the fleeting hips of a boy." Only "vaguely troubling" at first, her body becomes an obsession that he both indulges and resists.

Submitting to Patricia's appeal, he joins the cruise; reminding himself that he is a "fool . . . cursed of god" and that he has "work to do," he tries to ignore her. It is his fate, he tells himself, to find sustenance, not in "bread to the belly," but in "shapes cunningly sweated . . . out of chaos"; and to find warmth, not in the body of a woman, but in "whiskey . . . or a chisel and maul."

Later in *Mosquitoes* Faulkner gives Gordon words from a letter he had written to Helen Baird on the back of one of the pages of the typescript of *Mosquitoes*: "Your name is like a little golden bell hung on my heart."[55] In his first published poem, Faulkner had associated the sound of a bell stroke with the moment when lovers move from mere walking to dancing. Having written his letter, however, he did not mail it; and having thought these words, Gordon decides not to speak them. Shortly after they have come to mind, however, he refers to the play from which he took his version of them.[56] "Do you know," he asks Patricia, "what Cyrano said once?"

> "No: what?" she asked. But he only looked down upon her with his cavernous uncomfortable eyes. "What did he say?" she repeated. And then: "Was he in love with her?"
>
> "I think so. . . . Yes, he was in love with her. She couldn't leave him, either. Couldn't go away from him at all. . . . He had her locked up. In a book."
>
> "In a book?" she repeated. Then she comprehended. "Oh. . . . That's what you've done, isn't it? With that marble girl without any arms and legs you made? Hadn't you rather have a live one? Say, you haven't got any sweetheart or anything, have you?"
>
> "No," he answered. "How did you know?"

Faulkner wrote his unmailed letter to Helen knowing that she was gone, but the words with which he implored her to "come back" reflect deep anguish. In answering Gordon's query as to how she knew that he had no "sweetheart or anything," Patricia says no woman "is going to waste time on a man that's satisfied with a piece of wood or something." She thus glimpses what the sublimation Gordon practices implies: that he cultivates passion in order to sublimate it; that his deeper longing is for some internal image; and that his preferred substitute for that image is the work of art he creates. Earlier in the novel, she has noticed that she resembles his statue; now she senses the deeper implication of that resemblance: that he is infatuated with her because she resembles a statue that is in turn but an image of an image. "You ought to get out of yourself," she says. "You'll either bust all of a sudden someday, or just dry up."

In a novel in which self-involvement takes many forms, Gordon's is less peculiar than Patricia thinks. Earlier Dawson Fairchild has suggested that a man always writes for "some woman"; "Well, maybe," he adds almost as an afterthought, she's "only the symbol of a desire" rather than "a flesh and blood creature." The "old boys," he recalls, "never even bothered to sign their things."[57] Given her understanding of Gordon, Patricia's blindness to her own self-absorption is all the more telling. She spends most of her time following her brother Josh, who resembles her and, like her, seems faintly bisexual. Her avowed intention, despite his protests, is to follow him to New Haven when he enters Yale in the fall. What she seeks, and in this she resembles most of the characters of *Mosquitoes*, is not "counter-love, original response," but her "own love back in copy speech."[58]

Early in *Mosquitoes*, Gordon defines his ideal in terms that are even more extreme than Patricia's desire for her twin brother: "A virgin with no legs to leave me, no arms to hold me, no head to talk to me." For Mrs. Maurier, the patroness who organizes the expedition, the yacht itself is a kind of retreat or haven—a way of getting beyond the "rumors of the world." Of the many stratagems devoted to peace and control in *Mosquitoes*, art is merely the most interesting. *Mosquitoes* is full of echoes and evocations of painters, musicians, and poets. In it Dante serves as the supreme instance of a man who made art an improbable way of fulfilling his love: "Dante invented Beatrice," Julius Wiseman says late in the novel, "creating himself a maid that life had not had time to create, and laid upon her frail and unbowed shoulders the whole burden of man's history of his impossible heart's desire."[59]

In 1925, in one of his *Double Dealer* pieces, Faulkner suggests that poetry had simplified his early life by providing an "emotional counterpart" that required no partner. In 1922 he described Joseph Hergesheimer as a "strange case of sex crucifixion"; Hergesheimer resembled, Faulkner said, "an emasculate priest surrounded by the puppets he has carved and clothed and painted—a terrific world without motion or meaning." As Hergesheimer practiced it, art seemed to Faulkner a search for shelter—"a quiet region of light and shadow, soundless and beyond despair." Comparing Hergesheimer's works to "lovely Byzantine" friezes, Faulkner went on to "imagine Hergesheimer submerging himself in" his books "as in a still harbor where the age cannot hurt him and where rumor of the world reaches him only as a far faint sound of rain." The appeal of silence and stillness (of getting, as Frost put it, "out of all this now too much for us" into what Faulkner thought of as a world of "silent arrested motion, forever beyond the reach of time") Faulkner had felt early and knew well. In *Soldiers' Pay* Donald Mahon epitomizes psychic and physical withdrawal and retirement. In *Light in August*, another of Faulkner's remarkable cripples, Gail Hightower, finds in the church "shelter" and in his vocation hope of a life "intact and on all sides complete and inviolable, like a classic and serene vase, where the spirit could be born anew sheltered from the harsh gale of living . . . with only the far sound of the circumvented wind."[60]

Together these instances suggest why Faulkner's depiction of Gordon combined judgment and reluctance with force. In the piece on Herge-sheimer, Faulkner slightly misquotes a line of Italian from *Linda Condon*, "La figlia della sua mente, l'amorosa idea," which might be translated as "the daughter of his mind, the loving idea."[61] As perfectly as any line in Faulkner's early writings, this line anticipates his description in the early 1930s of what the writing of *The Sound and the Fury*, and particularly the creation of Caddy, would mean to him. Before he could come to such creation, however, he needed to make a further discovery. Before he could find in the "daughter of his mind" something other than "Little Sister Death," before he could find in the act of creating her something other than flight into a kind of internal heaven, or a dive into "a still harbor," he needed to find some way of maintaining what Albert Camus called equilibrium between reality and rejection of it.[62] Elmer Hodge is Faulkner's portrait of an artist who betrays the "vague shape" that calls him by abandoning the beauty of his thought for flesh, money, and a title. In the end, the real is all that matters to him. Gordon, on the other hand, epitomizes consecration: having briefly pursued Patricia, he goes back to the motionless and passionately eternal torso he has sculpted. In the process, however, he reveals the price as well as the appeal of consecration. Whereas Elmer enacts a fate Faulkner clearly hoped to avoid, Gordon embraces a fate Faulkner continued to resist. "Sufficient unto himself in the city of his arrogance" though he is, Gordon is, "in the marble tower of his loneliness and pride," alone.[63]

In September, with the manuscript of *Mosquitoes* finished, Faulkner stayed on in Pascagoula after his hosts, the Stones, had left. With his novel finished, he wanted to be alone. There were revisions to make, emotions and memories to sort out. Several days later he returned to Oxford, where Phil Stone helped him prepare a final typescript for Boni and Liveright. Having insisted on revisions that subdued the novel's discussion of writing as a kind of perversion and muted its overtly lesbian scenes, Liveright agreed to publish *Mosquitoes*.[64] Before it was released the next April, Faulkner had returned to New Orleans to visit old friends and collaborate with William Spratling on *Sherwood Anderson and Other Famous Creoles*—a work that includes caricatures of several people associated with the *Double Dealer* as well as an introduction by Faulkner written in the manner of Sherwood Anderson. Before he had finished his part of this second farewell to New Orleans, which he later described as "the unhappy caricature affair," he had begun work on two projects that fixed his vocation and completed his literary and imaginative return home. In the years to come, he would remain restless and so would continue moving in and out of Oxford, but he was almost ready now to live and work there again.[65]

FOUR 1927

The Great Discovery

In the year following his return to Oxford, Faulkner's life yielded several small events and one large discovery. Living at home, he fell easily into old patterns. He frequently took long walks in familiar woods, and when his restlessness mounted, he left for New Orleans, often alone, or for Memphis, usually with Phil Stone. Since Estelle Franklin was again living in Oxford with her parents, he saw her regularly. After years of experimenting with separations and reunions, she and Cornell Franklin had finally begun the long process of getting a divorce. The farther her marriage had gone, the more impossible it had become, and Faulkner knew that she was depending on him now more than ever before. At times he felt close to her, almost as before. What he had long suspected, he now knew: that one day soon he would have to decide whether or not to marry her. But with Helen Baird still on his mind, he was restless. In and out of Oxford, he continued seeing other women.

Soon, however, he was spending more time in Oxford and more time at work. By late April, when *Mosquitoes* was published, he had finished his collaboration with Spratling on *Sherwood Anderson and Other Famous Creoles*; had written, hand-lettered, and bound a fairy tale called *The Wishing Tree* for Estelle's daughter, Victoria; and had begun two new projects. He worked best in the mornings; often by noon he had written for five or six hours. With a new novel coming out, short stories circulating, and new fiction going well, his spirits were high. More and more, he felt confident about what he was doing. In the years just after the war, he had discovered that it would be his "fate . . . to keep on writing books." During his months in New Orleans, Paris, and Pascagoula, from early 1925 to late 1926, he had discovered more specifically what that fate implied. Gradually he had begun to master the ambivalence he felt toward art. He wanted to create—to serve "A Dream and a Fire" within him. But he wanted both to "shape this dream . . . in marble or sound, on canvas or paper, and [to] live." Like his vision, he was shapeless; and like it he needed form: "I, too, am but a shapeless lump of moist earth risen from pain, to laugh and strive and weep."[1] Early his contradictory impulses had led him to move back and forth between experiments in stillness and silence, on one side, and experiments with gunpowder and wings, on the other. Later they had entered both the language and the action of "Elmer" and *Mosquitoes*. One part of him wanted to move through his world like a living force, stirring beautiful women and living great adventures, and this part tended to be suspicious of words. "You begin to substitute words for things and deeds," Dawson Fairchild remarks in *Mosquitoes*, "like the withered cuckold husband that took the Decameron to bed with him every night."[2]

The kinds of substitution Faulkner had practiced, and to which in a sense he was committed, made him suspicious of the medium he was laboring to master. At times he seemed almost the epitome of the reluctant artist. It was not art's elitist implications that troubled him; it was the nature of his medium and his vocation. He had never wanted to prepare himself for art by ceasing to be interested in his "own emotions and experiences except as material." Even less was he interested in becoming a "perfect man of letters," one who creates "a fable in order to give himself the illusion of existing."[3] But for several reasons fiction had proved more liberating and enabling than poetry, and as a result it had done much to overcome the resistance within him. The project he had taken to New Orleans, "The Greening Bough," he had put aside for those he found there, the sketches and *Soldiers' Pay*. Avoiding any dramatic decision to abandon poetry, he had continued to write prose, first in Paris with "Elmer," later in Pascagoula with *Mosquitoes*. The writing of *Mosquitoes*, particularly the creation of Dawson Fairchild, constituted a turning point. Although doubts about his vocation and medium would persist to the end of his life, his faith already matched his doubt. Having described words as substitutes for acts, Fairchild adds that though they do not have life in themselves, they can be "brought into a happy conjunction" and so "produce something that lives."[4]

Believing that he could work out a relation between his own genius and that of art, Faulkner began moving confidently from project to project. Taken together, his next three projects point clearly to the possibilities now opening before him. In "Father Abraham," which contained the seeds of his Snopes saga, he began engaging the social, economic, and political developments that were transforming the South. In *Flags in the Dust*, which became *Sartoris*, he began drawing on regional and familial legends and traditions. In *The Sound and the Fury*, which became his first great novel, he returned to the family configuration of his earliest years and to memories out of his own childhood. Fiction had given him a new sense of art's viability as a vocation in part by enlarging his sense of its sources. Tentatively in *Soldiers' Pay* and more daringly in *Mosquitoes*, he had used his fiction to evoke and then dismiss himself as poet. In the process he had anticipated the move he was about to make—toward explorations of region, family, and self that would make his writing a mode of action rather than substitution, a form of adventure rather than evasion.

"It takes," as Northrop Frye once noted, "a great deal of will power to write poetry, but part of that will power must be employed in trying to relax the will, so making a large part of one's writing involuntary."[5] Why Faulkner could perform the second part of this act more readily in fiction than in poetry will take some time to show, but the place to begin is with his having heard and told stories as a child. Particularly in *Flags in the Dust* he began drawing heavily on the old tales and talking of his childhood and youth. As he moved back toward the oral traditions of his early years, he also moved back toward writers he had read early in his life, including Cervantes and Shakespeare. For years his reading had focused on the late nineteenth century, and his writings show the lasting consequences of that focus—in their self-conscious exploration of the structures of consciousness and imagination as they play with the surfaces and forces of life; in their self-conscious examination of language as a medium of play; and in their self-conscious demonstrations of the problematic relationship between fiction and reality. But these preoccupations, though intensely modern, are not new; they go back at least to Cervantes and Shakespeare, and thus to the era that gave birth to the novel. So what changed as Faulkner moved back toward the oral and written traditions of his youth were not the issues that concerned him so much as the depth of his awareness of those issues and, even more, his sense of which writers most profoundly engaged them. He discovered, as he later put it, that he preferred the "bad puns, bad history," and poor taste of William Shakespeare to the care and delicacy of Walter Pater.[6] In addition he went back to the great novelists of the nineteenth century, particularly Balzac and Dickens. Clearly in "Father Abraham" but also in *Flags in the Dust*, he displayed the major impulses behind nineteenth-century fiction: the will not only to mirror but to master "a threatening or at least bewildering historical reality by remaking it imaginatively."[7]

Together the literary and oral traditions of Faulkner's early years reinforced the dual commitment his experience had fostered, thus helping to make him both an intent realist and an intent imaginist. As a result, his conception of fiction was remarkably commodious. In it he could display the autonomous power of the fantasy world within him even as he labored to master the social world around him. By comparison, his conception of poetry remained rigid and impoverished. In an essay written in 1953, he attributes Sherwood Anderson's limitations as a writer to his commitment to perfection, or rather, to "the exactitude of purity." The search for perfect style, for pure art, which manifested itself in Anderson's slow, painful "fumbling for exactitude," Faulkner associated with a vocabulary and voice "controlled and even repressed."[8] One may dispute this description of Anderson, or even doubt that Faulkner learned much from Anderson about the dangers of seeking perfection, and still recognize the usefulness of Faulkner's terms for distinguishing his own practice as poet from his practice as fictionist. Despite his extended practice of it, poetry had remained for Faulkner almost wholly willed and controlled, which is to say repressed. To the end of his life, he conceived poetry as distinctly "literary" and overwhelmingly abstract. The poet, he remarked in 1955, "deals with something which is so pure and so esoteric that you cannot say he is English or Japanese—he deals in something that is universal."[9] The burden of this conception of poetry, the burden of purity and universality, deprived Faulkner of access to almost everything, leaving him only his own more obvious emotions and the words of other poets. His habit of borrowing from other writers had begun as an appropriative strategy only to become an evasive one; similarly, his habit of revising and rearranging his poems had begun as disciplined self-education only to become careful procrastination. As a fictionist, he remained a dedicated craftsman; his manuscripts, even that of *As I Lay Dying*, which was written with comparative ease, are clearly the work of a writer willing to labor without stint to improve his work. It was not carelessness but relaxation of will—deliverance from a too self-conscious straining after profundity of meaning and purity of style—that proved easier in prose.

As it did, Faulkner came to a new sense of self-trust. "I decided what seems to me now a long time ago," he wrote in 1941, "that something worth saying knew better than I did how it needed to be said, and that it was better said poorly even than not said."[10] Clearly the sense of trust described here, in the significance and the implicit form of the thing waiting to be said, involves deep self-trust. In Faulkner's formulation, however, the *I* is all consciousness, the thing waiting to be said all deeper than consciousness: it is as though the self he had come to trust was less the self of will and intention than the self of needs, desires, and memories, including remembered voices. Recalling the "warped and spartan solitude" of her childhood, Miss Rosa Coldfield of *Absalom, Absalom!* thinks of it as having taught her little except how "to listen before I could comprehend and to understand before I even heard." Like all great fiction, Faulkner's deals with things that we know only indirectly and therefore imperfectly; but like all great fiction, it also deals with things that we know, within and around us, yet fear to admit. If finding words for things we imperfectly know requires great prescience as well as great talent, finding words for things we resist requires great courage. For both parts of such discovery, indirection and even disguise possess obvious advantages.

In the same discussion in which he defined the poet in terms of the pure, the esoteric, and the universal, Faulkner added that the novelist "deals with his own traditions." As a boy he had begun to think of himself as a writer. Later he had discovered that prose fiction was his proper medium. Crucial though these acts were, they were less distinctive than his naming himself a provincial. Years later, recalling his months in New Orleans and Europe, he pictured himself living the purest form of exile—as "a tramp, a harmless possessionless vagabond," who dramatized the insignificance of place.[11] Although this picture exaggerates what Faulkner had actually experienced, it suggests the appeal rootlessness held for him. Earlier, in a poem called "Wild Geese" and in a fragment of a story called "And Now What's To Do," he had celebrated the wild, lonely flight of geese; later, in *As I Lay Dying*, he linked Addie Bundren's longing for freedom and fulfillment to the sounds of geese coming "faint and high and wild" out of the darkness.[12] He knew that flight could serve both as personal maneuver and as literary resource. Exile had become a dominant theme as well as a dominant pattern for writers of his generation; it was nothing if not a conspicuous alternative. For Eliot it meant appropriating a new home; for Joyce, Pound, and Hemingway, a series of new homes; for each of them it implied major redefinitions and heroic possibilities as well as new postures and accents. But Faulkner had discovered that his life was to be different: that he must experiment with exile while living commitment. Having observed his career and knowing as we do the cruciality of place in it, we see in his early writings scattered anticipations of the scene that became his signature and of the characters with whom he peopled it, giving to his discovery a sense of inevitability. In a piece published in the April 1925 *Double Dealer*, while he was living in New

Orleans, he thanked "whatever gods may be" that he was a provincial whose roots were planted in his native soil.[13] What he felt about himself, others saw in him. "You're a country boy," Sherwood Anderson said, "all you know is that little patch up there in Mississippi where you started from."[14] To say, however, that Oxford was all Faulkner knew is not to say that it was all he needed. Like Anderson, he remained an heir of Romanticism in several basic senses, including belief that human beings need larger participation in the life of the imagination. From this conviction their shared love of tall tales derived. Both men associated the staleness of the modern world with its having become so enamored of facts that it was prejudiced against the imagination; or, to quote one of Anderson's *Double Dealer* pieces, with its failing to find "time for a play of the imagination over the facts of life."[15]

Faulkner knew, however, that his own danger was that of becoming enamored of imagination, prejudiced against facts. More than most writers, he feared simple self-absorption—what he had earlier termed "a morbid interest" in one's own ego.[16] In exile he had tended to retreat within himself, as "Elmer" clearly shows. In addition, he feared abstraction, one of the perils he had dramatized in Gordon. As a fictionist, he needed customs and folkways, tales and legends as well as his own thoughts and desires. For his sensibility, stimulation was in large measure a function of familiarity: the more he knew of the folkways and stories of his region, the more they interested and agitated him. The terms in which he described his imaginative process—"sublimating the actual into the apocryphal"—tie his own practice to Gordon's. But in context they also suggested that his return to his "native soil" represented for him a turn toward "the actual," which he associated with a locale. Back in Oxford he resumed old hobbies and sought odd jobs. Writing in the mornings, he spent his afternoons and evenings playing golf or hunting, listening to stories or telling them. Now and then he took jobs painting houses or signs. Unlike his pastimes, his odd jobs brought in needed money. But like his pastimes, they were part of his strategy for becoming "a denizen" of Oxford and Lafayette County, Mississippi. Toward his world, he remained deeply ambivalent: drawn to it, he could half enter it; offended by it, he became uneasy and pulled back.[17] He knew that he needed the particulars of his world, and a part of him remained deeply committed to them. When boredom or pressure or offense intensified, however, he turned as one of his brothers put it, and stepped "off into a land of make-believe."[18]

Whereas James Joyce engaged in dramatic exile only to begin peering back into his lost home through a distant window, Faulkner returned home to ensure that he would look again and again at the immediate. The very intensity of his sensed estrangement made him aware of the need to stay close, and so avoid some more permanent flight. Still, in result if not intent, his return constituted a double strategy. For it not only ensured that he would attend the actual; it also intensified his need to sublimate the actual. Years later he obliquely linked his commitment to his region with his confinement in the post office—"my own little postage stamp of native soil." And in fact he associated his region not only with meagerness, or what he once termed "the bareness of the Southerner's life," but also with external pressure. "From this the poem springs," Stevens says, "that we live in a place/That is not our own." Oxford was what Faulkner knew, and his return committed him to it. Yet it never became completely his home. After the war, he had come back to find that he was "at home again in Oxford, Mississippi, yet at the same time . . . not at home."[19] It was an experience he repeated many times. To the end of his life, he continued experimenting with flight, making Oxford in several senses a "temporary address." A resource and an entertainment, the actualities of Oxford were also a pressure from without that generated a pressure from within, inspiring excursions. Withdrawing into a small room or study (the one at Rowan Oak would be deliberately plain, almost bare, recalling nothing so much as a monk's cell), taking the symbolic doorknob with him, he entered a world completely his own. There he engaged in a labor he described as "solitary" without there being anything "lonely about it." Later, leaving his imaginative realm behind, he returned to Oxford and Lafayette County. Going forth to the town square, he studied its monument to the Confederate dead; going out to nearby rivers, he observed their deer. Moving to and fro between two worlds, he gave his allegiance first to one, then to the other. For him, a sense of place not only provided equilibrium; it encouraged and controlled oscillation.[20]

Had Faulkner been less divided, he might have achieved a virtual merger of "his literary with his personal self," as Henry James had. Instead it was his fate to cultivate a kind of division. A writer, he said, "is one thing when he is a writer and . . . something else while he is a denizen of the world."[21] At times Faulkner as writer made Faulkner as denizen his effective sign—as in his dramatizations of the dandy and the bohemian. But the firmer his sense of his literary self became, the more his roles changed. Most of his later dramatizations—of the pilot, farmer, or hunt-clubber—were expressions of his shy social self. Later he habitually described himself as not a literary man but a writer, and as not only a writer but a farmer, just as Carlos Williams was a doctor as well as a poet.[22] In the process he obscured several important issues. Whereas Williams made his living as a doctor, Faulkner never supported himself as a farmer. He depended on writing and occasional odd jobs to earn money, which made money a big problem for a long time. Like his plane, boats, and horses, his farm, when it came, would be bought with money earned by writing and would become another expense. Yet, though he brought little of the intensity or the talent to life that he brought to writing, and though none of his activities, including farming, became remunerative, they remained an essential part of the divided life he lived.

Before and during his months as a wanderer, Faulkner wrote stories with settings that are rural and vaguely southern.[23] But in the projects begun just after his return to Oxford, his approach changed dramatically. He labored now both to relate and to differentiate the world he imagined and the region he could never wholly accept. If the world of imagination—the world as it might and should have been—was for him a kind of internal heaven, as in some sense it surely was, it was not a destination; or rather, as a destination it was "a still harbor," not a living kingdom. Like Frost's "swinger of birches," Faulkner often dreamed of going or climbing "*Toward* heaven," but he also feared the half-granted wish that would snatch him away, "Not to return." His deeper, more inclusive dream, therefore, was of "going and coming back."[24] Both of his worlds seemed to him to possess not only a promise of life but a threat of impoverishment, even extinction. It was, therefore, in oscillation that he saw possibility. To him each world was the only sufficient cure for the other. If one called him to imaginative flights or dives, and promised him harmony and control, the other called him to a kind of empirical gaiety, and promised him variety and change. His deepest recognition was the need both his life and his art had of both the flights and the gaiety. Whereupon he made his life one kind of mediation and his art another.

Finding in Oxford not only an engagement and a resource but a pressure from without, Faulkner became almost immediately generative. In mid-February, he wrote Horace Liveright that he was writing "on two things at once: a novel, and a collection of short stories of my townspeople." A few weeks earlier, Phil Stone had drawn up a news release describing two of Faulkner's projects, both "southern in setting"—one a comic tale of a large family "of typical 'poor white trash,'" the other "a tale of the aristocratic, chivalrous and ill-fated Sartoris family." During the months that followed, Faulkner journeyed through the land he first called Yocona toward the kingdom he later named Yoknapatawpha.[25]

That journey began in his determination to create an "evocative skeleton" of the world to which he had returned. At first he wrote "without much purpose"; then he realized that to make his work evocative, he would have to make it personal. Almost immediately, he began gathering characters. Some he "invented"; others he "created out of tales" he had heard as a boy. Since they were composed "partly from what they were in actual life," his characters evoked the world he could never wholly accept yet dreaded to lose. But since they were also composed "partly from what they should have been and were not," they belonged to the world of his thought and desire, the world as he would have had it.[26] The "aim of every artist," he said, is "to arrest motion, which is life, by artificial means and hold it fixed so that 100 years later when a stranger looks at it, it moves again since it is life." What he required, however, was not merely an image of life; it was an image of life heightened. He wanted to show what creatures, given the occasion and need, "could have done" and "would have done," perhaps even did when no one was "there to record the action."[27]

In this kind of oscillation Faulkner located the essence of his art. To create meant presenting an image of life as it was, modified by life as it "should have been." Earlier, in a book by Willard Huntington Wright called *The Creative Will*, he had found a definition of the artist as one who "takes the *essence* of his special world, color or document, and creates a new world of them."[28] Something like that was what he sought. What artificiality offered motion and form offered action was a kind of renewal, a "rectification of the world we live in"; and a kind of unity, a completion of "things that we can never consummate."[29] In a reduced world, "Back in a time made simple by the loss/Of detail," clear patterns, heroic possibilities, even forbidden completions—rectifications and consummations—might be easy. But the world thus simplified, "rid of the gnats and the tacks and the broken glass" of experience, the inhibitions and taboos, left with "only the peaceful pleasant things" or the dramatic, heroic ones, Faulkner associated with "not is, but was." Such reductions did not interest him. To be adequate, the created image had to evoke and master everything.[30] What a term like *rectification* implied was intensification as well as correction; what a term like *consummation* implied was performance and completion of forbidden as well as impossible acts.

As it turned out, the move Faulkner was prepared to make gave him access not only to a whole complex of traditions but to deeper levels of consciousness; not only to old tales and talking but to buried memories and desires. In the same essay in which he suggests that Anderson's example taught him to avoid the perils of exactitude and purity, he suggests that Anderson's advice helped to make him a regionalist: "I learned that, to be a writer, one has got to be what he is, what he was born." By placing existence under the aspect of inheritance and experience, however, this formulation suggests that Faulkner's return to Mississippi was also a return to childhood and family.[31]

Writing with a sense of great discovery, Faulkner worked simultaneously on two projects, one representing an effort to master the society around him; the other representing an effort to master family traditions and personal preoccupations as well as social forces. Called "Father Abraham," the first of these deals with the Snopes family.[32] Already, the setting is Frenchman's Bend, which is named for a man whose origins were "foreign" if not French; already, most of the area's inhabitants, the Armstids and Littlejohns, are of "Scottish and English blood"; already, Flem Snopes is working to displace the Varners; already, members of his inexhaustible family, Eck, I. O., Admiral Dewey, are coming from everywhere. Even the itinerant salesman, V. K. Ratliff, is present, though his name is V. K. Suratt.

"Father Abraham" is crude as well as unfinished, and Faulkner's various starts suggest what his abandoning it confirms: that he was not yet able to control what he had discovered. But "Father Abraham" is also a work of great importance. In it the past, seemingly distant and largely lost, belongs to a nameless man of large expectations. But "he is gone, with his family and slaves and splendor, his broad acres are parcelled out in small shiftless farms which the jungle is slowly taking again, and all that remains of him is the river bed where he straightened it out . . . and the skeleton of a huge colonial house." Will Varner is the central figure in the story's present—that is, the early 1900s. A man of considerable energy and property yet without pretensions, Varner is doomed to lose his place to Flem Snopes, the head of a "prolific and rootless and clannish" family descended "from a long line of shiftless tenant farmers." So in embryo the work contains several characters together with the history and processes that later yielded the Snopes stories and novels. Flem is already on his way toward the presidency of a bank; and he is already a bland yet ruthless descendant of the great nineteenth-century heroes of Dickens and Balzac. Like them, he devotes himself to making his fortune. Whereas they seek to enter their society and share in its power and wealth, Flem decides to take possession of his society—which is why he eventually destroys it as a community based on mutual respect for the human needs of its members, and why in turn he is eventually destroyed.

From his own experience and from his early reading, Faulkner had absorbed a fundamental tension between familial, social, and historical forces as they bear down on individual life; and individual needs and desires both as they inspire action and as they shape the structures of the imagination. During the nineteenth century the center of fiction "had shifted, broadly speaking, from consciousness and how it shaped the world around it to the world around and how it impinged with its specific gravity, its full concreteness, on consciousness." For Dickens and Balzac imaginative involvement with society and history mitigated against self-conscious, self-reflexive fiction. Still, what they accomplished was a redefinition, not a new beginning. As Robert Alter has noted, their works display "the autonomous power of their own fantasy-world even as they strive to make" a true image "of the world of contemporary society."[33]

Despite obvious differences in time and place, the forces that threatened Dickens and Balzac—wars and rumors of wars; drastic reorganiza-
tions of economic life; the shift of money, power, and prestige from one
social class to another; rapid technologic and demographic changes—had
much in common with the forces that troubled Faulkner. Faulkner knew
that "no matter how fine anything seems, it can't endure, because once
it stops, abandons motion, it is dead." He knew, too, that every age was
a mixed bag. In the world disappearing he saw both grandeur ("the
splendid fine things which are a part of man's past" but "which change
must destroy") and ruthlessness (a willingness to enslave a people and
destroy a wilderness in order to make the "earth grow something" that
could be sold "for a profit").[34] In the world emerging he saw both vulgarity ("Snopes's design was pretty base—he just wanted to get rich,
he didn't care how") and energy (which he admired even when he
detested the form it took).[35] Thus divided, he began rhetorically to tame
not only the mixed world around him but his own mixed response to it.
The imperial dimension of his enterprise, his stress upon the kingdom he
was making, asserted the power of his verbal art to outdo even the most
aggressive social and historical realities. He wanted the world he was
creating to possess all the salient features, all the wonderful and threatening qualities, of the world he knew—its grandeur and ruthlessness, its
vulgarity and energy—precisely because he wanted to master as well as
evoke it. Toward the world that had always seemed to him both familiar
and other, both appealing and threatening, his aim was territorial and
imperial. It was as though he had decided to transform it in order to make
it completely his own. He wanted nothing less than total possession
("William Faulkner/Sole Owner and Proprietor") and total mastery
("so I created a cosmos of my own. I can move these people around like
God, not only in space but in time too").[36]

Given hope that matched great need, Faulkner worked with deep
intensity. As he did, characters, families, and communities began to
proliferate, scenes and actions to multiply with such rapidity that his
imagination began leaping from one possibility to the next in frenetic
discovery. Separately, his projects contained multitudes; together, they
represented a staggering discovery of his region as a resource, of what he
called "sublimation" as an imaginative process, and of his mythical
kingdom as a creation. "I discovered," he later recalled, "that my own
little postage stamp of native soil was worth writing about and that I
would never live long enough to exhaust it, and by sublimating the actual
into [the] apocryphal I would have complete liberty to use whatever
talent I might have to its absolute top. It opened up a gold mine of other
peoples, so I created a cosmos of my own."[37] From very early on, Faulkner spoke of his kingdom as though it had presented itself to his mind

as a given locality with a history and processes of its own. Since each of its parts implied all the rest, it always included characters and adventures he had not recorded, corners he had not fully explored. If on one side it constituted a world of which he was the only adequate master, on the other it contained multitudes even he could not exhaust.[38]

With his sense of urgency mounting, Faulkner abandoned "Father Abraham" in order to concentrate on *Flags in the Dust*. Writing it, he found everything he had heard, seen, felt, and thought suddenly available: the sense of a shadowy past, at once cursed and glorious; of self-preoccupied individuals and families; of several entangled and doomed ancestors and descendants; of two entangled and doomed races, and two entangled and doomed sexes. During the summer of 1927 he returned to Pascagoula, where he continued writing with great excitement. There he finished his novel on 29 September 1927, four days after his thirtieth birthday. In the same place one year before, he had finished *Mosquitoes*. *Flags in the Dust* was a manuscript of nearly six hundred pages, and it needed some revision. But he was happy and confident. To Aunt Bama, the Old Colonel's youngest child and his own favorite relative, he wrote saying that his book was finished and that he was returning to Oxford to spend a month painting signs. To Horace Liveright he wrote saying that he had "written THE book," and that he needed an advance to go "on an expedition with a lady friend for purposes of biological research." Believing that he had written the best book any publisher would see that year and that he had given it a title no one could improve, he was already designing a jacket for the book.[39]

In both forms in which it was eventually published, as *Sartoris* and as *Flags in the Dust*, Faulkner's third novel is a flawed work. Still, it occupies a crucial place in his career—for two very different reasons. As no previous work had, it marked his emergence as a writer of great originality; it contains, as he once put it, the germ of his "apocrypha in it."[40] Implicit in the promise it contained and the greatness it announced was the direction his career would take. In addition, through the fate it met on its way to publication, it altered his life as a writer. Had *Flags in the Dust* been accepted and published immediately, Faulkner probably would have returned to "Father Abraham," and almost certainly would not have done what he did, which was to write *The Sound and the Fury*.

What *The Sound and the Fury* confirms, *Flags in the Dust* suggests: that the forces that threatened or at least troubled Faulkner were internal and psychological as well as external and social. The social, economic, and demographic displacements that are central to "Father Abraham" are present in *Flags*, as we see most clearly in its inclusion of several members of the Snopes clan. But in *Flags* other concerns, having to do with forbidden desires and forbidden acts, even specifically with the displacing of male rivals and the possessing of forbidden females, are dominant. Among several features that "Father Abraham" and *Flags* share is the presence of weak fathers and self-driven descendants. Despite its first title, the Snopes story belonged from the beginning to the Snopes descendants, especially to a firstborn son named Flem. In *Flags*, great-grandfathers, great-aunts, grandfathers, and sons dominate the scene while mothers and fathers are virtually deleted. In addition, there is a story of a brother named Horace Benbow whose life revolves around his hidden infatuation for his sister, Narcissa.

Flags in the Dust draws, then, on familial as well as regional sources. Recalling the violence, drama, and splendor of the Old Colonel, Faulkner created the aristocratic, ill-fated Sartoris family. Several crucial episodes in the life and death of Colonel John Sartoris—in particular, his conduct during the war, his building of the railroad, the way he dies, and the monument that towers over his grave—evoke the life and death of the Old Colonel. In the course of the novel we see Old Bayard, a somewhat crotchety yet imposing banker, musing over relics that had belonged to his father. Just as these relics resemble those Faulkner's grandfather had shown him at the Big Place, Old Bayard resembles the Young Colonel. During the novel Old Bayard, an aunt, and several friends and servants tell stories about the Colonel. The Falkner tradition of recounting the Old Colonel's adventures thus enters the novel directly, providing considerable interpolated material. Both Faulkner's dependence upon and his ambivalence toward his family's habit of mixing memory and elaboration also enter the novel directly, particularly through Aunt Jenny Sartoris Du Pre's account of the death of the Colonel's brother, the first Bayard: "She had told the story many times . . . and as she grew older the tale itself grew richer and richer . . . until what had been a hair-brained prank of two heedless and reckless boys wild with their own youth, was become a gallant and finely tragical focal-point."[41] Like his characters, however, Faulkner found freedom in the fluidity of his sources. Unlike the poetry he had read, which seemed fixed because written, the stories he knew existed only in oral tradition, many of them in more than one version. They not only permitted play, they invited it.

In addition to the Sartoris family, *Flags in the Dust* includes most of the social elements that become a part of Faulkner's Yoknapatawpha fiction. Only the Indians are missing. Among the black servants of the Sartoris family we meet some who are comic, some who are restive, and several who are both deeply resourceful and deeply pious. In the black family Bayard visits at Christmas, we see a family whose stoic resolve and traditional faith have enabled them to survive great adversity. In the MacCallums, another family Bayard visits, we see the hard-working, independent, and unpretentious yeomen Faulkner deeply admired. Several of the characters who figure in "Father Abraham," including members of the Snopes family and V. K. Suratt, also appear in *Flags in the Dust*. Descended of yeomen, Suratt retains their steady virtues even though he no longer lives on the land. Descended of once shiftless tenant farmers, the Snopeses represent indiscriminate and unprincipled ambition.

In *Flags* as in "Father Abraham," we feel a strong sense of place. The central town of Jefferson, several outlying villages, the rivers, and the railroad—in short, the central features of Yoknapatawpha—are all present. The world Faulkner presents is in many ways traditional. Informed by a sense of shared knowledge and sequence, it is a world of the village and of narrative. Throughout it we feel both Faulkner's "brooding love for the land where he was born and reared" and his lasting "delight in the weather."[42] From the ineluctable procession of the seasons, the novel takes its temporal framework: its action begins in the early spring of 1919 and ends in the spring and early summer of 1920. The strong presence of nature conveys a sense of something older than society or civilization, including several virtues that Faulkner particularly admired: independence, endurance, pride, courage, and discipline. Since the world Faulkner presents remains in many ways traditional and rural, the rhythm of the seasons interacts with human activities, making the work's structure unobtrusive.

Although *Flags in the Dust* shares characters, scenes, and devices with "Father Abraham," it differs from "Father Abraham" in several notable respects, including one of preeminent importance: it is informed by a strong sense of the past as well as a strong sense of place. In its opening scene, Old Bayard and one of his friends sit in the Sartoris bank talking of Old Bayard's father, the Colonel: "Freed as he was of time, he was a far more definite presence in the room than the two of them cemented by deafness to a dead time and drawn thin by the slow attenuation of days."[43] In "Father Abraham" we see signs of the past both in ruins and in local puzzles and legends, but the past does not weigh heavily on the minds of the living. Possessing few memories and no sense of familial history, the Snopes family displays considerable energy and expanding reach. The Sartoris family, on the other hand, carries heavy memories; and as their numbers dwindle, their burdens increase. Extending in time through four generations, their story begins when representatives of three of the four generations are still alive: the Old Colonel's sister, Virginia Sartoris Du Pre, belongs to the first; his son, Old Bayard, belongs to the second; and his great-grandson, Bayard, belongs to the fourth. Only the third, or parental, generation is missing. Born in 1893, Bayard has been an orphan since 1901.[44] During the Great War his only sibling, a twin brother named John, died. Haunted by a sense of doom as well as by guilt that he resents yet cannot escape, he moves recklessly across the somnolent scene of the novel, carrying the memory of his brother's melodramatic death with him. That death in turn recalls, and in spirit repeats, the death of the Old Colonel's younger brother, the first Bayard, in the Civil War. Left without parents, the living Bayard feels deserted; haunted by memories, he feels trapped. In a world that is for him at once too empty and too close, he feels doomed to repeat the pattern already repeated by his brother. In the end he does just that, and so enacts the danger implicit in being isolated in the present and yet held by the past.

Like *Soldiers' Pay, Flags in the Dust* focuses on a young man who returns from the war only to find adjustment to civilian life impossible. Unlike *Soldiers' Pay, Flags* focuses on the parallel Faulkner had earlier sensed between the Civil War and World War One. In the first of these wars a brother named John has survived a brother named Bayard, just as their sister, Virginia, has survived her husband. Both John and Virginia consistently honor, even glamorize, the daring defiance of their lost dead. But after the war Virginia has walked across the South to build a new life, while John has returned to realize his dream of building a railroad. In the stories they tell, we sense their fascination with glorious death; but in the things they do, we witness their commitment to life. In World War One, a brother named Bayard survives a brother named John. Conspicuously without parents, he feels restless and uneasy in his world. Whether drawn toward horses, cars, or airplanes, speed is his anodyne and danger is his love. Struggling with a wild stallion, he injures himself; driving a car, he precipitates the death of his grandfather; flying an obviously unsafe plane, he kills himself.[45]

The story of the Sartoris family, particularly its culmination in the life and death of Bayard, constitutes the largest element in the plot of *Flags in the Dust*. But another substantial element deals with two other orphans, Horace and Narcissa Benbow. Juxtaposing Narcissa and Aunt Jenny for one effect, and Horace and Bayard for another, Faulkner substantially enlarged his novel. Aunt Jenny's mixed disdain and delight for the wild foolishness of the Sartoris men has become in Narcissa cold contempt and fear: "There would be peace for her," she thinks at one point, "only in a world where there were no men at all."[46] Yet her life revolves around the creatures she cannot accept. Living with her effeminate brother, she keeps the anonymous love letters of Byron Snopes, secretly reading and rereading them. Later she finds herself drawn toward marriage with Bayard, who simultaneously repulses and fascinates her. At the end of the novel, she dedicates herself to saving her son from follies she associates with men.

Although Narcissa never becomes more than a hesitating wife to Bayard, she remains an ardent sister to Horace and becomes an ardent mother to her son. In Bayard we see one kind of romanticist, or at least one kind of romantic hero—a twentieth-century descendant of Arnold's voyaging "madman."[47] In Horace Benbow, another returning veteran, we see a very different kind of romanticist. Drawing on several earlier creations, including Elmer Hodge, Faulkner makes Horace both a descendant of the chivalric lover and a version of the fastidious aesthete. Called "a poet," Horace practices an art that is all substitution and sublimation. Whereas Bayard serves in the war as a combat aviator and returns with memories of his dead brother, Horace serves as a secretary to a YMCA unit in charge of canteens and returns with a glassblowing set. Working alone, Horace makes "one almost perfect vase of clear amber" that he keeps "always on his night table," calls "by his sister's name," and addresses "as Thou still unravished bride of quietude."[48]

If in Dawson Fairchild's picture of the withered man who "took the Decameron to bed with him every night" we observe one kind of substitution and in Horace's creation one kind of sublimation, in Horace's words we detect a clue to the link Faulkner sensed between substitution and sublimation. Not long after he finished *Flags in the Dust*, Faulkner began a novel whose relation to his own life he later described in terms that echo his depiction of Horace's vase and quiet bride. At the time he was writing *Flags in the Dust*, however, he found it easy to distance himself from both Bayard and Horace. His difficulty lay in satisfactorily conjoining their stories. At some points the novel seems to go over the same ground twice; at others it seems to go off in different directions simultaneously. Still, despite its faults, it deserved a better fate than it met, and it remains a more compelling novel than most critics have allowed. The earliest objection to it, that of Horace Liveright, in fact proved prophetic: Faulkner continued to write novels that strain their genre, not only because they draw different narrative strands together but also because they form parts of a larger whole. Characters from *Flags* would later appear in novels as different as *Sanctuary*, one of Faulkner's bitterest novels, and *The Unvanquished*, one of his most romantic.

We often sense a strong reciprocity among the works of writers who possess large, compelling imaginations. But what we observe in Faulkner's Yoknapatawpha fiction, clearly the heart of his imaginative achievement, is an overt interaction through which an implicit structure emerges. Three related facts—the enthusiasm Faulkner brought to Malcolm Cowley's suggestions for making *The Portable Faulkner*; the quickness with which Faulkner conceived it as "a Golden Book of my apocryphal county";[49] and the special place the project occupied in making Faulkner's greatness visible—point to a distinctive feature of the stories and novels that *Flags in the Dust* began: that they possess an integral as well as a differential logic, and that their integral logic, together with the interplay for which it accounts, is both complicating and enriching. Since Faulkner's fiction is not informed by any set of ideas or theories about southern history or southern society, and since his methods are not those of a historian or a sociologist, it is clearly wrongheaded to regard his Yoknapatawpha fiction as history or sociology. In their meaning his works "are more, and in their immediate application less, than" southern history or southern society in microcosm.[50] Yet such misreadings have important implications, for they suggest to what extent two contrary senses of his work balance one another—the sense, on one side, that it forms an imaginative kingdom; and the sense, on the other, that it derives from the world he could never quite accept as his home. Even before Faulkner's readers, critics, and neighbors turned the locating of sources and originals into a minor industry, his works suggested the kind of equilibrium that he sought in them to achieve and through them to maintain.[51] Returning to the Old Colonel's scene, he used the landscape, history, and demography of Tippah County and the village of Ripley; recalling the Young Colonel's scene, he used Lafayette County and the village of Oxford. But he used all of these things freely. For it was not finally to fact that he was committed but to what Anderson called the "play of the imagination over the facts of life." Blending and adding, revising and transforming, he created a world with features and processes of its own.[52]

In "Father Abraham" and *Flags in the Dust* Faulkner became a singer of familial and regional stories, legends, and myths that, because they were so much a part of him, he seems scarcely to have been conscious of using. When the people around him refused to endorse his singing by becoming his audience, his already strained relations with his culture became more strained.[53] Still, despite its failure to attract an audience, his imaginative return to Mississippi brought him back to several rich traditions. As V. K. Ratliff, V. K. Suratt later became a master of two of these traditions—a love of wild exaggeration essential to the tall tale; and a gift for wry, understated, self-deprecating humor. Following the Sartorises, other characters would adopt the elaborative, celebratory style that Faulkner associated with his own family. As a boy, he had also sat in Protestant churches, stood in front of political platforms, or attended local shows where "Thomas C. Trueblood, A.M., Prof. of Elocution and Oratory. University of Michigan" recited soliloquies from Shakespeare and Henry Watterson, a regional specialist, recited "Pickett's Charge" by Fred Emerson Brooks.[54] These and other traditions, together with rhythms found in Romantic poetry, merged in *Flags in the Dust*, which taught Faulkner to think of himself as a failed poet writing rich, cadenced prose.

Drawing upon the tradition of the novel, he evoked the world of actualities, which he associated with society as well as with nature. One part of him accepted the priority of nature and society, together with the sense that anything made of words must be comparatively insubstantial. But he shared with many turn-of-the-century writers a contrary conviction: that the prior world is fragmentary and unstable. Rather than simply bemoan this fact, he took consolation in it; for what the mutability of the world of act and deed implied, beyond loss, was opportunity. Several years later, he described his great-grandfather as epitomizing the heroic possibilities of the real, then noted that all the Old Colonel's achievements had faded: "There's nothing left in the old place, the house is gone and the plantation boundaries, nothing left of his work but a statue." Seemingly as an afterthought he added that he liked "it better that way," suggesting that it was as both living and dying force that his great ancestor appealed to him.[55] Years earlier, in *Flags in the Dust*, this double response had surfaced: although he took pride in the exploits of his great ancestor, he took pleasure in the relations and revisions he was free to work out. Among other things such doubleness suggests how far it was from accidental that his first completed engagement with Yoknapatawpha should be his most direct engagement with the life and times of the first W. C. Falkner.

The most powerful ancestors of the most powerful tribes, Nietzsche once remarked, must always be transfigured into gods.[56] In Faulkner's transfiguration of the Old Colonel into Colonel John Sartoris and his brother Bayard, we see the evocative and elaborative impulse Nietzsche described. The Sartoris family retraces Faulkner's deepest sense of his own family's story: *Flags in the Dust* is a tale of division so fundamental that it accounts for both the early heroism and the marked declension of a family. In it we move from a first generation that is predominantly courageous and creative to a second that is less vital and more divided yet remains committed to life and then to a fourth that comes to love and seek death. At least as surprising as the pattern thus established, however, is the missing parental generation. Asked years later about the generation he skipped, Faulkner said that the "twins' father didn't have a story," that he had lived only for the continuity of the family. Referring to the hidden intent of his own analyses, Freud once remarked that "the distortion of a text resembles a murder: the difficulty is not in perpetrating the deed, but getting rid of its traces."[57] In Faulkner's case, the trace is crucial: he set the date of the father's death as 1901, one year earlier than his own family's move from Ripley to Oxford. In this, Faulkner's most telling revision of his family's history, we can discern how intimately related the elaborative and the aggressive motions of his mind were. For what we observe is not simply distortion as a sign of repression

and revenge, or elaboration as a sign of benign transformation into meaning, but the two so interrelated as to be almost indistinguishable. Faced
with a writer of motives so mixed and strategies so complex, some readers
have concentrated on Faulkner's fidelity to facts and details, others on
his distortions of them. But in the great novels he was now prepared to
write, both fidelity and distortion would be crucial. For he was prepared
now to dramatize minds caught up in dismembering and reconstructing.
Musing over life, these minds discard and reclaim, displace and recreate,
leaving signs and traces everywhere. Even as they give life, making dead
figures seem potent and alive, they pass judgments, impose sentences, and
display mastery: they not only participate in their maker's great rhetorical
and imaginative gifts; they also share his mixed motives and complex
strategies.

　　Awaiting Liveright's response to *Flags in the Dust*, Faulkner felt at
once confident and impatient. At first he painted signs in order to finance
a trip with his anonymous lady friend. Still restless after his return to
Oxford, he accepted General Stone's invitation to join a hunting party.
In late November, Liveright's letter arrived. "It is with sorrow in my
heart," Liveright began—and then went on flatly to reject the novel
that Faulkner had believed would bring him commercial as well as critical
success. Explaining his rejection, Liveright completely contradicted
Faulkner's own sense of his career. *Soldiers' Pay*, he said, "was a very
fine book and should have done better"; *Mosquitoes* showed little spiritual
growth and no improvement in writing; and *Flags in the Dust* was "diffuse
and non-integral," lacking in "plot, dimension and projection." To Faulkner it seemed that he had discovered an inexhaustible kingdom; to his
publisher it seemed that he did not even "have any story to tell." Although Liveright claimed continuing interest in Faulkner's career, his
words were harsh. Viewing *Flags in the Dust* as an embarrassment, he
recommended that Faulkner not even "offer it for publication."[58]

　　Liveright's letter initiated one of the darkest periods in Faulkner's
life, and in the process redirected the first great phase in his career.
Responding to Liveright, Faulkner seemed cool, slightly detached, and
basically confident. "It's too bad you dont like Flags in the Dust," he
said; "I still believe it is the book which will make my name for me as
a writer." Admitting that he couldn't return the "super-advance" Liveright had given him, he still hoped Liveright would return his manuscript. He had two other projects in mind, one he hoped to finish by
spring, the other in three or four years. Perhaps Liveright would like one
of those. In the meantime, he wanted to try *Flags in the Dust* on another
publisher.[59] In fact, however, Faulkner felt too hurt and too baffled to
work. Trying to sort out his feelings, he found himself moving back and
forth between blind protest, furious denial, and efforts to be detached and

objective. In December Liveright returned the manuscript; in February he officially relinquished claim to it. He was willing to wait for the book Faulkner hoped to finish in the spring. But nothing was going right for Faulkner. In order to keep from sending one story to the same magazine twice, he carefully recorded the stories he mailed and the replies he received: his ledger showed no acceptances. Earlier he had been able to take rejections more or less in stride; now they deepened the disappointment and doubt Liveright's letter had triggered. Needing help, he turned to Ben Wasson. After practicing law for several years in Greenville, Mississippi, Wasson had moved to New York and gone to work for Leland Hayward at the American Play Company. The agency handled novelists as well as dramatists, and Wasson was also freelancing. Since he knew his way around publishing circles, he might have better luck placing the stories Faulkner had been sending out; at least he could relieve Faulkner of the trouble of mailing them and the frustration of recording rejections.[60]

Free of the stories, Faulkner tried again to revise *Flags in the Dust* and to write new fiction. It helped to think that he might at last make a little money from what he thought of as his commercial fiction. He had been trying to publish it for several years. Yet he still found it impossible to work. Rereading *Flags in the Dust*, he saw no way to revise it; turning to his new stories or his new novel, he wrote nothing that seemed right. At times he felt morbid as well as bitter. Worried about the money he owed Liveright, he wrote to say that he had turned his stories over to an agent and hoped they might bring in enough money to clear his debt: "Otherwise I dont know what we'll do about it, as I have a belly full of writing, now, since you folks in the publishing business claim that a book like that last one I sent you is blah. I think now that I'll sell my typewriter and go to work—though God knows, it's sacrilege to waste that talent for idleness which I possess."[61] In fact, he could not give up. Having worked on his manuscript for a time, he put it aside, determined to forget it, only to go back hoping to redo the whole thing. "Every day or so I burn some of it up and rewrite it," he wrote Aunt Bama, "and at present it is almost incoherent."[62] When he felt especially confused or hopeless, he gave the manuscript to friends, asking their advice. But nothing seemed to help. Finally he decided to retype the manuscript and send it to Ben Wasson. Someone might decide to publish it. Even if they did not, he might be able to go on to other things.[63]

Wasson tried about ten publishers before he finally showed it to Hal Smith, then an editor with Harcourt, Brace and Company. When Smith liked it, Alfred Harcourt agreed to publish it, with the stipulation that it had to be cut. Working under Smith's supervision and without Faulkner's participation, Ben Wasson apparently performed the operation. He deleted some of the Snopes material and large pieces of the Benbow story and so turned *Flags in the Dust* into *Sartoris*. In the process, he deprived the first Yoknapatawpha story of much of its fullness. In *Sartoris*, Bayard stands out almost alone. In *Flags*, he is surrounded by foils whose presences are more fully felt: by his more romantic brother; by the aesthete and dilettante, Horace Benbow; and by the strong, steady young yeoman, Buddy MacCallum.[64]

After the cutting, Faulkner added a dedication: "To Sherwood Anderson, through whose kindness I was first published, with the belief that this book will give him no reason to regret that fact." On 31 January 1929 the novel he had finished in October 1927 was published. Although he was glad to have it out, the wait had been too long, the ordeal surrounding it too painful. By 1929 most of Faulkner's relief and all of his elation focused on another novel. Born of that ordeal, and of another more intensely private, *The Sound and the Fury* was for him a very special book. He had let a friend cut *Flags in the Dust*, but when the time came to publish *The Sound and the Fury*, he effaced changes made by the same man.[65]

FIVE 1928-1929

The Self's Own Lamp

During the early months of 1928, Faulkner mixed spasmodic efforts to revise *Flags in the Dust* with other activities. He began several new stories and accepted occasional odd jobs, usually as a painter. At one time or another, he painted everything from the domes of large buildings to houses and signs; once or twice he even lacquered brass horns. During these months, he also made a second gift copy of *The Wishing Tree* "as a gesture of pity and compassion for a doomed child."[1] He had told his fairy tale to Margaret Brown many times; she was the youngest child in a family he had known for years. Now she was dying of cancer, and he wanted her parents to be able to read the story to her as often as she wished to hear it. Yet nothing seemed to help Faulkner, neither writing nor odd jobs nor acts of kindness. Failure was not new to him: he had gone along experiencing some of it and anticipating more, trying to prepare defenses that would mute its pain. But the disappointment he felt now was intense, and there was no one with whom he could share it. Although he remained close to his mother, he knew that her tolerance had never extended to complaints, let alone to failure. Relations with his father had eased over the years; by now he felt less shame about being the son of a failure, while his father felt less outrage about being the father of "a bum."[2] But Murry Falkner had never shared his disappointments with others or invited them to share theirs with him.

For different reasons, Faulkner also found it difficult to talk freely with Phil Stone or Estelle Franklin. Pride had always made it hard for him to express his need for tenderness, and now his relations with both Phil and Estelle had become strained. During the writing of *Flags in the Dust*, he had considered breaking with Phil altogether, apparently because he felt that Phil was trying to dictate what he should write. With *Flags* finished, he had enjoyed sharing his high expectations with Phil, and so the tension between them had eased.[3] But he was not ready to share disappointment and failure with Phil, and he had never felt more uncertain about his relations with Estelle. Her divorce would soon be final, and he knew that she was counting on him to marry her. He had continued seeing her so regularly that people in Oxford were gossiping. Yet he felt that he might be in love with someone else. In early 1928 he wrote a letter to his Aunt Bama in which he describes his efforts to revise *Flags* and mentions reviews of *Mosquitoes*. He also refers to a woman he does not name: "We all wish you would [come down]. I have something—someone, I mean—to show you, if you only would. Of course it's a woman. I would like to see you taken with her utter charm, and intrigued by her utter shallowness. Like a lovely vase. . . . She gets the days past for me, though. Thank God I've no money, or I'd marry her. So you see, even Poverty looks after its own."[4] Since Faulkner's lovely vase remained nameless, it is impossible to know whom he meant. But since Aunt Bama had long since met Estelle, it is clear whom he did not mean. Also unspecified in the letter are the barriers other than poverty that stood between him and his new love. If infatuation with his lovely vase kept him from confiding freely in Estelle, his sense of responsibility to Estelle probably made it difficult for him to confide in another woman. Feeling cut off, finding no one to help dispel his disappointment and doubt, he turned inward. Simply getting through the days became a problem. At odd moments he found himself singing morbid songs, thinking about how he might die, or wondering where he might be buried. "You know, after all," he said to a friend, "they put you in a pine box and in a few days the worms have you. Someone might cry for a day or two and after that they've forgotten all about you."[5]

Soon he was writing stories about some children named Compson. Taking a line from W. C. Handy's "St. Louis Blues," he called one of the stories "That Evening Sun Go Down." Another he called "A Justice."[6]

Both were based on memories out of his own childhood, and both concern children who face dark, foreboding experiences without adequate support or adequate sponsors. At the end of "A Justice" he depicts the children moving through a "strange, faintly sinister suspension of twilight."[7] As his imagination played with the Compson children, he began to see them quite clearly, poised at the end of childhood and the beginning of awareness—a moment that possessed particular poignancy for him, as scattered comments suggest, and as both the deep resonance and the making of the Compson stories confirm. "Art reminds us of our youth," Fairchild says in *Mosquitoes*, "of that age when life don't need to have her face lifted every so often for you to consider her beautiful." "It's over very soon," Faulkner later remarked as he observed his daughter moving toward adolescence. "This is the end of it. She'll grow into a woman."[8] At every turn the Compson children see things they cannot understand, feel things they cannot express. In "A Justice," as twilight descends around them and their world begins to fade, loss, consternation, and bafflement become almost all they know.

In early spring, Faulkner began a third story about the Compsons. Calling it "Twilight," he thought to make it an exploration of the moment "That Evening Sun" and "A Justice" had made the Compsons' inclusive moment. By the time he finished it, this third story had become *The Sound and the Fury*, his first great novel. Faulkner was capable, as he once remarked, of saying almost anything in an interview; on some subjects, he enjoyed contradicting himself.[9] In discussing *The Sound and the Fury*, he displayed remarkable consistency for thirty years. His statements vary, of course, in the quality of emotion they express and the quantity of information they convey, but they show that his fourth novel occupied a secure place in his memory, and they suggest that it occupied a special place in his experience. From his statements several facts emerge, all intimating that he wrote *The Sound and the Fury* in the midst of a crisis that was both personal and professional.

The professional dimension to that crisis is clear: Faulkner's high expectations for *Flags in the Dust* prepared for it, Liveright's harsh rejection initiated it, and Faulkner's response intensified it. More and more baffled as well as hurt, Faulkner soon found himself wondering again about his vocation. He probably knew that the threat to sell his typewriter and surrender his vocation was empty, but he apparently believed that he could alter his intentions and expectations—that he could teach himself to live without hope of recognition and reward. For several years he had written in order to publish. After publication of *Soldiers' Pay*, that had meant writing with Horace Liveright in mind. As his work became more satisfying to him personally, it had become less acceptable to his publisher. Refusing to go back to writing books as youthfully

glamorous as *Soldiers' Pay* or as trashily smart as *Mosquitoes*, he decided
to relinquish a part of his dream.[10] "One day I seemed to shut a door
between me and all publishers' addresses and book lists. I said to myself,
Now I can write"—by which he meant that he could write for himself
alone. Almost immediately, he felt free. Writing "without any accom-
panying feeling of drive or effort, or any following feeling of exhaustion
or relief or distaste," he began with no plan at all. He did not even think
of his manuscript as a book. "I was thinking of books, publication, only
in . . . reverse, in saying to myself, I won't have to worry about publishers
liking or not liking this at all."[11]

But Faulkner was also grappling with personal problems. Protecting
his privacy, he remained vague as to what they were. To Maurice Coindreau he spoke of the "severe strain" imposed by "difficulties of an
intimate kind" ("des difficultés d'ordre intime").[12] Though his problems
probably had something to do with Estelle and his "lovely vase," and
almost certainly had something to do with his loneliness and despair,
they remained unspecified. About them, we know only that they ran
deep and that they became intimately involved in the writing of *The
Sound and the Fury*. About the writing, we know that it brought Faulkner great joy, that it produced great fiction, and that it was carried on
with unusual secretiveness. Apparently no one, not even Estelle and Phil,
knew anything about *The Sound and the Fury* until it was virtually
finished.[13]

Like *Flags in the Dust, The Sound and the Fury* is set in Jefferson and
recalls family history. The Compson family, like the Sartoris family,
mirrors Faulkner's sense of his family's story as a story of declension.
But *The Sound and the Fury* is bleaker, more personal, and more compelling. Despite its pathos, *Flags* remained almost exuberant; and despite
its use of family legends, it remained open, accessible. Faulkner's changed
mood, his new attitude and needs, altered not only his way of working
but his way of writing. If writing for himself implied freedom to recover
more personal materials, writing without concern for publishers' addresses
implied freedom to become more experimental. The novel accordingly
represented a move back toward Faulkner's childhood and the family
configuration of his earliest years—a move into the past and into the
interior. At the same time, through the fictional techniques and strategies
that Faulkner used to discover, displace, and transfigure the memories he
found waiting for him, his novel represented an astonishing breakthrough.
A moving story of four children and their inadequate parents, *The Sound
and the Fury* is thematically regressive, stylistically and formally innovative.

Of the several corollaries implicit in its regressive principle, at least
two are crucial: first, the presence of the three Compson brothers, who

recall Faulkner's own family configuration; and second, memory and repetition as formal principles.[14] Faulkner possessed the three Compson brothers, as he later put it, almost before he put pen to paper. To anchor them in time and place, he took a central event and several images from his memory of the death of the grandmother he and his brothers called Damuddy, after whose lingering illness and funeral they were sent away from home so that the house could be fumigated. For Faulkner as for Gertrude Stein, memory is always repetition, being and living never repetition. *The Sound and the Fury,* he was fond of remarking, was a single story several times told. But since he used the remembered as he used the actual—less to denominate lived events, relationships, and configurations, with their attendant attributes and emotions, than to objectify them and so be free to analyze and play with them—the remembered was never for him simple repetition. To place the past under the aspect of the present, the present under the aspect of the past, was to start from the regressive and move toward the innovative. Like the novel's regressive principle, its innovative principle possessed several corollaries, including its gradual evocation of Caddy, the sister Faulkner added to memory, and its slow move from private worlds toward a more public world.[15]

The parental generation, which exists in *Flags in the Dust* only for the sake of family continuity, is crucial in *The Sound and the Fury.* Jason is aggressive in expressing the contempt he feels for his mother and especially his father. Attached to them, he nonetheless resents and hates them. Although Benjy feels neither resentment nor hatred, he does feel the vacancies his parents have left in his life. Although Quentin disguises his hostility, it surfaces. Like Benjy's and Quentin's obsessive attachments to Caddy, Jason's hatred of her originates in wounds inflicted by Mr. and Mrs. Compson. In short, each brother's discontent finds its focus in Caddy, as we see in their various evocations of her.

To the end of his life, Faulkner spoke of Caddy with deep devotion. She was, he suggested, both the sister of his imagination and "the daughter of his mind." Born of his own discontent, she was for him "the beautiful one," his "heart's darling." It was Caddy, or more precisely, Faulkner's feelings for Caddy, that turned a story called "Twilight" into a novel called *The Sound and the Fury*: "I loved her so much," he said, that "I couldn't decide to give her life just for the duration of a short story. She deserved more than that. So my novel was created, almost in spite of myself."[16]

In the same discussions in which Faulkner stressed the quality of his love for Caddy, he emphasized the extent to which his novel grew as he worked on it. One source of that growth was technical. The novel, he was fond of remarking, was a story that required four tellings. Having presented Benjy's experience, he found that it was so "incomprehensible, even I could not have told what was going on then, so I had to write another chapter." The second section accordingly became both a clarification and a counterpoint to the first, just as the third became both of these to the second.[17] The story moves from the remote and strange world of Benjy's idiocy and innocence, where sensations and basic responses are all we have; through the intensely subjective as well as private world of Quentin's bizarre idealism, where thought shapes sensation and feeling into a kind of decadent poetic prose full of idiosyncratic allusions and patterns; to the more familiar, even commonsensical meanness of Jason's materialism, where rage and self-pity find expression in colloquialisms and clichés. Because it is more conventional, Jason's section is more accessible, even more public. Yet it too describes a circle of its own.[18] Wanting to move from three peculiar and private worlds toward a more public and social one, Faulkner adopted a more detached voice. The fourth section comes to us as though from "an outsider." The story, as it finally emerged, tells not only of four children and their family, but of a larger world at twilight. "And that's how that book grew. That is, I wrote that same story four times. . . . That was not a deliberate *tour de force* at all, the book just grew that way. . . . I was still trying to tell one story which moved me very much and each time I failed."[19]

Given the novel's technical brilliance, it is easy to forget how simple and moving its basic story is. In it we observe four children come of age amid the decay and dissolution of their family. His sense of it began, Faulkner recalled, with "a brother and a sister splashing one another in the brook" where they have been sent to play during the funeral of a grandmother they call Damuddy. From this scene came one of the central images of the novel—Caddy's muddy drawers. As she clambers up a tree outside the Compson home to observe the funeral inside, we and her brothers see her drawers from below. From this sequence, Faulkner got several things: his sense of the brook as "the dark, harsh flowing of time" that was sweeping Caddy away from her brothers; his sense that the girl who had the courage to climb the tree would also find the courage to face change and loss; and his sense that her brothers, who had waited below, would respond very differently—that Benjy would fail to understand his loss; that Quentin would seek oblivion rather than face his; and that Jason would meet his with terrible rage and ambition.[20] The novel thus focuses not only on the three brothers Faulkner possessed when he began but also on Caddy, the figure he added to memory—which is to say, on the only child whose story he never directly told as well as on those whose stories he directly tells. His decision to approach Caddy only by indirection, through the eyes and needs and demands of her brothers, was in part technical; by the time he came to the fourth telling, he wanted a more public voice. In addition, he thought indirection more "passionate." It was, he said, more moving to present "the shadow of the branch, and let the mind create the tree."[21]

But in fact Caddy grew as she is presented, by indirection—in response to needs and strategies shared by Faulkner and his characters. Having discovered Benjy, in whom he saw "the blind, self-centeredness of inno- cence, typified by children," Faulkner became "interested in the relation- ship of the idiot to the world that he was in but would never be able to cope with." What particularly agitated him was whether and where such a one as Benjy could "get the tenderness, the help, to shield him."[22] The answer he hit upon had nothing to do with Mr. and Mrs. Compson, and only a little to do with Dilsey. Mr. Compson is a weak, nihilistic alcoholic who toys with the emotions and needs of his children. Even when he feels sympathy and compassion, he fails to show it effectively. Mrs. Compson is a cold, self-involved woman who expends her energies worrying about her ailments, complaining about her life, and clinging to her notions of respectability. "If I could say Mother. Mother," Quentin says to himself. Dilsey, who recalls Mammy Callie, epitomizes the kind of Christian Faulkner most admired. She is saved by a minimum of theology. Though her understanding is small, her wisdom and love are large. Living in the world of the Compsons, she commits herself to the immediate; she "does de bes" she can to fill the vacancies left in the lives of the children around her by their loveless and faithless parents. Since by virtue of her faith she is part of a larger world, she is able "to stand above the fallen ruins of the family."[23] She has seen, she says, the first and the last. But Dilsey's life combines a measure of effective action with a measure of pathetic resignation. Most of Benjy's needs for tender- ness and comfort, if not help and protection, he takes to his sister. And it was thus, Faulkner said, that "the character of his sister began to emerge."[24] Like Benjy, Quentin and Jason also turn toward Caddy, seeking to find in her some way of meeting needs frustrated by their parents. Treasuring some concept of family honor his parents seem to him to have forfeited, Quentin seeks to turn his fair and beautiful sister into a fair, unravished, and unravishable maiden. Believing that his parents have sold his birthright when they sold their land, yet still lusting after an inheritance, Jason tries to use Caddy's marriage to secure a substitute fortune.

The parental generation thus plays a crucial, destructive role in *The Sound and the Fury*. Several readers have felt that Faulkner's sympathies as a fictionist lie more with men than with women.[25] But his fathers, at least, rarely fare better than his mothers, the decisive direction of his sympathy being toward children, as we see not only in *The Sound and the Fury* but also in works that followed it. Jewel Bundren must live without a visible father, while Darl discovers that in some fundamental sense he "never had a mother." Thomas and Ellen Sutpen's children live and die without having either an adequate father or an adequate mother. Rosa Coldfield lives a long life only to discover that she had lost childhood before she possessed it. Held fast yet held without gentleness, these characters find repetition easy, independence and innovation almost impossible.

Although he is aggressive in expressing the hostility he feels for his parents, Jason is never able satisfactorily to avenge himself on them. Accordingly, he takes his victims where he finds them, his preference being for those who are most helpless, like Benjy and Luster, or most desperate, like Caddy. Enlarged, the contempt he feels for his family enables him to reject the past and embrace the New South, which he does without recognizing in himself vulgar versions of the materialism and self-pity that we associate with his mother. Left without sufficient tenderness and love, Quentin, Caddy, and Benjy turn toward Dilsey and each other. Without becoming aggressive, Benjy feels the vacancies his parents create in his life, and so tries to hold fast to those moments in which Caddy has met his need for tenderness. In Quentin we observe a very different desire: repulsed by the world around him, he determines to possess moments only in idealized form. Like the hero of Pound's *Cantos*, he lives wondering whether any sight can be worth the beauty of his thought. His dis-ease with the immediate, which becomes a desire to escape time itself, accounts for the strange convolutions of his mind and the strange transformations of his emotions. In the end it leads him to a still harbor where he fastidiously completes the logic of his father's life. Unlike her brothers, Caddy establishes her independence and achieves freedom. But her flight severs ties, making it impossible for her to help Quentin, comfort Benjy, or protect her daughter. Finally, freedom sweeps "her into dishonor and shame."[26] Deserted by her mother, Miss Quentin is left no one with whom to learn love, and so repeats her mother's dishonor and flight without knowing her tenderness. If in the story of Jason we observe the near-triumph of all that is repugnant, in the stories of Caddy and Miss Quentin we observe the degradation of all that is beautiful. No modern story has done more than theirs to explore Yeats's terrible vision of modernity in "The Second Coming," where the "best lack all conviction" while the "worst are full of passionate intensity."

Faulkner thus seems to have discovered Caddy in essentially the way he presents her—through the felt needs of her brothers. Only later did he realize that he had also been trying to meet needs of his own: that in Caddy he had created the sister he had wanted but never had and the daughter he was fated to lose, "though the former might have been apparent," he added, "from the fact that Caddy had three brothers almost before I wrote her name on paper." Taken together, then, the Compson brothers may be seen as manifesting the needs Faulkner expressed through his creation of Caddy. In Benjy's need for tenderness we see signs of the emotional confluence that preceded the writing of *The Sound and the Fury*. The ecstasy and relief Faulkner associated with the writing of the novel as a whole, he associated particularly with "the writing of Benjy's section."[27] In Jason's preoccupation with making a fortune, we see a vulgar version of the hope Faulkner was trying to relinquish. In Quentin's almost Manichaean revulsion toward all things material and physical, we see both a version of the imagination Allen Tate has called "angelic" and a version of the moral sensibility that Faulkner associated with the fastidious aesthete.[28] It is more than accident of imagery that Quentin, another of Faulkner's poets manqués, seeks refuge, first, in the frail "vessel" he calls Caddy, and then, in something very like the "still harbor" in which Faulkner had imagined Hergesheimer submerging himself— "where the age cannot hurt him and where rumor of the world reaches him only as a far faint sound of rain."[29]

In one of his more elaborate as well as more suggestive descriptions of what the creation of Caddy meant to him, Faulkner associated her with one of his favorite images. "I said to myself, Now I can write. Now I can make myself a vase like that which the old Roman kept at his bedside and wore the rim slowly away with kissing it. So I, who had never had a sister and was fated to lose my daughter in infancy, set out to make myself a beautiful and tragic little girl."[30] The image of the urn or vase had turned up in the Hergesheimer review, "Elmer," *Mosquitoes*, and *Flags in the Dust*; it had appeared recently in the letter to Aunt Bama describing his new love; and it would make several later appearances. It was an image, we may fairly assume, that possessed special force for Faulkner, and several connotations, including at least three of crucial significance.

The simplest of these connotations—stressing a desire for escape— Faulkner had earlier associated with Hergesheimer's "still harbor" and later associated with "the classic and serene vase" that shelters Gail Hightower "from the harsh gale of living."[31] In *The Sound and the Fury* Benjy comes to us as a wholly dependent creature seeking shelter. Sentenced to a truncated life of pain—"like something eyeless and voiceless which . . . existed merely because of its ability to suffer"[32] —he is all need and all helplessness. What loss of Caddy means to him is a life of unrelieved and meaningless suffering. For Quentin, on the other hand, loss of Caddy means despair. In him we observe a desire, first for relief and shelter, then for escape. In one of the New Orleans sketches, Faulkner introduces a girl who presents herself to her lover as "Little Sister Death." In the allegory he wrote for Helen Baird, a maiden of the same name turns up in the company of a courtly knight and lover—which is, of course, the role Quentin seeks to play.³³ At first all Quentin's desire seems to focus on Caddy as the maiden of his dreams. But as his desire becomes associated with "night and unrest," Caddy begins to merge with "Little Sister Death"—that is, with an incestuous love forbidden on threat of death. Rendered impotent by that threat, Quentin comes to love, not the body of his sister, nor even some concept of Compson honor, but death itself. In the end, he ceremoniously gives himself, not to Caddy but to the river. "The saddest thing about love," says a character in *Soldiers' Pay*, "is that not only the love cannot last forever, but even the heartbreak is soon forgotten."³⁴ Quentin kills himself in part as punishment for his forbidden desires; in part because Caddy proves corruptible; in part, perhaps, because he decides "that even she was not quite worth despair." But he also kills himself because he fears his own inconstancy. What he discovers in himself is deep psychological impotence that manifests itself in his inability to play either of the heroic roles—seducer or avenger—that he deems appropriate to his fiction of himself as a gallant, chivalric lover. But beyond the failure he experiences lies the failure he anticipates, a moment when Caddy's corruption no longer matters to him. Suicide thus completes his commitment to the only role left him, that of the despairing lover.

Never before had Faulkner expressed anxiety so deep and diverse. In Quentin it is not only immediate failure that we observe; it is the prospect of ultimate failure. Later, Faulkner associated the writing of *The Sound and the Fury* with anxiety about a moment "when not only the ecstasy of writing would be gone, but the unreluctance and the something worth saying too." In Quentin we see clearly Faulkner's sense that the desire to escape such anxiety was potentially destructive. If he wrote *The Sound and the Fury* in part to find shelter, he also wrote knowing that he would have to emerge from it. "I had made myself a vase," he said, though "I suppose I knew all the time that I could not live forever inside of it."³⁵ Having finished *The Sound and the Fury*, he found emergence traumatic. Still, it is probably fair to say that he knew all along that he would make that move. Certainly his novel possessed other possibilities for him, just as the image through which he sought to convey his sense of it possessed other connotations, including one that is clearly erotic and one that is clearly aesthetic.

We can begin untangling the erotic by examining the relation between the old Roman who kept the vase at his bedside so that he could kiss it and the withered cuckold husband who "took the Decameron to bed with him every night."³⁶ Both of these figures are committed to a kind of substitution, and practice a kind of autoeroticism. The old Roman is superior only if we assume that he is the maker of his vase—in which case he resembles Horace Benbow, maker of his own "almost perfect vase." With Horace and his vase we might seem to have come full circle, back to Faulkner and his "heart's darling."[37] For Horace not only keeps his vase by his bedside; he also calls it by his sister's name. In *The Sound and the Fury* affection of brother and sister replaces affection of parents and children as an archetype of love; and with Caddy and Quentin, the incestuous potential of that love clearly surfaces—as it had in "Elmer," *Mosquitoes*, and *Flags in the Dust*, and as it would in *Absalom, Absalom!*.

The circle, however, is less perfect than it might at first appear, since at least one difference between Horace Benbow and William Faulkner is crucial. Whereas Horace's amber vase is a substitute for a sister he has but is forbidden to possess, Faulkner's is a substitute for the sister he never had. In this regard Horace is closer to Elmer, Faulkner to Gordon in *Mosquitoes*. Elmer is in fact a more timid version of Horace. Working with his paints—"thick-bodied and female and at the same time phallic: hermaphroditic"—Elmer creates figures he associates with something "that he dreaded yet longed for." The thing he both seeks and shuns is a "vague shape" he holds in his mind; its origins are his mother and a sister named Jo-Addie. His art, like Horace's, is devoted to imaginative possession of figures he is forbidden and fears sexually to possess. When Horace calls his amber vase by his sister's name, he articulates what Elmer only feels. Like Elmer, however, Horace finds in indirect or imaginative possession a means of avoiding the fate Quentin enacts. Through their art, Elmer and Horace are able to achieve satisfaction that soothes one kind of despair without arousing guilt that might lead to another.

In *Mosquitoes* the origins of Gordon's "feminine ideal" remain obscure, though his art is clearly devoted to creating and possessing it. For Gordon as for Elmer and Horace, the erotic and the aesthetic are inseparable. A man is always writing, Dawson Fairchild remarks, "for some woman"; if she is not "a flesh and blood creature," she is at least "the symbol of a desire," and "she is feminine."[38] Elmer and Horace work in their art toward a figure that is actual; they make art a substitute for love of a real woman. Gordon, on the other hand, makes art a way of approaching an ideal whose identity remains vague. About it we know two things: that it is feminine and that it represents what Henry James called the beautiful circuit and subterfuge of thought and desire. Horace expresses his love for a real woman through his art, whereas Gordon expresses his devotion to his sculpted ideal by temporarily pursuing a woman who happens to resemble it.[39] Horace is a failed and minor artist, Gordon a consecrated one—the difference being that Gordon devotes his life as well as his art to a figure that exists perfectly only in thought and imagination.

On his way to Europe, shortly after finishing *Soldiers' Pay* and before beginning "Elmer" and *Mosquitoes*, Faulkner told William Spratling that he thought love and death the "only two basic compulsions on earth."[40]

What engaged his imagination as much as either of these, however, was his sense of the relation of each to the other and of both to art. The amber vase Horace calls Narcissa, he also addresses "Thou still unravished bride of quietude." "There is a story somewhere," Faulkner said,

> about an old Roman who kept at his bedside a Tyrrhenian vase which he loved and the rim of which he wore slowly away with kissing it. I had made myself a vase, but I suppose I knew all the time that I could not live forever inside of it, that perhaps to have it so that I too could lie in bed and look at it would be better; surely so when that day should come when not only the ecstasy of writing would be gone, but the unreluctance and the something worth saying too. It's fine to think that you will leave something behind you when you die, but it's better to have made something you can die with.[41]

In this brief statement the vase becomes both Caddy and *The Sound and the Fury*; both "the beautiful one" for whom he created the novel as a commodious space and the novel in which she found protection and privacy as well as expression. In its basic doubleness the vase is many things: a haven or shelter into which the artist may retreat; a feminine ideal to which he can give his devotion; a work of art that he can leave behind when he is dead; and a burial urn that will contain at least one expression of his self as an artist. If it is a mouth he may freely kiss, it is also a world in which he may find shelter; if it is a womb he may enter, it is also an urn in which his troubled spirit now finds temporary shelter and hopes to find lasting expression.[42]

Of all his novels, it was for *The Sound and the Fury* that Faulkner felt "the most tenderness." Writing it not only renewed his sense of purpose ("something to get up to tomorrow morning") and hope (a task he could "believe is valid"),[43] it also gave him an "emotion definite and physical and yet nebulous to describe." Working on it, he experienced a kind of ecstasy, particularly in the "eager and joyous faith and anticipation of surprise which the yet unmarred sheets beneath my hand held inviolate and unfailing."[44] Since, as Faulkner once noted, *The Sound and the Fury* is a "dark story of madness and hatred," and since writing it cost him dearly,[45] such statements may seem surprising. But he had discovered in *The Sound and the Fury* the kind of work he had anticipated in *Mosquitoes*: one "in which the hackneyed accidents which make up this world—love and life and death and sex and sorrow—brought together by chance in perfect proportions, take on a kind of splendid and timeless beauty."[46] In the years to come he continued to describe his fourth novel as a grand failure. Imperfect success would always be his ideal. To continue his effort to match his "dream of perfection," he needed dissatisfaction as well as hope. If failure might drive him to despair, success might deprive him of purpose: "It takes only one book to do it. It's not the sum of a lot of scribbling, it's one perfect book, you see. It's one single urn or shape that you want."[47]

In a letter to Malcolm Cowley, Faulkner once said that he wanted "to be, as a private individual, abolished and voided from history"; it was his aim to make his books the sole remaining sign of his life. Informing such statements was both a desire for privacy and a tacit conception of his relation to his art. Faulkner assumed that his authentic self was the self variously and nebulously yet definitely bodied forth by his fictions.[48] And it is in this slightly unusual sense that his fiction is deeply autobiographical. "I have never known anyone," a brother wrote, "who identified with his writings more than Bill did. . . . Sometimes it was hard to tell which was which, which one Bill was, himself or the one in the story. And yet you knew somehow that the two of them were the same, they were one and inseparable."[49] Faulkner knew that characters, "those shady but ingenious shapes," were indirect ways of exploring, projecting, and reaffirming both the life he lived and the tacit, secret life underlying it. At least once he was moved to wonder if he "had invented the world" of his fiction "or if it had invented me."[50]

Like imperfect success, however, indirect knowledge and indirect expression imply partial completion and carry several connotations. Both Faulkner's need to approach Caddy only by indirection and his need to describe his novel as a series of imperfect acts only partially completed ally it with the complex. His descriptions of *The Sound and the Fury* are in part a tribute to epistemological problems and in part an acknowledgement that beauty is difficult—that those things most worth seeing, knowing, and saying can never be directly or fully seen, known, and said. But the indirection and incompletion that his descriptions stress are also useful strategies for approaching forbidden scenes, uttering forbidden words, committing dangerous acts. For Elmer Hodge, both his sister Jo-Addie and behind her "the dark woman. The dark mother" are associated with a "vague shape [s]omewhere back in his mind"—the core for him of everything he dreads and desires. Since attainment, the only satisfying act, is not only dangerous but forbidden, and therefore both cannot and must be his aim, Elmer's life and art become crude strategies of approximation. The opposite of crude, the art of *The Sound and the Fury* is nonetheless an art of concealment as well as disclosure—of delay, avoidance, and evasion—particularly where Caddy is concerned. For the work that provides her expression also grants her shelter and even privacy. Beyond Faulkner's sense that indirection was more passionate lay his awareness that it was more permissive. For him both desire and hesitation touched almost everything, making his imagination as illusive as it is allusive, and his art preeminently an art of surmise and conjecture.

In *Flags in the Dust* Faulkner had taken ingenious possession of a heritage that he proceeded both to dismember and to reconstruct. In *The Sound and the Fury* he took possession of the pain and muted love of his childhood—its dislocations and vacancies, its forbidden needs and desires. The loss we observe in *The Sound and the Fury* is associated with parental weakness and inadequacy, with parental frigidity, judgment, and rejection. In the figure of Dilsey Faulkner recreated a haven of love he had learned early to count on; in the figure of Caddy he created one he had learned to long for. If the first of these figures is all maternal, the second is curiously mixed. In the figure of the sister he had never had, we see not only a sister but a mother (the role she most clearly plays for Benjy) and a lover (the possibility most clearly forbidden). Like the emotion Faulkner experienced in writing it, the novel's central figure comes to us as one "definite and physical and yet nebulous." Forced to avoid her even as he approached her, to conceal her even as he disclosed her, Faulkner created in Caddy a heroine who perfectly corresponds to her world: like *The Sound and the Fury*, she was born of regression and evasion, and like it, she transcends them.

By September 1928 Faulkner had finished the manuscript of *The Sound and the Fury* and had begun a typescript. Believing that he "would never be published again," he had no plan for submitting it to a publisher.[51] He wanted something he could bind for himself. Late in September, however, he received in the mail a contract for *Sartoris*. Harcourt, Brace was going to publish at least part of the novel Liveright had rejected. Almost immediately Faulkner decided to pack his manuscript and partial typescript and go to New York. He had a new three hundred dollar advance to live on; he had friends like Lyle Saxon, Bill Spratling, and Ben Wasson to visit; and he could revise and type as well in New York as in Oxford.

For a few days he stayed in Lyle Saxon's apartment; then, wanting a place to work, he found a room of his own. While Ben Wasson cut *Flags in the Dust*, Faulkner revised *The Sound and the Fury*. Although he had always revised with care, he worked now with deep intensity; sometimes his friends did not see him for several days at a time. In part his revisions reflect continuing commitment and affection: "I worked so hard at that book," he later asserted, "that I doubt if there's anything in it that didn't belong there."[52] But they also reflect growing hope that his book might be published. To himself and his friends, he still voiced doubt. He had no intention of building expectations only to see them dashed. It is "the damndest book I ever read," he wrote Aunt Bama. "I dont believe anyone will publish it for 10 years." Yet his revisions reflect a clear effort to enhance the novel's accessibility, to make it less exclusively his own. He increased the number of italicized passages indicating jumps in time; he added passages that clarified episodes; he made links and associations more explicit.[53]

Having finished the revision, Faulkner dated his typescript—"New York, N.Y./October 1928"—and gave it to Ben Wasson. It had been a long, intense, and satisfying labor. "I had just written my guts into *The Sound and the Fury*," he said later.[54] At first he felt exultant. "Read this, Bud," he said to Ben Wasson. "It's a real son-of-a-bitch."[55] But he had learned years before that for him the sense of completion often triggered depression and lifelessness, regret and guilt; that tomorrow he was likely to "wake up feeling rotten."[56] Writing *The Sound and the Fury* had been a deep excursion not only into his imaginative kingdom but into his own interior. Reversing direction proved almost impossible. The end he had labored hard to reach, he had dreaded, as though he dared not "risk cutting off the supply, destroying the source." Perhaps, like Proust and Rilke, he knew that "the gratitude of the completed" implied silence.[57] Perhaps it was not only silence but rejection and punishment that he anticipated. Certainly what he did in the days that followed both imposed silence and inflicted punishment.

Accustomed to the way he worked, his friends scarcely noticed his absence. One night two of them, Jim Devine and Leon Scales, happened by his flat, where they found him alone, unconscious, and lying on the floor, with empty bottles scattered around him. Seeing that he was ill and badly debilitated, they took him with them and nursed him back to health.[58] In later years there were several repetitions of this episode. Sometimes they came with little apparent reason, sometimes in response to painful tasks or unpleasant situations, often after prolonged, intensive writing. In *Mosquitoes* a character suggests that people not only seek but find moments of "timeless beatitude . . . through an outside agency like alcohol."[59] Although Faulkner's journeys into alcoholic twilight may not always have yielded such visions, they were clearly necessary for him. Sensing in the end of a novel the end of a world, and in the end of a world a final judgment, he often needed and sought an interface.

Able to write again, he stayed briefly with Devine and Scales in the apartment they shared with another friend, then moved in with an artist named Leon Crump. He had had enough of solitude for a time. Both he and Crump worked in the flat, and both worked hard, one painting while the other wrote. Faulkner remained skeptical about the future of *The Sound and the Fury*, but since Horace Liveright had released him from his contract, he was more hopeful. Harcourt, Brace had announced publication of *Sartoris*. In Ben Wasson, he had a loyal friend, in Hal Smith an editor who admired his work.

Wanting to publish and needing to make money, Faulkner began writing stories. He had finished *The Sound and the Fury* before reading any of it to anyone. Now he spent his evenings telling friends versions of the stories he worked on during the day. The war figured in some of them, his trip to Europe in others. In one, called "As I Lay Dying," he reworked material from "Father Abraham." Separately, both the material and the title would become famous; now, together, they found no publisher. Hoping to sell stories before he left New York, Faulkner asked Wasson to introduce him to some editors. Several gave him advice, and at least one, Alfred Dashiell of *Scribner's*, offered encouragement. For a time Faulkner thought he might stay in New York until after the January publication of *Sartoris*. But as Christmas drew near and money ran short, he changed his mind. No one was accepting his stories, and New York was beginning to irritate him. Having jotted down a few addresses, he packed his clothes and manuscripts and caught a train.[60]

Back in Oxford, he continued writing, hoping for some kind of breakthrough. At first his luck held steady; no one wanted anything. Then shortly after publication of *Sartoris*, 31 January 1929, he received a contract for *The Sound and the Fury*. He had been right about Harcourt, Brace. Having kept the manuscript for several weeks, Alfred Harcourt decided to let Hal Smith take it with him when he left to form the firm of Jonathan Cape & Harrison Smith.[61] It was, therefore, with a new publisher, his third, that Faulkner signed a contract for his fourth novel.

The Sound and the Fury was an ambitious undertaking for a new firm: it was a strange book, and it presented special printing problems. But Hal Smith was eager, and he had hired Ben Wasson as an editor. When the proofs arrived in July, Faulkner found changes everywhere. Wasson had removed all the italics and inserted spaces to indicate shifts in time; and he had made a few scattered additions to the text. Although Faulkner knew Wasson meant well, he was angry. Revising carefully, he restored the italics and removed the additions. Writing Wasson, he argued that italics worked as effectively as spacing, and that spacing was unsightly. And he insisted that his text not be tampered with: "Dont make any more additions to the script, bud," he added; "I know you mean well, but so do I. I effaced the 2 or 3 you made."[62] In October the novel was published with italics and without Wasson's additions. Almost immediately it began attracting attention. Even reviewers who found it baffling recognized that it was not simply another novel. But two weeks after its release the economy of the United States collapsed, discouraging sales. In 1931 two small printings followed the first. A total of about three thousand copies would last until 1946.

Between February, when he signed the contract for *The Sound and the Fury*, and July, when he read proof for it, Faulkner made two remarkable moves: he wrote a novel designed to make money, and he married Estelle Franklin. Writing *The Sound and the Fury* had redoubled his old uneasiness about writing for money and recognition. Working without any ulterior motive—not for fame, certainly not for profit—he had "discovered that there is actually something to which the shabby term Art not only can, but must, be applied."[63] Because it was free of ulterior, contaminating motives, *The Sound and the Fury* would always epitomize what he thought art should be. But he had never stopped needing recognition and money, and with publication of *Sartoris* his hope of them had revived: once again he was thinking of himself "as a printed object" and "of books in terms of possible money."[64] Such thoughts might seem base; one part of him, despising them, would always advocate repression.[65] But with *The Sound and the Fury* behind him, he had gone back to writing stories he thought of as public and commercial. Telling them to friends at night, he wrote and hawked them during the day.

His first weeks back in Oxford, he continued writing and pushing stories. At times Alfred Dashiell in particular seemed on the verge of accepting one. But as the mail continued to mix vague encouragement with clear rejections, Faulkner became angry. Internal resistance did nothing so much as redouble the humiliation of failure. It was bad enough to abuse one's talents; it was worse to find no buyers for the products of the abuse. For several years he had worked hard without ever making enough money to live on. Within a few months Estelle's divorce would be final. However uncertain he was about wanting to marry her, he knew that he did not want to do it on borrowed money. Yet he had a publisher for novels that made little or no money and a stack of stories that no one would publish.

As his frustration and anger deepened, Faulkner decided to write a novel that would make money when Hal Smith published it. In late January he began it; in late May he finished it.[66] He called it *Sanctuary*. Disturbed by his motives in writing it, he later disparaged the novel, confusing public response to it. It was, he said, "basely conceived. . . . I thought of the most horrific idea I could think of and wrote it" in order to make money.[67] Suggesting that the work itself must necessarily be contaminated, Faulkner did his novel a disservice. Many readers have followed his lead: assuming that it was basely conceived, they have concluded that it must be base. The disservice aside, however, it is probably fair to say that *Sanctuary* was written less out of injury than anger, and more for money than for itself; and it is certainly fair to say that it is one of Faulkner's bleakest, bitterest, and most brutal novels.

Faulkner began *The Sound and the Fury* knowing little about the direction it would take; he began *Sanctuary* knowing a great deal. Although writing it took several times the "three weeks" he allowed it in retrospect, it was in fact written quickly.[68] In part the speed suggests what the manuscript shows—that Faulkner wrote and revised it with less care than he had lavished on its predecessor. But Faulkner often played with the elements of a story for months, sometimes working them out in detail in his mind before writing a word, and several elements in *Sanctuary* had almost certainly undergone extended gestation. One element was the underworld of rural Mississippi, which revolved around the manufacture and sale of illegal whiskey. Faulkner had been doing business with small, independent "moonshiners" for years, and he admired their courage and resourcefulness, and even shared some of their contempt for "respectable" society. A second element was the gangster milieu of Memphis, where organized gangs battled for control not only of illegal whiskey but of gambling and prostitution. On excursions with Phil Stone, Faulkner had been visiting roadhouses and clubs controlled by Memphis gangs for years. Although he usually watched while Phil gambled, he enjoyed frequenting places like Reno De Vaux's. If most of the customers seemed ordinary, many of the gangsters seemed exotic. From his knowledge of the rural underworld, Faulkner created several crucial figures, including Lee Goodwin and Ruby Lamar, whom he clearly respects. From his knowledge of Memphis he created characters ranging from the comic Miss Reba to the grotesque Popeye. Miss Reba, who would reappear in the last of his novels, *The Reivers*, was based on a well-known Memphis "madam"; Popeye, who had turned up in an early unpublished story, "The Big Shot," was based on a notorious Memphis gangster named Popeye Pumphrey.[69]

Wanting his novel to be popular, Faulkner drew on two kinds of fiction, gangster stories and detective stories, which were read even in Mississippi. He had been reading as well as writing detective fiction for years, and he would continue to experiment with it. Despite the clear and relatively simple models that he had in mind, however, problems pertaining to plot persisted. He needed to find some way of joining the more sensational elements of the underworld to the more familiar social elements of Jefferson; even after several false starts, he continued to revise and shift. He also needed to find some way of controlling his discontent, which included society and men but focused on women. *Sanctuary* displays contempt for the male politicians who control society as well as for the middle-aged matrons who epitomize its hypocrisies. But its action centers on Popeye's brutal victimization of Temple Drake, who is young as well as female; and it reflects deep bitterness toward women. Whether or not this bitterness owes something to the shallow woman Faulkner described to Aunt Bama, or something to old wounds inflicted by Estelle and Helen, or something to the intimate difficulties Faulkner described to Maurice Coindreau, its focus and its depth are clear: as much as any work Faulkner wrote, *Sanctuary* suggests what Albert Guerard has termed a "persistent misogyny."[70] The scenes featuring Temple are so taut, spare, and detached as to seem almost clinical. In the sense that they center on action rather than thought and emotion, they are dramatic. Clearly they were conceived in part as a means of making *Sanctuary* more sensational and more remunerative. But these scences are curious on other grounds, primarily because the depravity in them is overwhelming. During the course of the novel we meet several familiar forms of corruption, from dishonest politicians and cynical socialites to murderers and prostitutes. But both the amoral impotence of Popeye and the corruption of Temple move far beyond usual bounds.

Through most of his life Faulkner felt a "rather strong distrust of women."[71] The move of a young girl through puberty to sexuality seemed to him almost to epitomize the Fall. "It's over very soon," he said later, as his daughter neared that fateful moment. "This is the end of it. She'll grow into a woman."[72] Temple enters *Sanctuary* as a young woman who, having already made this crucial move, is curious to discover its consequences. She loves parties; merely walking, she almost dances. Without fully understanding why, she is playful, flirtatious, provocative. Yet even to readers inclined to censure her curiosity and eagerness, her punishment must seem excessive.

"I am now writing a book," Faulkner told Ben Wasson, "about a girl who gets raped with a corn cob."[73] Having raped Temple, the impotent Popeye takes her to a room at Miss Reba's, where he watches while a surrogate lover named Red so thoroughly corrupts Temple that she becomes both willing and, finally, insatiable. In this curious triangle no character shows any tenderness or affection for another. They are all fascinated by violence and lust. Experiencing this fascination, Temple discovers evil within as well as around her. Because Popeye has introduced her to evil, she is drawn to him as well as repulsed by him. Soon after her rape she passes up a clear opportunity to escape, in part because she is already divided within herself. But her inaction also reflects the influence of her society. Escape, and perhaps survival, interest her less than keeping her refined and respectable friends from knowing what has happened to her because she knows that her society would rather condone evil than acknowledge it. Near the end of the novel, when she returns to the society from which she has been taken, she cynically cooperates in convicting Lee Goodwin of a murder she knows Popeye has committed. She thus comes to us as one who is both instinctually depraved and socially corrupt. Having found lust and violence magical, she becomes totally cynical. Flanked by her powerful father ("My father's a judge; my father's a judge") and four stalwart brothers, she calmly lies.

It may be that Faulkner fails to work out Temple's motivation in committing perjury and convicting an innocent man. But Temple's action presents fewer problems than many readers have suggested.[74] Even before she returns to society, others have begun conspiring to convict Lee Goodwin. The Memphis underworld wants Popeye protected; the district attorney of Jefferson, Eustace Graham, wants a conviction that will enhance his record and help him win election to Congress; Clarence Snopes wants to make a profit and curry influential friends; and Narcissa Benbow Sartoris wants to protect her good name by terminating a sensational trial in which her brother is defending a disreputable man. Although none of these characters commits perjury, none of them shows much interest in truth. Graham is far more interested in his career than in justice; and Narcissa is far less offended by the death of an innocent man than by the scandal of his common-law wife. In Jefferson the law is controlled by men who are interested in power and profit, and the church is controlled by "church ladies" who are interested in convenience and respectability.

Allied against these forces are Lee Goodwin, who knows that Jefferson is indifferent to truth; Ruby Lamar, his wife, who tries to help her husband without incensing the town; and Horace Benbow, Faulkner's improbable knight-errant. Part detective and part trial lawyer, Benbow insists that someone must care enough about truth and justice to pursue them. At times he is resourceful, even energetic and shrewd, and he experiences several fine moments. But in the end, he is overmatched, partly because he is too academic and timid, and partly because the forces allied against him possess great power. "Perhaps it is upon the instant that we realize, admit, that there is a logical pattern to evil, that we die," he thinks at one point. More than defeat, it is the totality of his capitulation that marks him with failure. If Temple's encounter with evil leaves her cynical, Horace's leaves him spent and resigned.

Like "Father Abraham," *Sanctuary* is set in the twentieth century; and like "Father Abraham," it uses the Old Frenchman's Place to evoke the shadowy beginnings of Faulkner's imaginative kingdom. Like *Flags in the Dust*, it suffered a strangely complicated fate between its completion and its publication; and like *Flags*, it underwent substantial revision in the process. While writing it, Faulkner's spirits continued to rise and fall, as they had over the last several years. The more he labored, the more he wanted his new novel to be a work he could regard with pride. But there were times when he felt that whatever he did, he would fail. Shortly before he finished *Sanctuary* he told Phil Stone that he had finally resigned himself: "I think I not only won't ever make any money out of what I write," he said, "I won't ever get any recognition either."[75] Still he could not relinquish hope. In early May, while he was revising and typing his manuscript, he received a new contract and a new advance from Hal Smith. A few weeks later, shortly after mailing his manuscript, he received a largely unexpected response. "Good God," Hal Smith wrote, "I can't publish this. We'd both be in jail."[76] Since Smith's reservations had little to do with the quality of the manuscript, he said nothing to disparage Faulkner's development as a writer. He also refrained from asking that Faulkner return the advance. But he made clear the shock felt by readers at the press, and he said nothing to offer encouragement. Once again Faulkner accepted his failure and hid his disappointment, this time without protest or feigned confidence: he did not even ask his publisher to return his manuscript so that he could try it on someone else. "You're damned," he said to himself, "You'll have to work now and then for the rest of your life."[77]

With his career at yet another turning point, Faulkner began trying to sort out his personal life. The question before him was what to do about Estelle. Her divorce had been granted in April, and he knew that she was waiting. Eleven years before he had felt certain. Now he was less sure, and the signs around him were mixed. Estelle wanted to get married—her younger sister, Dorothy, had called him to say that he should stop stalling. But Estelle's father remained adamant. Faulkner might be interesting, even likeable, but he seemed without prospects at an age when most men had established themselves. Faulkner's own family was scarcely less blunt. His father and brothers said he should get a job and earn some money before thinking about marriage. His mother did not want him marrying anyone, certainly not a divorced woman who was known to drink whiskey.[78] Given more advice than he had sought or wanted, Faulkner decided to ignore it. Some of it seemed to him irrelevant, and some of it presumptuous. He could borrow money to meet immediate expenses; later, if it became necessary, he could get a job. Even with the Depression deepening, he believed that he could earn enough money to support a family.

The larger problem was one of timing. The moment of which he and Estelle had dreamed was gone, and he knew that they could never go back. He may even have known that the residual bitterness within him ran deeper than time's power to heal. Certainly some of it had recently found expression in *Sanctuary*, where Temple's degradation reaches its culmination in scenes that put old preoccupations to new uses. Shortly after she arrives at Miss Reba's, Temple lies in bed remembering the dances she has loved. Later her tireless love of dancing leads directly to uncontrollable desire for fornication. "Call yourself a man, a bold, bad man, and let a girl dance you off your feet," she chides; and then, "Give it to me, daddy." In between these scenes, Popeye watches, "hanging over the foot of the bed," a pale slobbering Mephistopheles, while Red and Temple, "nekkid as two snakes," fornicate. But there was no reason to believe that further delay would soothe problems delay had exacerbated. And despite everything, marriage to Estelle seemed to him inevitable. The first time the Old Colonel had seen Lizzie Vance he had announced his intention to come back and marry her. Several years, one wife, and one child later, he had done just that. The first time Estelle had seen Faulkner, she had made a similar declaration. Now, several years, one husband, and two children later, she was going to do it.[79] There was reversal as well as repetition in the pattern, but both appealed to Faulkner. On 19 June 1929 he and Estelle drove to the courthouse in Oxford and got a marriage license. The next day he went alone to see his mother and Estelle's father. But his mood was no longer interrogative. He and Estelle had listened and waited long enough. With Dorothy as an attendant and a minister's wife as a witness, they were married.

SIX 1929-1931

Recognitions

Among those who opposed Faulkner's marriage, Phil Stone was one of the most specific and consistent. Eleven years earlier he had regarded Faulkner's wish to marry as foolish; since marriage was certain to multiply financial problems and create distractions, it was likely to hurt Faulkner's career and diminish his chance for recognition. The intervening years struck Phil as having worked few changes, none for the better. Although Estelle Franklin's two children, Victoria and Malcolm, were provided for by the divorce settlement, Estelle was not; and she was accustomed to spending more money on clothes than Faulkner could claim prospect of making. Money aside, Estelle and the children would require time and energy better devoted to writing. In such circumstances, Phil viewed willingness to forego marriage as a sign of commitment, its opposite as a sign of wavering and an invitation to failure.[1]

As it turned out, marriage forced major adjustments in Faulkner's life by drastically increasing personal entanglements, by requiring him to make money, and by creating a variety of other, less expected, difficulties.

Although they had known each other for more than twenty-five years, William and Estelle Faulkner seemed at times scarcely to recognize each other. Their wedding trip to Pascagoula turned out to be so strange and troubled that Estelle needed help from an acquaintance simply to survive it. The honeymoon over, problems having to do with family and money persisted. Several of the Oldhams and Falkners were slow to reconcile themselves to the marriage; a few, including Faulkner's mother, died without completing the process.[2] But marriage neither slowed Faulkner's production nor aborted his career. Although it imposed adjustments, it preceded several kinds of recognition.

As Faulkner and Estelle turned toward Pascagoula, they took many memories with them. Given its associations with Helen Baird, Pascagoula was a surprising place for Faulkner to take Estelle on a wedding trip. Estelle's interest in sand and surf was limited, her preference being for more formal surroundings; and she held no place in the associations Pascagoula possessed for Faulkner, though she may well have resented a few of them. Preparing for the trip, he packed several manuscripts and a few clothes, most of them the kind of beachcomber garb he enjoyed wearing. Estelle, on the other hand, had memories of her own and reminders of them. Her wardrobe was large and expensive, featuring imported gowns of silk and satin. A clear evocation of her glamorous days in Honolulu and Shanghai with Cornell Franklin, her clothes also belonged to the life for which she longed. The contrast between her gowns and her husband's rope belt was conspicuous, as was the contrast between her gowns and the ramshackle beach house in which they stayed. Although her first marriage had taught her much about unhappiness, it had taught her nothing about want of money and nothing about want of parties. Like life as Estelle Oldham, life as Mrs. Cornell Franklin had encouraged her to spend money freely. Even more, it had confirmed her early love of parties and dances, which she associated with gaiety as well as beautiful clothes.[3]

At times Faulkner shared Estelle's preferences. He could be elegant as well as gallant. Occasionally he enjoyed being with other people, even several at a time. But he sometimes wore clothes that were dirty as well as old; and he went without shaving almost as often as he went without shoes. In scattered moments and at a distance, such habits might seem merely eccentric or even exotic. As a daily routine and up close, they could be unpleasant, particularly to someone like Estelle, who, as Faulkner's brother John put it, had always been "petite, dainty," and had never liked "to get mussed up or dirty." As a boy Faulkner had purchased the clothes and acquired the habits of a dandy in part to impress Estelle; as a man, he proved considerably less accommodating.[4]

But more than worry about money or the dilapidated beach house or Faulkner's carelessness about clothes and hygiene, it was loneliness that gnawed at Estelle, the sense of being shut out. Sometimes Faulkner was warm and relaxed. During the mornings he crabbed and fished with Malcolm; in the afternoons, he walked on the beaches, talking with Estelle. In the evenings, sharing her mood, he dressed for dinner so that they could drink and eat ceremoniously. On such days, their place on the beach seemed pleasant to her, despite its inelegance. But his moods were unpredictable. Often he was silent, remote, preoccupied, careless of everything except the stories he was writing about the Snopeses and the Sartorises. Then, early in July, the proofs of *The Sound and the Fury* arrived, bearing Ben Wasson's revisions. As Faulkner discovered and corrected the changes, he became more agitated and withdrawn. His friend's meddling did nothing so much as reawaken the very special feeling that he retained for the Compsons and their story. Although he shared some of his characters easily, the Compsons were not among them. With Caddy, Quentin, and Benjy before him, his fictional kingdom tended to become both his primary reality and a thing essentially his own.[5]

Helped by a visit from her sister, Dorothy, Estelle got through the ordeal of *The Sound and the Fury*. A few days later, Faulkner put his manuscripts aside and took Estelle to New Orleans. Staying at the Monteleone, an old, elegant hotel, Estelle found life more to her liking. She preferred the narrow picturesque streets of the Vieux Carré to the beaches of Pascagoula. And since Faulkner was something of a celebrity, they were entertained by an assortment of thoughtful, lively people. Days that began with fashionable breakfasts ended with dinner, conversation, and music in places made for beautiful gowns.[6]

When they returned from the interlude in New Orleans, Estelle apparently found the contrast shocking. Like Faulkner, she drank regularly, and like him, she often drank too much, especially when loneliness and disappointment crowded in on her. One evening shortly after their return she ended several hours of concentrated drinking by attempting to drown herself. Dressed in a silk gown, one of her chosen garments, she walked down to the beach and waded out into the surf, seeking the place, some sixty or seventy yards away, where the shelf stopped and the channel began. Unable to stop her himself, Faulkner shouted for help. Hearing his call, a neighbor named Martin Shepherd raced through the shallow water; a few yards short of the shelf's edge, he caught Estelle. Struggling to reach the depth beyond, Estelle broke free long enough to make a final lunge, only to have Shepherd catch and subdue her.[7]

Although highly theatrical, Estelle's attempted suicide appears to have been serious. What it suggests, other facts support. Estelle had anticipated the disappointment, if not the pain, of her first marriage. On the day of the wedding she had toyed with the idea of running away.

Fearing her father's fury, she had decided that it was too late, and so had entered a marriage that not only proved untenable but also made her the central figure in one of Faulkner's earliest and deepest disappointments.[8] From the pain of that disappointment, he had been slow to recover. Later he had repeated it with Helen Baird. Later still he had reconciled himself to his vocation, discovered a kingdom, and built a life that he permitted others to enter, so far as possible, only on his own terms. He wanted to be independent—to be a "proud and self-sufficient beast," one who "walked by himself, needing nothing from anyone, or at least never letting them know it."[9] Of the female facility for enveloping and engulfing, he had become especially wary. Estelle, on the other hand, having emerged from disappointments of her own, had begun to count heavily on their long-delayed, unevenly sought marriage.[10] When it came, she not only discovered that Faulkner was leaving most of the required adjustments to her; she also discovered that she meant less to him as his wife than she had as his first love. In part it was a matter of the vocation he had found, the kingdom he had discovered, the life he had built. But it was a matter, too, of what in his case these things implied. In a figure like Caddy Compson he had brought many of his loves together. Creating for "himself a maid that life had not had time to create," he had "laid upon her frail and unbowed shoulders the whole burden of man's history of his impossible heart's desire."[11] In one way or another, he would go on doing something like this for the rest of his life. No woman, Patricia says in *Mosquitoes*, "is going to waste time on a man that's satisfied with a piece of wood or something."[12] The doubleness Faulkner had discovered and made his own meant that he would never be wholly satisfied with living in the world he imagined and so created; but it also meant that he would never really belong to the world around him or to the creatures of it. During the several years of her first marriage, Estelle had learned that she did not want to live without Faulkner; during the early months of her second, she seems to have learned that she would always have less of him than she needed. Since this was not a lesson for which mere warnings could prepare, her desire to resist it is finally less remarkable than her ability to accept it.

Given sedation and a few day's rest, Estelle recovered, and so brought their wedding trip to an end. Within a few days they were back in Oxford, living in an apartment in a large house. For several weeks Faulkner went on writing, hoping that someone would accept his short stories or that his novels would sell. In early October publication of *The Sound and the Fury* coincided with *Scribner's* rejection of "A Rose for Emily," one of Faulkner's finest short stories. Although Alfred Dashiell's letter of rejection offered encouragement, it showed little understanding of the story and no understanding of the mastery of short fiction that it signaled.[13]

Out of money and tired of borrowing it, Faulkner decided that he would have to take a job.

He found what he wanted in an improbable place: the power plant of the University of Mississippi. Although he worked a twelve-hour shift beginning at six in the evening, he had ample time to write. Later he pictured himself shoveling coal for several hours in a boiler room and then writing on a table made out of a wheelbarrow.[14] In fact his job was supervisory. Whether or not he found the hum of the dynamo soothing, as he also suggested, he clearly found his new routine acceptable. If he was not yet making a living as a writer, at least he was making a living while writing.[15]

Given a few hours' sleep in the mornings and short naps here and there, Faulkner was able to get as much rest as he wanted and still have free time during the day. Sometimes he went over the work he had done the night before; often he merely walked or played, cultivating what he called his "talent for idleness."[16] Concerned about the reviews and sales of his novels as well as responses to his circulating stories, he made regular stops at the post office. He also made daily visits to see his mother, a habit he had developed years before and continued for as long as Miss Maud lived (until 1960) without ever suggesting that he found it burdensome. Soon after his marriage he resumed the habit of making these visits alone. Despite Estelle's overtures, Miss Maud became distant and reserved in the presence of her daughter-in-law; she wanted and managed to have a part of most of her eldest son's days to herself.[17]

Late in October, as panic began to signal America's long economic nosedive, Faulkner began calmly writing a new novel. This time he knew exactly what he was doing and where he was going. Like *Sanctuary*, his new novel would be deliberate. But this time his intention was to demonstrate his mastery of fiction: "Before I began I said, I am going to write a book by which, at a pinch, I can stand or fall if I never touch ink again."[18] Using a title he had first given to a story about Flem Snopes, he called his novel *As I Lay Dying*. He also used a few characters, such as Henry Armstid, from his earliest Snopes stories. But the family whose story he was telling was new.

Like the Snopeses, the Bundrens are poor, and like the Compsons, they are close-knit. But they are not moved by large ambitions or haunted by loss of status and money. Their story focuses on the death of a mother named Addie rather than on the loss of a sister named Caddy, and it traces the journey they undertake in order to bury her. In part it is a story of disintegration—generally of the family, which loses its center, and specifically of a son named Darl, who moves toward madness as the novel moves toward its end. But it is also a story of ironic reconstitution. In its last pages, as the family turns toward home, we meet a new Mrs.

Bundren come to take the place of the old. Such doubleness fits, more-over, with the mixed tone of the novel. For the journey it recounts, through fire and flood toward Jefferson, is not only preposterous; it is often comic, occasionally heroic, and frequently grotesque. On one side it celebrates different modes of courage—Jewel's brave action, Cash's heroic suffering, and Darl's solitary efforts to end the travesty of the journey itself; on the other, it presents all motives as mixed and all cour-age as partly ridiculous.

Centering on a single family and tracing a continuous action, the novel begins at twilight just before Addie dies and ends just after she is buried. Throughout the novel events are shared, even public; friends and acquaint-ances, together with the members of the family, observe and participate in the journey. Yet all of the action comes to us through individual consciousnesses: the novel consists of fifty-nine sections of interior monologue of fifteen different characters. Although action is shared, perception and apprehension of it are not. Through his various characters Faulkner presents examples, or parodies, of every possible activity of consciousness, from the intuitive to the rational to the imaginative, from the primitive to the conventional to the bizarre. From Vardaman we get the confused metaphor of a child; from Cora, the self-righteous religiosity of a middle-aged church-goer; from Cash, something like the technical discourse of a craftsman; from Darl, the insights and confusions of a precariously balanced mind whose disposition is at once philosophic and poetic.

Such variety required a display of technical virtuosity, which Faulkner acknowledged by calling *As I Lay Dying* a tour de force. It was as though he had set out deliberately to make *As I Lay Dying* what Conrad Aiken thought *The Sound and the Fury* had become—a novelist's novel, a kind of textbook on the craft of fiction.[19] But Faulkner's control becomes all the more impressive when we note that the novel deals with a situation and themes, if not with a family, that were close to him. Like *The Sound and the Fury, As I Lay Dying* is not only the story of a family; it is the story of inadequate parents and their wounded children.

Anse Bundren, the father, spends his life trying to get other people to do things for him. Part hypochondriac and part con man, part parasite and part vulture, he manipulates language and people (children, friends, and strangers alike) so that he can devote himself to elaborate inactivity. Addie is considerably more vital and less villainous than Anse, but she is cripplingly cynical.[20] Mindful primarily of the discrepancy between what she has wanted and what life has given her, she appropriates her father's aphorism that "the reason for living is getting ready to stay dead" and so makes disillusionment not only an interpretive tool but a cause.

The different wounds Anse and Addie inflict cut deep. Like the Compson children, the Bundrens are held fast by the close-knit circle of their family. Neither Cash nor Darl ever makes any effort to establish a relationship beyond it. After she is pregnant, Dewey Dell lets Darl come "in between me and Lafe." After he has sacrificed to buy a horse of his own, Jewel sells it so that the family may continue its journey. He does this willingly, of course, but his sacrifice, like Cash's, serves the selfish request of his mother and the selfish wants of his father. At the novel's end his mother gets the grave she has chosen while his father gets a new wife and new teeth. From the family that holds them, on the other hand, none of the children receives adequate support. Within the larger circle of the family, each child forms a smaller circle; each of them is both held and isolated. We thus see in the Bundren family a different version of the tension we observe between the action of the novel, which stresses continuity, and its form, which stresses fragmentation. Like the society of which it is a part, the family restricts yet no longer sustains its members. The problem lies at the center: possessing no principles of order and no capacity for love, the parents fail to spread order and love around them.

Knowing containment without love, the Bundren children tend to become either stunted, like Cash, Dewey Dell, and Vardaman, or confused, like Darl and Jewel. The love Darl feels for Dewey Dell is both narcissistic and incestuous. The hostility he feels for Jewel, like the hostility Jewel feels for him, finally focuses on which one of them will possess and dispose of the body of their mother. After Jewel has triumphed, he caps his victory by disposing of Darl; having buried his mother, he conspires to incarcerate his brother. Behind these machinations lies the fact that each Bundren child is a kind of orphan even before Addie dies. It is not merely that Jewel is the child of an adulterous affair, or that Anse is a cipher both as a father and as a husband; it is rather that, for each child, one or both of the most fundamental relations is uncertain. In Darl, especially, we see the consequences of being born without an available mother; in Jewel, those of being born without an available father. "I cannot love my mother," Darl says, "because I have no mother"; and later, "Your mother was a horse, but who was your father, Jewel?" Both Darl and Jewel embody traits that are clearly compensatory. Haunted by motherlessness, Darl becomes internally profuse, intuitive, and imaginative, externally flexible and circuitous—qualities Faulkner associates in the novel with femininity. Given a question mark for a father, Jewel becomes internally meager and rational, externally direct, rigid, and active—qualities Faulkner associates in the novel with masculinity. Through Darl we observe the perils of limitlessness; it is death by diffusion and disintegration that threatens him. In Jewel we see the perils of rigid definition: the threat of impoverishment through exclusion.

Having finished *As I Lay Dying*, Faulkner "sent it to [Hal] Smith and wrote him that by it I would stand or fall." A few months later he stated that he had written it "in six weeks, without changing a word."[21] Both parts of this assertion, the second more than the first, are misleading. But both point to crucial facts about *As I Lay Dying*, and taken together they suggest why Faulkner felt so confident of his achievement. First, he wrote it with remarkable speed. He began his manuscript on 29 October 1929 and finished it on 11 December; by 12 January 1930 he had a revised typescript. Second, though he experimented with the order of a few sections, and though he changed a few names, many lines, and more words, he revised less than ever before. The manuscript is so clean that it would be remarkable even if the novel were simple and conventional. As the manuscript of a novel that is experimental and complex, it is astonishing. Most of the revisions come early, and many of its pages bear only one or two minor changes. In the years just after he finished it, Faulkner sometimes overpraised it, calling it his best novel. Later, terming it "a deliberate book" and a tour de force, he occasionally denigrated it.[22] But it clearly deserves to stand as one of his major achievements. Although it is less inspired than *The Sound and the Fury*, and finally is less moving, it represents remarkable control of great talent.

Moving quickly, Hal Smith published *As I Lay Dying* on 6 October 1930, less than a year after Faulkner began it. Like *The Sound and the Fury*, it attracted large notice and small sales, and so disappointed Faulkner. But nothing could diminish the boost writing *As I Lay Dying* had given his confidence: not even *The Sound and the Fury* had done so much to help him recapture the enthusiasm of discovering the Snopeses and Sartorises. Once again possibilities seemed to be opening on every side; and once again the conception of his whole cosmos was strong in him. "I found out," he said, "that not only each book had to have a design but the whole output or sum of an artist's work had to have a design."[23] From England word arrived of Richard Hughes's campaign to spread Faulkner's reputation. Known primarily as author of *A High Wind in Jamaica*, Hughes became a valuable sponsor. Having read several of Faulkner's works, Hughes persuaded Arnold Bennett to review *The Sound and the Fury* and convinced Chatto & Windus to secure British rights to Faulkner's works.[24] Paralleling Hughes's campaign on his behalf, Faulkner began one of his own.

It focused on his short stories, including many he had accumulated and several he was working on. Less than two weeks after mailing *As I Lay Dying*, he entered the first date (23 January 1930) on a piece of cardboard that he used to record attempts to place his short stories.[25] For 1930 and 1931 this carefully organized record correlates the names of magazines, the titles of stories, and the dates on which they were mailed. The titles of rejected stories, he struck with a single line; the titles of those accepted, he neatly circled. From this record we can draw three conclusions. First, Faulkner preferred better paying magazines—*Saturday Evening Post, Scribner's, American Mercury*—though he regularly sent stories to others as well. Second, he was more determined and more confident than ever before. Although some of the stories, such as "The Big Shot," remained unpublished when he died, he persisted in sending most of them out, undeterred by repeated rejections. Third, he began placing stories: of the forty or so stories recorded, twenty were accepted during the two years covered by the record.[26]

The breakthrough began with "A Rose for Emily," which the *Forum* published in April 1930—Faulkner's first publication in a major periodical since the *Double Dealer* pieces. By the time "A Rose for Emily" appeared, the *Saturday Evening Post* had accepted "Thrift" and the *American Mercury* had accepted "Honor"; in May, *Scribner's* followed by accepting "Drouth." Later Faulkner joked about the countless rejection slips he had received, suggesting that apprenticeship meant receiving hundreds of them.[27] They still arrived regularly. But mixed with them were acceptances, several of which brought substantial fees. At long last the work he conceived of as commercial was beginning to pay. From a simple story like "Thrift," the first piece published by the *Post*, Faulkner made $750— more than he had made from any of his novels.[28]

Encouraged by the news that he would soon be published in England and by scattered story successes, Faulkner decided to buy a home. He and Estelle wanted a place of their own, and both of them wanted something grand. The problem, of course, was money. Houses with aristocratic lineage and elegant appearance tended to be expensive, even during a depression. The solution Faulkner hit upon may well have been the only one open to him. He approached Mr. and Mrs. Will Bryant, who owned a large antebellum house called the Shegog Place, which had fallen into sad disrepair: if they would sell it to him, he would restore it. The Bryants had inherited the house and several acres surrounding it in 1923, but they lived on a fine estate near Coffeeville. Renting the Shegog Place from time to time, leaving it vacant occasionally, they had let it deteriorate. Having no desire to see it rot and no immediate need of money, they agreed to sell it and four acres of the land they owned on terms Faulkner felt he could manage. Foregoing a downpayment, they gave him a long-term, low-interest mortgage, with an option to buy more of the surrounding acreage—the Bailey Woods—later.[29]

In June 1930 the Faulkners moved from their comfortable apartment to their new home. Standing at the end of a long, curved, cedar-lined drive, facing south, the house had a graceful portico supported by large white columns, and it clearly suggested a kind of splendor. But it was barely habitable. The floors sagged and the roof leaked; it had no electricity

and no plumbing. Determined not only to reclaim it but to modernize
it, Faulkner put his writing aside. Through the summer of 1930 he gave to
the house the kind of unflagging effort that he had previously devoted
only to his writing. On several projects—such as painting, papering, and
screening the house and relandscaping the garden—Estelle, Victoria, and
Malcolm helped him. For others—such as rebuilding the foundation and
replacing the roof—he had to hire men to help with the heavy work. For
a few jobs—such as installing wiring and plumbing—he had to hire tech-
nicians. But much of the work he did himself, some of it alone.

Although the process of reclamation lasted several years, Faulkner
accomplished a great deal during the first summer. As the work progressed,
the bills mounted; paying them would be another long process. But
Faulkner spent the money as willingly as he gave the time. For what he
had in mind was more than a place to live. In one sense the house, and
especially the grounds, represented a recovery of his own past. As a boy
he had played games in the woods that surrounded the house, and after
the war he had returned to them, first with Dean and his friends and then
with his troop of boy scouts. But what he was seeking went back beyond
his own childhood to his family's history. In the household he was establishing, he made a place for Mammy Callie. Later, in dedicating *Go Down,
Moses* to her, he recalled both the long fidelity she had given his family,
"without stint or calculation of recompense," and the "immeasurable
devotion and love" she had given him. To head his staff of servants, he
turned to Uncle Ned Barnett, who had served both the Old Colonel and
the Young Colonel. Retaining his devotion to Faulkner's family,
treasuring the splendor it had once known, Uncle Ned still wore frock
coats and silk ties and still believed in a traditionally ordered and cere-
monious life. More even than Mammy Callie's arrival, Uncle Ned's
suggested what Faulkner was seeking. Soon he and Estelle would have a
child of their own—a baby was due in March. He was hoping for a girl,
whom he planned to name for Aunt Bama, the Old Colonel's favorite
child. In the meantime he wanted to establish a home so clearly evocative of his family's past that it would make him the acknowledged center
of his clan. While his father was paying to have a small brick house built in
the shadow of the Big Place, Faulkner was rebuilding an old mansion and
restoring an old estate. Seeking an appropriate name for his new home,
he decided to call it Rowan Oak—from the rowan tree, which Frazer
describes in *The Golden Bough* as symbolic of peace and security and as
indigenous to Scotland, the land Faulkner thought of as his ancestral
home.[30]

Although most people in Oxford deplored Faulkner's fiction, they
apparently approved his desire to reclaim Rowan Oak. What his return
to Oxford had started, his marriage and his home pushed farther. As

though to seal his reentry into the life of Oxford, the *Post* published "Thrift" on 6 September 1930. A straightforward war story, "Thrift" brought Faulkner far more local approval than *The Marble Faun* and his first several novels combined. A man who wrote poems full of nymphs and fauns and novels about perverts and idiots was one thing; a man who wrote stories you could read in beauty parlors and barbershops was something else. Besides, the *Post* was known to pay hundreds of dollars for one such story, and by September word was out that the same magazine had accepted two more of Faulkner's stories. One of these, "Red Leaves," was a wonderful story about the Indians of Yoknapatawpha; the other, "Lizards in Jamshyd's Courtyard," was about Flem Snopes. Each brought Faulkner $750, and both were stories people in Oxford could enjoy.[31]

As it turned out, Faulkner's new rapport with Oxford would not last long. Rougher days than any he had yet known lay ahead. But before more conflict set in, Faulkner found another way of expressing his reentry. In a local production of *Corporal Eagen*, a comedy about an Irish soldier in World War One, the title role was played by Phil Stone's brother, Jim, and that of Eagen's comic Jewish sidekick, Izzy Goldstein, by William Faulkner. Although several of Faulkner's friends were in the play, no one anticipated his decision to join the cast. Yet the role of Izzy Goldstein, a character at once familiar and alien, had at least the appeal of reflecting Faulkner's sense of his own position in Oxford, where, as he once put it, he felt at home yet at the same time not at home.[32]

Meanwhile Hal Smith had made a decision that would soon outrage Oxford: he had decided to publish *Sanctuary*. Earlier he had said that publishing the novel might land both author and publisher in jail; now he thought that it might make money not only for Faulkner but for the financially troubled firm of Jonathan Cape & Harrison Smith. In November Smith mailed the galleys, which Faulkner read, only to find himself offended by his own work. Faulkner knew that he had written *Sanctuary* out of anger and frustration and with the intention of making money. What surprised him was the crude transparency of his motives and the obvious cheapness of his work: "And I read it and it was so badly written, it was cheaply approached. The very impulse that caused me to write the book was so apparent, every word; and then I said I cannot let this go." Writing to Hal Smith, Faulkner suggested that they junk the novel. But since Smith now had money as well as hope invested in *Sanctuary*, and since he needed to make money rather than throw it away, he wrote back saying that he wanted to go on with the project. If *Sanctuary* had to be published, Faulkner replied, he would have to rewrite it—a condition on which he insisted even after Smith informed him that he would have to share equally the cost of resetting.[33]

Knowing that he would have "to pay for the privilege," Faulkner set about rewriting.[34] Still, though he made extensive changes at substantial cost, he did nothing to mute the novel's more horrific and violent scenes—the rape and seduction of Temple and the murders committed by Popeye. To them he added the brutal lynching of Lee Goodwin. In his deletions and revisions, he concentrated on material that was more personal and less integral, especially the role of Horace Benbow, the failed poet and former vase-maker turned lawyer.

In *Flags in the Dust* Horace Benbow is incestuously involved with his sister, Narcissa—an involvement that persists in *Sanctuary* despite his marriage to Belle Mitchell. "You're in love with your sister," his wife says to him. "What do the books call it? What kind of complex?" Offended by Belle's sexuality—by her being both sexually active and sexually available—Horace retreats into fantasies not only about his sister, Narcissa, but also about his step-daughter, Little Belle. For him the charm of incest persists, its secret being that it reconciles chastity with violent consummation. In *Flags* Horace sits on a bed with Narcissa, feeling "the wild repose of his hand lying on her covered knee." Like the protagonist of "Nympholepsy," Horace is content with this wild yet peaceful, intimate yet chaste episode precisely because it provides the only experiential basis he requires for building in fantasy "an incontrovertible consummation." In *Flags* he also watches Belle's husband, Harry Mitchell, fondle Little Belle, who in turn gazes at Horace "with radiant and melting diffidence." Like Quentin Compson in *The Sound and the Fury*, Horace associates the scent of honeysuckle with night and unrest, with hidden but only half-repressed desires. For Horace, however, these desires involve not only Narcissa and Little Belle but also his mother, and for him they are so strong as to make his dream world more vital than his life. At times he dreams of things mysteriously yet "irrevocably lost." At others he dreams of things evermore about to be. But always he moves from abbreviated experience to imagined consummation. Remembering moments in which he has felt Little Belle's fatal attraction, he recalls "the faint, furious uproar of the shucks" that he associates with reports of Temple's rape. Then, sitting alone, holding now not a vase called Narcissa but a photograph of Little Belle, he sees his step-daughter being ravished as she lies "bound naked on her back on a flat car moving at speed through a black tunnel."

In the revised *Sanctuary* Horace continues to play a major role. He also remains emotionally entangled and confused: he continues to practice several modes of displacement and substitution and to regard incest as the perfect form of love. But Faulkner's revisions change Horace's story considerably, particularly those parts of it that had made it "a Freudian study of. . . a man who is so much the victim of his half-hidden incestuous fantasies that he has no will of his own, cannot act, and possesses no courage."[35] In the first *Sanctuary* Horace's story competes with Temple's; in the second it extends rather than rivals Temple's story. Moving from episode to episode, encountering the victims of Popeye's perversions and violence, Horace tries to defend Lee Goodwin. Well-intentioned yet weak, he fails resoundingly. In the end he recognizes both the primacy of evil and the fact of his own inadequacy and guilt; he even comes to some awareness of the internal forces and conflicts that cripple him, including his own incestuous fantasies. But in the revised version of *Sanctuary*, he does these things without dividing the novel.

As he changed Horace's role, Faulkner also changed the roles of Narcissa and Little Belle, who in the second *Sanctuary* serve two important functions: they help to account for Horace's weaknesses; and they help to elucidate a conception of southern women that is crucial to our understanding of Temple and her story. Little Belle is less appealing than provocative, and less courageous than foolish, but she and Temple share several qualities, including felt sexuality. Narcissa, on the other hand, epitomizes the cult of respectability. Since she regards all expression of sexuality as both offensive and dangerous, she speaks consistently for repression. From Narcissa's point of view, Ruby Lamar's fidelity to Lee Goodwin counts as nothing, her complicity in a common-law marriage as everything. In this judgement we see not only Narcissa's commitment to repression but also her deepest assumptions: that society depends upon repression, particularly of sexual energy; that men can never be depended upon to exercise adequate restraint; and that women must therefore bear the burden of civilization.

In each of these opinions Narcissa is at one with her society. And like her society, she is more cynical than innocent, more easily offended than surprised. Of men she expects the worst—which means that neither Popeye's perversions nor her brother's fantasies, which once involved her and now center on the ravishing of his step-daughter, could finally outstrip her secret suspicions. Of women she demands much, believing that civilization depends on their willingness to exercise and impose control. Yet she makes her demands assuming that every woman's hold is precarious— that Little Belle's seductiveness is not new and that Ruby Lamar's flaunting of convention poses a threat as well as an offense. Temple's story, which takes her from playful flirtation and eager curiosity through desire and degradation to deliberate resumption of respectability, limns the only alternatives that Narcissa and her society perceive.

In part because the alternatives she sees are so sharp and in part because her hold on respectability is precarious, Narcissa is almost as distrustful of women as she is disdainful of men. Since we view her with disdain, however, and since no one can fail to view Temple's suffering and corruption as excessive, we are likely to feel that *Sanctuary* displays more sympathy for its men than for its women. Even Popeye, the novel's most obvious victimizer of women, finally emerges the victim of his mother. As a rule to which Ruby Lamar is the only significant exception, the novel's women tend toward one of two extremes: if they are not advocates of repression and enforcers of control, they are seducers of men and proponents of license. Together, these extremes very nearly exhaust possibility in *Sanctuary*. As soon as Temple begins to experiment with desire, she becomes provocative and challenging. As soon as she begins to express desire, she begins not only to wallow in filth but to taunt and humiliate men. As soon as she returns to the role endorsed by her society, she accepts her father and her brothers as protectors and lies in order to help them destroy Lee Goodwin.

Faulkner's work on *Sanctuary* represents a "minor miracle of revision."[36] Remembering his description of *Sanctuary* as basely conceived, many readers have forgot other assertions: that he paid "for the privilege of rewriting it" in order "to make out of it something which would not shame *The Sound and the Fury* and *As I Lay Dying*"; and that he "made a fair job" of it.[37] "I had done the best I could with it," he said. "The one that you didn't see was the the base and cheap one, which I went to what sacrifice I could in more money than I could afford, rather than to let it pass. The one you saw was one that I did everything possible to make . . . as honest and as moving and to have as much significance as I could put into it."[38] Sometime in December, after several weeks' hard work, Faulkner finished his revisions and mailed the new *Sanctuary* to Hal Smith.

The reclaiming of *Sanctuary* brought 1930 to a satisfying end. In *As I Lay Dying* Faulkner had given Addie words with which to attack language. Words, she says, "go straight up in a thin line, quick and harmless," while "doing goes along the earth, clinging to it"; "sin and love and fear are just sounds that people who never sinned nor loved nor feared have for what they never had and cannot have until they forget the words."[39] Later, in one of the stories accepted by the *Saturday Evening Post*, he had given Saucier Weddel words with which to celebrate language: "Our lives are summed up in sounds and made significant. Victory. Defeat. Peace. Home. That's why we must do so much to invent meanings for the sounds."[40] Addie's speech no less than Weddel's reflected the assurance Faulkner felt about his vocation. He knew that he would never be satisfied with words alone, but he also knew that he would never have to be; and he was certain now that he could never be content without them. In the year past he had rebuilt a mansion and established a home; soon he and Estelle would have a child. Yet he had gone on inventing meanings for sounds, exploring and expanding his mythical kingdom. Publishing more widely, he was making some money and gaining some recognition. Since his and Estelle's needs were expanding, money remained a problem. But he had another novel coming out, one he thought might finally make a great deal of money.

On 11 January 1931, about a month before Hal Smith published *Sanctuary*, the Faulkners' first child, a girl, was born. It had not been an easy pregnancy, and it was not an easy delivery. Estelle would be months recovering from it. But the child, though two months premature and very small, seemed fine. Faulkner had hoped his first child would be a daughter, in part because he wanted to name her for his favorite great-aunt, Alabama. The youngest of the Old Colonel's children, Aunt Bama had been the Old Colonel's favorite and had become Faulkner's. More than any other person, more even than Auntee Holland, Aunt Bama had given Faulkner the model for Aunt Jenny Sartoris Du Pre. Alabama might be an unusual name, but Estelle had agreed to it. Two days after their daughter's birth, he wired his great-aunt: "Alabama Faulkner born Sunday. Both well."[41]

A few days later Faulkner took his wife and daughter home. Although Alabama was very small, the doctor had said that she did not need an incubator; besides, the hospital did not possess one. With one nurse for Estelle and another for Alabama, and with the doctor visiting every day, both the mother and her daughter would be fine. Toward the end of the week, however, as Alabama began to weaken, Faulkner became alarmed. Driving to Memphis, he got an incubator and returned, only to find that he was too late. On Tuesday, 20 January, Alabama Faulkner died. Faulkner carried the small casket in his arms and then held it on his lap as he and the Falkners and the Oldhams drove to the cemetery. There he buried his daughter. Returning to Rowan Oak, he asked the nurse to give Estelle a sedative, then went in to tell her what had happened. It was, Estelle later recalled, the first time she had ever seen him cry.[42]

Refusing to drink, Faulkner tried to work, only to find that his grief ran too deep, touched too much. He had never liked or trusted Estelle's doctor. Now he was convinced that the doctor had been negligent. Later he bought and gave an incubator to a rival doctor's hospital, trying to assure that no other child would needlessly die. But he also wanted revenge, which he found not in acts performed but in fictions concocted. Soon rumors began circulating that the doctor was unable to work or was afraid to be seen. According to one account, Faulkner had gone to the doctor's office and shot him in the shoulder; in another, Faulkner had stood at the front door of Rowan Oak only to fire at the doctor and miss. Having spread such rumors around Oxford, Faulkner later spread them among friends and acquaintances in New York.[43]

Soon a different kind of notoriety began to mingle with Faulkner's bitter grief. Released on 9 February, *Sanctuary* attracted immediate

attention. There were more reviews than ever before, and they were
longer and more sensational. Describing themselves as offended,
sickened, or awed, reviewers mentioned technique and then stressed
Faulkner's preoccupation with violence and perversion. Within a few
weeks more people bought *Sanctuary* than had bought both *The Sound
and the Fury* and *As I Lay Dying*; by late April it had sold more copies
than all Faulkner's earlier books combined. Suddenly there were calls
for his earlier novels, even for *The Marble Faun*, as people went back,
hoping to find in earlier works the satisfactions they were finding in the
latest.[44]

Since the people of Oxford were not merely offended but insulted,
the rapport Faulkner had built up soon gave way to abuse. Without
admitting that they had read it, Faulkner's neighbors declared *Sanctuary*
an outrage. In January Faulkner's taciturn father had prayed movingly
over the grave of Alabama; in February "he tried to suppress" *Sanctuary*
by having "it withdrawn from the market." Without saying whether she
had read the novel, Miss Maud tried to defend her son. "Let him
alone, . . . " she said to her husband. "He writes what he has to"—a
remark few people in Oxford seemed capable of understanding. Feeling
affronted, they became cold, even hostile. Acknowledgment of Faulkner's
achievement would not finally come in Oxford, as one brother remarked,
until after he made large quantities of money.[45] Even then it would be
mixed with poorly repressed resentment, born of the feeling that he had
somehow shamed the people among whom he lived.

Needing money yet feeling too distracted to begin a long project,
Faulkner concentrated on trying to place stories. *Harper's* and *Woman's
Home Companion* had joined the list of magazines that occasionally
mailed acceptances. The *Post, Scribner's*, and *American Mercury* continued to show interest. But he still owed money for materials used in
restoring Rowan Oak, and medical expenses had been heavy for months.
In September the first royalties on *Sanctuary* should arrive. In the meantime both he and Hal Smith wanted to capitalize on its sensational reception. In May he signed a contract for *A Rose for Emily and Other Stories*,
which was published in September as *These 13*. As it turned out the
strategy paid off: the volume of mixed stories—four set in World War
One, six in Yoknapatawpha, and three in scattered places abroad—sold
better than any novel except *Sanctuary*.[46] Although his need of money
persisted, his prospects were improving. In April, Chatto & Windus added
The Sound and the Fury, and later that year *Sanctuary*, to a list that
included *Soldiers' Pay*. Richard Hughes was still supporting Faulkner by
writing helpful introductions. And now Maurice Coindreau wanted to do
translations so that Gaston Gallimard could publish Faulkner's novels
in France.[47]

Still, Faulkner remained troubled—by a shortage of money, the presence of hostility, the persistence of grief. Having dedicated *These 13* "To Estelle and Alabama," he began looking for some larger release. Soon he was working on a manuscript he called "Dark House." Like its title, the manuscript would change as he wrote and rewrote. Once again he would learn by writing what he had to write; and once again his labor would come as a kind of deliverance.[48]

Having resumed his familiar rhythm, he found the days passing more easily. Waking early, he wrote for several hours. During the afternoons he sometimes rode horses or hiked; more often, he worked on his house, stable, or garden. There were always odd jobs that needed doing, and he enjoyed working alone. In the evenings, as twilight descended, he and Estelle sat on the porch for a drink before dinner. Soon his novel seemed less a novel about a "Dark House" than another story of twilight—or rather, of "the lambent suspension of August into which night is about to fully come."[49]

As "Dark House" the novel focused on the Reverend Gail Hightower. Like Dr. Gavin Blount in "Rose of Lebanon," a story *Scribner's* had rejected in early August,[50] Gail Hightower is crippled by his preoccupation with his family's history. Like the Sartorises, he wants to be heroic; like the protagonist of "Carcassonne," the last of *These 13*, he wants "to perform something bold and tragical and austere."[51] As in *Flags in the Dust*, the dream of glory is associated with illustrious ancestors; as in "Carcassonne," it is associated with a galloping horse that thunders upward and outward into glorious oblivion. But in *Light in August* both the horse and the glory belong wholly to the past. Feeling that his grandfather has both epitomized and exhausted heroic possibility, Hightower wants to be better and braver "than he was afraid he" will be. Clinging to the example given him, he moves to Jefferson, the scene of his grandfather's death. There he tries to recapture in reverie and imagination the glory he is afraid he will never directly experience. Since his participation in glory is indirect and meager, it is never satisfying; and since it is never satisfying, he feels compelled to repeat it. Each evening at twilight, sitting alone in his darkening house, he circles again through the entrance of his grandfather's cavalry troop into Jefferson. As his existence comes to center on these moments, as he becomes an act of memory, the flow of his life stops. He fails his vocation, his congregation, his wife—all so that he may escape into a "past where some member of his family was brave enough to match the moment."[52]

Following several efforts to tell the story of Gail Hightower, Faulkner changed titles and shifted focus. As "Dark House" became *Light in August*, Lena Grove emerged as a central character. In contrast to Hightower, who circles through tortured reveries, Lena moves calmly through her world, getting around. She is never, as Faulkner later observed, "for one moment confused, frightened, alarmed." Privation and desertion account for most of what she has experienced, yet she is so resourceful and assured that she does "not even know that she [does not] need pity." Although she is an unwed mother in a conventional society, she feels no shame. Since she knows that it will be "her destiny to have a husband and children," she searches for a husband, just as she awaits the birth of her child, without haste or alarm.[53]

Entering *Light in August*, Lena gave Faulkner an unforgettable beginning. We see her first amid "the hot still pinewiney silence" of an August afternoon. Walking dusty roads, riding in anonymous mule-drawn wagons—"a succession of creakwheeled and limpeared avatars"—she has come "a far piece" from Alabama almost to Jefferson, carrying her unborn child and seeking her runaway husband. Around her we see the slow, deliberate world of the rural South—a world so traditional that she can take it in with "a single glance all-embracing, swift, innocent and profound." Through her, Faulkner deliberately evokes the pastoral world of Keats's "Ode on a Grecian Urn." In the world to which she belongs, she is a country woman traveling dusty roads; but in the context Faulkner creates for her, she is "like something moving forever and without progress across an urn."

Lena Grove provided a second major strand in the pattern Faulkner was trying to work out, and after her entrance the novel began to move more purposefully. As it turned out, she would give Faulkner an ending to match his beginning. But she did not provide the kind of complication he needed. The character who did, he called Joe Christmas. Perhaps the most divided and doomed of all Faulkner's major characters, Joe Christmas does not know what he is or what his destiny will be, though he regards both with alarm. Offended by women, fearful of progeny, he carries only his own life with him, "like it was a basket of eggs." Running along empty corridors and down "a thousand savage and lonely streets," seeking peace ("That was all I wanted," he says to himself), he moves from one terrible violence to the next. "Something is going to happen to me," he says: "I am going to do something." In the end he both inflicts and suffers death.

Almost as soon as he enters the novel, Joe Christmas begins to dominate it, in part because of what he represents and in part because his story requires a large number of supporting characters: the Hineses, the McEacherns, Joanna Burden, and Percy Grimm. To the pathos of Gail Hightower's life and the comedy of Lena Grove's, Joe Christmas adds the tragedy of a man who "didn't know what he was" and who had "no possible way in life . . . to find out."[54] Faulkner's concern with race had surfaced before and would surface again—not only in *Absalom*,

Absalom! and *Go Down, Moses*, but also in letters of the 1940s and speeches of the 1950s. In Joe Christmas that concern is both passionate and artistic, which accounts in part for the marked intensification of rhetoric that accompanies his entrance into the novel. Another purpose of Faulkner's rhetoric, however, is to define Joe Christmas as a hero so possessed of abstraction that his relations to the world around him are always strained. Later, with Thomas Sutpen in *Absalom, Absalom!* and Ike McCaslin in *Go Down, Moses*, Faulkner used highly rhetorical prose for similar purposes. Left without adequate parents or acceptable heritage, Thomas Sutpen conceives and pursues a grand design. Given a heritage he feels obliged to repudiate, Ike McCaslin commits himself to a set of abstract principles. Deprived of visible connections, Joe Christmas embraces an abstract fate. Since he is more divided, however, than either Sutpen or McCaslin, Joe Christmas remains ambivalent toward everything. Never before had Faulkner made so clear the relation he sensed between a man's attitude toward women and his disposition toward life. What he had approached in Quentin and Jason, Popeye and Horace, he realized in Joe Christmas. Like Gail Hightower, Joe seeks peace that is distinctly escapist; it is peace as release rather than peace as repose and generation that Joe desires. Early in the novel Faulkner associates Lena with an urn that connotes both motion and stasis, life and art. Late in the novel he associates Hightower with "a classic and serene vase" that offers shelter "from the harsh gale of living." In between he associates Joe Christmas with an urn that suggests, not life and art, or isolation and seclusion, but corruption and death.

Although men threaten and abuse Joe, women frighten and offend him. The "soft kindness" of Mrs. McEachern seems to him insidious because he believes that she wants to engulf him: "She was trying to make me cry. Then she thinks that they would have had me." The overt sexuality of Bobbie, on the other hand, both attracts and offends him; in moments of desire he pursues her, but in a nightmare vision, he associates her with "being sucked down into a bottomless morass." More even than with engulfment, however, it is with corruption that he associates women. Having learned that women are "doomed to be at stated and inescapable intervals victims of periodical filth," he says: "All right. It is so, then. But not to me. Not in my life and my love." Later, alone in the woods, "as though in a cave he seemed to see a diminishing row of suavely shaped urns in moonlight, blanched. And not one was perfect. Each one was cracked and from each crack there issued something liquid, death-colored, and foul. He touched a tree, leaning his propped arms against it, seeing the ranked and moonlit urns. He vomited." In the end Joe kills a woman and is killed by a man. Percy Grimm, his murderer and mutilator, emerges as a younger, more deeply twisted version of the militant Protestant we see in Hines and McEachern. In their preoccupations we see the forces that corrupt Joe Christmas even before they destroy him, just as they have corrupted Joanna Burden. Filth and abomination provide the categories in terms of which they understand most of life, including everyone who is either female or black. Partially descended of and corrupted by these men, Joe turns against the dark fecundity he associates with black people and the soft kindness and sexuality that he associates with women and toward the arrogant superciliousness and the love of violence that he associates with men. In the process he turns against the forces that ally him with pleasure and life and toward the forces that ally him with denial and death.

In the story of Joe Christmas, Faulkner virtually obliterates the distinction between victim and agent by stressing Joe's secret affiliation with the world that pursues and mutilates him. Early in the novel Joe moves back and forth between the feeling that *"Something is going to happen to me"* and the feeling that *"I am going to do something."* Later, before he has killed Joanna, he says to himself *"I had to do it"* already in the past tense; *"I had to do it. She said so herself."* Then, shortly before he commits the act that he accepts as fated, he calmly waits as Joanna tries to fire the pistol in which she has loaded exactly two chambers. Watching not the scene itself but its shadow "on the wall," he half-anticipates everything that is to be for him—not only the death and mutilation he will commit, but the death and mutilation he will suffer. When death comes to him, moreover, it comes not only as "desire and fulfillment" but as a kind of apotheosis; and it comes to him at the hands of another militant Protestant whose twin obsessions are sex and race. Like Doc Hines and Mr. McEachern, Percy Grimm is threatened and offended by the power of blackness, bitchery, and abomination even when these things exist only as figments of his twisted imagination. When Gail Hightower finally comes to the moment of luminosity in which he sees all of the faces that have come into his life, he sees most of them as composites that somehow remain simple and distinct—affiliated either with life or with death. The face of Joe Christmas, on the other hand, is different, in part because it is strangely allied with the face of Percy Grimm, and in part because it resembles the face of a confused, divided, lost child who wants simply to live yet feels himself drawn and doomed to die.

Before Faulkner was able to work out the story of Joe Christmas, or work it into the stories of Gail Hightower and Lena Grove, a trip to Virginia and New York interrupted him. It began with an invitation to attend a meeting of southern writers sponsored by the University of Virginia. At first Faulkner hesitated. He disliked literary gatherings and literary chitchat, and Estelle, who was still suffering from anemia, was in no condition to make a trip. But he felt restless, and when Hal Smith offered to finance the trip, then meet him in Virginia and accompany him to New York, Faulkner accepted the invitation. On 22 October he left for Charlottesville.[55]

The chief accomplishment of the conference in Charlottesville was to establish Faulkner's public reputation as a drinker. "Bill Faulkner had arrived and got drunk," Sherwood Anderson recalled. "From time to time he appeared, got drunk again immediately, and disappeared. He kept asking everyone for drinks. If they didn't give him any, he drank his own."[56] Most of those present (including Ellen Glasgow, James Branch Cabell, Donald Davidson, Allen Tate, Sherwood Anderson, and thirty or so lesser figures) enjoyed other literary people. Faulkner did not—in part because literary talk made him feel unlettered. Reminded that he was "a poet without education," he found himself thinking, like Proust's young artist, of nothing save his "lack of qualifications for a literary career." In addition literary talk reminded him of the "stupidity of words," the deadness of ideas, and so threatened his belief in the value of his work.[57] As a result, old anxieties about his life and his career tended to surface when he was around other writers. Feeling exposed, vulnerable, threatened, he reacted like a country hound dog, as he put it, that tried to hide under the wagon while its owner shopped in the general store. If nervous gestures, furtive glances, and abrupt responses failed to provide protection, he would yield to what he called "the chemistry of craving."[58]

But it was more than the double threat posed by literary talk that provoked the craving he felt in Charlottesville. The urge to drink descended on him even more when he felt "all of a turmoil inside" than when he felt trapped.[59] At times he associated alcohol with release—with the baggy pants and stumbling gait of the clown; at times he associated it with escape—with a haze or haven in which the sounds of life seemed neither sharp nor threatening. For several months he had worked hard on a story about a calm birth and a terrible death in an effort to master a painful memory; and during that time he had rigorously controlled his drinking. Alone, away from home, his control collapsed. Several times he suddenly spoke to people he scarcely knew about his lost child, and several times he alluded to the revenge he had taken.[60] Insomnia, which had troubled him before, was now so acute that he dreaded the coming of darkness. The more he drank, the less he ate, the weaker he became. Often merely quiet, he was occasionally rude; once he entered the rotunda of Farmington Country Club only to begin vomiting as people came forward to greet him.[61] And though parts of the pattern were old, Faulkner's situation was new. Several writers present were well known, but no one could match the interest Faulkner generated. People who made a point of being unimpressed by *Sanctuary* were awed by *The Sound and the Fury* and *As I Lay Dying*. When Faulkner skipped meetings or receptions, his absence was noted; when he attended them, he became, as one reporter noted, "beyond doubt, the focal point of every gaze."[62]

As it turned out, a longer stay in New York brought more of the same. During earlier visits Faulkner had spent most of his time with friends from Mississippi, like Stark Young and Ben Wasson, or friends from his New Orleans days, like Bill Spratling and Lyle Saxon. Now he was entertained by editors and publishers and introduced to fashionable writers, including those who wrote for Harold Ross and the *New Yorker*. Some of the people he met were merely curious, some were admiring, but some hoped to sign him to contracts. During his seven weeks' stay he spent weekends in Connecticut, joined the fashionable wits of the "round table" at the Algonquin, and attended parties given by people like Alfred Knopf and Bennett Cerf. "I have created quite a sensation," he wrote Estelle. "I have had luncheons in my honor by magazine editors every day for a week now, besides evening parties, or people who want to see what I look like. In fact, I have learned with astonishment that I am now the most important figure in American letters. . . . I'm glad I'm level-headed, not very vain. But I dont think it has gone to my head."[63]

To the more perceptive of those around him, Faulkner seemed less a lion than a shy, vulnerable man. "You just wanted to protect him," Dorothy Parker said.[64] Flattered, interested, and tense, Faulkner tried to recapture his New Orleans habit of intense listening. Most of the people he met liked to talk and welcomed listeners, and listening was a role he felt comfortable in, at least at times. Occasionally it yielded unexpected results. One of Dorothy Parker's friends, Robert Lovett, told a story about the young British volunteers who had served heroically in Coastal Motor Boats during the war. Modeling Captain Bogard on Robert Lovett, Faulkner promptly began a story called "Turn About," the core of which came from Lovett. Within a few months the *Saturday Evening Post* published it; later it became the first of Faulkner's stories to be made into a movie. When the conversation turned away from books Faulkner was more apt to mix talking with listening. He enjoyed swapping hunting tales with Nathanael West at the Hotel Sutton, and he spent hours talking with Dashiell Hammett and Lillian Hellman. Hammett had done almost everything before becoming a writer. Like Faulkner, he liked telling stories; and like Faulkner, he enjoyed drinking, sometimes for days at a time.[65]

But nothing altered the basic uneasiness Faulkner felt, even around people he wanted or needed to meet. One of the things he shared with Hammett was antipathy for stilted literary conversation; another was antipathy for the fashionable, and to them false, milieu that Alfred Knopf epitomized. "I don't like literary people," he told one reporter. "I never associate with other writers. I don't know why—I'm just not social. I can't stand 'literary groups.'" Feeling beset and vulnerable, Faulkner drank so hard that at times he moved in a deep alcoholic haze. Repeating his Virginia performances, he embarrassed himself several times in New York. At Alfred Knopf's, after Hammett had passed out, Faulkner collapsed in a heap, unable to walk. At Bennett Cerf's he offended guests by refusing to give free autographs.[66]

Yet in the mornings he was apparently still trying to write.[67] He had taken *Light in August* with him, and he had picked up other projects in New York. Bennett Cerf wanted him to write an "Introduction" for the Modern Library edition of *Sanctuary*, and several magazine editors wanted to see stories. "I have taken in about 300.00 since I got here," he wrote Estelle early in November, "and I believe that I can make 1000.00 more in a month." In debt in Oxford and behind on his house payments, he needed money. Before leaving New York he was able to pay all that was due on the house and to settle several overdue bills in Oxford.[68]

Some of the pressure and excitement Faulkner felt came from writers and editors, some of it from publishers. Bennett Cerf's decision to add *Sanctuary* to the Modern Library list was part of a campaign to sign Faulkner for Random House, another part of which was his decision to issue a limited, signed edition of "Idyll in the Desert," a story Faulkner had been trying to place for months. Cerf's plan was merely the most concerted of several. Although he disapproved of Faulkner's manners, Alfred Knopf wanted to sign him to a contract, as did Harold Guinzburg of Viking. In part such interest reflected Faulkner's changed status; in part it reflected the collapse of Jonathan Cape & Harrison Smith. Troubled for months, the firm had gone under, owing Faulkner royalties on *Sanctuary* that he would never collect. Hoping to sign Faulkner before Hal Smith could recoup and form a new company, publishers began appearing "with contracts in their hands and the advance and percentage left blank."[69] Cerf and others talked of special editions, Hollywood connections, and large sums of money. "It's just like I was some strange and valuable beast," Faulkner wrote Estelle.[70]

In the end Faulkner signed with Harrison Smith and his new partner, Robert Haas—an act of admirable loyalty and dubious judgment. Hal Smith had given him help when he needed it most, and he remained, Faulkner said, "my one friend in the North, one man I like."[71] Meanwhile the drinking continued along with the negotiations, interviews, and parties. By mid-November Ben Wasson and Hal Smith were worried. Neither of them thought Faulkner could continue the pace he had set, yet neither of them could do anything to change it. Finally Wasson wired Estelle, asking her to come as soon as she could manage it. Within a few days she joined Faulkner in New York at the Algonquin, hoping to persuade him to return to Oxford. He agreed, but he wanted to wait until "Idyll in the Desert" was published, particularly since Bennett Cerf had agreed to advance the date from 15 December to 10 December. Meanwhile, the frantic pace continued. Editors like Alfred Dashiell, new acquaintances like Robert Lovett, old friends like Hal Smith and Ben Wasson, publishers like Bennett Cerf—all gave parties in honor of Estelle and William Faulkner. But with Estelle, Faulkner found the occasions less gruelling, in part because he knew she was enjoying them, and in part because he knew they would be home for Christmas.[72]

SEVEN 1932-1936

Three Trips to Babylon

Back in Oxford, Faulkner began writing immediately, unflustered by the recognitions and embarrassments of New York. He preferred vindication to neglect, but he knew it offered no lasting satisfaction. Even the money he had collected was quickly disappearing. Already he felt "a little amused at the sudden enthusiasm" of people who earlier had ignored or dismissed him.[1] Some of his wilder escapades troubled him, in part because they were sure to find their way into the stories people told about him. But he had fed those stories with fictions about his life as well as episodes from it for years. In an interview soon after his return, he spoke cautiously when queried about his war experiences. But since a part of him enjoyed being a writer "about whom legends of all kinds collect," his caution was sure to fade.[2] He would go on as he had begun, trading occasional embarrassment for the pleasure of being outrageous.[3] Although the Virginia and New York audiences had been new, the aftermath of his performance was familiar. What he wanted now was to get back to work, first on the story he had discovered in New York, then on the novel he had taken with him.

In early January, less than a month after his return, he mailed a finished version of "Turn About" to Ben Wasson. By March, when the *Saturday Evening Post* published the story, Faulkner was finishing *Light in August*. "I will warn you," he wrote Anthony Buttitta, inviting him to stay at Rowan Oak in January, "that I am trying to finish my novel, and so I am going to let you entertain yourself during the forenoons. But in the afternoons and evenings we can get together." Faulkner turned out, Buttitta reported, "to be something of a conventional Southern host"— solicitous about his guest's comfort and apologetic about the condition of Rowan Oak. On one occasion he invited Buttitta into the study where he worked. There Buttitta saw the manuscripts and typescripts of Faulkner's books, from *The Marble Faun* to *Sanctuary*, as well as a large file of unpublished stories, "many rejected and paperclip-stained."[4] Yet Faulkner obviously did not permit the visit to interfere with his work. On 19 February 1932 he completed the manuscript of *Light in August*; by mid-March the revised typescript of his seventh novel was on its way to Ben Wasson and Hal Smith. Despite his trip to Virginia and New York, he had completed it in less than eight months. "This one," he said, "is a novel: not an anecdote"—by which he meant that it was a long story with a large cast and a complicated action.[5]

As it turned out, *Light in August* brought Faulkner's first great period to an end. Many months passed before he again wrote with sustained intensity. Several publishers in New York had mentioned Hollywood, always in connection with big money. The depression notwithstanding, movie-makers paid large salaries, even to writers. Soon after Faulkner's return to Oxford, Samuel Marx of Metro-Goldwyn-Mayer telegraphed Faulkner's agent in New York, asking whether Faulkner was available and at what price.[6] Suspecting that Estelle would favor the move, Faulkner rejected the offer without consulting her. Money, it seems, was already a source of contention between them. "I will be better off here until the novel is finished," he wrote Ben Wasson. "Maybe I can try the movies later on."[7] Still, he needed money badly. Rowan Oak was large, its renovation and modernization a continuing and costly process, particularly since Faulkner thought it required such things as the hand-hammered locks he had recently ordered.[8] Despite his intermittent interests in economizing, he had expensive tastes, as Elizabeth Prall Anderson had noted, and he was developing expensive habits. He enjoyed spending money freely, and he liked loaning or giving it to relatives. Such largess was a part of the grand style he associated with his grandfather and great-grandfather. Although she knew as little about frugality as Faulkner, Estelle knew more about writing checks and opening charge accounts. As a result, their finances were always in a shambles. At times they may well have needed more than he made. And since they quickly spent everything that came in, they certainly would have been better off had their money come in smaller, more regular installments. But both of them wanted more than they really needed, and neither was tolerant of the other's extravagances. Before he could finish *Light in August*, they were in debt again. "Sorry to bother you," he wrote Hal Smith, asking for $250 immediately. "But it's either this, or put the novel aside and go whoring again with short stories. When it's convenient, send me another slug."[9]

With *Light in August* behind him and money tighter, Faulkner began examining his prospects more systematically. For years he had gone on trying to write stories for the *Post*, hoping and failing to make enough money to support himself. From *Sanctuary*, his most successful commercial venture, he had received almost no royalties. In March, when Jonathan Cape's new firm went into receivership owing him thousands of dollars, Faulkner saw his chances of collecting take another plunge. Remembering the recent fanfare in New York and hoping to avoid both "whoring again with short stories" and selling out to Hollywood, he decided to try serializing *Light in August*—if it could be arranged on his own terms: "I will not want to take less than $5000.00 for it," he wrote Ben Wasson, "and not a word to be changed." As prospects of this dimmed, however, while circumstances tightened, his thoughts turned again to short stories and movies. Finally, with the promise of larger, more regular checks before him, he opted for Hollywood. "If you can get $5000.00 with no changes," he wrote Wasson, "take it. If not, and the movie offer is still open, that should tide me along."[10] In April, serialization having failed, he signed with MGM for a term of six weeks, at a salary of $500 per week, with no options.[11]

Faulkner reported to Sam Marx's office on 7 May 1932, two days early, and promptly requested assignment to either Mickey Mouse films (the property of another studio) or newsreels—"the only pictures I like," he added.[12] Told that he had been assigned to work with Harry Rapf on a picture called *Flesh*, he disappeared for a week. "The truth," he said later, "is that I was scared . . . [and] got flustered."[13] When he returned with reports that he had been wandering in Death Valley, MGM's producers, including Harry Rapf, turned wary. Having no place to put him, Marx asked him to work on original stories. Determined to earn his pay, Faulkner began trying to adapt some of his rejected stories to screen use.[14] In fact, however, he had never seen a screen play, much less written one, and so possessed little notion of how to proceed. When the material he submitted showed his inexperience, Marx tried pairing him with an experienced writer. Still, with his six weeks' term running out, MGM had little to show for its money, which was about the only thing he had to show for his time. He had enjoyed talking and drinking with Laurence Stallings, James Boyd, and a few other writers; he had gained some facility in using screen idiom; and he had saved a little money. But he had no faith in the work he had done for MGM; and though some of the stories he had brought with him, particularly those about the Snopeses, continued to interest him, he had had no luck working on them. Offered a longer term at lower pay, he decided to go home, only to have a conversation with Howard Hawks change his mind. Hawks was about to make a movie of "Turn About," and he wanted Faulkner to write a quick script: if Hawks rejected it, Faulkner would have another week's salary to show for his effort; if Hawks accepted it, Faulkner would sign for good money.[15]

Excited for the first time since his arrival in Hollywood, Faulkner accepted the terms and went to work, writing quickly.[16] When Hawks showed the script to Irving Thalberg, MGM's vice-president in charge of production, Thalberg said, "Shoot it as it is."[17] Changes had to be made, of course, particularly after Hawks decided to add a role for Joan Crawford to a story about men. But working on "Turn About" with Hawks had salvaged as well as prolonged Faulkner's first stay in California. Although he might never feel comfortable in Hollywood, or fully engaged by the work he did there, he respected Hawks and knew that Hawks respected him—not only for the books he had written but for his skill as a screenwriter, particularly in doctoring specific scenes.[18]

The first test of Hawks's esteem came on 7 August 1932, when Murry Falkner died. Faulkner needed to return to Oxford, and he wanted to stay there for several weeks without losing pay. It was an unusual request, but Hawks, having agreed to it, persuaded Sam Marx to approve it—with two stipulations, first, that Faulkner continue working on "Turn About" in Mississippi, and second, that he return to California when Hawks needed him.[19]

Murry Falkner had died of a heart attack ten days before his sixty-second birthday. During the last years of his life he had become more and more defeated. His life with Miss Maud had long since drifted into a kind of coexistence born less of affection than of resignation and obligation. But for several years his duties at the University of Mississippi had helped to fill his life, as had his youngest son, Dean. An outstanding athlete both in high school and at the university, Dean had given his father many hours of pleasure and pride. Then, at about the time Dean's days on the playing fields of Ole Miss ended, Murry Falkner lost his job in a political shuffle. After that, as his diversions narrowed and his duties dwindled, he became more lost and lonely, until finally he "got tired of living," as his eldest son put it, and "just gave up."[20]

Faulkner felt the pathos of his father's life—he knew that Murry

Falkner's dying had been gradual, that no one in the family had done more than his father to define life as preparation for staying dead. Moving promptly, he took steps to replace his father as the undisputed head of the clan: he took charge of his mother's financial affairs and possession of the family Bible. "Dad left Mother solvent for only about 1 year," he wrote Ben Wasson. "Then it is me."[21] In the Bible he recorded names and dates that his father had declined to add, including the dates of his and Estelle's wedding and of Alabama's birth and death. Then he went back to writing for Howard Hawks and reading galleys for Hal Smith. Soon he would know whether Paramount was going to exercise an option to purchase film rights to *Sanctuary*. If they did, he would receive more than $6000. Combined with what he was making from "Turn About," the $6000 would enable him to get back to writing fiction.

By mid-October Faulkner was back in California, touching up the script that Hawks had renamed "Today We Live" and waiting to hear what Paramount was going to do about *Sanctuary*. But he felt tired of California's monotonous sun and lonely for Mississippi's unpredictable skies.[22] When the contract for *Sanctuary* arrived, he signed it and went back to Rowan Oak. "Here I am home again, thank God," he wrote Hal Smith. "I made enough jack in Hollywood to do a lot of repairs on the house." For a time his writing seemed to go almost as well as the repairs. Having earlier persuaded Smith to publish a volume of poems, Faulkner began sifting through the poems he had written a decade or so before. Selecting some and rejecting others, revising lines and experimenting with titles (which he later discarded altogether), he settled on forty-four poems: "I chose the best ms and built a volume just like a novel," he said.[23] In part an act of loyalty to the ambition he had taken with him to New Orleans, *A Green Bough* was also an act of loyalty to his oldest and deepest sense of himself as a writer: that of a genius writing in the romantic tradition, not for money, nor even for fame, but to satisfy himself and his muse. "I've often thought that I wrote the novels because I found I couldn't write the poetry, that maybe . . . I think of myself as a poet."[24] But his poems could hardly take him back to any such self-conception without reminding him, too, of what he had become: a professional who, whatever larger cause he served, published wherever he could in order to make money.

As he turned from selecting poems to writing fiction, his sense of relief vanished and his efforts scattered. He worked briefly on a kind of chronicle, "The Golden Book of Jefferson and Yoknapatawpha County," and then on stories about the Sartorises and Snopeses.[25] But neither summation nor extension of his kingdom fully engaged him. Promising stories to Ben Wasson and a novel to Hal Smith, he found himself working on several projects spasmodically and none concertedly.[26] Although he

was back in his familiar study, following his old routine, he seemed unable
to accomplish anything. A year earlier he had said that he wrote when the
spirit moved him and that the spirit moved him every day; now he found
himself wondering whether he had forgot how to write. As though to remind himself of what he had done and could do, he began going through
his file of rejected stories. A few he decided to send out; others he tried to
patch up or rewrite. Occasionally an old story suggested a new one. "I
have turned out three short stories since I quit the movies," he wrote Hal
Smith eight or nine months after his return, "so I have not forgot how to
write." But his new stories were few and labored. Having finished one, he
wondered if it was just another dud. On the nameless novel for which he
had contracted and received an advance, he could make no progress.[27]

For several years Faulkner had gone on writing novels and stories
filled with voices that sang to him, and so had turned the bareness of his
workroom into a kingdom and the loneliness and pain of his life into a
thousand things. Sitting alone looking out a window upon scenes he already knew, he had performed a labor that he described as solitary without there being anything lonely about it.[28] Much of what he had written
on the sheets before him had come strangely, involuntarily. Tentatively
in *Flags in the Dust*, more concertedly with the stories of the Compson
children, decisively with the voice of Benjy as it called forth the figure of
Caddy, he had discovered a series of remarkable voices. Together they had
enabled him to create great art; and together they had given him the entertainment, the affection, the tenderness he required. Now, as he sat alone,
the voices came, if at all, only with great effort and for short stays.

Needing a diversion, he revived an old interest. On 2 February 1933 he
took his first flying lesson, the need for which he explained by suggesting
that he was just an old veteran learning to fly new planes. Soon he was
flying regularly. It is, he said, "about the only fun I have." On 12 April
"Today We Live" had its national premiere in Oxford; on 20 April *A
Green Bough* was published in New York and Faulkner soloed in Memphis. A few months later he obtained his license and purchased a plane.
Later he went into business with Vernon Omlie, who had taught him to
fly, and Dean, whose flying he encouraged and financed. Together they
sponsored air shows in Ripley and Oxford, complete with stunt flying and
parachute jumping.[29]

Like flying, the continuing renovation and improvement of Rowan
Oak provided a needed diversion. But the major event of 1933 was the
birth of another daughter. In June, just after he and Estelle had enlarged
their house and increased their acreage, a daughter they decided to name
Jill was delivered by the doctor to whom her parents had given an incubator after their first daughter's death. Jill, too, was small, but she was
healthy. "Well, bud," Faulkner wrote Ben Wasson, "we've got us a gal

baby named Jill. Born Saturday [June 24] and both well." Having waited a long time to become a father, Faulkner promptly became a doting one. At first Jill's presence also seemed to ease tension between her parents, both of whom took delight in the duties and the rituals of their roles. With some prompting, Hal Smith came all the way from New York to witness Jill's christening.[30]

Yet nothing relieved the need Faulkner felt to write again. For a time he worked on an introduction to a special limited edition of *The Sound and the Fury* that Bennett Cerf was talking about publishing.[31] In it he recalled the "beautiful one" he had named Caddy,.together with the sister he had never had and the daughter he had been fated to lose. It was that earlier intensity and joy that he needed to recapture. Instead he moved from one project to another, making no progress. Having mailed one version of the introduction to Bennett Cerf in August, he turned again to "the Snopes book"; balking there, he toyed with a novel he called *Requiem for a Nun*. But with money a nagging problem, words refused to come. "It has been almost 16 months since I have written anything original or even thought in such terms," he confessed to Hal Smith. Perhaps they could publish a book of stories they wouldn't "be ashamed of." If things did not break soon, he added, "I shall have to . . . go back to Hollywood, which I dont want to do."[32]

Gradually stories began to come. Some were new versions of old work, including one drawn from "Elmer" that failed to find a publisher; but among the stories Faulkner mailed to his new agent, Morton Goldman, at least one was new. Called "A Bear Hunt," it soon appeared in the *Post*.[33] In addition, there was a new novel with an old title. Through the introduction he had been working on, he had finally discovered a way of telling the story of Thomas Sutpen, with whom he had been conjuring for several months. "I have put both the Snopes and the Nun one aside," he wrote Hal Smith:

> The one I am writing now will be called DARK HOUSE or something of that nature. It is the more or less violent breakup of a household or family from 1860 to about 1910. It is not as heavy as it sounds. The story is an anecdote which occurred during and right after the civil war; the climax is another anecdote which happened about 1910 and which explains the story. Roughly, the theme is a man who outraged the land, and the land then turned and destroyed the man's family. Quentin Compson, of the Sound & Fury, tells it, or ties it together; he is the protagonist so that it is not complete apocrypha. I use him because it is just before he is to commit suicide because of his sister, and I use his bitterness which he has projected on the South in the form of hatred of it and its people to get more out of the story itself than a historical novel would be.[34]

Having decided to use Quentin Compson's preoccupations to discover Sutpen's story, Faulkner was confident that his new novel would get itself written. He could, he believed, "promise it for fall." Yet it too went the

way of "the Snopes and the Nun"—first in mid-February, so he could attend an air show opening the Shushan Airport in New Orleans; then in
March, so he could try to make money.

"I always need money bad," he wrote Morton Goldman soon after the
New Orleans trip, "but this time I am desperate."[35] Earlier he had planned to wait for the spring publication of *Doctor Martino and Other Stories*,
hoping it would bring in the money he needed. Now, finding that he could
not wait, he turned again to writing stories specifically for the *Post*. Having finished one about the Snopeses called "Mule in the Yard," he wrote
one about the Sartorises called "Ambuscade." In 1927 his creation of
these two families had given him a feeling of great discovery. In 1934 his
return to them brought great relief, in part because he began to feel that
he might again make money, and in part because he began to feel that he
could still write fiction of authentic power. As he began following his old
work habits and reviving old memories, he began writing with deeper intensity and confidence than he had felt in several months. Taking episodes
from the life of the Old Colonel, he filled out some of the story of Colonel John Sartoris and much of the story of John Sartoris's son Bayard.
In *Flags in the Dust* we see Bayard as an old man; in "Ambuscade" we see
him as a boy of twelve. In creating Old Bayard, Faulkner had drawn on
memories of his grandfather, John Wesley Thompson Falkner ("the
Young Colonel"); in creating Old Bayard's youth, he drew on several family stories, including some the Young Colonel had told him on the porch
of The Big Place. As he immersed himself in memories and stories, writing
came more easily. At once familiar and distant, detailed yet fluid, his
sources presented themselves as an invitation and an opportunity. Although ghosts and voices were everywhere, they were neither fixed nor
imperious. Having finished "Ambuscade," he went on immediately to
write "Retreat" and then "Raid." In a matter of weeks, he had written
three substantial stories, each longer and richer than its predecessor.

In Bayard, Ringo, John Sartoris, and Granny Millard, Faulkner began
discovering or rediscovering characters who would eventually yield a
novel. With their Civil War adventures recounted, however, he found himself stymied. Since the *Post* was interested in publishing the whole series,
he wanted almost desperately to finish it, which meant cooking "up three
more [stories] with a single thread of continuity . . . with the scene during
Reconstruction time." Yet, despite repeated efforts, he could not "get
started." For several weeks he had felt good; now he felt blocked. Disappointed with himself and annoyed at how little the *Post* proposed to
pay, he decided to return to Hollywood. In the spring he had responded
to Howard Hawks's overtures by giving Hawks "the go-by." In June, after
his writing had slowed and Hawks's offer had improved, he signed a contract obligating him to report in July for an unspecified period at a salary

of $1000 per week. Since Hawks was willing to let him work some of the time in Mississippi, Faulkner left Oxford hoping to limit his stay in Hollywood to a few weeks while drawing pay for several months.[36]

For once things went almost exactly as he had hoped. He missed Jill deeply and often found his work boring. But there were acquaintances like Laurence Stallings and Marc Connelly to visit, and friends to see. Having earlier left Mississippi for New York, Ben Wasson had recently left New York for California. Another misplaced Mississippian, Hubert Starr, asked Faulkner to stay at his place "down on the beach, in a canyon," where he was able to "hide out and work." Waiting for Hawks to read the material he had turned in, he sometimes felt that he was wasting time— "that's what frets me about this business." But he liked the beach and the surf, and soon he was able to work again, not on the stories that had stymied him but on the story of Thomas Sutpen, which he still called "Dark House." Before he left, it had a new title.[37]

In less than a month he was back in Oxford with a script to finish, stories to write, and a novel to continue. "I have a title" for the novel, he wrote Hal Smith: "ABSALOM, ABSALOM; the story is of a man who wanted a son through pride, and got too many of them and they destroyed him." But the novel seemed to him "not quite ripe yet"; "I have a mass of stuff, but only one chapter that suits me; I am considering putting it aside and going back to REQUIEM FOR A NUN, which will be a short one, like AS I LAY DYING, while the present one will probably be longer than LIGHT IN AUGUST." More immediately, however, he had a script to finish. Writing in the mornings, he spent the afternoons and evenings doing odd jobs, playing with Jill, or fooling around with one of his hobbies. Sometimes he flew with Vernon Omlie or his brother Dean. He had a tennis court now and played regularly. On days when it was too hot for tennis, he played croquet or chess. Occasionally he felt impatient with the script, even with the stories; he wanted "to write something better than a pulp series." But he had had nothing to drink for almost a year, and he was working well.[38] During August he finished the script, and by late September, two more stories about the Sartorises. In the fourth story, called "The Unvanquished," Buck McCaslin and Ab Snopes, as well as Bayard, Ringo, and Granny Millard, play prominent roles. He was pushing the Sartoris saga farther, expanding and interrelating different parts of his kingdom. In the fifth story, called "Vendée," we see Bayard and Ringo emerge without sponsors to avenge Granny's murder.

"Vendée" completed the series of five stories published in the *Post*, and it also marked the temporary conclusion of Faulkner's last major extension of the story of the Sartoris family.[39] During the next few weeks he added an episode called "Skirmish at Sartoris"; a few years later he revised the stories and wrote a final chapter called "An Odor of Verbena."

Renaming the fourth episode "Riposte in Tertio," he shaped his stories into a novel called *The Unvanquished*. Ostensibly the story of a family and a region caught up in a war and its aftermath, *The Unvanquished* is essentially the story of two boys. In it we observe the growth of Ringo and especially of Bayard.[40] In the last episode they are young men in their mid-twenties, and they have been tested several times. Near the middle of the novel they lose Granny Millard; near its end, Colonel John Sartoris. Deprived of sponsors, they retain memories that enable them to survive with honor.

There is great energy and skill in *The Unvanquished*, and there is also genuine delight in some of the exploits of Granny, Ringo, and Bayard. Through his treatment of Ringo and Bayard, Faulkner was able to push farther the concern about race that had found compelling expression in *Light in August*. But he was of at least two minds about his tendency to romanticize southern resistance, just as he was about the *Post*'s conception of fiction. The stories he called "a pulp series," he also called "trash."[41] Although *The Unvanquished* is more than "glib romanticizing,"[42] it is less than major fiction, as Faulkner clearly understood. Having completed the series for the *Post*, he turned to the "mass of stuff" he called *Absalom, Absalom!*, knowing that it was a work of a different order. Almost immediately he found himself in trouble. In Thomas Sutpen and his story, he possessed the core of the novel's action; in Quentin Compson, the major teller of the tale; and in their juxtaposition, the basic structure of the novel. Yet the story still seemed to him "not quite ripe yet." Several months earlier he had written a story called "This Kind of Courage," which had found no publisher. In October 1934, stymied in his effort to complete *Absalom, Absalom!*, he decided to make a novel out of his failed air story.[43]

He called the novel *Pylon* and based it on events surrounding the opening of Shushan Airport, New Orleans, February 1934. Having finished the novel, he wrote Hal Smith wondering whether someone might notice similarities between the novel and the Shushan opening and "see a chance for a suit": New Valois was a "thinly disguised" New Orleans; Feinman Airport resembled Shushan and, like it, was named for a politician; one of his characters had certain things in common with Jimmy Weddell, who had flown at New Orleans and had "held the land plane speed record at one time." Yet, though he listed a series of parallels, Faulkner also insisted that the story, action, and characters of *Pylon* were "all fictional."[44] And certainly it is clear that the novel grew out of interests much older and deeper than any Faulkner had in the Shushan opening. A year before, he had realized his dream of becoming a pilot. More than a decade earlier, he had begun writing stories about flyers. Two of those stories, "Honor" and "Death Drag," deal specifically with barnstormers.

In "Honor" we encounter a ménage à trois that involves a pilot, his wife, and his wing-walker; in *Pylon* we encounter one that involves a pilot, his wife, and a parachute-jumper. Several characters in *Pylon* act out of the kind of reckless courage Faulkner located in the last Bayard Sartoris, and like Bayard one of them dies flying a plane he knows to be unsafe. In "Honor" and "Death Drag" as well as *Flags*, we see versions of themes that are crucial to *Pylon*.[45]

In structure, however, *Pylon* is closer to *Absalom, Absalom!* than to any novel Faulkner had yet written. Its action centers on four barn-stormers and a child: a pilot named Roger Shumann; his lover and wife, Laverne; a parachute-jumper named Holmes, who is also Laverne's lover; a mechanic named Jiggs; and a boy named Jack, who is Laverne's son, probably by Roger, though possibly by Holmes. Together these characters epitomize the appeal of flight and rootlessness. Each of the adults has re-jected a mundane, ordinary existence in order to become a homeless ad-venturer. Born in an airplane hangar in California, Jack has never known anything except a nomadic life. To him, as to the people with whom he travels, the airplane is an almost perfectly expressive symbol: it bespeaks both an antipathy to all terrestrial ties and a love of danger. Spatially, Faulkner's barnstormers belong to any and every place: since they feel no rapport with any locale, their gaits and manners reflect some "irrevocable homelessness" even when they walk familiar streets. Temporally, they live only in the present: they possess almost no sense of the past and feel no commitment to the future. The little lives they have left behind they as-sociate with parents like Roger's father, Dr. Shumann, and small towns in Ohio, Iowa, and Kansas. In those lives we detect traces of ancient rhythms and ancient aspirations: Roger's father had always hoped that his son would become a doctor too. But Roger, Laverne, and Holmes think of their rejected lives only in terms of what they precluded: true adventure and true sex, the two things their less structured lives celebrate. Speed and risk are for them not only anodynes but aphrodisiacs. In a remarkable scene, just as Laverne is about to make her first parachute jump, she climbs back into the cockpit and demands that Shumann make love with her. Astonished, frightened, yet excited, he responds, whereupon Laverne makes her jump—having for once conjoined the two great excitements she and her lovers treasure.

Faulkner's barnstormers express themselves in acts and deeds rather than words. As a result they embody heroic if not tragic potential. Most of what we learn about them, however, comes from a character called the Reporter—and it is in this juxtaposition that *Pylon* anticipates *Absalom, Absalom!*. Like the people whose story he follows, the Reporter is root-less: he has no recorded place of origin and no recorded name. Unlike them, he expresses himself in words rather than acts. Physically he resembles

Elmer Hodge; he is both tall and awkward. Temperamentally he resembles both Elmer Hodge and Horace Benbow: like them, he is a quixotic idealist as well as a romanticist; and like them, he is at least half an artist. Although he differs from the barnstormers in several crucial respects, he shares not only their rootlessness but also their fascination with sex and danger. He finds Laverne strangely boyish yet irresistibly appealing, and he finds Shumann and Holmes heroic. By befriending and following these people he hopes to understand the needs that inform their lives, and thereby the needs that define his own. In the process he hopes vicariously to experience thrills that will answer the needs he feels yet cannot act out. Having written about Shumann's adventures, he goes to bed and fantasizes about Laverne's body. To the adventure of the one, he comes no closer than thinking himself into a cockpit; to the body of the second, he comes no closer than touching the sheets of a bed on which she has slept. Finally, however, his quest for vicarious experience replaces rather than extends his quest for understanding. Although he conveys much information, he gains little in understanding. Like the compulsions he shares with them, the people he follows remain too cloudy. Like the compulsions that make him distinctive, the logic of his own life remains too obscure.

The barnstormers' flight from conventional existence toward heroism and sexuality is compromised both by the assumptions from which it arises and by the form it takes. The quality that distinguishes them—the readiness with which they risk their lives merely to win "enough money to live, to get to the next place to race again"—also diminishes them. For the risks they run are too tenuously related to the causes they serve. About their heroism the Reporter remains too uncritical and vague—in part perhaps because, given the sleaziness and corruption of the world around him, his need for heroes is too great. Colonel Feinman, the man society honors, combines petty meanness, fundamental dishonesty, and ruthless efficiency, and so represents a world in which all values go dead.[46] The barnstormers, on the other hand, though almost totally dispossessed, retain from the past a code of courage and honor, their glory being that what they love, they love well. Their energy and courage make them superior to the city of waste and death over which they soar. Through them Faulkner evokes the heroism that alone makes meaningful judgments possible. Before *Pylon* ends, he gives each of his barnstormers a special chance to act honorably. In so doing, especially since he permits each of them to pass the test, he not only shows particular fondness for them; he also enables them to justify his Reporter's faith in them. "It's all right," the Reporter says to Laverne, after she has assured him that she has told the truth. "I would believe you even if I knew you had lied." Since their code is dissociated from the context in which it possessed larger meaning, however, it evokes horror as well as admiration. For what it finally inspires is a frenetic pursuit of danger. The victories they win, like the defeats they suffer, are too nearly empty, making their lives seem almost as doomed and "ephemeral as the butterfly that's born this morning with no stomach and will be gone tomorrow."[47]

Like *Sanctuary, Pylon* is a bleak, uncompromising novel. Its world is so hopelessly mean and evil as to inspire cynicism and even despair. Like *Sanctuary, Pylon* was written in haste and remains uneven. Unlike *Sanctuary*, however, its weaknesses derive primarily from its failure to realize its own structure. It brings active, unreflective characters into promising conjunction with an inactive, reflective Reporter. In *Absalom, Absalom!* a similar structure would yield astonishing results. In *Pylon* it yielded disappointing results, largely because the Reporter remains too timid, too easily satisfied, too derivative. The loyalty that he gives to the people whose lives he reads and reports constricts him, making independence impossible. In the end, he defines his task in reductive terms. He is so completely a reporter that he needs no name. As a result, *Pylon* is most powerful in depicting its flyers, where it is closer to "Honor," "Death Drag," and *Flags in the Dust*; and it is most disappointing in depicting the Reporter, whose timidity and ineffectuality are finally crippling. His weakness is not infidelity or unreliability; in a narrow sense he is a good reader and reporter. But he creates no contexts of his own and so remains only marginally interesting.[48]

Sometime before he finished it, Faulkner began hoping that Hollywood would buy *Pylon*: the more stories he sold the movies, the less time he would have to give them. For weeks he had been trying to get back to *Absalom, Absalom!*, only to find himself hounded by need of money—a condition that had become almost constant. In addition to his and Estelle's usual needs and extravagances, he wanted to buy more land around Rowan Oak. Over the last few years his old dream of owning Bailey's Woods had been reinforced by a desire to protect his home from frequent intrusions. Disrupted and weary, he began trying to find ways "to boil the pot again."[49] Hoping to avoid Hollywood, he turned to short stories, again with the *Post* in mind. And again the strategy failed. Even when the stories came, the *Post* proved unpredictable; and even when the *Post* said yes, their fees failed to match his needs. However much he wanted to be free "from bourgeoise material petty impediments and compulsion," he was not. The more money he made, the more he seemed to need. Over the last several years his income had risen dramatically, yet he still had "butchers and grocers bills and insurance hanging over" his head. It was demeaning as well as distracting to be in debt, always worried about money, particularly since he feared as well as dreaded Hollywood, the only solution he saw. His dilemma was simple: he was a writer who could make sufficient money only by doing things that impaired his ability to write.

"The trouble about the movies," he said, "is not so much the time I waste there but the time it takes me to recover and settle down again; I am 37 now and of course not as supple and impervious as I once was."[50]

Feeling cornered, he began drinking, and for several days did little else. Then as abruptly as he had begun, he stopped, determined to write what he wanted to write. Turning again to the story of Thomas Sutpen, he found what seemed to him "inchoate fragments that wouldn't co-alesce," and so decided to make a new start, which he did, on 30 March 1935. Earlier he had felt that the novel was not "ripe yet"—that he did not "know enough" or that his "feeling toward it wasn't passiónate enough or pure enough"; now he moved with assurance.[51] The basic structure he had earlier devised remained unchanged: it would be a story about events of the nineteenth century recovered and recounted in the early twentieth century; Thomas Sutpen would be the dominant figure in the action of the story, Quentin Compson the central figure in telling or tying it together. Soon Faulkner had charted the two basic lines of information leading to Quentin, one from Sutpen to Miss Rosa Coldfield to Quentin, and one from Sutpen to General Compson to Mr. Compson to Quentin.[52] Through late spring and early summer he continued to hunt and began to fish more, but he also continued to write with great intensity. In late April, he, Vernon Omlie, and Dean sponsored an air show over Oxford. Still his work went well. As new narrative voices surfaced and began speaking to him, his novel became more varied and more compelling. Once again he was telling a story several times, and once again he was finding in the drama of the telling interest that rivaled the drama of the story being told.[53]

In mid-August, with four chapters completed, Faulkner put his manuscript aside to face a mounting financial crisis. He owed merchants in Memphis and Oxford, was behind on insurance and taxes, and had no available cash. To salvage the situation he required several thousand dollars; otherwise he faced the danger of bankruptcy and the loss of his "house and insurance and all." Since he had sold his airplane to Dean (at a low price on easy terms) he had no assets except his house and his manuscripts. Hating the prospect before him, he inquired about the possibility of selling some of his manuscripts. "It's all written in long hand," he wrote Martin Goldman; "besides the short stories, I have SOUND & FURY, AS I LAY DYING, SANCTUARY, LIGHT IN AUGUST, PYLON. Will there be any market for it?" Not knowing what the manuscripts would bring, or whether, if he found a buyer, he could make himself part with them, he decided to go to New York. Perhaps he could find an editor who would serialize *Absalom, Absalom!*; or perhaps he could negotiate a better contract. If not, he would have to try to borrow money from Hal Smith and Robert Haas.[54]

Faulkner tried several schemes. He approached two or three editors about serializing *Absalom, Absalom!*, and he talked to Bennett Cerf, who remained interested in signing him for Random House. But he found no one interested in serialization, and he owed Hal Smith and Robert Haas a novel on an old contract. A few months later, before he could finish *Absalom, Absalom!*, Smith and Haas would join Cerf at Random House, taking Faulkner's contract with them: *Absalom, Absalom!* would be Faulkner's first book with his last publisher. But since the merger was not yet set, Faulkner had to settle for a loan from Smith and Haas, and even it came with conditions: "There are strings to it, of course," he wrote Estelle, "and I have agreed to go to California for 8 weeks in March if Hal can get me a contract and so pay back the money which they loaned me." They would have nothing to spare, he warned, just enough to pay all the bills, taxes, and insurance, and to buy winter clothes for her and the children. "We will shop carefully and pay cash, and it will do."[55]

Faulkner returned to Oxford 13 October, having surprised everyone in New York by how little he drank.[56] Two days later he began the fifth chapter of *Absalom, Absalom!*, and may well have surprised himself. For he was writing with undiminished intensity. Nothing, it seemed, could distract him—neither a several weeks' break nor the unexpected news that Phil Stone, a bachelor of forty-two, had left for New Orleans to marry a young woman named Emily Whitehurst. Then, on 10 November 1935, word came that Dean, who had turned twenty-eight in August, was dead.[57]

Three years earlier, when Murry Falkner died, Dean had been restless, unsettled, wild—unable, it seemed, to find anything to compare with the satisfactions he had found on high school and college playing fields. Worried about his younger brother, Faulkner had encouraged and financed his becoming a pilot. Almost at once the plan began to work. Given the exhilaration of flying, Dean felt less need for unnecessary danger, and so became a reasonably careful pilot. Given his unusual skills, he became a talented and confident one. A few months after his first lessons he was giving exhibitions and instruction as a partner of Vernon Omlie—a large, talented, safety-minded man from whom three of the Faulkner brothers had taken lessons. A year before his death, Dean married Louise Hale. A week before it "The Flying Faulkners" had sponsored an air show in Oxford. Then Dean was dead, killed in a plane that Faulkner had bought before Dean could fly, at an air show in Pontotoc that Faulkner had judged too routine to attend.

The days and weeks that followed were as painful as any Faulkner had known. After a long night in a Pontotoc mortuary, where he engaged in a futile effort to help prepare the mangled body and face of his brother so his mother could see the body of her youngest son, he returned to Oxford to choose a stone for his brother's grave. As an inscription he chose the epitaph he had given John Sartoris in the first of his Yoknapatawpha novels: "I bare him on eagles' wings and brought him unto Me." Following the funeral Faulkner moved into the small brick house his father had built, where he spent several days taking care of his mother, who was so distraught she was talking of suicide, and Louise, who was several months pregnant. Filling his days with routine tasks, he spent much of each night writing. After his mother and sister-in-law were asleep, he arranged his manuscript on the dining room table and wrote into the night. Once during these days his self-control collapsed, but for the most part he found in writing both a necessary task and a needed release from guilt and grief.

By early December Faulkner was convinced that his novel was good and that another month would "see it done."[58] As it turned out, Hal Smith and Robert Haas had already negotiated a contract with Howard Hawks calling for a salary of one thousand dollars per week. Intending to work long enough to repay the money he owed and build up a small reserve, Faulkner packed his unfinished manuscript and left for Hollywood on 10 December. Living alone in a convenient, inexpensive hotel where he hoped to work on *Absalom, Absalom!*, he began collaborating with Joel Sayre on a script called *Wooden Crosses*, later retitled *The Road to Glory*.[59] After a shaky start, both projects went well. By late December script and manuscript were virtually complete, at which point the restraint he had shown for several months dissolved. A single night's celebration with Sayre triggered an extended collapse. Having handed a startled friend the manuscript of *Absalom, Absalom!*, declaring it "the best novel yet written by an American," he stopped eating and began drinking, as though to prove that "there's a lot of nourishment in an acre of corn." During much of January he continued to drink—first in California, where Hawks and Sayre took care of him, then in Mississippi, where his family finally took him to a sanitarium outside Byhalia for an updated version of "the Keeley cure."[60]

By late January he was sufficiently recovered to date his manuscript and commence his final revisions and typing. The long making of *Absalom, Absalom!*, his ninth novel, had cost him much agony, but it had left him confident of its greatness. As though to acknowledge the special place of *Absalom, Absalom!* in his work, he added a chronology, genealogy, and map that gave it an appearance of summation. What these additions suggest, the novel justified. For it is certainly his most inclusive novel, and is probably his greatest. It touches not only the geography and history but also the prehistory of Yoknapatawpha, and it makes contact with each of its social elements—including dispossessed Indians, enslaved blacks, and a variety of whites, from Wash Jones and the Coldfields to the Compsons. Through its action it reaches back into the early nineteenth century, when Yoknapatawpha was "still frontier."[61] Through its French architect it reaches back to Europe. Through Thomas Sutpen's family it reaches back both to the splendor of Tidewater Virginia and to the simplicity of a primitive Appalachian community. Through Sutpen's slaves it reaches back to the West Indies and Africa. It provides, therefore, a sense not only of the people and history of Yoknapatawpha, but of its sources. Through two of its narrators it takes us beyond Yoknapatawpha to Cambridge, Massachusetts. And since the man whose story they tell recalls Biblical kings yet remains intensely modern and intensely American as well as southern, his story reaches out in several directions at once.[62]

A part of the force of *Absalom, Absalom!* derives from its inclusiveness: by engaging the entangled relations among several generations of several doomed families, three doomed races, and two doomed sexes, it not only touches large segments of history but also expresses longstanding concerns—concerns that had structured Faulkner's fiction from *Flags in the Dust* to *Light in August*, the other novel he first called "Dark House." Another part of its force derives from its allusional density: its evocation of stories from the Old Testament; from Greek drama and myth; from Cervantes, Shakespeare, Melville, and Conrad. But the larger source of the power of *Absalom, Absalom!* is formal. On one side it is the story of Thomas Sutpen's effort to realize his grand design: its action flows from his attempt to build a mansion and found a dynasty. On the other side it is the story of the characters Faulkner got "out of the attic" of his imagination to tell Sutpen's story.[63] Together Faulkner's narrators—Miss Rosa Coldfield, Mr. Compson, Quentin Compson, and Shreve McCannon—try to construct not a mansion but a narrative. They must form, out of old tales and talking, together with scattered memories, ancient grievances, and abiding preoccupations, the story of Sutpen's design. Corresponding to the novel's double focus are two physical and two temporal settings. Most of its action takes place in Yoknapatawpha in the nineteenth century; most of its telling takes place in Cambridge, Massachusetts, in the twentieth century. The novel thus stretches from a time when people were trying to conquer a wilderness and build mansions through a period of war and devastation to a time when people sit, looking backward, thinking about their ravaged fields and decaying homes. The result is a novel almost perfectly balanced between two different kinds of intensity—between great dramatic moments, on one side, and great psychological and intellectual complexities, on the other. It is a novel full of unexpected turns and twists, yet its surprises grow out of incredible repetition. There are great dramatic moments, in which wills and purposes collide and from which destinies emerge. Each of these confrontations (Sutpen standing at the door of the mansion; Sutpen putting Eulalia Bon aside; Sutpen confronting the people of Jefferson; Sutpen rejecting Charles Bon; Sutpen dispatching Henry to stop Charles; Sutpen affronting Miss Rosa; Sutpen betraying Milly and Wash Jones—to name some of the most obvious) comes to us several times, often with pieces missing, sometimes with

conjectures and surmises added. They thus lead into and become inseparable from the psychological, intellectual, and even specifically metaphori-
cal surprises that give the novel another kind of intensity.[64]

Early in his story Sutpen emerges as a creator. Following a precise
schedule and pursuing a single fixed goal, he directs the conquering of a
"hundred square miles of tranquil and astonished earth." Naming his kingdom Sutpen's Hundred, he builds a magnificent mansion and surrounds it
with formal gardens. In his desire to make himself a king and found a line
of princes, he seeks not only to create something "to represent his own
blood, his own passion" but also to avenge an affront suffered in his boyhood.[65] As a small ragged boy, innocently running an errand, he has been
rebuffed at the front door of a mansion by a servant who tells him to go
to the back. Injured as well as insulted, he retreats into a cave, where he
sits in stillness and silence, reviewing the whole of his life. What he has
previously accepted without thinking about it—the futility and brutishness
of his family's life, the countless ways in which he and they have been insulted and exploited—becomes clear to him as he remembers and resees
episodes from his past. Feeling that he must do something, he thinks first
of killing the servant who has affronted him, then of killing the man
whose agent the servant is. But since he desires vindication, shelter, and
protection more than revenge, he determines to build a mansion of his
own. What he does, he does in part for himself, so that he can live with
himself for the rest of his life; in part for his forbears, who have lived
"without hope or purpose," performing labor that was "brutish and stu-
pidly out of proportion to its reward"; and in part for the boy he was, or
more precisely, for the "boy-symbol" that the boy he was has become,
for all of the "forlorn nameless and homeless lost" children who have
been sentenced to live without adequate parents and without adequate
tenderness and love.

Feeling the eyes of his failed forbears and his forlorn children upon
him (he thinks of them as waiting, watching to see whether he will set
things right), Sutpen gives himself to his design without stint. Since he
wants to avoid the failure that marks his family, particularly his father,
he adopts the plantation owner as a model: his specific goal is to match
or even surpass that man's power and grandeur. In *Absalom* as in *Light in
August*, Faulkner intensifies the rhetoric of his novel in order to portray
a hero possessed by abstraction. During the course of the story we hear
Sutpen speak of his grand design; to accomplish it, he says, "I should require money, a house, a plantation, slaves, a family—incidentally of course
a wife." In pursuing his design Sutpen displays great energy, courage, and
resolve. In one sense he creates the action of the novel; it takes him, as
one of the narrators puts it, "to make" all the rest. On two separate occasions he nears the "triumphant coronation" that he seeks, only to have

his life crumble around him. Having discovered that his first wife is part black, he puts her aside, and so leaves her without a husband and their son without a "visible father." Moving on, he begins again. Having built another mansion, found another wife, and sired other children, he discovers that the boy about to marry his daughter is the part-black son of his first marriage. Repeating the affront he has once suffered and already once repeated, he turns his firstborn son away from the door of his mansion. Later, when that son persists in the courtship, he makes his second son the instrument (the "outraged father's pistol-hand") of his revenge. Sensing final defeat, knowing that time is running out on him, he moves quickly from affront to affront. Before he is through he betrays both Rosa Coldfield, his dead wife's sister, and Milly Jones, the daughter of a man who trusts and admires him. The plantation he has named Sutpen's Hundred shrinks and falls fallow. He dies, cut down by the rusty scythe of Wash Jones. Having fallen into disrepair, his mansion becomes, first, a "rotten mausoleum" where his second son waits to die, and then a fire-gutted ruin. His only known descendant, a part-black idiot, heads west, not even bearing Sutpen's name.

Toward the end of his life, with defeat staring him in the face, Sutpen begins to rehearse the basic facts of his life. Through "patient amazed recapitulation," he tries to force some illumination of his failure. Baffled and offended, he ends as he began, in review and repetition. Like other parts of his story, however, his recounting comes to us only by indirection. In part because they share his sense of bafflement and in part because they share his sense of significance, several different people continue Sutpen's struggle to understand his story. In *Pylon* Faulkner had juxtaposed several people who express themselves through action with one person who expresses himself through words. In *Absalom, Absalom!* he juxtaposes one character who instigates an action with several who try to narrate it. The greater force of *Absalom* owes something to this proliferation of narrators. It also owes something to Sutpen's stature: to the fact that "integer for integer" he is "larger, more heroic" than any character in *Pylon*. But it owes most to Faulkner's making the act of narration itself a source of great drama. Compared with the figure whose story they tell, Faulkner's narrators live meager, attenuated lives. Like the Reporter of *Pylon*, they practice substitution, as we see most clearly in Quentin. Unlike the Reporter, they practice revenge, as we see most clearly in Miss Rosa. Examining the past, they seek vicarious satisfactions and effect vicarious revenge: they sympathize and share, delete and dismember. Like the motions of their minds, their motives are mixed. In some moments they repeat and circle as though hoping to achieve illumination through incantation. In others they regale us with facts ("forty-three years"; "forty-three summers") for which we can find no immediate use. In still others they seem to withhold the one fact we need. Even at the end they remain uncertain about their home, about their heroes, about their own emotions, and about the meanings of their own story. Nothing is easy for them, and they rarely make anything easy for us.

Through the ordeals of his narrators, Faulkner broadens and intensifies his novel. For they share not only a task but a variety of gifts and a variety of wounds and grievances. They know literature, and they possess a gift for language, even a love of it. But as they begin to work with their sources—with "the rag-tag and bob-ends of old tales and talking," with "a few old mouth-to-mouth tales"—we begin to see that their claim to authority has only a little to do with gifts and less to do with precision and objectivity. Although they tell a story that is "probably true enough," they discover it through the wounds they hide and the grievances they bear. Time and again they are able to locate correspondences between stories they have read, the stories they have lived, and the story they are trying to tell. In *The Sound and the Fury* Faulkner makes regression a means of transcendence; in *Absalom, Absalom!* he makes repetition a source of great innovation. His narrators repeat their sources and themselves and each other almost endlessly. But their sources are fragmentary and fluid: they are pieces rather than patterns, and they are oral rather than written. As a result, they invite play. Working in the dark, Faulkner's deputies fear failure. Still they go on trying, compelled by their hope that the correspondences they discover and the analogies they establish will disclose some informing pattern. Although none of them finally succeeds, each of them achieves moments of genuine insight and so participates in Faulkner's effort, which does succeed. As a result *Absalom, Absalom!* becomes both a narration of great action and an exploration of human minds and imaginations engaged in acts of discovering what will suffice. Although we can never be sure what liberties the narrators have taken with their multiple and fluid sources, as they hear and speak, recount and interpret, deconstruct and reconstruct, we trust them because they are at once engaged and engaging.[66]

The story Faulkner's narrators labor to tell has much to do with heroes and history, and much to do with families—with parents and children or, more precisely, with inadequate parents and wounded children. In the novel's opening scene the elderly Miss Rosa Coldfield appears wan, haggard, and haunted. Sitting in a too-tall chair, she resembles "a crucified child." Every essential relationship in her life is painfully confused. Having lost her mother at birth, she has been reared by a pitifully weak father. Ellen, her only sibling, is twenty-five years her senior and seems at least as much an aunt as a sister. Ellen's son and daughter, who are six and four when Rosa is born, seem at least as much her brother and sister as her nephew and niece. The only man ever to propose marriage to her, Thomas

Sutpen, is not only old enough to be her father; he is the widower of her only sister. After she has accepted his proposal he changes it to an insulting proposition and so makes her a widow without having made her a bride. By becoming her "nothusband," he sentences her to live out her life in "long embattled virginity." Her effort to tell his story becomes, among other things, an effort to sort out her thwarted, confused, failed relations. The closest she comes to peace and reconciliation is when she enters the names of her father and nothusband in the neglected family Bible—at which point the story she has labored to tell, the fall of the house of Sutpen, merges with the story she has lived, the fall of the house of Coldfield.

The interlacing we see between the story Miss Rosa tells and the one she lives is crucial, in several important ways, to our understanding of *Absalom, Absalom!*. Behind Faulkner's writing of *Absalom, Absalom!* lay at least three acts—the arranging of *A Green Bough*, the writing of two versions of an introduction to *The Sound and the Fury*, and the beginning of "The Golden Book of Jefferson and Yoknapatawpha County"—that took him back into his own life. In different ways, each of these acts influenced *Absalom, Absalom!*. *A Green Bough* had taken him back to that conception of himself that always seemed earliest and best. Among several things that delayed completion of *Absalom, Absalom!* was his desire to wait until his feeling for it seemed to him both passionate and pure. His "Golden Book," which was to be a kind of genealogical chronicle, is reflected not only in the chronology, genealogy, and map that he added to *Absalom, Absalom!*, but also in its inclusive, summarial tone. The writing of the introductions to *The Sound and the Fury* took Faulkner back toward the novel for which his feeling remained most passionate and pure. It also took him back to his first anticipation of a moment that now troubled him more and more: the moment when he would know that he had "forgot how to write."[67] But the introductions did so much more than this that their impact is felt everywhere. First, they focused Faulkner's attention on the problematic relations between a novelist and his novels. Second, they provided the occasion for his discovery of Quentin Compson as a narrator of Thomas Sutpen's story. As it turned out, these two developments (fascination with the relations between teller and tale, and Quentin as teller of Sutpen's story) became interrelated. Since Faulkner found Quentin too limited a teller, he went on to create other narrators—in part because he needed them to discover his story, and in part because his fascination with the ordeal of narration was inexhaustible. But in the process he made the second of these developments (Quentin as narrator) a way of exploring the first (the relation between teller and tale).

Together these developments enriched the novel's structure in two remarkable ways. First, the extrinsic, reciprocal relations that characterize all of Faulkner's fiction—his effort to give the whole of his work a design

of its own—reach their fullest expression in the enormously complex relations between *The Sound and the Fury* and *Absalom, Absalom!*. In this
sense these works epitomize Faulkner's imaginative achievement: which
means that he had the happy good fortune, or the extraordinary genius, to
make his most distinctive works also his most powerful and moving. Second, *Absalom, Absalom!* stands as the supreme expression of his longstanding concern with the relation between poet and poem, teller and tale,
experience and imaginative construct, history and art, Lafayette and Yoknapatawpha.

Born in a region and into a family turned in upon themselves, Quentin
is too self-involved in *The Sound and the Fury* to love even his sister. He
prefers abstract ideals, such as honor, or abstract concepts, such as fate.
Yet Faulkner uses Quentin's maladies to enter and discover Sutpen's story,
thus establishing intricate relations between *Absalom, Absalom!* and *The
Sound and the Fury*. Through Quentin Compson we discover that several
themes crucial to *The Sound and the Fury* are also crucial to *Absalom,
Absalom!*—particularly the themes of repetition and fate, self-involvement
and incest. Yet, in addition to entering both novels, these themes inform
the relations between them. More crucially, they suggest ways of defining
the relations between the lives and the stories of *Absalom*'s narrators.

In *The Sound and the Fury* Quentin's love for Caddy expresses his
devotion to the ideal that he insists she embody. Similarly, his suicide is
a substitute for, even a version of, the homicide he cannot bring himself
to commit in defense of her honor. In *Absalom, Absalom!* Quentin identifies with Henry Sutpen, who defends his sister's honor by killing his
brother—a deeper, darker self who intends to commit incest rather than
just talk about it. Like Quentin, Henry is a failed son and brother, but unlike him, he avoids overt suicide. By living alone in an attic, where he can
practice stillness and silence, Henry manages to become a ghost before he
becomes a corpse, and so makes his life a long substitute for suicide. Thus,
although one aspect of Quentin's self finds expression in the story he lives
(in *The Sound and the Fury*), another finds expression in the story he tells
(in *Absalom, Absalom!*). *Absalom* is for him both elaborative and corrob-
orative: an analogue to the story he lives, it extends, perhaps delays, and
certainly mirrors the murder and incest of which he dreams and the suicide that he commits in *The Sound and the Fury*.[68]

In *Absalom, Absalom!*, more than in any other of Faulkner's novels,
the stories the narrators tell illuminate and are illuminated by the stories
they live. The pages of the novel are littered with tokens of obsession and
traces of compensatory strategies and fantasies. Its crippled, unpromising
narrators engage in special pleading and strange self-justification; they permit their preoccupations and needs to shape what they see; and they
commit a variety of narrative atrocities—they withhold, disguise, distort.

Yet Faulkner not only treats them with compassion, he makes their flawed acts of narration the opposite of reductive. Together they create, out of old tales and talking, as well as old preoccupations and obsessions, a story that becomes a thousand things. Even if they fail in their efforts to recover their "faith in human misfortune and folly," they still manage "to salvage at least from the humble indicted dust something anyway of the old lost enchantment of the heart."

As it builds on detection, assumption, and surmise, and insists on the power of its own rhetoric, *Absalom* draws its readers into its imaginative and linguistic play. Soon we begin to act as if we believe implausible things or know things we cannot directly know.[69] Having described himself as possessing "an illimitable courage for rhetoric," Faulkner added "(personal pleasure in it too: I admit it)."[70] One part of the unusual delight that informs *Absalom, Absalom!* derives from Faulkner's pleasure in playing his imaginative and rhetorical games. Another part derives from his pleasure in making us play them, too. Finally, however, the novel is not so much self-indulgent or aggressive as generous. The larger component to its delight derives from Faulkner's sharing the pleasure and the pain of its creation. The "happy marriage of speaking and hearing" that it celebrates touches characters, author, and reader alike. Such confluence is made possible by the play of minds and imaginations as they move, now in exuberance, now in desperation, "discarding the false and conserving what seemed true." In the process of this play, mind and imagination go back toward images hidden in darkness, shadows accepted before they are known; and they go forward toward discovery of patterns that promise illumination and formulations that promise meaning. As readers no less than as amateur detectives and historians, Faulkner's narrators engage in a search for truth. Through them Faulkner commits himself to fact. But his narrators are also creatures of imagination, amateur poets, as well as creatures with hidden wounds and hidden needs. Before they finish, they learn that facts can't and don't explain; they even learn that facts can't be and aren't separable from man's conjecturing, surmising consciousness. Early in the novel available facts—"forty-three summers"; "forty-three years"—outstrip understanding. Later, understanding begins to leap beyond facts, tying narration by detection to narration by surmise.

Absalom successfully resists reduction partly because of this happy marriage: in its plenty every discovery occasions revisions and elaborations. It also resists reduction through its insistence that it will go on giving us the sense of beginnings and the sense of endings without giving us anything more, since more would be impossible or at least false. From the recollected conversation with which it begins, we surmise that the telling of Sutpen's story has been going on a long time. In Quentin's concluding assertion, we sense the presence of ambivalence and anguish and the absence of resolution. We know, in short, that only death can end his striving, that as long as he has breath he will go on as he has begun, trying to solve puzzles, find patterns, unlock doors. Like Sutpen, Quentin and Miss Rosa want finality: they not only conceive patterns and answers, they try desperately to believe in them. But even as they insist on inter-pretations—on familiar demarcations, expectations, and destinations—they articulate their uncertainty. Sometimes directly ("something is missing"; the facts "dont explain"), and sometimes obliquely ("I dont hate it. . . . I dont. I dont."), their doubt and insecurity surface. Caught between the sense that the lives they live and the stories they tell both "cant" and "must" matter, they go on seeking final meaning in a novel that goes on simultaneously approaching and avoiding it. Like *The Sound and the Fury*, *Absalom, Absalom!* is a story several times told and resolutely unfinished.

In February, with the revising and typing of *Absalom, Absalom!* near-ly completed, Faulkner returned to Hollywood to work for Howard Hawks. The pay was good, the term unspecified, and the work no more objectionable than usual. Although he avoided large parties, he met movie stars like Claudette Colbert, Za Su Pitts, and Clark Gable. Sensing that some terrible depression threatened him, Hawks and others did what they could to entertain and protect him. With acquaintances like Marc Con-nelly, Dorothy Parker, and Nathanael West, all of whom had made the move from New York to California, and with friends like Ben Wasson, Joel Sayre, and David Hempstead, he played tennis and poker occasional-ly. Once or twice he and West hunted doves or wild pigs. But he spent most of his time with Meta Doherty Carpenter.[71]

Meta Doherty worked for Hawks, first as a secretary and receptionist, later as a script clerk and supervisor. Earlier, in July or perhaps December, she and Faulkner had met and become lovers.[72] In March, April, and May their affair became a deep entanglement. Later it figured prominently in the making of *The Wild Palms*; on other counts, too, it was a sign of things to come. More immediately, it intensified problems that had been devel-oping for several years.

The rebuilding of Rowan Oak and the prospect of having a child had temporarily eased tensions between Estelle and William Faulkner. Strained by Alabama's death, which Faulkner blamed on a doctor retained at Es-telle's insistence, the marriage had later rebounded. In the months sur-rounding Jill's birth in June 1933, it had warmed. "We are fine," he wrote Ben Wasson in August. "Jill getting fatter and fatter. Estelle has never been so well." Soon, however, a tone of resentment and mistrust crept in-to Faulkner's letters. One problem was money: he became afraid to have checks sent to Rowan Oak when he was not there, lest they "be misap-plied."[73] He and Estelle shared a few extravagances, such as improving

Rowan Oak and indulging Jill, but they also shared suspicions and resentments. Estelle's love of expensive clothes and finery seemed to Faulkner frivolous, one of the terms she associated with his desire to own and fly airplanes. Whereas she resented the money he gave his mother and the help he had given Dean and was giving Dean's widow and daughter, he resented her father's conduct as guardian of Victoria and Malcolm, particularly his withholding of the monthly child-support payments that came from Cornell Franklin.[74] Such irritants did nothing so much as arouse deeper resentments. Faulkner had never learned to share Estelle's interest in parties and dances, and she had never learned to share his preference for privacy. To him, the labor and worry of their lives seemed all his, its leisure and peace all hers; to her, the glamor of their lives seemed all his, its isolation all hers. Even when he was at Rowan Oak, he showed little interest in going out or having people in; often he simply withdrew into his workroom for hours, taking "the door knob . . . with him."[75] On all of his journeys into Yoknapatawpha, as on most of his trips to New York and Hollywood, he left her behind. There were people in Oxford Estelle had known all her life, but few of them shared her habits or interests. Years before, amid the glamor of Honolulu and Shanghai, she had felt what she now felt amid the poorer provincialities of Oxford. What was new was not the sense of being deserted and forsaken; it was the constant carping about money. In Oxford as in Shanghai, she found herself alone, fighting a running battle against suicide with alcohol and drugs.[76]

What Faulkner later termed the great unhappiness of their marriage was clearly more than financial, however, and was almost certainly sexual. What he told Meta Doherty—that he and Estelle never resumed sexual relations after the birth of Jill—is at least plausible. After four difficult births and several miscarriages, Estelle had reason to avoid pregnancy. After two troubled honeymoons and two difficult marriages, she may well have wanted nothing more to do with sex. That, in any case, is what Faulkner told Meta during the months in which she was becoming the third great love of his life.[77]

To Meta, as to Estelle and Helen, Faulkner quoted Keats, Swinburne, and Housman. For her he also wrote poems—some that echoed the poems he had been quoting; some that seemed stilted and stylized; and some that were openly erotic.[78] Since money was short, their pleasures were simple. They ate at the Musso and Frank Grill, a friendly, inexpensive restaurant that Faulkner and his friends called Musso Frank's; they played miniature golf; they walked and talked; and they made love. On a few special weekends they stayed at the Miramar Hotel in Santa Monica near the sand and sea. With Meta as with Estelle and Helen, Faulkner was a deeply romantic lover, as his poems and letters show. Once, on a special evening near the Pacific, he sprinkled their bed with gardenia and jasmine petals. With

Meta, however, he also became, perhaps for the first time in his life, an unabashedly erotic lover as well.

Born in Memphis and reared in Tunica, Mississippi, Meta Doherty thought of herself as southern and traditional, which in many ways she was. But she had married early and divorced soon. Ten years younger than Faulkner, she enjoyed the sense of being his beloved—of feeling herself the object of his passion as well as his devotion. In *The Wild Palms* Faulkner would create a character named Charlotte Rittenmeyer, who owes much to both Helen Baird and Meta Doherty. An aggressive, insistent, and fearless woman, Charlotte delivers Harry Wilbourne from an orderly, secure world free of women by inspiring in him a great, complicating passion. Although Meta was probably too conventional fully to play such a role, she apparently seemed to Faulkner both unrestrained and reassuring. Painfully conscious of his size, he had always worried about himself "with women a whole lot."[79] Whatever else it had done, his marriage seems to have left him still worried, even anxious. Like *The Wild Palms*, the poems and letters Faulkner wrote to Meta suggest that he found release with her. "For Meta," he wrote in one letter, "my heart, my jasmine garden, my April and May cunt"—as though deliberately to relate innocence and initiation, the ideal and the erotic.[80]

A playful as well as ardent lover, Faulkner found both guilt and purity magical. There was in him deep reticence, which derived from associating sex with the forbidden, and though this reticence made sex difficult, it also made illicit sex exciting. Meta was "his love's long girl's body sweet to fuck"; entering the darkness with her, he felt free to "clip and kiss." For her, he wrote erotic verse and drew erotic sketches. And with her, at least for a time, he became something like the high-bouncing, irresistible, and insatiable lover he had always wanted to be.[81] But even from the beginning, he was moved as much by the magic of purity as by the magic of guilt. There was in him a kind of romanticism that associated passion with release and release with self-transcendence. Some of the drawings Meta Doherty describes are apparently so highly stylized as to resemble inspired outlines of lovers; and several of his poems speak not of immersion in passion but of escape from it:

> Ah, let this fade: it doth and must.
> Nor grieve.
> Forever shall I dream
> And she be fair.
> Meta, my darling, my love.[82]

Behind the tension between his eroticized and idealized versions of his and Meta's love were associations buried somewhere back in Faulkner's mind, as we see by the way he revised Meta's life. "Although he made love to me as a man to a woman," Meta Doherty reports, "there were times when he saw me as being far younger than I was." "With one flourish of his mental blue pencil," he edited his love's life. Removing birthdays, a marriage, and work, he did what he could to turn her "into a sweet, tremulous girl," or more radically, his "girl-child."[83] If on one side these revisions reduced Faulkner's fear of being engulfed, on another they reduced his fear of being contaminated. For he was taking his lover back not only to a time when she was sweet and timid but also to a time before the onset of "periodical filth." In one of his poems to Meta, he wrote

Dainty is couth
Couch thy moons.
Mid with me then
In the darkness
Clip and kiss.[84]

Years before, in *The Sound and the Fury*, Quentin Compson had recalled his father's sense of women in terms of "Delicate equilibrium of periodical filth between two moons balanced." In *Light in August* Joe Christmas greets knowledge of menstruation with horror. Only after he has knelt to soak his hands in the warm blood of a dying sheep is he able to accept what he has learned, and then only conditionally: "It was as if he said, illogical and desperately calm *All right. It is so then. But not to me. Not in my life and my love.*" Through removals and dissociations, Faulkner attempted to move Meta toward conjunction with an acceptably pure shape —that of a young girl. But even as he took her back toward purity, he took her toward the figure of a child in whom merged several shapes buried in his mind—the daughter of his mind, the sister of his imagination, perhaps even the dark mother. As a result he remained a cautious as well as adoring lover. In particular, he avoided actually living with Meta. Fearful of being dominated, wary of displaying and discerning flaws, he declined to share another day-to-day life. "It would be a grievous error," he said. "Let us be faultless one to the other."[85]

Although he did not want to leave Meta, Faulkner needed and "wanted to go back to Rowan Oak and to Jill." Promising Meta only that he would write, he prepared to leave.[86] In late May, his plans already firm, he inscribed several pages of the typescript of *Absalom, Absalom!*, along with copies of the chronology and genealogy he had added to the novel, "to Meta Doherty."[87] Earlier he had signed a contract that obligated him to return to Hollywood in August for twenty weeks. Having hoped for better terms, he was disappointed, but he saw no other way of making the money he needed. The writing of *Absalom, Absalom!* had got him "out of the habit of writing trash," and though he hoped to recover the skill, he could not count on it.[88] In the meantime he would have to take what Hollywood offered.

The need for money was in fact more acute than he knew. Back in

Oxford, he found himself dangerously in debt—behind on insurance and mortgage payments and owing most of the merchants in Oxford and several in Memphis. The problem, as he saw it, was Estelle's wild use of charge accounts and checkbooks, and he was determined to remedy it. In late June newspapers in Memphis and Oxford carried notices in which he disclaimed further responsibility "for any debt incurred or bills made, or notes or checks signed by Mrs. William Faulkner or Mrs. Estelle Oldham Faulkner."[89] Although he knew such action was drastic, he may well have been surprised by the attention it received and the resentment it engendered. After interviews with reporters from *Time* and an ugly confrontation with Estelle's father, he decided to stop publication of the statement. In letters to Meta, and perhaps in conversations with Estelle, he continued talking about separation and divorce. A part of him wanted to make a new start. But he was not ready for divorce if it meant, as seemed likely, that he would lose the "girl-child" named Jill.[90]

As August approached, Faulkner decided to take his family and two servants with him when he returned to Hollywood. He knew that the time he had spent there during the last four years had unsettled more than his ability to write, and this trip was going to last several months, perhaps a year. To salvage their marriage, he and Estelle needed to acknowledge the large role Hollywood was playing in their lives. Perhaps by consolidating households they could cut expenses; and perhaps by being together in a new setting they could recover a sense of order and stability if not of happiness.

EIGHT 1936-1942

Two Gestures of Gianthood

When Faulkner reported for work at the studios of Twentieth Century-Fox on 1 August 1936, he was still looking for a house large enough to accommodate his family and servants, Jack Oliver and Narcissus McEwen. Soon he found a place, just north of Santa Monica, complete with servants' quarters and a view. On a clear day he could see both the San Gabriel Mountains and Catalina Island. The house was too far from the studio and it cost too much, but both he and Estelle liked it; and since they had a car, a chauffeur, and a big salary, they decided to take it.[1]

To people in Hollywood, the Faulkners' life may have seemed private. When he was not working, Faulkner liked to take Jill to the beach. It was a good place to walk and tell stories, and he enjoyed watching Jill play with other children. To William and Estelle, however, their life seemed social. They entertained or went out occasionally—with neighbors like Val Lewton, another screenwriter, and his wife; with friends like Ben Wasson and Joel Sayre; even with celebrities like Clark Gable, the Howard Hawkses, or the Ronald Colemans. They were pleasantly situated, and though money remained a source of contention, it was no longer a major problem. Still, they failed to escape the pattern of resentment, jealousy, anger, and violence that held them. As the weeks passed, both of them continued to drink hard, she regularly, he sporadically; and both began showing bruises and scratches to their friends as marks of the other's wrath.[2]

The friend to whom Faulkner carried most of his complaints was Meta Doherty. During Faulkner's stay in Oxford, Meta had become involved with a pianist named Wolfgang Rebner. Now, with Rebner gone on tour and Faulkner back from Oxford, she found herself in love again.[3] In their conversations she and Faulkner continued to talk as though he and Estelle might "reach some accommodation" and so arrange a divorce that would not damage Jill, Victoria, and Malcolm. But Faulkner apparently knew the odds were against it, for he made no promises. "Let me say it this way," he told Meta, "I want you for my own always, but I don't know—I do not know—whether it can ever be."[4] Content for the time being with vague hope and scattered meetings, they resumed their affair. Usually they went out alone to places like Musso Frank's, or met at Meta's apartment. Occasionally Meta joined Faulkner and Jill on their excursions to the beach. One evening he arranged for her to come to dinner at the house he and Estelle had rented, where he introduced her to Estelle as a friend of Ben Wasson. To Meta, Estelle seemed small, sad, wasted. Later, however, when Estelle learned whose friend Meta really was, she proved fierce and determined. She was willing to make adjustments, especially if they meant that she could live a more independent life. But she had no intention of agreeing to a divorce that would necessitate another new start, or of giving up anything that she wanted, which included her name, her home, and her daughter.[5]

Threatened by notoriety and her thirtieth birthday, Meta became fearful of continuing the life she had made with Faulkner. Soon she began moving toward Rebner, who not only talked of marriage but proposed it. Before September ended she was listening; by December she had agreed. Although she continued seeing Faulkner, who went on hoping that she would give them "a little more time," she, too, was determined. Earlier, soon after they had become lovers, Faulkner had watched her dance with other men to tunes written by George Gershwin, Cole Porter, and Richard Rodgers. When it became clear that other old patterns were going to repeat themselves, he played his part out to the end. Calling on Meta, he talked to her of the work he was doing and the love he felt, all the while asking her to change her mind. Then, with the wedding day almost upon them, he wished her well and walked away. Soon she was gone on a wedding trip that took her to New York, London, and Germany.[6] "For Meta Carpenter," Faulkner wrote on the first of the three hundred copies of the limited edition of *Absalom, Absalom!*, "wherever she may be."[7]

Faulkner tried to keep his troubled marriage and painful love affair from interfering with his work at the studio. He dressed conservatively, favoring neatly tailored tweed jackets, and spoke in a reserved, rather formal voice; together his clothes and manners gave him something of "the grave air of a High Court justice." But it was he who was on trial, and he knew it. For there was a clause in his contract cancelling it if he drank on the job.[8] Needing a renewal rather than a cancellation, he went about performing his assigned tasks without ever suggesting that they were beneath him. Although he had never fully enjoyed writing scripts, and had never done his best work on them, he still tried to do a creditable job.

Despite his efforts, the results were mixed. Once again he produced an astonishing amount of copy. Most of the people around him learned to respect him; several of them began to regard him with affection and loyalty. But much of the work he did failed to serve its intended purposes. At times his scripts seemed disjointed and confusing, as though other stories had broken in, distracting him; even when they followed the story line, they sometimes proved useless. "Bill wrote magnificent things," David Hempstead later remarked, "but they had little to do with what was then motion pictures."[9]

At first Faulkner moved from one assignment to another—from *Slave Ship* to *The Giant Swing* to *Splinter Fleet* to *Dance Hall*; occasionally he was left "unassigned"; from March to June of 1937 he worked steadily on *Drums Along the Mohawk*. Everything varied except two facts: that the words he wrote for Twentieth Century-Fox, as it was being run by Darryl Zanuck, did little to shape scripts and less to give him pleasure. He had always hated the idea of working for money, yet that was precisely what he was doing. "I just kept telling myself," he said later, "'They're gonna pay me Saturday, they're gonna pay me Saturday.'"[10]

As it became clear that Faulkner was ill-suited to his tasks—that he was both more and less than an accomplished screenwriter—the good will of the people around him proved valuable. When he began to drink on the job and to miss paydays "for illness," it became crucial. Even when he was drinking regularly, he usually exercised considerable control. When his resistance failed completely, however, as it did several times in the fall of 1936, when Meta was preparing to marry Rebner, and again in the spring of 1937, when loneliness and frustration overcame him, he was likely to "wake up in one of those ovens"—his term for the Cedars of Lebanon and the Good Samaritan hospitals. The way back from unconsciousness and debilitation, always difficult, apparently seemed to him particularly humiliating against the backdrop of a hospital's white efficiency.[11]

Faulkner had of course been drinking off and on for years, often conspicuously and sometimes heavily. In some moods he liked to "play drunk," just as he had enjoyed playing the clown years before. In other moods he liked to dramatize the amount of whiskey he could drink without getting drunk. Not long after the war he had begun presenting himself as one for whom alcohol was an anodyne to some terrible pain or terrible woe. Like other roles, this one served at once to mythify and to protect him. For the most part, however, he had been able to take whiskey "or leave it alone."[12] After Jill's birth he had abstained for more than a year. Only when something had happened to get him "all of a turmoil inside" had his control vanished.[13]

Still, the ordeal of the suffering drinker was an experience he had lived as well as played, and in California, in late 1936 and early 1937, he began playing it less and living it more. A partial explanation of the change lay in the misery he shared with Estelle. In ways that would not be clear until he published *The Wild Palms* (1939), Meta's coming and going had hurt him deeply. But there were other less obvious explanations, too. He genuinely disliked Hollywood: no one would live there, he told one of his brothers, "except to get what money they could out of it."[14] He missed familiar sources of relief, particularly those associated with living at Rowan Oak and being near the hills and woods around Oxford. The most popular diversions at hand, he detested: Hollywood had done nothing to diminish his contempt for parties and cocktail chatter. In August, almost exactly nine months after Dean's death, Vernon Omlie, veteran barnstormer and instructor, died as a passenger on a regularly scheduled flight of the Chicago and Southern Airlines. One month later, Faulkner resumed flying. But flying alone in planes rented at Mines Field was more than lonely. Memories of his lost brother and lost friend triggered fear as well as pain. It would be months before flying became again a diversion rather than a grim test of will.[15]

More than his usual diversions, however, it was the scenes and satisfactions of work that he missed. Neither the house where he lived nor the bungalow where he worked provided a room essentially his own, complete with detachable doorknob. Up to his neck, as he put it, in moving pictures, he found it almost impossible to do work of his own. With the reading of the galleys of *Absalom, Absalom!* behind and nothing before him, he very nearly collapsed. Despite talk of writing new stories or a new novel, the only projects that took hold centered on old work—the first on *Absalom, Absalom!*, the second on the series of stories he had written for the *Post*. Since he was in Hollywood, he decided to try selling the story of Thomas Sutpen to the movies. As his own agent, he might make enough money to free himself from movies altogether. But having reduced his price from "one hundred thousand dollars . . . or nothing" to fifty thousand without finding a taker, he let his plan die.[16] Later, as his restlessness again mounted, he went back to the stories of Bayard and Ringo. What would Random House think, he wrote Bennett Cerf in December, about his turning the stories he had written for the *Post* into a book?[17]

Given his other duties, and especially his distracted, downcast state, the making of *The Unvanquished* was a perfect project for him. It involved substantial revision and adaptation but only a modest amount of new writing; and the easier parts of the work, revising and adapting, tended to suggest the more difficult, including the only extended expansion—a long, concluding episode called "An Odor of Verbena." By drawing on earlier episodes, "An Odor of Verbena" brings *The Unvanquished* to a kind of resolution and so transforms a series of stories into a novel. Still, though faced with relatively easy tasks, Faulkner moved slowly. It was spring before he could make much progress on the revisions, and it was mid-July before he could finish the piece that brought his work to conclusion.

By the time Faulkner sent the last of *The Unvanquished* to Random House, he was alone, once again preparing to leave Hollywood. In May Estelle and Jill had returned to Oxford; in July Twentieth Century-Fox announced that they would not take up the next option on his contract. Since he was "tired of movies, worn out with them," and since he was almost desperate in his loneliness for Jill, he probably felt some relief at the prospect before him. But it was mainly defeat that he felt. The money had been too good: he had earned nearly $20,000 in Hollywood during 1936 and more than $21,000 during the first eight months of 1937. To fulfill his old dream of being free from worry about money, he needed another renewal and a larger salary, not termination.[18]

During his last weeks in Hollywood, Faulkner worked a little, flew a little, and drank a little. Then, having said goodbye to a few friends, he made an appointment with Darryl Zanuck in order to tell him what he thought of him and his studio.[19] By September he was back in Oxford, playing with his daughter, walking and riding in Bailey's Woods. Having taken an option on the thirty-acre tract in April, he decided to purchase it as a present to himself and his family on his fortieth birthday, 25 September 1937.[20]

Although he had been away from home for more than a year, he soon left again. By mid-October he was in New York, with several things—publication of *The Unvanquished*, money, and Meta Doherty Rebner—on his mind. Hal Smith had remained with Random House long enough to see *Absalom, Absalom!* through publication, but he had since moved to the *Saturday Review*. For the first time since *Sartoris*, Faulkner was publishing a novel without Smith, and he wanted to see it through a final revision in the office of his new editor, Saxe Commins. In addition, he wanted to talk to Robert Haas. If Random House would agree to hold the money he had saved, sending him specific amounts at regular intervals, he might avoid seeing it squandered.[21]

Faulkner worked easily with Commins and Haas, and at first even the social parts of his visit went well. Working a little and making a few scheduled appearances, he still had plenty of time to see such old friends as Hal Smith, Jim Devine, and Meta Rebner.[22] One afternoon at an ordinary cocktail party he saw Sherwood Anderson and decided to go over and speak. As the awkwardness between them passed, they talked for the first time in years. From that encounter, Faulkner kept a clear memory of a moment in which his old friend suddenly "appeared taller, bigger than anything he ever wrote. Then I remembered *Winesburg, Ohio* and *The Triumph of the Egg* and some of the pieces in *Horses and Men*, and I knew that I had seen, was looking at, a giant in an earth populated to a great—too great—extent by pygmies, even if he did make but the two or perhaps three gestures commensurate with gianthood."[23]

Although this reconciliation with Anderson meant much to Faulkner, he soon paid a heavy price for his trip to New York. Having gradually increased, his drinking finally became almost constant, primarily because seeing Meta had proved too wrenching. A few weeks before his decision to make the trip, she had written to say that she wanted to see him again. Hoping to rekindle her love, he had agreed to meet her, only to discover that she was not ready to become his lover.[24] Shortly after his return to Oxford he would retreat into his study and begin writing a novel in an effort "to stave off what I thought was heart-break"[25]; in New York he retreated into his room at the Algonquin and drank himself into unconsciousness. Noting Faulkner's absence and remembering the aftermath of *The Sound and the Fury*, Jim Devine began a search. When Devine found him, Faulkner was lying alone, unconscious on the floor, clad in his undershorts, surrounded by bottles. This time, besides being badly debilitated, he had sustained a third-degree burn on his back, directly over his kidney, apparently from prolonged contact with a steam pipe.[26]

With the help of a doctor and a few friends, Devine began nursing Faulkner back to health. A few days into the recovery, as signs of tension increased, Devine became worried. Was there someone Faulkner would particularly like to see, he asked. Joel Sayre was the answer, or Sherwood Anderson. Hearing of his old friend's request, Anderson came. As he sat by Faulkner's bed, he talked softly and easily, with perfect understanding of a situation and needs he never directly acknowledged. It was the last time they saw each other.[27]

When Faulkner was able to travel, Devine accompanied him to Rowan Oak and stayed with him for a few days, until his strength began to return. "I am feeling a little better," Faulkner wrote Robert Haas, "though it will take my back some time to heal." The recovery, as it turned out, took longer than he guessed: there would be many scrapings, a few grafts and infections, much pain, a permanent scar. Yet within a few weeks he was at work on a novel he called "If I Forget Thee, Jerusalem," a title he reluctantly changed to *The Wild Palms*. Having finished it, he asked Bennett Cerf to send copies of it to three people—Jim Devine, Sherwood Anderson, and Meta Rebner.[28]

The writing went well at first. Since pain was troubling his sleep, he began writing at night—for the first time since *As I Lay Dying*. Although he worked more slowly in 1938 than he had in 1929, he had less trouble than he had feared getting back into the habit of writing. "The novel is coming pretty well," he wrote Haas in December, adding that he expected it to be done by May. Later, after the pain increased and the writing slowed, he revised his target date. It was late June rather than early May before he was able to mail his typescript to Random House.[29]

He began his novel with Charlotte Rittenmeyer and Harry Wilbourne, who sacrifice security, respectability, and money for love. The demands Charlotte and Harry make on life are extravagant, as those of great lovers tend to be; and the price they pay is severe.[30] As though to stress the dismalness of their fate, Faulkner made the beginning of their story the end of their romance. The novel opens with language and action that are painful, agonizing, almost hysterical, as Charlotte lies dying in a shabby cottage on the Mississippi coast, the victim of a luckless abortion that Harry has mishandled. In a futile effort to help her, Harry brings in an aging doctor. Having presided over her dying, the doctor helps to convict Harry. Charlotte and Harry thus lose not only those things they have willingly risked—money, respectability, security—but things they have treasured—Harry his freedom and Charlotte her life.

After he had discovered and entered the painful story of Charlotte and Harry, Faulkner began to feel "that something was missing." In meeting the need he felt, he made a decision or discovery that turned a conventional novel into an experimental one. As a counterpoint to "Wild Palms" he began writing "Old Man." What he sought was not a rival to his story, but a way of enlarging its context and controlling its intensity. Composing "the two stories by alternate chapters," he began developing thematic and narrative parallels and inversions.[31] Harry Wilbourne begins in the orderly, secure world of a hospital; the Tall Convict begins in the simplified, restricted world of a prison. What an invitation to a party does for Harry, a flood does for the Tall Convict: each man finds himself dislodged from the simplified world into which he has retreated; and each finds himself entangled with a strange woman. Jerked out of their ordered worlds, they face perilous adventures, with women providing the primary complications, entanglements, and inducements. One of the men successfully delivers a child; the other botches an abortion. With their adventures behind them, both end in Parchman Prison.

Of the two men, the Tall Convict is clearly a more traditional hero.

Facing the perils that flood and fate force upon him, he proves himself
both resourceful and courageous. He does "what he has to do, with what
he has to do it with." Despite his heroism, however, the Tall Convict
seems stunted, primarily because the peace he seeks is empty and the order he serves is reductive. As a young man he has read the *Detectives'*
Gazette. From it he has acquired a false notion of heroics and a silly plan,
and so, armed with a mail-order lantern, weapon, and handkerchief, has
tried to rob a train. Betrayed by his reading and then by the ripe young
girl he has hoped to impress with his heroics and money, he has become
permanently disillusioned. For the rest of his life he has lived with one
idea in mind: to have as little as possible to do with life and nothing to
do with women. Having been jerked out of his little life by the flood, he
displays remarkable endurance, shrewdness, and courage. Still he remains
single-minded, and so returns to the prison from which the flood has dislodged him. Parchman is his Jerusalem. He opts for its limited, diminished
life, in part because he feels obliged to do it, but primarily because it both
relieves him of the uncertainties of freedom and removes him from the
reach of women. "Women," he says at the end, "shit!"[32]

Like the Tall Convict, Harry is fearful and distrustful of life and women. For him the hospital is a sanctuary where the sounds and stirrings of
life enter only as intimations, and so never become alarming. In such retreats he has lived for twenty-seven years, taking no chances at all. When
he meets Charlotte Rittenmeyer he is still a virgin, whose clear intention
is to make each day a replica of the one before it. Still, there is yearning
in Harry as well as much timidity and reluctance, and since Charlotte is
all yearning, it is yearning that she sees in him. As a girl she has read stories of romantic love. From them she has come to believe that love should
"be all honeymoon, always. Forever and ever, until one of us dies." To
such expectations, her marriage to an ordinary businessman is a mockery.
What she wants, furthermore, is precisely what she sees the better part of
Harry as wanting: deliverance from mundane existence through discovery
of a grand, consuming love.

Dislodged from his secure, circumscribed world, Harry finds himself
surprised by passion. Since both the larger vision and the larger passion
are Charlotte's, Harry becomes her follower as well as her lover. From
their New Orleans hotel room they go to Chicago, Utah, and Mississippi.
Having shared the Tall Convict's deepest suspicions and fears, and having
experimented with retreat, Harry rejects them. The tension we see in him,
like the oscillation we observe in the novel, bespeaks deep ambivalence.
But the choice that Harry makes with Charlotte's promptings, and keeps
with her memory, is for the larger way of joy and pain rather than the
smaller way of security and peace. In the end, despite suffering that is
extreme and loss that touches everything, he believes that love and suffering

are better than peace, respectability, and wealth: "Yes," he thought, "between grief and nothing I will take grief." Feeling pain, he is moved to self-pity; feeling loss, he is moved to remorse and bitterness. But he does not fill his life with vain regret, and he does not name prison his Jerusalem. He endures prison for having experienced everything that the Tall Convict embraces prison in order to avoid. Although their stories take them to the same place, Harry goes involuntarily, for crimes committed against society in the name of love.

Since *The Wild Palms* is not finally a novel, we possess no term to describe it. That Faulkner thought of it as a unified work (that he conceived the story of the Tall Convict "simply to underline the story of Charlotte and Harry" and wrote the two stories as alternating chapters)[33] does not mean his experiment in coupling succeeded. Most readers apparently have felt that it did not, in part because, despite several kinds of links, the stories remain too discrete; and in part because "Old Man" suffers from none of the uncertainty and from little of the unevenness of "Wild Palms." Having said these things, however, we must add at least two things. First, despite the strangeness of its form, its two stories are enhanced by their juxtaposition. Read by itself, "Old Man" seems slight and overextended; read by itself, "Wild Palms" is too consistently painful, too clearly extreme in both its exultations and its agonies.[34] If the sharp intensity of "Wild Palms" benefits from being muted, the lesser intensity of "Old Man" benefits from being heightened. Second, the larger problems in the book have little to do with its form but much to do with its women—or more precisely, with one of its women, since the lethargic young country woman of "Old Man" troubles no one except the Tall Convict.

Charlotte Rittenmeyer, on the other hand, is clearly the most compelling figure in the novel. She creates the love she shares with Harry, and she presides over the disaster they meet. Her demands are extravagant, her commitment absolute. There is no claim she is not prepared to renounce: having deserted her husband and children, she insists upon aborting her unborn child—all in the name of what she calls "bitching," her term for the pursuit of erotic passion. Yet what she seeks in the passion she pursues is surely nothing less than love, or at least some hope of it. "I told you before," she says, "that maybe what I was trying to say was hope." The fulfillment that Addie Bundren wants yet finally despairs of finding, Charlotte seeks without stint. Her dream includes the kind of desire that Addie associates with wild geese and sounds that come "faint and high and wild out of the wild darkness";[35] but it also involves union and in a sense even marriage. Charlotte detests institutions, of course, and has no interest in the marriage of mere minds, however noble. But the lust that becomes the marvel of her life is finally true passion. She rages against all limitations, especially the twin enemies of love—society and time—just as she dreams of a union so perfect that desire is transcended, silencing all emotion and stilling all motion. "She doesn't love me now," Harry thinks, before a moment of coupling she has not so much sought as demanded, "She doesn't love anything now."

Charlotte knows, of course, that lovers are vulnerable, and like Harry, she suspects that they are doomed: "Something is about to happen to me," he thinks, anticipating disaster.[36] But she still believes and teaches that love is better than peace, grief better than nothing. Longing for a life of timeless moments, she seeks a scattering of them for herself and for Harry. In them she becomes an inspired outline of herself. And since she is another of Faulkner's intensely feminine yet faintly masculine women, to be that is to be everything: not only "the female principle," eternal Aphrodite made flesh, but "all polymath love's androgynous advocate."[37]

The Wild Palms is a novel, then, of extreme cases, just as it is a novel of extreme narrative strategies. The Tall Convict is a diminished man who deals with the whole range of desires by renouncing them. Although Harry moves beyond renunciation to follow Charlotte, he fails to match her vision and courage; she remains, as he says at one point, the "better man."[38] Being unworthy of her, he fails to swerve her determined effort to fulfill her dream of pure passion and so find on the far side of desire something like the peace, the stasis, the Jerusalem, that the Tall Convict seeks through renunciation. "It can't be anything else," she says to Harry. "Either heaven, or hell: no comfortable safe peaceful purgatory." In the end her absolute demands and her courage merge with Harry's hesitations and his failure of nerve to destroy them.

In *Pylon* Faulkner's characters follow a similar course. Like Charlotte and Harry, Shumann, Laverne, and Holmes reject mundane, ordinary lives in the name of great adventure; and like Charlotte, Shumann pays with his life. In the barnstormers, sexual love is subordinated to pursuit of danger; in Charlotte and Harry, sexual love is clearly dominant. But in both works, the two pursuits are interrelated, and in both they lead to death. Harry's anticipation of disaster, itself an echo of Joe Christmas's premonition ("something is about to happen to me"), is finally but an extension of Charlotte's deepest insight that "love and suffering are the same thing."[39] Because she believes that love alone deserves devotion, Charlotte scorns compromise, but she does so knowing that the heaven true lovers seek always lies beyond harm's way.

What complicates *The Wild Palms* even more than its unusual structure is the ambivalent tone it displays toward each of its major characters. It often mixes sympathy with irony, and it occasionally mixes pity with disdain. The result, as Cleanth Brooks has noted, may well be "too complex for the good of the novel."[40] To understand it we need to look at the particular agony that informed its making. For it was written out of pain that was physical, marital, and personal. Halfway through it, after months of "pretty constant pain and inability to sleep," Faulkner began to think himself a little mad. "I have lived for the last six months," he wrote Robert Haas, soon after finishing the novel,

> in such a peculiar state of family complications and back complications that I still am not able to tell if the novel is all right or absolute drivel. To me, it was written just as if I had sat on the one side of a wall and the paper was on the other and my hand with the pen thrust through the wall and writing not only on invisible paper but in pitch darkness too, so that I could not even know if the pen still wrote on paper or not.[41]

Clearly, then, the context out of which Faulkner wrote *The Wild Palms* was dominated by personal problems as well as by pain and heartbreak.[42]

It is tempting, of course, to associate Faulkner's pain with his back, his heartbreak with Meta, and his "family complications" with Estelle, and to a large extent the evidence requires such a view. Finally, however, the evidence, including that within the novel, squares with a more general crisis. During the winter that began in 1937, Faulkner spent hours talking and reading poetry to Estelle's daughter, Victoria. A few weeks after the birth of her first child, Victoria's husband had deserted her, leaving her on the edge of despair. Later she recalled the hours Faulkner spent helping her to recover hope: "He kept me alive," she said.[43] But it seems probable that Faulkner gained as well as gave assurance through the process of articulating it. At the Algonquin he had felt rising in him an instinct he knew from earlier flirtations with disaster. In the record of the next several months there are signs everywhere of doubt and consternation as well as "pretty constant pain." Harry Wilbourne's description of himself as a painter recalls not only Elmer Hodge but Faulkner's own early career. Similarly, the attitudes Harry brings to bear on the sleazy stories he writes for pulp magazines echo Faulkner's reservations about his commercial fiction and his work in Hollywood. Although she owes much to Meta, Charlotte Rittenmeyer recalls several women from Faulkner's earlier fiction as well as several from his life, particularly Helen Baird. The burns Charlotte has suffered as a child tie her to Faulkner and his recent injury. But they also correspond closely to an injury Helen had suffered in her childhood. Like Helen, Charlotte bears several scars from an early burn; and like Helen, she habitually tells people about them "before they would have time not to ask."[44]

Further, though the novel treats Charlotte's toughness and gallantry with genuine admiration, it also manifests deep suspicion and rancor toward women. The several comments on Charlotte's talent for arranging illicit affairs square on one level with the Tall Convict's deepest conviction: that women possess an affinity for evil and a desire to entangle men in it. The consequences of this sensed affinity are in turn felt at every point in the novel. Charlotte suffers a brutal fate; and both the Tall Convict and Harry end up imprisoned, owing in large part to their entanglements with women. Within the novel, man's longing for early retirement, not only from sex but from life, flows directly from his sense that women make retreat man's only alternative to destruction. The appeal of retirement had interested Faulkner for many years: it finds expression in characters ranging from Horace Benbow to Gail Hightower. But during the mid-1930s it had begun to haunt him. Several years later he suggested that Sherwood Anderson "might have been happier if he had been a monk," "if he could have retired completely into a monastery . . . where nobody could hurt him."[45] A few years earlier he had purchased Rowan Oak, surely in part as a haven, and within it he had created a deeper retreat, a plain, almost cell-like room wholly his own. Shortly before he began writing *The Wild Palms* he completed arrangements for enlarging his sanctuary. Later he worked hard to enlarge it again, in part for the purpose of protecting his privacy. Within it, he insisted upon living a formal, ceremonial life: as he made clear in another context, his ideal remained "ante-bellum and stately."[46] Yet another part of him had always resisted retreat and retirement, and so he had continued making excursions both into Yoknapatawpha and out into the world. He feared nothing more deeply than the artist's reluctance to brave "chance and circumstance."[47] A part of him had long fought all signs of surrender to such fear, particularly as it manifested itself in fear of women. Even his dream of achieving financial security and being delivered from worry about money was hardly more than half a desire; in practice, at least, he avoided it more effectively than he sought it. He had always wanted to be an athlete, a hunter, a flyer, as well as a poet and a lover. In February 1938, while he was writing *The Wild Palms*, he realized his dream of becoming a farmer by buying a 320-acre farm that he named Greenfield. For Faulkner no less than for W. B. Yeats, increased awareness of mortality intensified the desire to live as well as the desire to write. Between heartbreak, grief, or pain and nothing, he preferred heartbreak, grief, pain, but he was finally more deeply divided than Charlotte or Harry. If a part of him wanted to create a novel celebrating love as worth the price it exacts, another part insisted on making the price extreme. Like Charlotte and Harry, he had to pay his way as he went. Against love he allies not only society and respectability, all hope of approval, but also rationality, all hope of survival and freedom. Viewed in this light, the vision of *The Wild Palms* is even more extreme than its strategies. In it love is not only illicit but doomed. The disaster Harry anticipates—"Something is going to happen to me"—bespeaks deep prescience; but it also bespeaks hidden guilt. *The Wild Palms* was written, then, not so much to stave off pain and division as to explore and express them.[48]

Although *The Wild Palms* remains a flawed work, it did much to re-store Faulkner's sense of confidence and purpose as a writer.[49] Within a few months he was launched on another major project. In the meantime he had money to spend, most of it provided by the $25,000 MGM had agreed to pay for *The Unvanquished*. Having purchased Greenfield Farm, Faulkner wrote Morton Goldman to say that at last he would be able to write when and what he wanted, as he had "always . . . fondly dreamed."[50] During the summer, with *The Wild Palms* finished, he spent much of his time stocking his farm. Years before, in the first of his Yoknapatawpha novels, he had celebrated the mule's imperviousness to time and circum-stance; its loyalty "to the land when all else faltered"; and finally its insis-tent singularity. It possessed, he recalled, a built-in principle of retirement, and so resisted the most entangling of alliances: "Father and mother he does not resemble, sons and daughters he will never have." Now, despite the protests of his brother John, who had agreed to run Greenfield Farm for him, Faulkner insisted that they raise mules rather than cattle.[51]

By late September, when he went to New York for the final revision of *The Wild Palms*, Faulkner was writing about characters who resembled both the Tall Convict and the hill folk who lived around Greenfield Farm. During his visit to New York, he changed the name of his novel and en-gaged Harold Ober as his agent.[52] He also attended the usual parties and visited old friends, including Meta Rebner and Jim Devine. In less than a year, however, his mood had changed so drastically that nothing seemed to fluster him. A few days after his arrival, he wrote Jill that he had fin-ished the story he had brought with him and was already typing it.[53]

The story Faulkner was working on continued to engage him after he returned to Oxford. Called "Barn Burning," it focused on Ab Snopes and his ten-year-old son, Colonel Sartoris Snopes. After *Harper's* published it, it won the O. Henry Award as the best short story of the year. More im-portant, it took Faulkner back toward "Father Abraham" and forward toward work of major importance. By mid-December the structure, though not the titles, of the entire Snopes trilogy was clearly before him: led by Flem, the Snopes clan would descend on Yoknapatawpha and gradually consume it. The first volume ("The Peasants") would trace Flem's career from his beginning in the country through his taking of a small village. There his last coup would give him a foothold in Jefferson. In the second volume ("Rus in Urbe") Flem would rise from being half-owner of a back-street restaurant through various grades of city employ-ment to become the president of a bank. In the process he would fill each of his vacated positions with another Snopes from the country. In the third volume ("Ilium Falling") Flem would consume Jefferson; having corrupted its government, he would begin demolishing its antebellum mansions in order to build subdivisions and enlarge his fortune.[54]

By the time he wrote Haas, Faulkner was writing with deep intensity and pleasure. His plan was to finish the first volume in three months so that he could move quickly to the second. In fact, writing the first volume took him almost exactly a year—in part because his story turned out to be longer than he anticipated; in part because he had to stop and write stories for the *Post*; and in part because he was interrupted several times by unexpected circumstances. By late 1939, when he mailed the last part of the typescript to Saxe Commins, he had changed the titles to *The Hamlet, The Town,* and *The Mansion,* and his sense of leisure had vanished. He was again embroiled in financial difficulties, and they were steadily worsening.[55] Yet despite interruptions and distractions, writing *The Hamlet* was for him a striking adventure. In April, reporting to Haas on his progress and plans, he added, apropos of nothing save his own sense of mastery, "I am the best in America, by God."[56]

Although there were no signs that this opinion was widespread, there were several indications that Faulkner's reputation was spreading. In mid-January he was named a member of the National Institute of Arts and Letters. On 23 January 1939 his picture appeared on the cover of *Time* magazine—as a rather solemn twentieth-century Walt Whitman, wearing an open shirt and no tie. Although the people of Oxford remained cool, events were running against them. They could not go on indefinitely ignoring a native son whom *Time* was turning into tourist-bait.[57] In December, in preparation for the *Time* story, Faulkner granted an interview in which he talked briefly about his parents and extensively about the Old Colonel. "There's nothing left in the old place," he told Robert Cantwell, "The house is gone and the plantation boundaries, nothing left of his work but a statue. But he rode through that country like a living force. I like it better that way."[58] Later he took Cantwell to Mammy Callie's cabin at Rowan Oak and to Greenfield Farm to meet Uncle Ned Barnett. But he was writing with ease and confidence, and he was determined to let nothing break his rhythm. By mid-January he thought he was nearly half done; in February he described himself as nearly finished.[59]

In March he learned that Phil Stone stood on the edge of bankruptcy. Two years earlier Stone's father and older brother had died, leaving the family estate seriously encumbered. Phil Stone had tried to order his affairs only to fail, apparently because, as his wife later put it, he was already "burned out."[60] Seeing his old friend in trouble, Faulkner responded with the kind of loyalty and generosity that he had recognized and counted on in Sherwood Anderson. Considerable tension had developed between him and Phil Stone over the years, but Faulkner was determined to help, even if it meant endangering his own security. He would sell or mortgage anything, he wrote Robert Haas, including his manuscripts; and he would "sign any thing, contracts, etc." But he needed money, and he needed it quickly.[61]

With the $1200 advanced by Random House and the $4800 he collected against an insurance policy, Faulkner provided most of the $7000 that Phil Stone needed to settle the suit brought against him.[62] Less than a month later Faulkner heard from another old friend who needed money. It was Meta Rebner, saying that her marriage to Wolfgang was over and that she needed trainfare to get to her parents' new home in Arizona. Sending the money, Faulkner asked her to meet him in New Orleans. There he showed her the buildings, streets, and cafes that he remembered from his life a decade earlier. Soon he was talking not only of old memories but of the stories he was writing, the books he planned. There, in a hotel in the Vieux Carré, he and Meta became lovers again. Within a few days, however, he was back in Oxford with his manuscript; and following a short stay in Arizona, Meta was back in New York with her husband.[63] Knowing that their reunion had failed, Faulkner found himself able to work only in fits and starts. As weeks stretched into months, he was forced to make another loan against future royalties, and then to put *The Hamlet* aside in order to write stories for the *Post*. By October, when he finally mailed the last of his novel to Saxe Commins, he had decided to dedicate it to Phil Stone.[64]

The Hamlet was for Faulkner a return—to the work that he had called "Father Abraham"; to several stories that he had published, including "Spotted Horses," "The Hound," "Lizards in Jamshyd's Courtyard," and "Fool About a Horse"; and to other stories he had been telling friends for years.[65] Yet his mood was expansive. A partial explanation lay in the sense of mastery *The Hamlet* restored: he knew that he had demonstrated remarkable power both in revising and in extending his old material. But a further explanation lay in a new sense of freedom that *The Hamlet* instilled. In his stories of the Compsons and Sartorises, much of the energy and most of the grandeur belong to past generations: living without hope of independent adequacy, Young Bayard and Quentin endure for a time and then die as faint, diminished copies of ancestors they at once revere and resent. In *Pylon* and *The Wild Palms*, characters make extravagant demands and take dramatic chances in the present. Yet for a variety of reasons, including Faulkner's own affiliations and ambivalences, his control of *Pylon* and *The Wild Palms* had faltered. In Flem Snopes he possessed another character who acts with energy and purpose in the present; in addition he possessed a character whose differences happily distanced him.[66]

Morally, Flem Snopes is terrifying, as Faulkner several times remarked.[67] But he is free in ways that were for Faulkner liberating: no traditions, patterns, or models hound him. His grossest failings, including sexual impotence, scarcely trouble him. Even when he repeats man's oldest games and vices, he does not know it. Neither ancestors, predecessors, nor influences cause him anxiety. The aristocrat who once dominated Frenchman's Bend, with his dream of a mansion, a fortune, and a dynasty, is not merely dead; he is forgotten. It is not known that he was French, and it would mean nothing to Flem if it were. Left without ancestors or heritage, Flem does not even know that he lacks them. In the genealogies with which Faulkner liked to play, the Compsons and Sartorises possess great historical depth and narrowing reach, the Snopeses little depth and seemingly inexhaustible reach. Among the Compsons and Sartorises, names are passed from generation to generation, along with legends and patterns, land and guilt. Among the Snopeses, children are named for neighbors (Colonel Sartoris), or saints (St. Elmo), or politicians (Bilbo and Vardaman), or animals (Mink), or heroes (Admiral Dewey), or mail-order houses (Montgomery Ward), or poets (Virgil and Byron), or historical events (Wallstreet Panic). But they are never named for mothers and fathers, grandfathers or great-grandfathers. In this contrast we can see a crucial feature of the saga Faulkner was creating, and in it we can locate one source of the expansiveness he felt.

Although the people of Frenchman's Bend find Flem appalling, they also find him refreshing.[68] Snopes-watching had entertained Faulkner off and on for a decade, in Lafayette as well as Yoknapatawpha. In *The Hamlet* it is an activity he enjoys, as a loquacious, curious, accommodating narrative presence; and it is also an activity he shares—with Ratliff and his porch-sitting tale-swappers, and with his reader. In one episode after another, characters, author, and reader alike find themselves watching Flem: wondering what it is that he wants now, how he intends to get it, and how far he is willing to go. If we are offended that Flem feels no guilt for the crimes he commits, surely we are relieved that he possesses no records and no curiosity about the sins of his fathers, nor any incapacitating guilt for crimes he has only contemplated. Even his lack of reverence delights as well as offends. He moves through his world as a creature of convenience, playing with the rules and keeping some of the sabbaths, along with everything else he can lay his hands on. But he remains ready to burn any barn he finds, any bridge he crosses.

Since Flem's story is basically a progress or history, the story of a rise and fall, its essential element is change—specifically, a dramatic change in status and fortune. Unmistakably modern, Flem is always in motion; compared with him, the world of Frenchman's Bend seems scarcely to move at all. Whereas a history tracing change is the proper form for Flem, a journal detailing activities is the proper form for Frenchman's Bend. Although it is not especially mindful of its past or reverent toward its ancestors, Frenchman's Bend is a world of slow time. In it many things happen, but few things change rapidly—until Flem's coming.

With that coming everything changes, including money, power, and status. Before he moves on to Jefferson, Flem takes possession of most of Frenchman's Bend. Even the community's most fundamental activity—swapping or trading—is altered. In earlier Snopes stories, swapping is an entertainment as well as a business activity. Part ritual and part game, a swap depends upon certain conventions and requires certain skills; part deal, it culminates in the exchange of everything from money and notes to machines and horses. For committed traders like Ratliff and his friends, one performance always implies another: they swap tales about their swapping as often as they swap horses or mules. And in telling no less than in trading, elements of ritual and contest mingle. For Ratliff, who delights in the process of telling as well as in the resolution of the tale, every performance has a double purpose: he entertains himself and his listeners as he goes, but in the end his listeners must learn, too late, that they have been fooled by a master storyteller. Ratliff never tells his best story first, and he never botches a telling: his control of tone and complication remain flawless, even when he recounts a swap in which he has lost more than he has gained.

In the day-to-day world of Frenchman's Bend, the trades tend to be small, the tales tall. Almost everyone can afford the first, and almost everyone enjoys the second. It is this fundamental situation, along with the center of power and wealth, that Flem changes. He differs in part because he takes so little delight in the process of swapping, his interest being only in the result; in part because his interest stops with the deal itself; and in part because his deals are large, interrelated, consuming. The epitome of the coolly efficient and joyless trader, he is even stingier with words than with money. He is also ruthless and insatiable—so overwhelming that he reduces other men to watching and wondering, as he becomes the stuff of which legends are made.

The Snopeses are Faulkner's greatest comic creation. At times *The Hamlet* seems distinctly old-fashioned—in the presence of direct and full rendering; and in the absence of the kind of conscious formal experimentation we see in *The Sound and the Fury, As I Lay Dying,* and *Absalom, Absalom!*. But it is remarkable for its self-assurance, not its carelessness, and it is a strikingly original contribution to modern literature. The voice that speaks to us in it manifestly enjoys itself and clearly knows what it is about. In the end, as much as character and action, it is that voice in its varied styles that stamps itself on memory: its sense of plenitude, as though there were no end of Snopeses or of stories so long as one attends the days and works of man and possesses an inventive mind; and its sense of leisure, as though the ending toward which its larger story moves were so distant yet so inevitable that neither author nor reader need worry about it at all. Into what is basically a third-person narrative, with Flem the principal actor and Ratliff the principal watcher, Faulkner accommodates

several tall tales and a few remarkable interludes. In the process he remains a genial, accommodating, yet reserved host. Among the freedoms he
explores, two are his own: the freedom to tell his story as he sees fit, making whatever shifts seem to him proper, and the freedom to keep his distance. Both the reader, with whom he shares so many pleasant surprises,
and the porch-sitters, with whom he shares so many habits of mind and
turns of speech, remain other. Even Ratliff, for whom he clearly feels affection, he keeps at a distance.[69] Having made Ratliff central in book one,
he casually abandons him in book two. Having later moved Ratliff back
slowly toward heroism, he permits greed and vanity to make him another
of Flem's victims. Finally it is not so much by making Ratliff heroic that
Faulkner favors him as by making him private. More than any other protagonist Faulkner was ever to create, Ratliff balances involvement and detachment, which are the qualities Faulkner brings to his novel. Ratliff
moves to and fro, in and out. Never has an itinerant salesman been so af-
fable yet so ascetic. Although most people, including Ike, count with him,
none counts too much. He moves in and out of his community, living a
life that seems almost monastic and is celibate.

Several of Faulkner's greatest novels, including *The Sound and the
Fury* and *Absalom, Absalom!*, move back and forth between familial,
social, and historical contexts in which action occurs, on one side, and
minds and voices through which that action is refracted and given form,
on the other. *The Hamlet* is grounded socially and historically as firmly as
any novel Faulkner ever wrote. Unlike several of its great predecessors,
however, it does not dramatize minds and voices engaged in the crucial
acts of knowing and articulating, and so does not overtly play with its
own fictive status. Put another way, it pays little direct attention to the
operations of the mind and imagination, and therefore displays little concern for possible disparities between the categories of the mind, the processes of intellection, the structures of imagination, and the forms of
articulation, on one side, and things as they are, on the other. If we are
to understand what these omissions signify, however, we must proceed
with caution. For they imply, not simplification, but a double focus, one
that is overt and one that is not.

The overt focus is clear, and it takes *The Hamlet* in the direction of
what we usually call "realism." *The Hamlet* includes more social history,
economics, and politics than any of Faulkner's earlier novels. With mini-
mal strain, it could bear an updated version of the subtitle Stendhal gave
The Red and the Black: "A Chronicle of 1830." With no strain, it could
bear the subtitle George Eliot gave *Middlemarch*: "A Study of Provincial
Life." Had Faulkner gone on immediately to complete his trilogy, he
might have found use for "the most paradigmatic of these 'reportial'
titles": Balzac's *Etudes de moeurs au XIXe siècle*.[70] What these correlations

suggest is crucial: that *The Hamlet* owes much to the great realist enter-
prises of the nineteenth century. Like them it shows a determination to
make room in fiction for social history, economics, and politics; and like
them it is scrupulous in rendering the particularities of its social, economic, and political milieu, as well as the customs and folkways of its people.

In addition to its overt focus, however, or more aptly, through it, *The
Hamlet* displays a sense of imaginative mastery. It attends and renders not
only with scrupulous care but also with astonishing confidence. The remark Faulkner made to Robert Haas declaring himself "the best in America" constitutes an appropriate gloss on the tone of the book he was
writing. The realities to which *The Hamlet* offers an imaginative response
clearly offended as well as amused Faulkner; at times they may have be-
wildered or even threatened him. "Of the Snopes," he said, "I'm terri-
fied."[71] Yet he moves with great assurance in *The Hamlet*, as though
confident that there is no reality he cannot outdo. He maintains his distance and his control, demonstrating the amplitude, variety, and authority
of his voice. Confident of the strengths he possesses, he willingly shares
them with his characters—even the Snopeses, whom Faulkner later described as responding to rapid change and coping "with it pretty well"; and
especially Ratliff, whom he described as accepting "a change in culture, a
change in environment" without anguish or grief. As he shares control,
however, he also demonstrates it—by insisting on such interpolations,
interludes, and narrative shifts as he pleases; and by keeping his distance.
Even more than Ratliff, he is prepared to accept "what's now and do the
best he can with it because he is—possesses what you might call a moral,
spiritual eupepsia, that his digestion is good, all right, nothing alarms
him."[72]

In contrast to the control evident in *The Hamlet*, Faulkner's personal
and financial affairs were in a shambles. He had lived in 1939 on a modest
income only by exhausting the last of his reserves. Examining his situation, he hit upon a new version of an old plan, the first of several schemes
for surviving without Hollywood. He would devote six months of the next
year to writing the kind of fiction that would make money, so that he
might then have six months for writing when and what he liked. The danger of such a plan, Faulkner knew well: the *Post* still rejected more of his
stories that it accepted—often, he once remarked, for the obvious reason
that he needed money.[73]

In late January 1940, while Faulkner was reading galleys of *The Hamlet* and thinking about stories for the *Post*, Mammy Callie died. In a service
at Rowan Oak, he spoke of the devotion she had given his family and of
the affection and security she had given his childhood. For a time her
death left him with "little of heart or time either for work."[74] Soon, however, he was writing again, on stories about the Beauchamps, including one

named Molly, who clearly resembles Mammy Callie. In the weeks and months to come, he began his most concerted effort to enter the experience of the black people of Yoknapatawpha. For several weeks he wrote easily and well. In quick succession he sent Harold Ober "A Point of Law," "Gold Is Not Always," "The Fire on the Hearth," and "Pantaloon in Black."

A year before, when need of money had forced him to put *The Hamlet* aside, Faulkner had written a story called "The Old People." It was a hunting story, set at Major de Spain's camp, and it involved several hunters, including Sam Fathers, Boon Hogganbeck, and Ike McCaslin. After writing the stories about the Beauchamps, he decided to merge them with the hunting stories to form a single work centering on the black and white members of one large family. By late April, the basic structure of his next novel, his seventeenth book, had taken shape. What he had in mind was a work similar in method to *The Unvanquished*. The problem, as usual, was money. His six-month plan had worked well in one respect: he had written six stories by 15 March. But in another it had failed. As the quality of his stories increased, editors' interest in them declined. In rejecting "Pantaloon in Black," surely one of the finest stories he had written, the editors of *Collier's* described it as the strongest of his stories they had read, adding that it clearly had no place in their magazine. By late April only one of the six new stories had sold.[75]

Frustrated by repeated rejections and worried about notes that were coming due, he began trying to devise yet another plan. Otherwise he did not dare devote six months to finishing his new novel. What he wanted, he wrote Haas, was a regular income from his writing, not necessarily large but dependable. When money came in large sums, he and Estelle spent it; and when it ran out, they borrowed, assuming that a check would arrive in the next mail. Could Random House help him, he asked, by agreeing to provide a regular monthly income? They could, Haas replied, but not as much as Faulkner thought he needed.[76] Over the next several months Faulkner moved from proposal to counterproposal, from plan to plan, seeking some way of coping with his mounting debts. In June he very nearly left Random House for Viking Press; one month later, after a hectic trip to New York, he was still with Random House and still in trouble. By then it seemed to him that his situation had been worsening for so long it was certain to explode.[77]

As it turned out, it merely deteriorated—not steadily, since the *Post* and *Collier's* were as unpredictable as ever, but drastically. In 1936, 1937, and 1938, Faulkner made more than $20,000 a year; in 1941, a year after the government announced that he owed substantial back taxes, he made just over $3800.[78] In the meantime he and Estelle had mixed new efforts to economize with old habits of extravagance. Not long after he described himself as virtually bankrupt, he appeared for a quail hunt armed with a new handcrafted, custom-made shotgun and dressed in a Duxbak hunting suit.[79] In fits of self-pity he sometimes described himself as weighed down by extravagant, incompetent, and ungrateful dependents. In one remarkable letter he depicts his situation in terms of "this really quite alarming paradox": that whereas an artist "should be free even of his own economic responsibilities and with no moral conscience at all," he was damned by a strict sense of integrity and saddled with sole responsibility for a large family. Whereupon he lists more than ten men, women, and children as his dependents, not counting servants. But these spells "of raging and impotent exasperation" alternated with moments of understanding. He knew that he either ignored money, practicing and encouraging extravagance, or worried about it incessantly. Early in *The Hamlet* he had pictured Will Varner pondering the Old Frenchman's vanity, "trying to find out what it must have felt like to be the fool that would need all this." Writing to Haas, he noted that it was "probably vanity as much as anything else" that made him want to keep not only a farm in the country but "35 acres of wooded parkland inside Oxford corporate limits," and he added that it was "a larger parcel of it than anybody else in town." Still he wanted it, in part simply to humble all the relatives and fellow townsmen who had prophesied that he would "never be more than a bum."[80]

As he worried and struggled, trying to solve his problems and still keep his land, his writing suffered gravely. In the spring of 1940 he had been working well; by midyear it seemed to him that he couldn't and that he didn't even want to write. Tired yet unable to sleep, his efforts scattered. Once again he found it easier to describe projects than to write fiction: "I have a blood-and-thunder mystery novel which should sell"; "I think I have a good one . . . a sort of Huck Finn" story. As his weariness and depression deepened, his caution mounted: perhaps they could collect the magazine stories he had published since *Doctor Martino and Other Stories*.[81] Now and again a new story came, including "Go Down, Moses" in July and "Delta Autumn" in December. But as 1940 ended and 1941 began, his state of mind darkened. When the threat of bankruptcy was not worrying him, the threat of war was. He had added sailing to his diversions, which already included farming, hunting, riding, and flying. As his work slowed, such activities, particularly flying, filled more of his days. "I am flying fairly steadily," he wrote Haas in March 1941, "still very restless. Civilian Pilot Training is not enough. If I had money to take care of my family and dependents, I would try for England under my old commission. Perhaps I can yet. If not (and when and if I get money) I will try the U.S. air corps. I could navigate, or teach navigation, even if I could not fly service jobs because of my age."[82]

During the next several months he went on worrying about money and playing with his old dream of becoming a warrior. Yet by May he was writing again. A year earlier he had conceived a book made up of stories, some that he had already written, a few that he intended to write, their "general theme being relationship between white and negro races here." He had a title for it now, *Go Down, Moses*, and a clear notion of what writing it would entail. He would revise the stories he had written, assuming that "some additional material might invent itself in process." In any case he should be able to finish the job quickly.[83]

When Faulkner began *Go Down, Moses* he had the example of *The Unvanquished* in mind, not only as to size and method but as to ease and money. He did not even "want to gamble the time and effort," he said, unless he could be sure the book would make money.[84] Soon after "The Bear" started inventing itself, he decided to write a shorter, simpler version of it for the *Post*. As rumors of war multiplied, they disturbed him more and more. In December 1941, when he finished *Go Down, Moses*, he was seriously considering either entering the war or returning to Hollywood. Yet the farther he got into his project, the more it absorbed him, first, in scattered moments, and then long enough to become another major achievement. "My promise re mss. Dec 1 is already broken," he wrote on 2 December. "There is more meat in it than I thought, a section now that I am going to be proud of and which requires careful writing and rewriting to get it exactly right. I am at it steadily, and have been. If I make another definite promise, it might be broken too. But I think I will send the rest of it in by Dec. 15. Sooner of course if possible."[85]

Go Down, Moses marked, as many readers have sensed, a crucial point in Faulkner's career, in part because it was followed by a silence that lasted nearly six years, and in part because it brought much work that had preceded it to a kind of culmination. Like *The Hamlet*, it represented reworking of earlier work; and like *The Unvanquished*, it evolved from stories first conceived as commercial. In *The Unvanquished*, Faulkner had simplified his longstanding concern with history, family, inheritance, and guilt. In the juxtaposition of Bayard and Ringo he had brought his longstanding concern for black-white relations to a new point. In *The Hamlet*, having distanced himself from several familiar themes, he had extended both his sense of nature's permanence and fecundity and his exploration of society. In *Go Down, Moses* he focused on the largest and most complexly entangled of all Yoknapatawpha families, the McCaslins, and through them engaged all of his familiar preoccupations, including such explicitly moral ones as slavery and the land and man's hunger for possession and power. His new novel's ties go back, therefore, not only to *The Unvanquished* and *Light in August*, but to several other works, including *Absalom, Absalom!* For like *Absalom*, it is at once inclusive and profoundly experimental.

Since the founder of the McCaslins is another bold, ruthless conqueror of the wilderness, *Go Down, Moses* begins with the beginning. In part it is a story of a founder, Lucius Quintus Carothers McCaslin, of whom we may say what Shreve said of Thomas Sutpen: that it took him to make the rest. But *Go Down, Moses* is primarily the story of what it means to be a descendant and an inheritor. In its opening pages, Ike McCaslin comes to us as one who has inherited at birth not merely, nor even primarily, a father and a mother, but a grandfather and aunts and uncles and cousins, one of whom, "McCaslin Edmonds, grandson of Isaac's father's sister and so descended by the distaff," is "rather his brother than cousin and rather his father than either," and several of whom are descendants not only of the founder but of his slaves. In addition to scores of complicated relations, Ike has inherited property, dependents, and servants that he never desired; and he has also inherited experiences, stories, and tales "out of the old times, the old days," which he has not "participated in or even seen." The past is always with him, and it is often more vivid and alive than the present. From it come countless tales; and like the tales and talking of *Absalom, Absalom!*, they are scattered and oral, fragmentary and fluid as well as occasionally written. To the opportunity provided by these texts, both Ike and his maker respond. *Go Down, Moses* comes to us, then, as a text of a text. It is conspicuously fragmentary and cryptic, and so is engaging without being fixed.

The McCaslins, who in fact developed slowly, seem an almost deliberate culmination of Faulkner's original conception of Yoknapatawpha, so perfectly do they correspond to its fictional possibilities. A part of what we encounter formally in *Go Down, Moses* is also familiar: the manipulation of information through which Faulkner controls how and what we know, and the manipulation of understanding. Often variations and repetitions are introduced too subtly to be noticed, and often chronology is so jumbled and relations so entangled that we know more (that is, possess more facts) than we can possibly understand. By forcing us to sort facts, to piece information, to establish chronology, Faulkner forces us to participate actively in his story. One aspect of the work's suspense depends on what its characters do, another on what they understand, and yet another on what happens to them. But its suspense is tied, too, to its readers, and specifically to what we can know, understand, figure out.

In *Absalom, Absalom!* we follow Sutpen's interpreters into these activities; they make beginnings and provide models for tasks we must continue. In *Go Down, Moses* beginnings are made and models are provided, but much of the interpretive activity required to clarify what the novel begins must be carried on beyond the text by its readers. There are advantages to this, of course, particularly in the large role it creates for the reader. *Go Down, Moses* is a participatory reader's perfect text, there being no activity of mind and imagination that it does not reward. A part of this reward, as it turns out, is crucial. More than any other novel Faulkner wrote, *Go Down, Moses* defines every text as a pre-text, making the act of reading a continuation of the act of narration. If *Absalom, Absalom!* may be said to be Faulkner's paradigm of a teller's relations to his tale, *Go Down, Moses* may be said to be his paradigm of a reader's relations to his text. During the course of *Go Down, Moses* we read fragments of the cryptic text Ike has read. Like Ike we find ourselves determined, ardent, and compelled. Although our text is finally larger than his, we too move back and forth between hope and frustration, illumination and darkness, victory and defeat, finding meanings that we must then revise.

But there are disadvantages as well as advantages to shifting focus from teller and tale to reader and text—the big one being that much drama is removed from the novel. In *Absalom, Absalom!* Faulkner captured both the drama of great action and the drama of troubled telling. In it we see heroic action—colliding wills, astonishing destinies. A part of its great richness flows from its large action. But it also enacts several interpretive narrations, ranging from Miss Rosa's Biblical poetics and Mr. Compson's Classical contexts to Quentin's personal tale and Shreve's relatively detached sympathy and irony. To these narrators, Faulkner gives not only a variety of oral traditions (scores of remembered speeches, years of old tales and talking), but also a few scattered texts (a few fragments of letters). In the process he works into his dominant paradigm, of the teller's relation to his tale, an implicit paradigm, of the reader's relation to his text. He also establishes each of these as a version of the other and both as versions of the artist's relation to his work. *Go Down, Moses* represents, among other things, a variation on this complex structure: in it the dominant paradigm is that of reader and text, the implicit paradigm is that of teller and tale. But it less fully renders the dramatic potential of these paradigms than *Absalom, Absalom!* Although old Carothers McCaslin is clearly more prolific than Thomas Sutpen, he appears less prodigious. Although Isaac McCaslin is morally more exercised than the interpreters of *Absalom, Absalom!*, he is not as compelling a reader and teller. What we have, then, is a lesser greatness and a greater timidity, with the relations between the two only partially worked out.

Behind these limitations lay two principles of simplification, both of which were built into *Go Down, Moses* by virtue of the way Faulkner wrote it. It was publisher, and not author, Faulkner made clear, who thought of *Go Down, Moses* as a collection of stories, and so added *and Other Stories* to its title. For Faulkner it was "indeed a novel."[86] Still, it is composed of smaller units, and this creates problems as well as freedoms. Although the parts must contribute to a larger pattern even as they create smaller patterns of their own, they also justify jumps and gaps.

Consequently, though its historical reach is greater than that of *Absalom, Absalom!*, *Go Down, Moses* is a shorter and simpler book precisely because its structure allows so many omissions. Furthermore, insofar as it consists of units that are also stories, it approximates the "good, lucid, simple method" that Faulkner associated with short, commercial fiction.[87] The complexities of disclosure and technical experimentation we associate with Faulkner's early great novels enter *Go Down, Moses* fully only in "The Bear," the part of the novel that invented itself while he was turning his stories into a novel. Whereas the stories were written in simpler form, then complicated and enriched for the novel, "The Bear" was written in its fuller, more complicated form, then simplified into commercial fiction.[88] If this fact accounts in part for the tension some readers have sensed between "The Bear" and its context, it also suggests why *Go Down, Moses* remains partially allied with the simplifications that informed much of Faulkner's short fiction.

As though to match the simpler narrative techniques of *Go Down, Moses*, Faulkner moved toward greater thematic directness. It is clearly wrongheaded to regard Ike McCaslin as Faulkner's spokesman.[89] Ike's idealism is not only disputed by other characters, most effectively by Cass Edmonds; it is undercut by "Delta Autumn." Outside as well as within the novel, Faulkner sought to make clear that Ike was too puritanic and separatist, and therefore too easily given to renunciation and retirement: "Well, I think a man ought to do more than just repudiate," he later remarked.[90] Preoccupied with maintaining his own purity, Ike ends in virtual isolation. Knowing that his forefathers have seized the earth and claimed ownership of it and other men for profit, he makes Sam Fathers his surrogate father and then renounces his heritage. Knowing that his ancestors have permitted lust and vanity to lead them into incest, he contents himself with being "uncle to half a county and father to no one."

Besides remaining too simply an uncle, Ike becomes too reductive an imitation of Jesus. He protects his purity by living a life that is less than human. Without entanglements, including those introduced by ownership, sex, and progeny, too little of life is left. Since Ike's preoccupations correspond to the novel's themes, Faulkner presents the power of Ike's idealism. Since Ike's solutions are his own, however, and are inadequate, Faulkner dramatizes their limitations, specifically by allying them with repudiation, withdrawal, and retirement. The problem thus created is twofold, for what we have is a novelist's qualified repudiation of his character's almost total repudiation. In a curious way, moreover, this problem takes us back to the reader and his implied tasks. The novel defines every text as an ur-text and pre-text, and then requires us to begin making connections and patterns that we must then revise or even repudiate. Similarly, it gives us moral problems together with apparent solutions that it then

partially repudiates as inadequate because they are run through with repudiation. In one case we have ur-texts (both the text with which we begin and the texts we have made and then at least partially rejected) that go
on looking for a reader who can make them a text. In the other case we
have moral problems (both those with which Ike grapples and those we
create when we judge his grappling) that go on looking for a moralist who
can resolve them. Despite its apparent closure, *Go Down, Moses* is as
open-ended as *Absalom, Absalom!.*

When Faulkner mailed his typescript to Saxe Commins in mid-
December, the United States was at war, and he was badly distracted.
Still, knowing that he had written another great work, he made his in-
structions plain: "Set as written," he said at one point; "DO NOT
CHANGE PUNCTUATION NOR CONSTRUCTION," at another.[91] A
month later he sent Robert Haas a dedication—the most moving and appropriate he would ever write. *Go Down, Moses* is a novel made up of
old tales and talking about the old times and the old people as well as
the new; and it is the story of a boy from a large and storied family who,
being a kind of orphan, must seek a sponsor of his own. More directly
than any of his earlier novels, it explores familiar themes such as "honor,
truth, pity, consideration, the capacity to endure well grief and misfortune and injustice," in terms of individuals who try to observe and adhere
to them.[92] In dedicating it to Caroline Barr, Faulkner recalled not only
the rare length but the rare nobility of her life: that despite the injustice
done her, she had given his "family a fidelity without stint or calculation
of recompense"; and that recognizing the unspoken needs of a small boy,
she had given him "immeasurable devotion and love."

During the early months of 1942 Faulkner worked sporadically on
stories that would eventually become a part of *Knight's Gambit*. But he
was soon too distracted to work. He had been living on credit for months.
Having cashed in his last insurance policy, he had no remaining reserves.
If "I were sued by anyone, all my property except my home would go and
my daughter and mother and wife would have nothing." It was time, he
thought, for a change of scene. Perhaps if he could find a place free of
hounding creditors, he could work again.[93]

One of the avenues he saw before him led to Washington and war, the
other to Hollywood and movies. Following the first, he went to Washington, hoping to secure a commission. But there was no way he could qual-
ify, at age forty-four, for the kind of service he wanted—a plane and
combat, preferably over France. Hollywood, on the other hand, suddenly
wanted him. As early as October 1938 Faulkner had begun exploring the
possibility of returning to Hollywood. When no offers followed, he began
to suspect that the studios had become wary of him. In May 1941, when
a young agent named William Herndon wrote to say that he could arrange

a contract, Faulkner told him to see what he could do, then went back to work on *Go Down, Moses.* A year later, when Warner Brothers suddenly expressed interest, Faulkner was pleased as well as surprised.[94]

In the weeks that followed, as negotiations became more confused and acrimonious, the pleasure faded. The problem was simple: Faulkner was being represented in Hollywood by two agents, William Herndon, who had contacted Faulkner directly, and H. N. Swanson, who handled all of Harold Ober's West Coast affairs.[95] From this basic situation, confusion spread to touch almost everything. Swanson was clearly the better agent, and his connection with Faulkner was of a more usual sort. But Herndon, who was young and determined, had made the first contact with Warner Brothers. When it appeared that Swanson was about to arrange a contract, Herndon not only accused Faulkner of having "failed in integrity," he also threatened to "cause trouble." Faulkner's first response was anger; he resented both the accusation and the threat. Soon, however, he began to feel that Herndon, however naive, mistaken, and incompetent, was sincere.[96] Asking for the good wishes of Swanson and Ober, he agreed to accept Herndon's terms of $300 per week rather than Swanson's of $500. Yet, even to a man chronically in need of money, the difference in salary meant less than other provisions in the contract. By going with Herndon, Faulkner had given Warner Brothers options totalling seven years.[97]

NINE 1942-1950

The Dark Years and Beyond

Faulkner arrived in Hollywood in late July 1942. Soon after, he learned that the *Post* had accepted "Shingles for the Lord," a comic story about country people and a country church. It was welcome news. There had been too many rejections, and his need of money was acute. He had come to California burdened with a carefully organized ledger containing the names of his creditors. Since he was not "quite a boat's length ahead of the sheriff," he needed to save money and pay off his debts.[1]

Over the next several years he did just that, but he also stopped publishing. It was six years before he finished another novel, and seven before he published another story in a major magazine. He had suffered other dry spells, when he was worried about money or was having trouble getting Hollywood out of his system. In 1932, following publication of *Light in August* and his first trip to Hollywood, he had struggled for several months, unable to complete anything. But the drought that began in 1942 was so long and intense as to seem fundamentally different. About it we know several things: that it came just after he had completed work of authentic originality and greatness; that he entered it reluctantly; that he struggled against it repeatedly; and that it marked him permanently. Since Faulkner had worked hard all of his life, he may well have needed a rest; certainly he may be said to have earned one. But he was not a man who knew how to live without work. Even his hobbies he enjoyed mainly as a change of pace, which meant that the pleasure they gave him, though genuine, was not independent. Without the prior satisfaction of a long morning's work, an afternoon of sun and woods and horses lost its shimmer. The neglect into which he had fallen made it difficult for him to take pleasure in what he had done. Looking back he saw a long string of books, most of which were out of print. But, neglect aside, he had always been more interested in what he was doing than in what he had done. To a surprising extent, particularly for one to whom the past was so important and for whom work was so necessary, he had also been an "occasional" novelist: many of his novels—ranging in time from *Mosquitoes* to *Go Down, Moses* and in quality from *Pylon* to *The Sound and the Fury*—had represented his response to immediate experiences or crises. Most of his life he had learned by going where he had to go. The larger design of his work was more discovered than willed; it was something he found waiting for him in the words he had written. All of his life he had gone along finding—in rejections, frustrations, and disappointments, in striking reversals of fortune, failed romances, and untimely deaths—contexts that hurt him into fiction. And despite a thousand distractions, most of them having to do with family, women, and money, he had gone along finding the only other thing that he required: a room of his own and long hours in which to write.

Although Hollywood and World War Two provided many distractions, their impact on Faulkner had less to do with the distractions they brought than with the power they displayed. Although Faulkner disliked Hollywood and deplored the war, he found both compelling. Beside them mere words seemed not so much inadequate as futile. What came soon and stayed long was the sense that time was running out—the sense that he was doomed to live and die without leaving any significant "mark on this our pointless chronicle."[2] For many years he had believed that he could master any experience and outdo any reality, however bewildering or threatening, with nothing but solitude, words, and the power of his imagination. In some works he had stressed the reality of his own imagined worlds; in others he had played with the fictive status of those worlds. But in both kinds of works—recently in *The Hamlet* and *Go Down, Moses*—he had moved beyond worry about the artificiality of art to faith in its power. Now, with time and energy running out, he found himself at yet another critical juncture, only to discover that circumstances were "bad for writing."[3] This experience, as it turned out, changed everything, including his

writing. From it he emerged as a more didactic or at least prophetic novelist and as a more outspoken citizen, particularly about race and war. What
is curious about this development, however, aside from its helping him to
gain needed visibility and recognition, is the way it drew upon two very
different literary experiences. When it finally came, his new work—especially *A Fable*—would reflect the influence not only of skills acquired in
Hollywood but also of attitudes that dated back to his early career as a
poet.

When he learned the details of the Herndon contract his first impulse
was to run. "It is a long series of options, 13-13-26-26, then a series of 52
week options," he wrote Harold Ober. But he had little choice and knew
it. Within a week he had signed, believing the assurances given by Warner
Brothers's representative James Geller that the studio would negotiate a
new contract later, permitting him to work "in Oxford practically for
whatever periods of time I desire." By the time he signed, he was living in
a room at the Highland, an inexpensive residential hotel, and was working
with Robert Buckner on a film about Charles De Gaulle. The regimen he
set for himself was simple: he planned to work hard in order to keep his
job and improve his contract; and he planned to live frugally in order to
save money and pay his debts. At times the routine grated. It could be, he
said, "a damned dull life." But he took satisfaction in seeing his debts reduced, and he enjoyed seeing old friends, particularly Meta Rebner.[4]

Shortly after her meeting with Faulkner in New Orleans in April 1939,
Meta Rebner had returned to New York, hoping to mend her marriage.
The next January she and Wolfgang moved to California, still hoping to
make a new start. There she resumed her career, and there, following a
brief recovery, her marriage disintegrated. Hearing of her return to New
York, Faulkner wrote, combining fond memories with bitterness. What he
needed, he said, was a new woman, "a physical spittoon"; yet what he had
known with Meta made other women impossible. Later, informed by Meta
that she had moved to California and that her marriage was collapsing,
he replied that he too might be returning to Hollywood. Later still, he
wrote saying that despite false starts and delays, he was coming. Then, late
one July afternoon, Meta pulled up in front of her apartment to find him
sitting there "cross-legged . . . his luggage stacked neatly on the steps."[5]

Five years had passed since the two of them walked down Hollywood
Boulevard to drink and eat at Musso Frank's, and many things had changed,
including Faulkner's age and status. In 1937 he had still seemed young
and he had been making $1250 per week; in 1942 "he had aged percepti-
bly" (his hair had turned gray and his eyes had acquired an "old guarded
eagle look"), and he was making $300. Ignoring what they could not alter,
they tried to begin again "as though no time at all had passed," only to
discover that their life together "was not the same and could never again

be as it was." Hoping to recapture what they had lost, Meta suggested that they try living together; wanting to protect what they had once known, Faulkner replied that attempting it in Hollywood "would be a grievous error." What they needed was a timeless place, "ante-bellum and stately," where they might "be faultness one to the other." Once, believing in such a possibility, he had attempted it. But having had too much of marriage, he had no intention of trying anything like it again, especially not in the crude, tinsel world he knew as Hollywood. As fastidious if less ardent lovers, and as loyal friends, they might recommence their love without damaging the memory of their great romance.[6] At first they spent long hours together, eating, drinking, and making love. Much of the time they talked—about old times; about Jill; about Meta's work and Faulkner's dismal contract; about his recent attempts to become a soldier; about the books he had written and hoped to write. But having resumed their "night-after-night pattern," they soon abandoned it. Both of them needed more independence. Meta's career as a script clerk was in full swing now, and she wanted to protect it. Faulkner liked visiting Dorothy Parker and spending evenings with other writers at Musso Frank's, Preston Sturges' Players on Sunset Boulevard, or LaRue's.[7] Occasionally he joined Howard Hawks and Clark Gable on hunting or fishing expeditions. Now and then he went to zany parties with Ruth Ford—a young actress he had first met when she was a coed dating Dean Faulkner. Later, hoping to become her lover, he would ask to be "promoted," but for the time being he took pleasure in being her "gentleman friend."[8]

At the studio he worked on a series of scripts, most of them having to do with the war. His first assignment was junked when De Gaulle fell into disfavor in London and Washington; but since Hollywood was turning out movies at a record rate, there were plenty of scripts to go around. With *The De Gaulle Story* still in progress, he helped Howard Hawks briefly on *Air Force*. With De Gaulle abandoned, he moved on to *Liberator Story, Life and Death of a Bomber,* and *Battle Cry*. Since Jack Warner treated all writers the same, with contempt ("schmucks with Underwoods," he called them), the writers in The Ward shared an enemy as well as a calling.[9] Faulkner found most of his coworkers, including Richard Aldington, Stephen Longstreet, and Tom Job, friendly and agreeable. Frederick Faust, who was better known as Max Brand, turned out to be a prodigious drinker as well as an admirer of Faulkner's fiction. Jo Pagano and especially Albert Isaac (Buzz) Bezzerides, author of a novel called *The Long Haul*, became lasting friends. Some Hollywood writers, notably Jules Furthman, cared nothing about literature and so were ignorant of Faulkner's larger gifts. To them he seemed inept. But Faulkner respected good craftsmanship, even in Hollywood and even when the craftsman seemed benighted. Besides, he was aware of his limitations as a screenwriter. What he did best was the kind of patching or doctoring that Hawks gave him to do. Focused on a particular scene, he was less likely to write the long narrative sequences and the long, uninterrupted speeches that other screenwriters came to think of as his signature. Since he found the war absorbing, he found most of his assignments at least mildly interesting. A few turned out to be engaging. If he were ever going to work on movies, the time at least seemed right. "I feel pretty well," he wrote, "sober, am writing to the satisfaction of the studio."[10]

As the first thirteen-week period neared its end, he waited, hoping that the studio would make good its promise by giving him a new contract at a fair salary. When Jack Warner used the old contract to bind him for another period at a small raise, Faulkner shut himself in his office and drank himself into unconsciousness. Secreted out of the studio by Buzz and Meta, he was back at work within a few days, grateful that his friends had saved his job. But he was bitter as well as relieved. He knew that Jack Warner was treating him shabbily, and he felt "the indignity of making far less money" than other writers of smaller literary reputation and similar movie experience. His acute need of money, which so limited his choices, compounded his resentment. Under his present contract he could keep his creditors at bay but would be years paying off his debts.[11]

Seeking some relief, he asked for a month's leave so that he could spend Christmas at Rowan Oak, a request Jack Warner granted on condition that he continue working on *Liberator Story*.[12] Given a little more money than they had come to expect, he and his family had a good Christmas. His stepson, Malcolm, and his nephew James Faulkner would soon be leaving Oxford for Europe or the Pacific, and he had wanted to talk with them before they left. Most of all he enjoyed seeing Jill, whom he had never got over missing. The only bad news came from Random House, informing him that his royalties for 1942 totaled $300. But even this merely confirmed what he already knew: that he was going to have to resign himself "to being a part-time script writer at least."

Knowing that he must leave Rowan Oak in order to have it to come "back to," Faulkner returned to Hollywood hoping to save more money and shorten his stay. By January he was planning a several months' leave beginning in April. Perhaps then he could get back to his own work.[13] When April and May passed without a leave, his resolve wavered and his drinking increased. During most of June he moved back and forth between dependence on doctors and nurses and dependence on friends like Buzz, Meta, and Jo Pagano. Sick of Hollywood and Warner Brothers, he half hoped the studio would let his contract lapse. In July, however, despite his record of June, the studio took up another option—this time for fifty-two weeks at $400 per week. Buoyed by a decision he had dreaded yet needed, he went back to work with Hawks on *Battle Cry*, an assignment abandoned in April. From time to time Hawks had talked of setting himself up as an independent producer and hiring Faulkner as a writer. Soon the script Faulkner had earlier deserted struck him as a crucial test. If he could satisfy both the studio and the director, he wrote Estelle, he could accomplish two things at once: he could free himself "from the seven-year contract" that Warner Brothers now promised to destroy as soon as he had written a successful picture; and he could establish himself with Hawks and thus relieve himself of having "to worry again about going broke temporarily."[14]

As Faulkner's spirits soared, Estelle began to suspect "that Mr. Hawks must have his old secretary back," though by now, she added, she neither begrudged him his pleasure nor found the idea of Meta very frightening.[15] Although Estelle was right about Meta Doherty's presence, she was wrong about the basis of Faulkner's enthusiasm. For several weeks Warner and Hawks had gone along arguing about money. In early August, a few weeks after Faulkner's letter to Estelle, outlining another version of his old hope of coupling freedom and financial security, Hawks quit. Hearing that *Battle Cry* had been abandoned, Faulkner headed for the nearest bar. Trying to skirt a collapse, he requested a leave. He wanted six months, and he was willing to take it without pay. By mid-August he was free, though the term stated was for three months rather than six.[16]

Faulkner had tried to work in California, both in his room at the Highland and on an adjoining terrace. He wanted and needed "to begin a new novel" and write new stories. In letters to Harold Ober and Robert Haas, he mentioned projects from time to time. In November 1942 he sent Harold Ober "a 3-page poem, 'Old Ace,'" about young pilots and old.[17]

> There's still a patrol for you to lead
> Of young men who, like us in our old time,
> Ask only of death that dying's no new sell-out
> By the new usurers of the same old wrongs and shames.[18]

But war and movies about war, together with Herndon and contracts, dominated his correspondence even as they filled his life. For years he had gone along needing and making excursions. But now his excursions took him to a strange land and lasted too long. Back in Oxford he took up familiar tasks as though hoping that they would help him to recapture some forgotten rhythm. He supervised needed repairs on Rowan Oak and looked after livestock, crops, and equipment at Greenfield Farm. In an interview with the Oxford *Eagle* he suggested that he had been writing all along—that he had merely stopped publishing because his contract gave everything he wrote to Warner Brothers.[19] But even as he talked of new stories and a new novel, his anxiety deepened. Early in his life he had

worried about substituting words for deeds; now he worried about substituting planned words for written ones.

By late September, when he finally got back to writing, he wrote in a
style and on a subject that owed much to Hollywood. About the time
Hawks walked out on *Battle Cry*, Faulkner started talking with Henry
Hathaway, a director, and William Bacher, a producer, about a project
that had nothing to do with Warner Brothers. In these conversations they
reached several agreements: first, that they would collaborate in making a
movie based on the World War One legend of the Unknown Soldier; second, that they might tie that legend to the Passion Story; third, that
Faulkner could write, in addition to the script they would share, a novel
or play of his own; and fourth, that he would write a synopsis early and a
full script later, after he was free of Warner Brothers. "I am working on a
thing now," Faulkner wrote Harold Ober. "It will be about 10-15 thousand words. It is a fable, an indictment of war perhaps, and for that reason
may not be acceptable now. I am writing it out in a sort of synopsis."[20]

It took Faulkner ten years to finish the work begun in 1943, and nearly that long to name it *A Fable*. Before completing it he learned to think
of it as his masterpiece. Writing it proved difficult beyond anything he
could have imagined. Over the years he accumulated a mass of deleted
pages, including revised or rejected versions of virtually every scene in the
book; and he experienced both great weariness and great exaltation. "If I
were only older, and had the big book behind me," he wrote Saxe Commins, "I would be almost tempted to break the pencil here and throw it
away."[21] This contains, he said to a startled acquaintance, indicating an
overfull briefcase, "the manuscript of the book that is possibly the greatest of our time."[22] Yet, despite the tortured writing and the shifting
moods, the basic character of the work was set early. More than any other
book he had written, including *Go Down, Moses*, his new work was a
dramatization of ideas: what he had in mind from the beginning was
something deliberate, abstract, and didactic, and therefore more allegorical than analogical.[23]

In all of these respects the new project reflected a shift in Faulkner's
basic conception of his role as an artist. The war, he said, was "bad for writing." It usurped energy and preempted attention, leaving art nothing. And
it had come at the wrong time, when he was "too young to be unmoved"
yet too old to fight. He felt both the drama of the event and the need it
could answer. It is a strange thing, he wrote his stepson, "how a man, no
matter how intelligent, will cling to the public proof of his masculinity: his
courage and endurance, his willingness to sacrifice himself for the land which
shaped his ancestors." Longing to prove that he could do "as much as anyone else," yet knowing that he was too old, he came reluctantly to admit
that he would never know the glory of answering the trumpet call.[24]

Following another elusive war he had concocted stories designed to demonstrate a hero's willingness and appropriate a hero's glory. Over the years he had remained uneasy with those concoctions, even as he had remained unwilling, or unable, to surrender them. To one of his family's young warriors he made a gift of his R.A.F. pip, explaining that he had lost his dog tag in Germany. Perhaps his nephew's commanding officer would let him wear the pip as a good-luck charm when he learned that it came from a godfather who had been an R.A.F. man. But it was not on stories or tokens of past glory that he was counting; it was on a small role during and a large role after the war. While younger men were making "the liberty sure first, in the field," he would "stay in civilian clothes to look after things for us when everybody comes back home again." Although he was too old to fight, he could make films celebrating heroes and write letters advising, preparing, and encouraging them. The ones he wrote to his stepson and nephew tended, as he noted, to be "long . . . and preachified too." Still, he had never thought mere caretaking an adequate task, and his deeper intention focused on a day beyond the war. "Then perhaps the time of the older men will come" again.[25]

The question, of course, was what older men might then do, particularly such a one as he, who could not "do anything but use words." The answer he hit upon had to do with two fundamental changes he foresaw, or forehoped, one of which was familiar, the other surprising, and both of which he spelled out in letters to Malcolm Franklin, who had become his "dear son." "We are fighting, as always, the long battalioned ghosts of old wrongs and shames that each generation of us both inherits and creates. We will win this one, then we must, we must, clean the world's house so that man can live in peace in it again. I believe we will." If this, the first change he anticipated, seems obvious, a World War Two version of a World War One hope, the other seems almost visionary. Having become what the first great war was supposed to be, a prelude to peace, the second great war must also usher in a new era of racial justice. A squadron of Negro pilots, he wrote, had finally persuaded Congress to allow them to risk their lives for their country. While they were doing that in Pantelleria, "a mob of white men and white policemen killed 20 negroes in Detroit. Suppose you and me and a few others of us lived in the Congo, freed seventy-seven years ago by ukase; of course we cant live in the same apartment hut with the black folks, nor always ride in the same car nor eat in the same restaurant, but we are free because the Great Black Father says so." Then there is a war, and at "last we persuade the Great Black Father to let us fight too," only to be told that while we were fighting, twenty of our people had "been killed by a mixed mob of civilians and cops. . . . What would you think?" "A change will come out of this war," he continued. "If it doesn't, if the politicians and the people who run this country are not forced to make good the shibboleth they glibly talk about freedom, liberty, human rights, then you young men who live through it will have wasted your precious time, and those who dont live through it will have died in vain."[26]

Although Faulkner knew that he would have to wait out the war, he had no intention of waiting out the changes it would make possible. In the day beyond the war, he wrote Malcolm, there "will be a part for me, who cant do anything but use words, in the re-arranging of the house so that all mankind can live in peace in it." Then, he had written earlier, "the time of the older men will come, the ones like me who are articulate in the national voice, who are too old to be soldiers, but are old enough and have been vocal long enough to be listened to, yet are not so old that we too have become another batch of decrepit old men looking stubbornly backward at a point 25 or 50 years in the past."[27]

Faulkner's view of the war as a kind of interim in which art had no place is less surprising, finally, than his sense of it as a kind of personal watershed—as an event that marked the end of the kind of fiction he had written and the beginning of the kind of fiction he was now attempting. In October 1943 he extended his leave in order to finish the synopsis he had begun in September. By January, when he began revising it, his conception of it had changed. He now thought of it more as a book than as a movie, and he wanted more time to work on it. Still, the didacticism of his conception remained undiminished. The work he had described in September as "a fable, an indictment of war perhaps," he described in January as an argument, the gist of which was that man dare not waste his "final chance" to secure peace.[28]

Anticipating changes the war would make possible, Faulkner worried that it might outlast his endurance. He was prepared to move from short stories and novels toward exempla and fables, from indirectness toward directness, from modes of fiction that made "nothing happen" toward modes that were at least arguments for change. But he felt that time was running out. "I have a considerable talent, perhaps as good as any coeval," he wrote Harold Ober. "But I am 46 now. So what I will mean soon by 'have' is 'had.'" If the war presented one problem ("It's too bad I lived now though"), money presented another: circumstances forced him to give too much time to making it. Yet he already anticipated a more serious problem: that writing his fable would be painfully difficult not simply because he was older and wrote less rapidly, but because he was trying to master a literary mode that was less congenial with his talent.[29]

With the revised synopsis finished, it was time to go back to "the salt mine." Although he had hoped at one point to prolong his leave and continue his fable, he still made the journey West with less dread than he had felt a year before. The longer break had helped, particularly by enabling him to get back to work of his own. Perhaps he could gradually work out a new version of his old six-month plan. If he knew that by staying in Hollywood he could have equal time in Oxford, he might find the journeys less disruptive. What he wanted was some way of keeping the two scenes of his life "locked off" from one another so that the work he had to do would not contaminate the work he wanted to do.[30]

Soon after his return Faulkner exchanged his room at the Highland for a spare room with Buzz Bezzerides and his family, in a pleasant area just north of Santa Monica. Although the house was several miles from the studio and he had no car, living there worked well. He liked commuting with Buzz, he had pleasant surroundings, and he felt less lonely. For several months work, too, went better. After a rocky start, when it looked as though he might be made to work with Hal Wallis on a movie about Robert Lee Scott and the Flying Tigers, he began writing a script based on Ernest Hemingway's *To Have and Have Not.*[31]

Even with Jules Furthman as a collaborator Faulkner found *To Have and Have Not* the best situation Hollywood had offered him since "Turn About." Although it was financed by Warner Brothers, the venture belonged to Hawks. To demonstrate his independence, he simply stopped work when Jack Warner approached the set. Hawks preferred crews that worked hard yet had fun, and he had a knack for gathering them. Since he liked to improvise as he went along, his writers worked closely with him and his crew. Meta Doherty was there, and so were Humphrey Bogart, Lauren Bacall, and Hoagy Carmichael. Years later Faulkner expressed particular admiration for Humphrey Bogart, the star of *To Have and Have Not.* But he enjoyed drinking and talking with Hoagy Carmichael, and watching and working with Lauren Bacall. "She's like a young colt," he told Ruth Ford.[32]

By May, when his work on *To Have and Have Not* ended, Faulkner had rented a room in a private home closer to the studio. Besides feeling that he had imposed too long on the Bezzerides family, he had grown restless. Since his debts had decreased, he wanted to spend more time at Musso Frank's, talking, eating, and drinking with friends—not only with Meta but with Jean and Jo Pagano, a Warner Brothers writer who had left Colorado hoping to become a novelist; with Owen and Betty Francis, who had come to California hoping to make enough money to return to New Orleans; and with Edmund Kohn, an artist who had worked his way out of the tenements of Philadelphia and Brooklyn. In some ways it was an improbable group. But its members shared several stray interests as well as a few obvious ones. Owen Francis had been a friend of Thomas Wolfe, a writer Faulkner always overpraised. Like Faulkner, Edmund Kohn liked to recite Shakespeare. Only Jo Pagano and Edmund Kohn seem to have read much of Faulkner's fiction, yet all of the group liked to hear Faulkner

talk of home, of the Snopeses and their schemes, of the Mississippi woods
and their deer, bear, and coon. Years later Betty Francis remembered his
telling scores of "little creature stories" about the homes and habits of
small wood animals. They were precious and funny stories, she said,
"wonderful in the real sense of the word," particularly to someone suffering from the malaise of life in Hollywood.[33]

Faulkner's work on *To Have and Have Not* earned him "strong respect
around the studio," and he emerged from it collected. Still, as he began a
series of new assignments, with people like Jerry Wald on scripts called
The Damned Don't Cry and *The Adventures of Don Juan*, his old anxieties mounted and his control failed. He had come back to Hollywood in
January, hoping to write. In mid-May his manuscript remained unchanged.
The frantic efforts of movies to justify themselves "in a time of strife and
terror" did nothing so much as redouble his feeling that art was one of the
things suspended for the duration. Yet his own dependence on writing remained: he would never be able to stop it for long without feeling lost and
fearing that he might never find his way back. "When and if I get at it
again," he told Harold Ober, "I will write you." But he made no promises,
invited no queries.[34]

Not even hope of renewed recognition relieved his depression. Early in
May he began an answer to a letter from Malcolm Cowley. Cowley planned to write a long essay designed to help "redress the balance between
[Faulkner's] worth and his reputation," and he wanted to know whether
Faulkner would cooperate by meeting him and answering "questions
about his life and his aims." Faulkner had reservations about "the biography
part," but he would be happy to meet and talk, and he was grateful. "I
would like very much to have the piece done," he said. Then, as though
glimpsing what the fateful correspondence might mean, he went on to
suggest the hope he retained despite the weariness he felt. "I think (at 46)
that I have worked too hard at my (elected or doomed, I don't know
which) trade, with pride but I believe not vanity, with plenty of ego but
with humility too . . . to leave no better mark on this our pointless chronicle than I seem to be about to leave."[35]

It took a fortunate distraction as well as considerable will to ward off
a major collapse. The distraction came in the spring, when Faulkner began
looking for an apartment large enough for him, Estelle, and Jill. In late
April he found one. It was small and had no yard, he wrote, but it was "in
a quiet, convenient *not Hollywood* neighborhood." It would be a big
change from Rowan Oak, but they might like it, and at least they would
be together. Feeling betrayed by Faulkner's decision to bring Estelle and
Jill to California, Meta Doherty had stopped seeing him. And since Faulkner was shifting from one boring assignment to another, from *Fog over
London* to *Stranger in Our Midst*, and yet remained unable to write fiction,

he had more free time than in any summer he could remember. During June, July, and August of 1944 Estelle in a minor way and Jill in a major one filled his life. He was making one-third the salary he had made in 1936 and 1937, when they had rented a spacious house, complete with servants' quarters for a cook and a chauffeur. Now they had a small apartment, no servants, and no car. Yet their life was less tortured as well as less glamorous. They went to a few parties, made the usual sightseeing tours, and ate out often. On June 24 they celebrated Jill's eleventh birthday. Over the next several weeks she took riding lessons at the school Elizabeth Taylor was attending. On scattered weekdays and most weekends she rode at Jack House's Glendale Stables, once with her mother, often with her father.[36]

Since it was riding that made Jill happy that summer, it was riding that saved Faulkner's job. Bored with his work, he was prepared to quit it and take Jill home if she became unhappy. But the riding also brought Jill closer to her father. Regretting that they had been separated so often and knowing that she was nearing the end of childhood, Faulkner treasured their time together that summer. Although his own childhood had been punctuated with disappointment and pain, he continued to look back on it with tenderness. In the years that had come after it he had searched without success for rules that seemed to work and for forms that did not simplify in advance. Now more and more he was haunted by the sense not merely that his powers were declining but also that he was lost. Looking backward through Jill to childhood, he recalled the only time when life had seemed to him so whole and blessed as to be acceptable without the imaginative tamings that he had once termed periodic faceliftings but that he most often thought of as sublimations of the actual. Studying a photograph made by Buzz of Jill striding out of the surf, he saw not a world that lay before her like a dream but a world that was already fading. Although he knew that Jill's childhood had been troubled, he still thought of childhood as the best part of life. "It's over very soon," he said to his friend. "This is the end of it. She'll grow into a woman."[37]

Had Faulkner been given another poor assignment he probably could not have tolerated the departure of Jill and Estelle for Oxford and another school year. From May to August he had moved from script to script, finding nothing that engaged him. In August he began writing with Hawks on Raymond Chandler's *The Big Sleep*. Although Jules Furthman received partial credit for the screenplay, Faulkner's major collaborator was a young writer named Leigh Brackett, with whom he worked easily. Since he still tended to write dialogue that "did not fit comfortably the actors' mouths," as his young collaborator later put it, they had to make many changes on the set. But Hawks liked it that way, and Humphrey Bogart and Lauren Bacall had grown accustomed to it.[38]

So long as filming of *The Big Sleep* continued, Faulkner stayed sober enough to work hard. In mid-November, when it ended, he virtually collapsed. He was living with friends again, in part to cut his expenses, in part to relieve his loneliness, and he was also riding horses occasionally. But nothing seemed to help, not even Meta Doherty. Hearing that Estelle had left and that Faulkner was drinking too hard, Meta had come to see him. Working together on *The Big Sleep*, seeing each other regularly, they had recaptured a part of what they had shared "at the beginning."[39] But he had been away from Rowan Oak almost a year now, and away from writing. "Sometimes I think if I do one more treatment or screenplay, I'll lose whatever power I have as a writer," he said. In July Malcolm Cowley had written, reminding him of what he already knew: that in publishing circles his name was mud. On 29 October 1944, in the first of three essays, Cowley prefaced his call for a major reappraisal of Faulkner's achievement by reminding his readers that only one of Faulkner's seventeen books remained in print.[40]

With loneliness and depression crowding upon him, Faulkner began drinking more heavily. His friends, particularly Buzz, Meta, and Jo Pagano, did what they could. Knowing how much he hated the places he called ovens and jails, they tried to take care of him themselves. At work they covered for him; in the evenings they tried to hide or ration his whiskey. Still there were times when he drank so much that they had to take him to one of the Valley's private hospitals. Recognizing the self-destruction implicit in his friend's drinking, Buzz tried to dissuade him. "Don't go that way, Bill," he said. "You're too precious." But neither help nor appeal could deter Faulkner. Finally he asked for a leave. He needed out, and he was willing to settle for a three-month suspension without pay. If they would let him get started on his way back to Mississippi, he would even agree to do additional rewriting on his own time, free of charge.[41]

By 15 December he was back at Rowan Oak, and within a week his spirits lifted. Writing to Cowley to express gratitude and answer queries, he also voiced frustration and bitterness. The South, he said, was not particularly important to him; it was simply the place he knew, neither better nor worse than another. Life, he continued, "is a phenomenon but not a novelty, the same frantic steeplechase toward nothing everywhere and man stinks the same stink no matter where in time." Yet the sense of entrapment was gone. Assuming that he would be able to extend his leave to six months, he felt not only "free of Hollywood" but in control of it. "I can work at Hollywood 6 months, stay at home 6, am used to it now and have movie work locked off into another room."[42]

By January he was working again on his fable, having arranged with Random House for an advance of "say 2 or 3 thousand if I need it, about March." Through most of his career, he wrote his publishers, he had been "a poet without education, who possessed only instinct and a fierce conviction and belief in the worth and truth of what he was doing, and an illimitable courage for rhetoric (personal pleasure in it too: I admit it) and who knew and cared for little else." Now he was "writing and rewriting, weighing every word." The change meant that writing would take longer now, a fact that bothered him, but he thought of it as signifying new maturity: "I have grown up at last," he said.[43]

In fact, his new work showed a fundamental shift of a different kind. It was as though the parts of his writing that had been not so much subordinate as predominantly preconscious had become all conscious. In a letter to Malcolm Cowley he noted that he had always "tried to present characters rather than ideas," even in what were structurally his most complex and experimental novels. Cowley had been right about *Absalom, Absalom!*, he said: "I was first of all (I still think) telling what I thought was a good story, and I believed Quentin could do it better than I in this case. But I accept gratefully all your implications, even though I didn't carry them consciously and simultaneously in the writing of it." In his fable, on the other hand, he was carrying the ideas and symbolism consciously, simultaneously, deliberately at every step.[44]

Several years later, shortly before he had finished *A Fable*, Faulkner depicted Sherwood Anderson's career—"his whole biography"—as revealed in one anecdote or parable: a purported dream in which Anderson pictured himself "walking for miles along country roads, leading a horse which he was trying to swap for a night's sleep—not for a simple bed for the night, but for the sleep itself." In Faulkner's explication of Anderson's dream, the horse becomes the world that Anderson could never wholly accept, "his own America," and Anderson's life becomes one in which he has offered "with humor and patience and humility, but mostly with patience and humility, to swap" the world given him "for his own dream of purity and integrity and hard and unremitting work and accomplishment, of which *Winesburg, Ohio* and *The Triumph of the Egg* had been symptoms and symbols."[45]

Faulkner's explication of Anderson's dream-parable is interesting in several ways, one of which—its usefulness in understanding the labored style of his own poetry—I have already noted. But Faulkner's picture of Anderson's "fumbling for exactitude" also bears a large relevance to Faulkner's practice in writing *A Fable*. Anderson worked, Faulkner said, "laboriously and tediously and indefatigably. . . . It was as if he said to himself: 'This anyway will, shall, must be invulnerable.' It was as though he wrote not even out of the consuming unsleeping appeaseless thirst for glory . . . but for what to him was more important and urgent: not even for mere truth, but for purity, the exactitude of purity." Earlier, in moving from poetry toward fiction, Faulkner had learned to believe in the value and the implicit form of what was waiting within him to be said. Now, in writing *A Fable*, he was "weighing every word" as though convinced that if "he kept the style pure and intact" it would be enough.[46] What he thought of as new maturity accordingly bears a striking resemblance to his practice as a poet. Once again he was committing himself to extreme purity and deliberate universality, qualities that are probably even less compatible with fiction than with poetry.

The results were several, the big one being that Faulkner seemed to be working in two different modes without having first settled the issue of priority and direction. In all of his fiction realistic and fabulous elements mingle: throughout it we encounter recurring themes as well as recurring scenes; improbable, even incredible events as well as remarkable specificity and circumstantiality. But even his most abstract pieces of fiction—"Carcassonne," for example—began with obsessive images rather than big ideas; and his greatest work had begun with compelling characters (Caddy Compson, Thomas Sutpen) as well as obsessive images (Caddy climbing the tree, Sutpen knocking at the door of the mansion). Waiting in such characters and scenes he had discovered actions that effected explorations and yielded meanings. But the givens of his new work—the legend of the Unknown Soldier, the Passion story, and the notion of combining the two into "a fable, an indictment of war perhaps"—were so fundamentally different as to entail a reversal of his characteristic fictional process. It was as though he had begun trying to transmute the apocryphal into the actual. Once again he found himself straining not only for stylistic perfection but for moral directness, not only for purity but for prophetic relevance.

Almost the epitome of deliberateness, the writing proved not so much slow as inconclusive: "It will take some time yet to finish the mss. It may be my epic poem. . . . I had about 100,000 words, rewrote them down to about 15,000 now." From so deliberate a process, something like direct examination of self and career seemed to follow almost as a matter of course. Like the writing, the examination proved slow, painful, and never more than partially conclusive. Uncertain about the worth of what he had accomplished as well as what he was doing, he knew only that he felt trapped and that time was running out. Always in danger of having either "to pot boil, or go back to the salt mine," he circled again through hope and beyond it—to realization that he would have to "go back to Warner about June 1st." Having dreamed his "usual vague foundationless dream" of being able to get enough money to live on while he finished his book, he had come to his usual conclusion: that he would never "earn enough outside of pictures to stay out of debt."[47]

By 7 June 1945, a month after V-E Day, he was back in California, determined to carry on with his fable by "rewriting the whole thing."[48] For several weeks he held to a set schedule: before leaving for the studio, he put in four hours' writing. Living with the Bezzerides family and commuting with Buzz, he surprised those who remembered him from the previous December both with the discipline he brought to writing and with the restraint he brought to drinking. At the studio he began adapting a novel by Stephen Longstreet called *Stallion Road*, confident that he could keep it from interfering with his own work. His script was "wild, wonderful, mad"; although it had little to do with what the studio wanted, it was, Longstreet recalled, "a magnificent thing" that might later have been "made as a New Wave film."[49]

Faulkner's orderly life did not, as it turned out, last long. Always in need of extra money, he accepted a moonlighting job on a non-Warner Brothers property, Jean Renoir's film based on George Sessions Perry's story about tenant farmers, *Hold Autumn in Your Hand*. Later he agreed to work with Malcolm Cowley on the Viking *Portable Faulkner*. With all of his novels except *Sanctuary* out of print, it was clear that an anthology could not hurt. Besides, what Cowley had in mind (presenting a picture of his "work as a whole") sounded like a project he had conceived years before: "By all means let us make a Golden Book of my apocryphal county. I have thought of spending my old age doing something of that nature: an alphabetical, rambling genealogy of the people, father to son to son."[50]

Writing to Cowley, Faulkner expressed mainly excitement. Talking to Meta and writing to Harold Ober, he expressed deepening frustration. For several years he had gone on believing Warner Brothers's promises about contracts that would pay more for work he could do in Oxford. But in June the studio had taken up another fifty-two week option on the Herndon contract. Jack Warner continued to boast of buying America's greatest writer for $300 per week. At times Faulkner felt that he could handle Hollywood, could lock it off, performing the tasks it required while doing his own work. But three years had passed since he had finished anything that mattered to him. He knew that his books had never sold and were out of print. He no longer expected the "labor (the creation of my apocryphal country) of my life" to make money. But he had "a few things yet to add to it," and he needed an alternative to Hollywood. He would try any kind of hack-writing or editorial work so long as he could do them at home. "I think I have had about all of Hollywood I can stand," he said. "I feel bad, depressed, dreadful sense of wasting time, I imagine most of the symptoms of some kind of blow-up or collapse."[51]

A month earlier Faulkner had tried to reach an agreement with William Herndon, who had gone on collecting 10 percent of Faulkner's earnings for three years. But Herndon's having negotiated a poor contract without regard to his client's welfare had no legal status, nor for Herndon any moral significance. Although he had collected far more than he had earned, he wanted to collect more. If Faulkner would shut up and work several more years, Herndon would make another twenty thousand dollars in commissions. If, on the other hand, Faulkner wanted to be free, Herndon would settle for direct payments from Faulkner of only $100 per week for two years.[52]

For several weeks Faulkner continued trying to reach an agreement, but neither the studio nor his agent would budge. As a condition of leave, Warner Brothers insisted that he assign them rights to everything he wrote; siding with the studio, Herndon said he would sue unless Faulkner accepted the plan presented him. Both tired and thwarted, Faulkner wrote Harold Ober, asking what would happen if he simply pulled out; and in Ober's reply, he found the only encouragement he required. Assuming that Warner Brothers must surely possess some sense of shame even if Herndon did not, Ober thought it unlikely that they would want the facts of Faulkner's "contract brought out in arbitration."[53] Herndon and Jack Warner aside, Faulkner had had enough. He "was through with Hollywood, finished with screenwriting." He would not accept the studio's or Herndon's proposal, and he could not stay in Hollywood. The last several years had moved him closer and closer to despair—to the sense that life was no longer "worth the living" and perhaps never had been.[54]

In September he said a long goodbye to Meta Doherty. Despite the injuries she had suffered, Meta had gone on hoping that they might somehow marry. Loving Faulkner, she seems scarcely to have noticed the persistence with which he had avoided sharing day-to-day life with her. Several years before, he had discovered what he wanted from their love. Now that age was intervening with all its matter-of-factness, his desire was clearer, and it was for a timeless romance to remember rather than another imperfect existence to share. More even than the threat of being dominated or engulfed, it was the threat of losing their love in some shabby way that haunted him. He wanted to be tender, supportive, but he needed to keep his distance. Although he preferred grief to nothing, he preferred one kind of grief to another: "I know," he wrote her later, that "grief is the inevictable part of it, the thing that makes it cohere; that grief is the only thing you are capable of sustaining, keeping; that what is valuable is what you have lost, since then you never had the chance to wear out and so lose it shabbily." Drawn to a man she could not fully understand, Meta Doherty moved back and forth between bitterness and love: two nights before he left, she rejected him; their last night together, she forgave and embraced him. The next morning her outstretched hand was the last thing he touched as he turned toward Mississippi.[55]

In the weeks just after his return, Faulkner celebrated his forty-eighth birthday and worked on a kind of "Appendix" to *The Sound and the Fury* that he had promised to write for the *Portable Faulkner*. He wrote without rereading *The Sound and the Fury* and without worrying about inconsistencies, and as he did his characters seemed to come alive. Writing quickly and easily, he made his last engagement with the story of the Compsons a genealogy of the family, extending from 1699 to 1945. Although it differed from everything else in Cowley's Golden Book of Yoknapatawpha, it resembled the genealogy of the Sartorises Faulkner had conceived as his own Golden Book. Later he spoke of it as a fifth telling of his tale and as a last effort to complete his story.[56] Finally, however, the appendix is more than a revival of an old project and more than a retelling of an old story. In several ways it suggests what Faulkner was increasingly drawn to: the making of fiction out of his own fictions. Feeling anxious about what age, neglect, and Hollywood were doing to his talent and career, he was turning a longstanding concern into a fictional resource: what the appendix represents is less a recapitulation of an established text than a revision of fluid memories. Tracing the sources and roots of the Compson family, Faulkner leads us on a journey from Scotland through Carolina and Kentucky to Mississippi. Evoking a "dispossessed American king" named Ikkemotubbe, a President named Jackson, and an explorer "named Boon or Boone," he takes us out into American history. In addition, he presents as the architect of the Compson mansion a figure who clearly recalls Sutpen's architect. Even the Compsons' furniture, brought by "steamboat from France and New Orleans," recalls some of Sutpen's imported prizes. Although some characters, notably Jason, Benjy, Dilsey, and Luster, seem little changed, Quentin seems somehow simplified and Caddy somehow diminished. Leaving indirection behind, Faulkner presents an account, or synopsis, of Caddy's life in which we see her standing beside an expensive sports car with a German staff general. Although Faulkner treats Caddy tenderly, he limns out a fate for her that is in some ways more terrible than the one he conceived for Charlotte. Holding what is probably a picture of Caddy in her hand, Dilsey folds it carefully, without identifying it; crying quietly, she knows that she doesn't want to know whether it is Caddy "because she knows Caddy doesn't want to be saved hasn't anything anymore worth being saved for nothing worth being lost that she can lose."

By mid-October, when he finished the appendix, Faulkner was also trying to limit the biographical material included in Cowley's long introduction, particularly as it pertained to World War One. In the end he succeeded in what was clearly a double strategy: he avoided having to admit that he had not served heroically in France by persuading Cowley to say only that he had been a member of the R.A.F. in 1918. When *The Portable Faulkner* was published, in April 1946, it neither confirmed nor denied Faulkner's status as a wounded hero.[57]

Nothing else he attempted in late 1945 and early 1946 went nearly so well. In October he decided to make a direct appeal to Jack Warner.

Stressing his failure as a script writer, he suggested that the studio had got too little for its money. Noting that he was forty-seven, he pointed out that he had misspent time that was precious to him. "And I dont dare mis-spend any more of it. . . . So I repeat my request that the studio release me from my contract." It was a moving plea, but it overestimated Warner's basic humanity. The reply came from Warner's attorney rather than from Warner. Rejecting Faulkner's request, it advised him to sign promptly the leave agreement and assignment he had already refused to sign.[58]

Determined to make no further request of Warner, Faulkner tried to write. Having finished the material promised Cowley, he worked doggedly on his fable, unable to establish any rhythm or make any progress. Doubly distracted—threatened on one side by legal action that might force him to fulfill the Herndon contract and on the other by a shrinking bank account that might starve him into it—he found himself virtually paralyzed.[59] By February he had resigned himself to going back in March. A few days before his scheduled departure Harold Ober and Robert Haas intervened, prepared to do whatever proved necessary to free him from both of his distractions. Urging him to wait in Oxford, they asked Bennett Cerf, who knew Jack Warner, to intercede. Appealed to by someone he thought of as a businessman rather than a schmuck, Warner agreed: Warner Brothers would grant Faulkner an indefinite leave and renounce claim to his novel. Informed of Warner's concession and told that Random House would advance him $500 per month until he could finish his fable, Faulkner responded with simple relief. "I feel fine," he wrote Haas in March 1946, "am happy now, thanks to Harold and you."[60]

Soon Faulkner's spirits were bolstered by other good news, including publication and reviews of *The Portable Faulkner*. Eventually Cowley's project would help to inaugurate a major critical reevaluation of Faulkner's achievement. More immediately, it helped persuade Random House to reissue *The Sound and the Fury* and *As I Lay Dying* in a Modern Library edition, which in turn helped to bring other novels back into print. During the summer Harold Ober informed him that RKO wanted to buy rights to "Death Drag" and "Honor," and that Cagney Productions wanted to buy rights to "Two Soldiers." Together these sales totaled more than $10,000. In November and December he got the kind of movie job he was always hoping for: work he could do quickly in Oxford for good money.[61]

The problem, he soon discovered, was writing. When the writing went well, as it did occasionally, he labored with deep intensity, convinced that his fable would be his "magnum o." When it slowed he realized how different and difficult his new mode of fiction was for him. When it stopped, as also happened, he began to fear that Hollywood had ruined him or that he was simply burned out. For days at a time, he wrote slowly, reluctantly, as though the act were now all will. It was not simply that he had written scores of words for every one he had to show Random House; he had always done a lot of writing. The problem ran deeper, and it touched everything. The whole process had become agonizing. He made "mistakes slower now," and he corrected "them slower."[62]

Over the years he had grown accustomed to accepting advances. Once he had joked about being "so busy borrowing money from Random House" that he had no time left to write. Another time he had described himself as the only writer he knew "who got advances from his agent." Now, as he became less and less sure of himself, he began to feel that Haas and Ober must surely be worried too. How could they go on extending, or he accepting, advances when he seemed unable to do anything new? Earlier he had joked of wanting "to keep" the distinction of taking advances from his agent "constant." Now he wanted his publisher and his agent to know that they could stop what they had begun. Anytime you feel you have gone far enough, he wrote, "so do I."[63]

As his feeling of uncertainty and restlessness mounted, Faulkner began visiting Greenfield Farm more regularly and riding more recklessly. Now and then he talked of taking longer trips. "It's a dull life here," he wrote Cowley. "I need some new people, above all probably a new young woman." Perhaps he should come to New York, he wrote Haas, to tell them about the story he was writing. That way they would know where it was going and what it would be. Still he persisted, sustained not so much by what he had written as by "the whole pattern" he saw before him.[64]

It took a double development to divert him. During the summer of 1947, almost two years after his return from Hollywood, he began a "new chapter" of his fable that he described as "a good story, a complete novelette." In the book the tale would be an interpolation, "one single adjectival clause," as he put it.[65] Yet it proved fateful out of all proportion both to its role in *A Fable* and to its quality as a story—in part because it took him back toward Yoknapatawpha, his heart's country, and in part because it deepened his crisis of confidence. As he worked on it, his "new chapter" engaged him more than any writing he had done for months. In it he traces the adventures of "a white man and an old Negro preacher and the preacher's 14 year old grandson" as they dodge "from one little back country track to the next racing" a stolen horse.[66] After it had been published separately, in a limited, signed edition by the Levee Press as *Notes on a Horsethief* (1951), it would become a part of *A Fable* (1954). But first it was rejected by the *Partisan Review*.

It was late November 1947 when Faulkner learned of the rejection. One part of his disappointment was financial: he needed money for taxes, and now he would have to "ask Bob [Haas] for it." But since he had more confidence in the novelette than in the fable, doubting it called everything into question. Soon he was swinging again between confidence and uncertainty. For every assertion ("There is nothing wrong with the book as it will be") there were several questions ("What is your opinion of this section in question? Dull? Too prolix? Diffuse?"). Ober had nearly five hundred pages of the most heavily rewritten and confusing manuscript Faulkner had ever written. However much faith Faulkner might have in the pattern perceived by his mind's eye, he knew that he had worked hard yet made little progress toward realizing it. And he knew that he had "been on Random H's cuff a long time now."[67]

In January 1948 he "put the big mss aside" in order to write a short murder-mystery story set in Yoknapatawpha. Like the long, ongoing project, the short one would be morally didactic; unlike the long project, the short one would be about race rather than peace, and it would get itself written quickly. Its theme, he wrote Ober, "is more relationship between Negro and white, . . . the premise being that the white people in the South, before the North or the govt. or anyone else, owe and must pay a responsibility to the Negro."[68] In this description as in the work itself, we see reflected both Faulkner's longstanding concern with race and his newly explicit sense of moral urgency. In other ways, too, particularly its clipped dialogue and its strong, carefully plotted action, his new story reflected recent lessons, including those reiterated by Hollywood. But as he moved back toward Yoknapatawpha and its familiar characters and voices, Faulkner began writing with expectation rather than reluctance. Soon he was working with something like his old sense of confidence. By late February he had a completed manuscript, by late April, a revised typescript and a title.

Intruder in the Dust shares several themes with *Light in August* and several characters as well as themes with *Go Down, Moses*, and it is more complex and less sentimental than many readers have suggested. Still, despite the enthusiasm and care with which he worked on it, particularly in revision, Faulkner failed to give it the intensity and resonance we associate with his finest work. The crucial place it occupies in his career derives in part from the themes it engages, in part from the shift in self-conception that it announced, and in part from the money and attention it garnered. In one sense it took Faulkner back toward *Go Down, Moses* —specifically in the theme of black-white relations and the characters of Lucas Beauchamp, who plays a major role in both novels, and Gavin Stevens, who plays an important one near the end of *Go Down, Moses* and throughout *Intruder in the Dust*. But *Intruder* also carried Faulkner forward, toward a more didactic and prophetic fiction, as we see especially in the career of Gavin Stevens. A limited character initially, too much of his time and place, Stevens gradually changes. Moved by the tenacity and courage of Lucas Beauchamp and the innocence and faith of Charles Mallison, he begins to discard prejudices that have blinded and tainted him, and then to speak with the authority of wisdom as well as truth. Through this remarkable reclamation, however, one of the major problems with the novel surfaces. Long before Stevens stops talking, he begins moralizing, leading the reader to associate his voice with a term like "message": to the North that it should permit the South to solve its own problems; to the South that it must stop living with "injustice and outrage and dishonor and shame."[69]

Intruder in the Dust not only represented Faulkner's first finished attempt to become "articulate in the national voice," it also marked his final move toward fame and fortune. The money and recognition that had eluded a series of major achievements now came easily to a minor performance. Although reviews were mixed on both the art and the ideology of *Intruder in the Dust*, they came from every corner, and they came in such numbers as to convince even the Oxford *Eagle* that Faulkner was "Oxford's great novelist." Before publication had come or recognition begun, Bennett Cerf sold the movie rights to MGM for $50,000.[70] A few months earlier Faulkner had written Cowley expressing disgust for the "vast and growing mass of inanimate junk, possessions" that cluttered his life without offering him any real satisfaction.[71] Now, with money in the bank, there were trips to make, a sailboat to buy, clothes and books to purchase, a house to enlarge. Since his desire for such things, like Estelle's and Jill's, would continue to grow, the $50,000 would disappear quickly. But since there were other big paydays to follow, his worry about money was over. Never again would his and his family's desire for money far outstrip his ability to make it.

During the summer he worked with friends building and launching a houseboat, the *M/S Minmagary*, on Sardis Reservoir. As signs of success increased, his enthusiasm for other projects revived. Earlier he had talked of collecting his stories. Hoping to give the collection a form of its own, he was ready to get back to it. Even his fable seemed possible again. But first he wanted a "vacation from the nest-and-hearth."[72] Waiting for September publication of *Intruder in the Dust*, he left for New York. Between the parties and interviews, he found time to drink and talk with old friends like Hal Smith and Jim Devine, and new ones like Malcolm Cowley. But it was Ruth Ford that drew most of his attention. In Hollywood he had been content to remain her gentleman friend. In New York he offered to become her lover: "I've been your gentleman friend for quite a while now," he said. "Ain't it time I was promoted?"[73] Perhaps because the answer he received disappointed him, his mood changed. At first he had seemed lively and funny; now he began to drink more and talk less. Finally he retreated to his room at the Algonquin and drank himself

to near unconsciousness. Finding him weak and debilitated, friends took
him to a sanitorium. From there they moved him to Malcolm Cowley's
home in Sherman, Connecticut, where he completed his recovery. He
showed extreme self-control, Cowley recalled, and seemed not only small
and vulnerable but determined, too. Feeling better, he returned to New
York, where he had dinner at Ruth's and held several conversations with
Albert Erskine, Saxe Commins, and Robert Haas at Random House. Then
he was ready to go back to nest and hearth, another of his vacations behind him.[74]

Soon he was at work again, briefly on the collected stories and his
fable, then concertedly on a book of six related stories he called *Knight's
Gambit*. More or less detective fiction, the stories of *Knight's Gambit* feature Gavin Stevens in his effort not simply to solve or prevent crimes but
"to protect the weak, right injustice, or punish evil." Although several of
the stories had already been published, the title story had been rejected
repeatedly. Convinced now that "Knight's Gambit" had been turned
down because it wanted to be a novella rather than a story, Faulkner proposed to expand it. Together, he wrote Saxe Commins, the Gavin Stevens
stories would make a book about the length of *Intruder*. Encouraged by
Random House, he began work in early 1949, showing neither strain nor
reluctance. Working in the mornings, he spent most afternoons at Greenhill Farm or Sardis Reservoir, where he could relax on the *Minmagary* or
sail *The Ring Dove*. With Oxford excited by the filming of *Intruder in the
Dust*, the farm and lake had become important retreats. Still he was working well. By mid-May he had a finished manuscript; by June, a typescript.[75]

Although *Knight's Gambit* is clearly a minor performance, it is important on several counts, including the way in which its title story, the
only piece Faulkner substantially revised, draws on his life as well as his
earlier fiction. "Knight's Gambit" recalls such things as the Sartoris love
of airplanes, and it recounts Gavin Stevens's effort to regain his childhood
sweetheart. In age and appearance, Stevens resembles Phil Stone; in his
long preoccupation with his first sweetheart, he resembles his creator.[76]
Faulkner had always enjoyed echoing his earlier works. After his desire to
give his works a larger design and felt reciprocity had surfaced, he had
moved toward more complex echoes and relations. But the anxiety fostered by the long silence between *Go Down, Moses* and *Intruder in the
Dust* had given this habit a new edge. "Knight's Gambit" is a work of
deep resonances, and Gavin Stevens is a character who embodies an
especially suggestive kind of uncertainty and self-involvement. On one
side Stevens is defined by the persistence with which he is devoted to
his first love; on the other he is defined by hesitations and reassess-
ments. He moves through his world with deep dis-ease, questioning

yet demonstrating both his own constancy and the value of his causes.

Earlier in the book, in a story called "Monk," we encounter language that specifies as well as reflects Faulkner's own continuing interest in detective fiction. In the story's opening paragraphs, Charles Mallison comes to us not merely as a detective but as a prototype of man in his aspect of curiosity and bafflement—which is to say that he possesses several habits and a disposition that make him one of Faulkner's representative men. As a result of his habits and disposition, however, Mallison engages in activities that we associate with two other crucial figures—the narrator and the reader. For he is troubled not only by circumstances that clown and ciphers that refuse to add up, but also by words that "do not make sense." In order to discern the logic of Monk's story ("to make something out of . . . the nebulous and inexplicable material" given him), he must become half a detective, half an artist, and all a reader. "Monk" accordingly becomes at least as much the story of its narrator (or, more radically, its reader) as the story of its subject. For not only does it derive much of its force from the drama with which Faulkner invests the interpretive act, it also defines that act in terms that tie it to the art of detection, the art of narration, and the art of reading. Charles Mallison labors in troubled faith that, through interpretation, "the paradoxical and even mutually negativing" aspects of Monk's life "can be juxtaposed and annealed . . . into verisimilitude and credibility." But he does so knowing that his only hope resides in the skill with which he uses "the nebulous tools of supposition and inference and invention."

Between completion of *Knight's Gambit* and the world premiere of the movie *Intruder in the Dust*, in Oxford on 11 October 1949, Faulkner continued to work on his big manuscript. He also continued to hunt, sail, and farm.[77] A few days before the premiere he announced that he preferred not to attend. For years only a few friends, notably Mac Reed and Phil Stone, had remained loyal to him. Though he welcomed vindication, Oxford's turnabout had come too late. Embarrassed, his family tried to change his mind, only to fail. Finally playing her trump, Estelle called Aunt Bama, who in turn called Faulkner to say that she planned to see him take his bow and that she expected him to be properly dressed for the occasion.[78]

Early in 1950, about the time work on his fable slowed again, Faulkner got a note from Saxe Commins saying that Random House wanted to go ahead with the *Collected Stories*. A year earlier, before putting the project aside for *Knight's Gambit*, Faulkner had decided on an organization that pleased him. Since he still liked what he had set up then, he had nothing more to do. The volume would consist of forty-two stories divided into six unequal sections, The Country, The Village, The Wilderness, The Wasteland, The Middle Ground, and Beyond.[79] What he had in mind as a diversion from his fable was a different work altogether—a play. It would take far longer than he expected to complete, and before he had finished it, it would become another strange compound work, neither play nor novel. From the beginning, however, it reached out in several interesting directions.

A sequel of sorts to *Sanctuary*, *Requiem for a Nun* extends the story of Temple Drake and her suitor, Gowan Stevens. In addition, Nancy of "That Evening Sun" becomes Nancy Mannigoe in *Requiem*. *Requiem* differs from the earlier works, however, in tone as well as in genre. It treats themes having to do with race and justice, with public institutions and public awareness, so directly as to make it seem even more didactic than *Intruder in the Dust*. Like *Mosquitoes* and *The Wild Palms*, however, *Requiem* also has important extraneous relations, one of which involved Ruth Ford. Earlier Ruth Ford had asked Faulkner to write a play for her; later he announced that he had written *Requiem* with her in mind.[80] Beyond this extended entanglement, however, was a deeper one with a younger woman.

In August 1949, shortly before Faulkner began writing *Requiem*, Joan Williams had come down from her home in Memphis hoping that a friend would take her to Rowan Oak. Soon she would be going back to Bard College to begin her senior year. Slender, pretty, and intelligent, she wanted to become a writer and wanted to meet William Faulkner. Finding their first meeting brief and inconclusive, she wrote a letter that seemed to Faulkner "like something remembered out of youth." Since it had made him feel young "again and brave and clean and durable," he agreed to answer any questions she might want to ask of "a middle-aged writer."[81] She responded with a list of what seemed to him "the wrong questions"— questions a woman could ask a man only when they were lying peacefully in bed on the edge of sleep. Yet she should not grieve over having "to wait, even to ask them," he said, nor over having questions without answers, even when hope of answers seemed slight, since questions were the kindest gift the gods could give the young.[82]

For several months Faulkner kept his distance, playing mentor to Joan's talents. He read things she wrote and sent her lists of things to read: the Bible and Shakespeare, Housman, Malraux, and Bergson. Not long after they met, she sent him a story called "Rain Later" that had been accepted by *Mademoiselle*. Soon he found it impossible to remain distant. Although he had felt many things over the last several years, he had not felt young and durable for what seemed a very long time, and he was drawn toward the only person able to move him to it again. He would go on, he said, trying to write letters about literature, but he thought she should know that he wanted to write of love. Perhaps if they could collaborate on the play he was beginning, he could take his love and create "a poet out of her."[83]

The collaboration begun by post in January 1950 continued in meet-ings in New York in February, by which time Faulkner had an outline of what would become the first act of his play. As he became more ardent, direct, and persistent, however, Joan became uneasy; and as she became hesitant, he became unhappy. Although the idea of collaboration had not taken hold, he continued to work on the play and to write Joan about his progress. He would try, he said, to be whatever she wanted him to be to her. But he was "capable not only of imagining anything and every-thing, but even of hoping and believing it."[84]

As late spring approached with no resolution in sight, his unhappiness deepened. Neither farming nor sailing nor riding brought satisfaction; even when it went well, work was "not really enough." What "he wanted was to walk in April again for a day, an hour."[85] With Joan he felt young and clean and durable; without her he found reminders of decay everywhere. Soon it seemed to him that he had lost even his ability to work. You know, he told Jim Devine, as he sat looking out the window of his work-room at Rowan Oak, "there were a lot of days when I sat and looked out this window and knew I was workin'. Now I sit and look out this window and know I ain't workin'."[86] In a letter to the American Academy ac-knowledging the Howells Medal, his tone was distinctly elegaic. Earlier in his life he had moved from book to book feeling that each was imperfect but that "there was always another one" to write. "Then one day I was fifty and I looked back at it, and I decided that it was all pretty good—and then in the same instant I realized that that was the worst of all since that meant only that a little nearer now was the moment, instant, night: dark: sleep: when I would put it all away forever that I anguished and sweated over, and it would never trouble me anymore."[87]

While Joan demurred and Faulkner brooded, Estelle began to seethe. Not even the reluctant adjustment she had made to Meta Doherty pre-pared her for what she now faced. Joan was only a few years older than Jill, and Memphis was much too close to Oxford. Worried and angry, Estelle tried to intercept letters and contact Joan's parents, and so embar-rassed herself even more than she inconvenienced the collaborators. Hoping to placate Estelle, Faulkner talked of backing off. But he wanted to walk again in April more than he could admit or control. Still hoping and believing in some idyll "not in a garden but in the woods maybe," and still preferring grief to nothing, he went on trying to calm Estelle's ire and rekindle Joan's ardor.[88]

As summer gave way to fall, the stalemate continued. Neither Joan nor Estelle nor Faulkner seemed able to make a decisive move. Then, early on the morning of 10 November 1950, the telephone rang, signalling an extended interruption. The call was from New York, and it announced award of the Nobel Prize for 1949, in acknowledgment of Faulkner's "powerful and independent artistic contribution."[89] Faulkner had known for some time that his American reputation lagged behind his European reputation. "Pour les jeunes en France," Jean Paul Sartre had told Cowley, "Faulkner c'est un dieu."[90] On several occasions, rumors had linked his name specifically with the Nobel Prize. In March 1946 Thorsten Jonsson, one of his Swedish translators, had predicted that he would receive it. In the fall of 1949, when no award had been announced, the rumors had become more numerous and more explicit.[91] In 1950, when the moment finally came, Faulkner repeated the response he had made to the invitation to the premiere of *Intruder in the Dust*: it was a nice honor and he was grateful, but he preferred to stay at home. When requests from family, friends, and State Department emissaries failed, Estelle once again devised a scheme that worked. She appealed to her unenthusiastic daughter, and Jill in turn persuaded her father not only to go but to take her with him: she was a senior in high school, she had never been to Europe, and she wanted the trip as a graduation gift.[92]

Having agreed to go, Faulkner very nearly aborted the journey by drinking steadily for several days before his scheduled departure. Finally on his way, he described himself as "damn sick and tired" of being told to do his duty. But it was finally his duty that he most wanted to do. "I want," he said to the American ambassador to Sweden, "to do the right thing."[93] Tired, frightened, and weak, he needed help, as he had before and would again, from family, friends, and even strangers. But he had often been fortunate in finding help, and he was again—at several points from Jill; in New York from the Haases and Comminses; and in Sweden from the ambassador, Walton Butterworth, from an English valet named Geoffrey Button, and from Else Jonsson, widow of Thorsten. Several years before, amid darkness that was personal and global, he had written to a boy going to war about a time when he might become "articulate in the national voice." He wanted now, he said, to use the moment given him as a pinnacle from which he might be listened to by the young. As it turned out, he was so shy, hurried, and soft-spoken as to be inaudible: "We did not know what he had said until the next morning," Else Jonsson reported.[94] But he found, as he had before, that some silences are articulate after all. Before he was done, it would be as though he had spoken from a pinnacle to voice longstanding concerns and convictions. Those concerns (that we are consumed by fear, and that fear is the basest of all emotions) and those convictions (that the problems of the human heart in conflict with itself alone make good writing, and that stories written without love and honor and pity and pride and compassion and sacrifice are ephemeral and doomed) are less simply related to his great fiction than he sometimes assumed. But he felt them deeply, as his letters of the 1940s—particularly those written to Warren Beck and Malcolm Cowley about his fiction, and to his stepson and nephew about the war—clearly show.[95]

Many artists carefully avoid articulating their simpler convictions. Some do so out of fear of simplifying their art; others out of fear of evoking ridicule—of being termed an aging scout master or a doddering fool. But Faulkner had always been better at taking chances than at exercising caution. What the Stockholm speech signalled was readiness to take chances of a different kind. With the ceremony behind him ("It was as long as a Mississippi funeral," he told reporters), he took Jill to Paris and then through London to New York.[96] By Christmas they were home again. A few years earlier he had felt himself trapped by neglect: "I eke out a hack's motion picture wages," he said, "by winning second prize in a manufactured mystery story contest." Now reporters met him at every stop; a full-page advertisement greeted him in the Oxford *Eagle*; and friends hovered around him wondering what he had meant by saying that he hoped to spend the $30,000 in prize money in a way "commensurate with the purpose and significance of its origin."[97]

TEN 1951-1962

The Faces of Fame

With the Nobel ordeal and Christmas behind him, Faulkner returned to his two unfinished projects. If the end of his fable seemed far away, the end of *Requiem for a Nun* lay clearly before him. Yet, a few good weeks were more than he could put together. His suspended affair with Joan Williams did nothing so much as make him restless. Once "nothing nothing nothing else but writing" sufficed to give him peace; now nothing gave him peace.[1] Able to write only with great effort, he began seeking the kinds of distractions he had once avoided. Within a few weeks he had fallen into a pattern that defined the next several months of his life. Unable to write, he began moving from place to place.

Following a short trip to Greenville, he left for a several weeks' stay in Hollywood. In Greenville, he signed copies of the Levee Press edition of *Notes on a Horsethief*; in Hollywood he worked for Howard Hawks, writing a script based on William Barrett's *The Left Hand of God*. The first of these ventures, undertaken as a favor to Ben Wasson and Hodding Carter, made little money; the second paid $14,000 in five weeks. Yet the larger difference between the two had to do with duration. For it was time more than money that troubled him now; what he needed were ways of filling his days. Unable to work, he discovered that his talent for idleness had deserted him. Having returned to Rowan Oak in March, he found neither of his manuscripts engaging; nor were any of his usual diversions entertaining. It was as though the pain and self-doubt of his youth had suddenly merged with the disappointment and bitterness of his maturity. Now that great success had come, bringing reward and recognition, he found it empty. In April, not long after France decided to make him an officer of the Legion of Honor, he decided that he needed to see Verdun in order to write his fable.

Despite his heavy drinking (it was on this trip that a young acquaintance sat in astonishment, counting as he downed twenty-three martinis in one day), the journey went well enough. On his way through New York he saw Ruth Ford, who was waiting for him to finish *Requiem*. Having landed in France, he spent more time in Paris than Verdun. Walking the streets of Paris with a young writer-editor, Monique Salomon, who worked for Gallimard, he recalled memories of his first trip to France when, as a possessionless vagabond, he had visited the battlefields of slain heroes and the haunts of literary giants.[2]

On his way home he stopped in New York to see Joan Williams, who seemed to fear his intensity almost as much as she desired his presence. But it was writing that he needed, and he knew it. Back in Oxford he finished the commencement address he had agreed to deliver at Jill's graduation. On 28 May 1951, at age fifty-four, he attended his first graduation ceremony and delivered a short speech emphasizing themes prominent in his Nobel address.[3] But by then he was also working on *Requiem*, this time with enough staying power to finish it.

Like the Appendix to *The Sound and the Fury* and *Knight's Gambit*, *Requiem for a Nun* looks backward in several interesting ways. In its clipped, terse dialogue, it reflects lessons learned in Hollywood. In its mannered style, it recalls *The Marionettes*. In its basic action, it resumes the story of Temple Drake. Between the final scene of *Sanctuary* and the beginning of *Requiem* lie a series of crucial events. Following her return from Europe with her father, Temple has married Gowan and the two have settled down to a life of dull respectability. Unable to forget her sojourn with Red and Popeye in the Memphis brothel, however, Temple has hired Nancy Mannigoe, a reformed prostitute and dope-addict, as her maid. With Nancy as her confidant, Temple has recalled the one great and terrible adventure of her life. Later, after Red's brother appears with threats of blackmail, her affinity for evil has resurfaced. Troubled and confused, fearing the worst for Temple and her children, Nancy has tried to save Temple's home by killing one of Temple's children, an act she

commits out of love rather than malice and with the intention of sacrific-
ing herself as well.

Concerned with the resolution of these events, and particularly their
consequences for Temple and Nancy, *Requiem for a Nun* focuses on conflicts that are internal as well as external. Whereas Nancy's fate is virtually
fixed, Temple's hangs in the balance. Leaving the state to preside over
Nancy's trial and execution, Gavin Stevens concerns himself with Temple's moral awakening. By engaging her in a kind of moral dialectic, he
seeks to bring her to new self-recognition and then to confession. Through
the play's action we accordingly become mindful of the distance between
the state's concern and Gavin Stevens's. In its avid desire to execute
Nancy, the state manifests concern only for legalities and respectability.
To the fate of individuals, to shadings of innocence and guilt, to the possibility of confession and redemption, it remains indifferent.

The gulf created, between society's preoccupations and Stevens's,
Faulkner explores in part with dialogue and action and in part with prose
prefaces. Having initially conceived *Requiem for a Nun* as a three-act play,
he gradually changed his conception of it. Then, several months before his
final push to complete it, he decided to introduce each act with a prose
preface that took as its starting point the scene of the act it precedes. He
thus changed his work from a play into "some kind of novel" and broad-
ened it in two ways: he placed its action firmly within the history of Yoknapatawpha, and he tied the history of Yoknapatawpha to the history of
Mississippi.[4]

The first of the prefaces, called "The Courthouse (A Name for the
City)," focuses on the history of Faulkner's mythical kingdom, which it
traces from the time when Yoknapatawpha was still frontier to the play's
present. In this piece Faulkner not only recalls the names of the settlers
of his county, he also voices a distinct antimodernism. He associates the
past with slow time and clear purpose, the present with frenetic travel, a
love of speed, a commitment to mere motion. The second of the prefaces,
considerably shorter, deals with Jackson and Mississippi. Called "The
Golden Dome (Beginning Was the Word)," it combines historical sweep
with miscellaneous data.[5] As a result, Jackson appears more standardized
and nondescript than Yoknapatawpha. Still, though it is clearly not mythical, Jackson is finally too modern and typical to be historical. The third
of the prefaces, "The Jail (Nor Even Yet Quite Relinquish—)," returns to
the story of Jefferson and Yoknapatawpha. Once again familiar names begin to circulate, familiar motives to dominate. Its central episode takes us
back nearly a century—to a doomed girl who has scratched her name,
Cecilia Farmer, and the date, 16 April 1861, on a window of the jail. A
gesture of defiance, a way of saying *no* to oblivion, her act ties her not
only to Nancy Mannigoe but to Faulkner's definition of the artist as one

who knows that life is short, "that the day will come when he must pass through the wall of oblivion," and who determines that he will "leave a scratch on that wall."[6]

Faulkner conceived his prose pieces as integral to the acts they pre-ceded. They were necessary, he later remarked, to give the work "the contrapuntal effect which comes in orchestration." By providing some-thing a little mystical, they sharpened "the hard simple give-and-take of the dialogue."[7] In addition to serving these purposes, however, they created a double problem, first, because they do not lend themselves to dramatic presentation, and second, because they are rhetorically more forceful than the dramatic core of the work.

If the second part of this problem emerged only after the work was published, on 27 September 1951, the first part became clear almost im-mediately. By the time he finished writing *Requiem*, Faulkner was so "tired of ink and paper" that he was planning to devote his summer to horses and crops. As it turned out, he spent much of the summer and some of the fall in New York and Boston, trying to turn the work he had written into a play Ruth Ford could get produced.[8] Eventually he left the adaptation to other hands; and eventually the play was staged in more than a dozen countries, including Germany (1955), Spain (1956), France (1956), and Greece (1957), as well as England and America. Seeing it as translated by Albert Camus, and recognizing in its stylized tragedy several elements familiar to their own theater, the French responded enthusiasti-cally. But in 1959, when it finally reached New York, *Requiem*'s run was too short and undistinguished to match the dream Faulkner had shared with Joan Williams in scattered moments and with Ruth Ford for several years.[9]

Having put *Requiem* aside, Faulkner returned to Oxford, hoping to finish the "big book." Farming, sailing, or riding in the afternoons and evenings, he tried to write in the mornings. But Joan Williams continued to preoccupy him, making play difficult and work almost impossible. Before long he found himself wondering whether he would ever finish what he had begun. "I am too old to have to miss a girl of twenty-three, . . ." he wrote Joan. "By now, I should have earned the right to be free of that." Hoping that he was "getting ready, storing up energy . . . to start again," he tried to wait out the stalemate. But when the awaited moment failed to come, he became not only restless but reckless. In February and again in March 1952, he fell from horses, the second time sustaining a severe back injury. Tired of waiting, he decided to spend April in Europe.[10]

First in Stockholm, where he visited Else Jonsson, and then in Paris, where he visited Monique Salomon, her husband, and new baby, he sought relief. Still peace eluded him. His back, injured several times, became extremely painful. Whiskey, his favorite medicine, not only weakened him but aggravated his insomnia, which had worsened over the years. After an intense drinking spree he was hospitalized in Paris, where doctors told him that he had fractured two vertebrae, that there were clear signs of arthritic complications, and that surgical fusion was advisable. Refusing surgery, he moved on to Oslo, where he found temporary relief in a program of physical therapy.[11]

Determined to break out of the circle that held and frightened him, he started home. On his way through Memphis he visited Joan; back in Oxford he wrote, trying to describe their situation as he saw it. Had they been free to meet whenever they liked, to walk and talk freely, he might have been able to accept the limits she had set.` "But as it is," he concluded, "I wont get any peace until we have finished the beginning of it." For three years he had been part mentor, part father, part suitor. But he loved her, and he wanted no substitute.[12]

Years before he had described a man who found it "unbearable to believe that he had never had the power to stir women." It was, he now knew, almost as unbearable to believe it a power one no longer possessed. Convinced of his need, Joan became his lover sometime in the summer of 1952. In the weeks that followed, however, he found pain rather than peace. Feeling trapped, Joan fled; feeling rejected, he grieved. Telling her that she need not grieve because his capacity for grief was great enough for both of them, he tried to prepare himself for what he saw coming: if the end of their beginning was to be only an end, he wrote, "that's all right too; haven't I been telling you something: that between grief and nothing, I will take grief?"[13]

For a time he explored his grief, hoping to turn it into poetry—as he had in *Mosquitoes* and *The Wild Palms*. Feeling rotten, he "dug out the mss. of the big book and went to work at it." But writing no longer seemed to work as a way of fighting unhappiness, depression, heartbreak. "Maybe I shall have to cut completely away from my present life," he wrote Harold Ober, "at least for a time. I seem to have lost heart for working. I cant find anything to work, write, *for*." The great trouble, he wrote Else Jonsson, was a general malaise, an almost consuming unhappiness, such that he had "lost heart for everything."[14]

Years earlier he had constructed a life that maximized his dependence on his created cosmos and minimized his dependence on other people, making him a "proud and self-sufficient beast." Walking alone, he had needed "nothing from anyone." And in those days he had believed that "there is a God that looks after the true artist because there is nothing as important as that and He knows it." But he had always been more a writer than a reader and had always found more pleasure in what he was doing than in what he had done. As his hold on his fictional world loosened—

as his sense of access and viable relationship to it faltered—his needs began to shift, his faith to waver.[15]

Much of the fall of 1952 he spent moving in and out of hospitals. Drinking remained the most reliable barometer, and he was drinking heavily. But he was also suffering occasional convulsive seizures. Having long since learned that he combined the rarest gifts of imagination with crippling faults of personality, he knew that his psychic survival required the playing of dangerous games as well as the cultivation of considerable self-deception. Drinking in particular had long been a recourse as well as a sign. Still, coupled with his more usual oscillations, the seizures frightened him. Feeling that something was wrong, that something was about to happen to him, he was willing to try anything that might help him recover his equilibrium. In New York in November, he underwent a series of electro-shock treatments, after which his doctor reported that he seemed gentle and dependent, almost childlike in his need for affection and tenderness.[16]

In an interview in Princeton shortly before he was hospitalized in New York, Faulkner recalled André Gide's remark that "he admired only those books whose authors had almost died in order to write them." When he returned to Oxford in December, he was determined to make a last great effort to finish his fable. Still the words seemed to come either in short spurts or not at all, and often when they came, they did not seem right. Within a few weeks he was back in New York, prepared to stay for several months. Perhaps there, close to Joan and with the help of Saxe Commins, he could get started again.[17]

The experiment began ominously, in a hospital. Then Faulkner began writing, on his fable now and again, and on short pieces, too. After "Weekend Revisited," the story of a man who drinks in order to discover meaning through suffering, he wrote two essays that seemed distinctly elegiac.[18] In the first of these he tenderly recalled his days in New Orleans with Sherwood Anderson. In the second he looked back nostalgically toward the land of which he had made his mythical kingdom and toward the years after the Great War when he had been "a tramp, a harmless possessionless vagabond," who yearned to be a poet.[19]

It felt good to be writing after two years of near silence—even though the big work continued to move slowly, and even though looking back reinforced his sense that most of his work lay behind him. He felt nothing more distinctly than the distance between the writer he had been and the man he was, unless it was awe for what he had created. Thinking of the books he had written, he seemed to see some antecedent self performing amazing feats. "And now I realise for the first time," he wrote Joan Williams in April 1953, "what an amazing gift I had: uneducated in every formal sense . . . yet to have made the things I made."[20]

Following a sudden trip to Oxford in April, after Estelle had suffered
a near fatal hemorrhage, he made a short trip to Massachusetts in June to
see Jill graduated from Pine Manor. But he was ready now to return to
Oxford for another last effort. Through the early and middle summer he
worked with something like his old intensity. Following early resistance
to his entanglement with Joan, Estelle had finally accepted it. Hoping
her sanction might lend the affair a guise of respectable collaboration, she
had once offered to invite Joan to stay and work at Rowan Oak. But Estelle had also begun to live a more independent life. With Faulkner working
on his manuscript at Rowan Oak and visiting Joan in Memphis, she decided to leave for Mexico City, where Jill planned to enroll in the university.[21]

For the first time in many months, Faulkner's ability to work lasted.
By late September he had a nearly completed manuscript. One chapter
and more revision than he suspected remained, but the work he had begun
a decade before was at last almost finished.[22] A few months earlier he had
asserted that "a great book is always accompanied by a painful birth."
Now, as though to show how painful had been *A Fable*'s birth, he began
to oscillate wildly between elation and depression. More than usually complicated, his recovery took him in and out of hospitals in Memphis and
Byhalia.[23]

While Faulkner tried to collect himself in order to begin the process of
revision, Robert Coughlan published a two-part piece in *Life* magazine
titled "The Private World of William Faulkner" (28 September 1953) and
"The Man Behind the Myth" (5 October 1953). Describing Faulkner as
"a small, wiry man with closely cropped iron-gray hair"; a darker moustache; a thin, high-bridged aquiline nose; heavy-lidded, deep-set dark eyes;
and a tanned, weathered face, Coughlan went on to stress Faulkner's love
of pipe-smoking and his legendary drinking. Faulkner was, Coughlan reported, "not an alcoholic but perhaps more accurately an alcoholic refugee, self-pursued."[24] Still insisting that his private life should be private,
Faulkner left Oxford for New York, planning to pick Joan up in Memphis.
He was ready now to revise the book he had decided to call *A Fable*.
Through October and into November, he continued shifting and rewriting.
The work he had begun in Oxford in December 1944, he finished in
Princeton in November 1953.[25]

A Fable contains many fine episodes, including two justifiably praised
by Cleanth Brooks: the comic search for a body to place in the tomb of
the Unknown Soldier, and the killing of General Gragnon by three strangely
allied American soldiers—a white farmer from Iowa, a black man from
Mississippi, and a gangster from Brooklyn.[26] Several moments in the confrontation between the Corporal and the Old Marshall are compelling. In
the opening scene, where setting and atmosphere are crucial, Faulkner

writes with great power. Yet despite moments in which it is nearly as good as Faulkner wanted it to be, *A Fable* is deeply flawed. It is not only strained and awkward; it is too deliberate and too self-conscious, too direct and too abstract. Of all Faulkner's books, it is the clearest example of the fumbling search for exactitude and purity that he associated with Sherwood Anderson.

The reasons for the work's failure are several, and they touch both its source and its protracted making. If its origins committed it to abstractness, its long, complicated history not only encouraged confusions but imposed burdens. There were finally too many versions of too many scenes, too many changing ideas and opinions, and above all too much sense that the delay had to be justified by greater purity and profundity. Hoping for universality, Faulkner created a protagonist called the Corporal whose life happens to parallel the life of Christ in one striking detail after another. Hoping for purity, he made his young protagonist simple and uneducated: the Corporal carries the trappings of no particular culture with him; and though he remains loving and faithful, he is not specifically religious—he makes no mention of God and claims no special tie to anyone. What he possesses is belief in the ability of human beings to act with selfless generosity and love. Having discovered the remarkable powers this faith gives him, he gathers twelve disciples and begins persuading Allied and German troops to put down their weapons and stop the killing.

A Fable moves slowly, through a series of subplots, digressions, and interpolations, to a confrontation between the Allied high command and the Corporal. When that scene comes we learn, as we often do in stories about foundlings, that the Corporal is no ordinary foundling at all. To the contrary, he is the son of the Old Marshall, who is the head of the Allied high command. Acting in his official capacity, the Old Marshall tries to persuade his son to renounce the cause of peace; and when he fails, he orders his son executed. What the Corporal's mysterious origins do, however, aside from linking his story to the story of Tom Jones as well as the story of Jesus Christ, is to confuse things considerably. What are we to make of a Christ-like protagonist whose father has an affiliation with war that forces him to play both tempter and destroyer of his son? What, above all, are we to make of a steadfast son who refuses to explain or complain—who stands, almost silent, making occasional statements and asking a few questions, yet refusing to disclose, except in the vaguest and most laconic way, what it is that he believes. By contrast the Old Marshall sets forth his position in great detail and with considerable rhetorical force —the problem being, first, that he is almost as free as his son is stingy with words; and second, that he contradicts himself repeatedly. As a consequence, the moment toward which the novel slowly and elaborately moves—the confrontation between the Old Marshall and the young

Corporal—delivers too little. None of its possibilities—realist versus idealist; elitist ruler versus simple commoner; father versus son—is fully realized. In the end we have little more than a conflict between an old prolix man of time and history and a young, quiet man of eternity, between a father associated with authority, position, and responsibility, and a son associated with ideals and principles.

In several notable respects this confrontation resembles the one between Cass Edmonds and Ike McCaslin in *Go Down, Moses*.[27] Both *A Fable* and *Go Down, Moses* tend, moreover, toward abstraction and didacticism, just as their protagonists, Ike and the Corporal, tend toward abnegation and martyrdom. Furthermore, in both works Faulkner's sympathies are divided, in part because old preoccupations, having to do with parents and children, life and art, lay imbedded in the confrontations that he depicts. Finally, however, the balance within the two works between the fictional elements and the allegorical is so strikingly different as to suggest that for Faulkner the question of which came first was crucial. "To me," he once remarked, "the New Testament is full of ideas and I don't know much about ideas. The Old Testament is full of people . . . heroes and blackguards . . . and I like to read the Old Testament because it's full of people, not ideas."[28]

From the distinction thus set up, two crucial observations follow: that *A Fable*'s basic affinity as well as much of its obtrusive framework lay with the New Testament, and that Faulkner's talents as a writer coincided with his preferences as a reader. Clearly underway in *Go Down, Moses*, his move toward a fiction of ideas, toward more overt ideological awareness and greater moral directness, had accelerated first with the coming of old age and weariness, then with the coming of World War Two, and again with the coming of fame: as podiums began multiplying, his need to utter proclamations had increased. In *A Fable* we see the consequences of this process. It discloses what Faulkner's emergence as a moralist had meant to his life as a fictionist. It was almost as though his creative self were being forced to serve a foreign dictator. Early in his career Faulkner had come to share deep theoretical interests as well as sincere moral concerns with other writers. Still, through much of his career—and particularly in his greatest novels, *The Sound and the Fury, Light in August, Absalom, Absalom!*—his distrust of abstractions and his suspicion of systems had balanced both his theoretical interests and his moral concerns. As a result he had written novels that dramatized possibilities without defending positions. In *A Fable*, on the other hand, as in many of his public statements, he moved decisively toward the kinds of simplifications that proposals require.

Of *A Fable* Faulkner once said what he might also have said of *Absalom, Absalom!*: "I was primarily telling what to me was a tragic story, of the father who had to choose between the sacrifice or the saving of his son."[29] Since one such telling became a masterpiece, the other a work sadly flawed, we may well wonder whether, in addition to the abstractness that characterized its origins and the fumbling that characterized its making, *A Fable* does not betray some deeper impediment. *A Fable* is after all not just another story of conflict between parent and child; it is specifically the story of a son who conspires, in fetching and almost unwitting innocence, to overthrow his father. The father's response is carefully considered, and it comes to an expectant son. What is striking in all of this, beyond the seeming inevitability of the father's victory, even beyond the stillness and silence of the son's resignation, is Faulkner's unmastered ambivalence. Earlier he had given children much of his sympathy and many of his words. In *A Fable* some of his sympathy goes toward the Corporal, but most of his words and most of the power go to the Old Marshall. In addition, all of the women in the book remain remote. The Corporal has his Mary and Martha, and after he is dead his body is turned over to his sister for burial. But peace—of the largest, most abstract kind—is the only cause that truly moves him. He is, to the end, a single-minded and astonishingly detached man, and he finds the fulfillment that he seeks in the death that he suffers. Even when he bespeaks resistance, he seems to yearn for dismissal.

The ordeal of *A Fable* at an end, Faulkner boarded a plane for Europe.[30] For months he had been preparing for endings, but he still found the prospect of them troubling. Jill was almost twenty-one, and was eager for independence. As "a gesture when she became of age," he dedicated *A Fable* to her.[31] To Joan Williams, the other of his heart's darlings, he had already given the manuscript of *The Sound and the Fury*.[32] But Joan, too, was visibly restless, and he knew that his career as her lover was over. Earlier, in a letter to Harold Ober, he had talked of making a complete break with his present life. Instead, he accepted a new assignment: working with Howard Hawks on a movie called *Land of the Pharaohs*.[33]

Faulkner left New York on 30 November 1953, bound for Paris and armed with a bottle. Over the next several weeks—in Paris briefly; then in Stresa, Italy, on Lake Maggiore; then in St. Moritz, Switzerland—he tried to work with Hawks and Harry Kurnitz on a script. He liked Stresa better than St. Moritz, where there were too many actors and tourists. But in neither place was he able to work. Shifting restlessly about, he visited Else Jonsson in Stockholm, Monique and Jean-Jacques Salomon in Paris, and Harold Raymond of Chatto & Windus in Kent, England. In January he joined Hawks and Kurnitz in Rome to begin casting. He liked Rome, particularly its fountains; and he found Kurnitz an understanding as well as talented collaborator. But Faulkner was drinking heavily. "Well, with one martini ah feel bigger, wiser, taller, and with two it goes to the superlative, and ah feel biggest, wisest, tallest," he told Lauren Bacall, "and with three there ain't no holdin' me."[34]

And in fact it was becoming difficult to hold him. In February, when the crew left for Cairo, Faulkner returned to Paris. A few days later, awaiting his arrival in Cairo, Hawks and Kurnitz watched in disbelief as an ambulance roared out to carry him from the plane on a stretcher. Following several days' convalescence, first in a hospital, then in a hotel, he tried to get back to work.[35] But script-writing was clearly no answer to his depressions. In December he had written Joan Williams trying to assure her "that nothing basic has changed with us." He had wanted, he said, to be a father to her, to be "the one . . . who desired, tried, to put always first your hopes and dreams and happiness." Above all, he wanted her not to regret the things they had done as lovers. "I know I am better for it," he said, "and I know that some day you will know that you are too."[36] But the sense that things had changed haunted him. "I love the book," he wrote Saxe Commins in February, recalling *A Fable*'s origins and the long years he had given to writing it. But he could not overcome his fear that it might turn out to be a "bust." In March he learned that Joan had married Ezra Bowen. A few weeks later Jill wrote saying that she wished to marry a young West Point graduate named Paul Summers, Jr.[37]

Wanting to spend a part of April in Paris and then return home, Faulkner asked Howard Hawks to let him go. But this release, though it came quickly, did nothing to reverse Faulkner's dive. He hated hospitals: their whiteness, their sterility, their regimen, reminded him of jails, ovens, death. Yet he could not control the drinking that kept landing him in them. Neither old friends, like Else Jonsson and Monique Salomon, nor new friends, like Jean Stein, seemed able to help. He had met Jean Stein in St. Moritz. She was young, intelligent, attractive, and responsive, and she knew and admired his fiction. He had seen her in Paris in December, in Rome in January, in Paris in February, and now again in Paris in April. Already he had begun to depend on her. But Jill, Joan, and *A Fable* had become involved in an emotional tangle that resisted substitution as well as resolution. What pressed on him from all sides was the sense of endings.

He had gone on dreading the quick, harsh flowing of time that was making Jill a woman. Her move toward maturity and independence had interacted as well as coincided with Joan's coming. With Joan he had sought, apparently with mixed results, "to walk in April again." In *The Wintering*, her fictionalized account of her affair with Faulkner, Joan Williams depicts a young girl-woman named Amy Howard ("I'm neither a woman or a girl," she writes) who finally accepts a famous and aging novelist named Jeff Almoner as her lover. Almoner is a short man whose manners are courtly and old-fashioned. He walks with a noticeably erect back, practices silence, and drinks heavily. In addition, he is burdened with a wife who not only drinks and takes codeine but has tried to burn at least one of his manuscripts.[38] When Amy enters his life, Almoner intends merely to help and advise her. He wants to free her from her middle-class manners and mores and to make a poet of her. Soon, however, he finds himself in love. With her as his lover, he feels that he might not only live but write again. Soon she becomes for him the perfect embodiment of the ideal figure he has always kept locked away in his mind: "I never intended to fall in love with you when all of this began," he writes her. "But yours is the girl-woman face and figure I see when I close my eyes." As the embodiment of the image for which he writes, Amy has turned him from "the cat who walked by himself" into a man enthralled. Or, still more radically, as the embodiment of the forbidden figure of whom he has always dreamed, she becomes the one for whom he has always written: "I've learned something about my life recently," he says. "Everything I've done was for you . . . even when you were still in darkness. . . . Yes, even before you were born."[39]

Perhaps it was as a token of some such feeling as this that Faulkner gave Joan Williams the manuscript of the story of Caddy Compson, the girl he still thought of as his heart's darling. For he almost certainly regarded Joan as the culmination of many things. In *Mosquitoes* Gordon says that Pat Robyn's "name is like a little golden bell hung in my heart," a line he later associates with Edmond Rostand's *Cyrano de Bergerac*. While writing *Mosquitoes*, Faulkner had used this line in a letter to Helen Baird. In *The Wintering* it comes up several times. Jeff not only quotes and translates it for Amy; he later gives her a small golden bell to wear so that she will always remember him. In letters to Joan Williams, Faulkner used other lines that he associated specifically with Meta Doherty and *The Wild Palms*—lines that are also echoed in *The Wintering*.[40] Given such confluence, we may fairly assume that Joan became several things for Faulkner—not only his heart's darling, nor merely one he had tried through love to shape into a poet, but also the daughter of his mind. Late in *The Wintering* Jeff speaks words to Amy that bear clear resemblance to words Faulkner had recently written to Joan: "I'm better for all that's happened to us," he says. "I hope, someday, you'll feel you are." Just before he speaks these words, however, Jeff speaks others that make explicit the light in which he views the love he and Amy have shared: "No matter what course your life takes, there are some things between us that can't change. There's a bond that nothing can break. There's been love between us, but sin. No I'm not talking about morality. I know I was the father you wanted. We've committed incest, then. That alone will always hold us together. Now, are you going to run?"[41]

These lines are remarkable in at least two ways. First, they bear a clear resemblance to Quentin Compson's view of incest in *The Sound and the*

Fury. Although Quentin only contemplates and talks of incest, he too sees
it as a way of transmuting perishable love into enduring bond. Second,
they bring the freedom and renewal Faulkner had found with Joan under
the aspect of old compulsions. From one perspective we may say that
Amy and Jeff freely express their desires: she for her father and he both
for his daughter and for the figure buried back in his mind. Furthermore,
compared to the price the Corporal pays for seeking to overthrow his
father in *A Fable*, the price Amy and Jeff pay for "incest" is mild. In saying this, however, we also define their freedom as a form of compulsion,
their expression as a mode of substitution. Even as he pursues and courts
Amy, Jeff works on another novel. At about the time he completes his
novel, their affair ends. Yet despite this remarkable reciprocity, their affair and his novel move to different conclusions. For *The Wintering* is a
story of prolonged, courtly pursuit and abbreviated consummation. It
contains more than its fair share of false starts, hesitations, and deferrals.
And when consummation comes, it is over before it begins. "I had waited
for you too long," Jeff says plaintively, looking toward the moment he
knows is certain, when his lover will be gone.[42]

Jeff Almoner loves knowing that he is fated to lose the girl-woman,
daughter-lover named Amy Howard—that in the end "the face and figure"
locked away in his mind will be all that is left him. When that moment
comes, he is almost prepared. When a similar moment came to Faulkner, it
proved painful beyond anything he had anticipated, even in telling Joan that
he preferred grief to nothing. He had known, obviously, that he was fated
to lose Jill and Joan to other men, but he could find no beginning to relieve the pain of such endings. The long, protracted, painful making of *A
Fable* had left him half-convinced that his life as an artist, like his life as
loving father and courtly lover, was over. Within a few days of his arrival
in Paris, he repeated the Cairo routine: a brief stay in a hospital followed
by a longer convalescence in a hotel. Confused and frightened, he decided
to go home.[43]

Through most of May he worked on Greenfield Farm, hoping to reclaim it from neglect while working himself "back into proper physical
condition." But his old activities soon seemed to him almost useless. Even
as a way "to get time passed," farming had lost its appeal: in late May he
sold his stock and leased his farm.[44] While Jill and Estelle busied themselves preparing for an August wedding, he stood by, looking on, wondering what ghastly amount the affair would cost and knowing that he
needed something to do. Suddenly a telephone call brought an unexpected diversion. It came from Muna Lee, a State Department employee
who wanted to know whether Faulkner would be willing to attend an in-
ternational writers' conference in São Paulo, Brazil, from 6 August to 16
August 1954, for the purpose of improving relations between the United

States and the countries of South America. Since Faulkner possessed little experience as a goodwill ambassador and remained shy and unpredictable, it was in some ways a surprising invitation. People had known for years that he could be rude as well as courtly. Less than a year had passed since *Life* magazine described him as "an alcoholic refugee, self-pursued." But the Nobel Prize had given him great visibility, and he had developed some skill as well as a need for making public statements. He had always liked the idea of serving his country, and over the last several years he had come especially to admire André Malraux's double life as novelist and statesman.[45]

During a brief appearance in Peru, en route to Brazil, Faulkner handled a news conference and a cocktail party with seeming ease. Fielding questions on race and art as well as his own novels, he appeared neither shy nor nervous. Suddenly, somewhere between Lima and São Paulo, he started drinking steadily, as though to abort the entire venture. With the help of a doctor and several officials, he was able to resume what he had begun, and soon his mood began to change. For months he had been looking for a new task; now he felt that perhaps he had found it. In the United States, confronted by reporters who seemed to him presumptuous, he was sometimes surly and misleading. "I never tell the truth to reporters," he once told a startled woman who had caught him in a lie. But in São Paulo, it was his ease that reporters noticed, whether the questions had to do with fiction or social problems. There for the first time publicly, he admitted disappointment with *A Fable*. And there he directly confronted an issue that was more and more to occupy him: racism, he said, was the world's great problem, tolerance its only hope.[46]

For years Faulkner had regarded himself as a person who had chosen art over the provincial values and prejudices that were a part of his heritage. Over the last several years he had been exploring the social implications of that self-conception.[47] Since he was not a systematic thinker, however, his statements on peace and especially race continued to move uneasily from position to position rather than along a single, clearly developed line. On one side he wanted the United States in general and the South in particular to denounce racial attitudes and policies that he associated with "injustice and outrage and dishonor and shame"; on the other he was suspicious of governmental intervention and especially of forced desegregation.[48] Stressing now one of these things and then the other, he disappointed or angered his countrymen as often as he pleased them. In foreign countries, however, where discussions remained more general and where local pressures, including threats of violence, were remote, he was free to proclaim the moral repugnance and mounting danger of racism without having to recommend caution and patience. As a result, it was abroad that he felt more relaxed in dealing with social issues, and it was there that he met with greater success.

Within a week of his return, Jill's wedding day had come and gone, leaving him and Estelle spent and depressed. Finding little comfort in each other, they resumed their separate lives. Shortly after Estelle left for Manila to visit Victoria, Bill, and Vicky Fielden, her daughter, son-in-law, and granddaughter, Faulkner left for New York, planning to see Jean Stein and hoping to find another task that felt right. Following his return from Brazil he had written Harold Howland of the State Department to say that he had enjoyed the trip and would be available again. Although he was "too inexperienced yet to judge" his effectiveness, he wanted Howland to know that he was willing to "answer in detail any questions," that he had become "suddenly interested in what" he was trying to do, and that he would be in New York in the fall ready to discuss other "possibilities, situations, capacities" in which he might serve. When the discussions brought no new assignment, Faulkner felt let down. Left without a task to engage him, he began swinging back and forth between New York and Oxford, spending a month here, a month there. "I do a lot of moving about these days," he wrote Else Jonsson.[49] Now and then a story came. In New York in September 1954 he finished "Race at Morning," a hunting tale about Ike McCaslin and other familiar figures. Later he wrote a Snopes story called "By the People." But it was restlessness that consumed him and death that preoccupied him—often as a darkness into which he would not walk, occasionally as a deliverance "from the anguish and grief and inhumanity of mankind."[50]

Hoping to overcome the uneasiness he felt, Faulkner began accepting new assignments and reworking old material. For *Sports Illustrated* he covered a hockey match in January and the Kentucky Derby in May. In between, he and Saxe Commins designed a volume called *Big Woods* (1955), another partly old and partly new book. Handsomely made, it brought together four hunting stories—"The Bear," "The Old People," "A Bear Hunt," and "Race at Morning"—with drawings by Edward Shenton. In the care with which Faulkner worked on the book we see two continuing interests (in hunting and hunting stories) and two revived interests (in drawing and book design). In several ways *Big Woods* was a perfect project for him. It took him back into contact with work that still moved him, and, at a time when he was clearly tired, it gave him the sense of work without the agony of it. But in addition to showing that Faulkner was still a writer, *Big Woods* was undertaken to give his moral concerns artistic form. To stories that he had already written, some of them more than twenty years earlier, Faulkner added five short prose pieces ("interrupted catalysts," he termed them) that linked the stories to each other and also tied them to the history of Yoknapatawpha.[51] In the stories we encounter several scattered episodes out of Yoknapatawpha's past. In the short prose pieces we go back to the beginning, when Yoknapatawpha was

still unspoiled wilderness, and forward almost to the present, when Ike
McCaslin is nearly eighty—that is, from a time when the virgin land was
"rich deep black alluvial" to a time when it has been "deswamped and de-
nuded and derivered" by men whose only concern is making money.[52]
Finally, however, this attempted reach accentuates the problem the book
as a whole raises. For, despite the shared scene and some overlapping interests, there is marked tension between the stories that provide an occasion for the sketches and the sketches that provide a context for the stories.
In the stories, meaning originates in characters who act in specific situations; in the sketches, Faulkner's rhetoric and ideology seem obtrusive.

What the latter in fact resemble are the speeches Faulkner was giving
and the essays he was writing in connection with the public role he had
come to play. During World War Two he had anticipated changes that
would force "the politicians . . . to make good the shibboleth they glibly
talk about freedom, liberty, human rights." As the question of "the thirst
and need of the Negro" for justice began to come up with greater fre-
quency and intensity, Faulkner began to take a more public stance. "It
was about this time," his brother John wrote later, "that Bill started writing and talking integration. It did not set well with the rest of us."[53]

While members of his family were writing letters and making statements designed to shun his opinions, Faulkner's neighbors were threatening to retaliate. Calling him names like "Weeping Willie Faulkner" and
"nigger-lover," they harassed and challenged him. "Of course, as soon as
Bill started talking integration he became subject to anonymous phone
calls at odd hours. Mysterious voices cursed him, and his mail was filled
with abusive anonymous letters. Since none of us agreed with Bill's views
we said, 'It serves him right. He ought to have known this would happen.'"
At times the controversy engaged and even exhilarated Faulkner. His
cause was good, his targets easy, his rejoinders witty. But he was often
deeply disturbed—not only because he knew that he might be forced to
leave his native state, but also because he knew that the "folly and savagery
and inhumanity" around him might lead to large-scale disaster.[54]

With the "tragic trouble in Mississippi" still intensifying, Faulkner decided to accept a State Department assignment that would take him
around the world. On 29 July 1955 he left Oxford bound for Tokyo and
a three weeks' stay in Japan. After hours of travel with too little sleep and
too much whiskey, he found himself surrounded by people, their questions prepared, their pencils poised. Sometimes he joked about being "an
old veteran sixth-grader." But there were times when he felt genuinely disadvantaged. In a relaxed, confident mood, he enjoyed expressing his opinions and convictions; sometimes he came close to pontificating. But when
he sensed that people expected him to be lettered, erudite, and wise, he
tended to withdraw, and he tended to drink. Once again he needed

assistance to avoid a collapse, and once again he found it—from a doctor and a perceptive official named Leon Picon.[55]

With great effort and considerable help, Faulkner turned near-disaster into his finest moment as an envoy. He fared better, Picon noticed, when there was little time for concerted drinking, when meetings with students outnumbered meetings with professors, and when there were pretty girls in the audience. Given shrewdly arranged schedules and carefully arranged audiences, Faulkner talked easily about books, war, and race, hunting, farming, and sailing. Although his manners remained formal and his replies formulaic, he seemed poised and responsive. Finding his demeanor almost oriental, the Japanese liked him.[56]

In late August he flew to Manila, where he made public appearances and visited Victoria, Bill, and Vicki Fielden. Then he left for Rome, where he joined Jean Stein. What he had in mind was a few days' relaxation before undertaking another round of State Department appearances. Shortly after his arrival, however, news of the murder and mutilation of a fourteen-year-old boy named Emmett Till reached Europe. In a brief press dispatch Faulkner described the murder, by two Mississippi white men of "an afflicted Negro child," as an act of fear. If we in America, he continued, "have reached that point in our desperate culture when we must murder children, no matter for what reason or what color, we don't deserve to survive, and probably won't." Having issued his statement and completed his European tour, he met Jean Stein again, this time in Paris, then went on to England and Iceland, the last two stops on his official itinerary. By the time he reached New York, in mid-October, he felt that he had finally worked out his restlessness. After spending a few days in New York he planned to "go back to Mississippi . . . and get to work again." Perhaps he still had not only a need to write but things to add to his "imaginary country and county."[57]

Word that his mother, now eighty-four, had suffered a cerebral hemorrhage hastened his return. When he got to Oxford he found that his mother was recovering and that his wife had joined Alcoholics Anonymous. Although she had been ill off and on for years, Estelle had gone on drinking heavily. Helped by Jill, she had decided to make a fresh start. Hoping to make a start of his own, Faulkner decided to take up the long-delayed sequel to The Hamlet. But first there were two trips he wanted to make, one to Washington and New York for official debriefing, the other to New Orleans and Pascagoula on a kind of pilgrimage.[58] Over the years he had walked the narrow streets of the Vieux Carré and the beaches of Pascagoula with Helen and Estelle, Meta and Joan. Now he wanted to walk them with Jean Stein.

By December he was back in Oxford, writing about the Snopeses. At first the words came slowly, or refused to come at all. As a young poet he had tried to create something wholly new, only to have the echoing voices of ancestors and predecessors almost paralyze him. Now it was not so much the presence of ancestors and predecessors as the shadow of his younger self that haunted him. More and more he found it impossible to believe that he could match his own earlier feats. The sense he attributes to Gavin Stevens—of standing "suzerain and solitary above the whole sum of your life beneath the incessant ephemeral spangling"—was what he wanted and needed to feel as well as imagine. But it was weariness and fear that he felt, not power and dominance. Soon he began to think that he might be "burned out," that he might never again catch "fire in the old way." Like *A Fable*, *The Town* would reflect in its length his need to write big books, and in its tone his need to give advice and utter profundities. But he still needed a woman to write for, a woman he knew believed in him. "I feel pretty good over your reaction to the new Snopes stuff," he wrote Jean in January. Later, as good days alternated with bad, his letters to Jean mixed reports of progress with doubts about whether he would ever again write with "fire, force, passion." But since Jean believed in him, he was determined to go on, especially since he wanted to believe that she was right and he wrong.[59]

Despite a series of interruptions, he persisted. In late January he was writing so well that it frightened him. In February and March, when racial controversy embroiled him, he slowed almost to a stop.[60] In pieces like "A Letter to the North" and "On Fear: The South in Labor," he tried to work out a position that would bring about reform without leading to violence. But his efforts pleased no one. While W. E. B. Du Bois was challenging him to public debate, angry voices were daring him to "come over to the Delta to test them."[61] Troubled about the land in which he lived and uncertain about his ability to write, he drank heavily and rode recklessly. If drinking made him feel "bigger, wiser, taller," and then simply superlative, riding made him feel bigger and stronger. Large, unruly horses, like the one he called Tempy, posed a challenge he required: "something deep and profound in his emotional nature and need," a "desire for physical supremacy, victory."[62]

During the late winter and early spring Faulkner made little progress on his larger challenge. But he continued to work at it, first in Oxford; then in Charlottesville, where Jill's first child was born; then in New York, where Jean was working for the *Paris Review*; then again in Oxford. In late spring and through the summer, as he spent more time in Oxford, he began to work with greater intensity. In July his hesitation and uncertainty faded. By late August, when he completed his manuscript, he thought his new book sad as well as funny.[63]

The Town took Faulkner back to "Father Abraham" of the late twenties, to pieces like "Mule in the Yard" (1934), and to the work outlined in a letter to Robert Haas in 1938. Whereas *A Fable* was a long time in process, *The Town* was a long time in gestation. He had been thinking and talking about parts of it for thirty years. Reluctant to admit that the book reflected "tiredness" with his fictional kingdom, he acknowledged that it might have been "put off too long" and grown "a little stale."[64]

In fact *The Town* reflects what readers have sensed and what Faulkner admitted—guardedly in interviews, more openly in letters—that he was not only older but tired when he finally got around to writing it. One of its most poignant moments comes when, at age thirty-eight, Eula Varner Snopes commits suicide. In *The Town* as in *The Hamlet*, Eula exudes sexuality. But in *The Town* she is more imperial than bovine, and she becomes tragic. She dies in part to save her daughter from scandal; but she also dies because her meager, rapacious world contains no person worthy of her life and love: "She was bored," Ratliff says. "She loved, had a capacity to love, for love, to give and accept love. Only she tried twice and failed twice to find somebody not just strong enough to deserve, earn it, match it, but even brave enough to accept it." Like this remarkable reclamation of Eula, however, the work's unevenness is only in part a result of weariness; it is also a result of dissociation between the man who conceived the Snopes saga and the man who wrote *The Town*. The tension we feel in *A Fable* is between intention and genius; of all Faulkner's work, it most clearly reflects the consequences of his having determined to write a book alien to his gifts. In it, however, donnée and intention are allied: it was abstract and didactic from its conception to its completion. In *The Town*, on the other hand, genius and donnée are allied, this being one of the primary implications of its early conception. What damaged it, in addition to waning energy, was divided intention—the intention of the man who wrote it being different from the intention of the man who conceived it. If *A Fable* suggests that Faulkner's effort to make himself a different kind of writer had met with partial success, *The Town* suggests that the change had been substantial.

Although some of the energy and delight of *The Hamlet* enter *The Town*, we feel them most clearly in sections written earlier, like the "Mule in the Yard" episode; or in elements introduced earlier, like Ratliff's wry determination to oppose Flem's inexorable march toward the presidency of the Sartoris bank. Joined by Gavin Stevens and Charles Mallison, Ratliff goes on trying to do something to stop Flem. Of all characters in *The Town*, however, it was of two women—Eula and her daughter Linda—that Faulkner said he felt especially proud.[65] Clearly Flem and Stevens continued to hold his interest, and Ratliff his affection. Yet he found himself moved most deeply by Eula's failed search to find a love and a place of her own. Although she lacks Caddy's will to survive, Eula shares Caddy's capacity for love. She dies essentially of heartbreak, having despaired of finding what she needs. Linda, too, is interesting on several counts, including the resemblances she bears. In her problematic birth, she recalls Miss Quentin; in other ways, she resembles Joan Williams, just as her mentor, Gavin Stevens, resembles both Phil Stone and William Faulkner. Like Stone, Stevens is a tall, wordy lawyer and a frustrated teacher. Concerned about his reputation and Linda's, and mindful that his protegé is very young, Stevens tries with Linda, as Faulkner had with Joan, to give his emotion a proper direction. For a time he thinks of himself primarily as her father and tutor. He wants to direct her reading, form her mind, and shape her destiny. Since he feels restricted, however, he thinks of Linda as feeling repressed. Soon he is not only a father nurturing his daughter and a tutor educating his student, he is a knight, and he wants to be a lover. As a knight, he hopes to free his maiden from the inadequate mores that inhibit her; as a lover, he longs to possess as well as shape and free her.[66]

If in Eula we observe something of the darkness that was coming to fill Faulkner's life—his rising sense that he would never find a love commensurate with his capacity for wonder—in Linda we see the drama of longstanding dissatisfactions. Early in his life Faulkner had begun raising dissatisfactions with his region and his family to the level of grand observation, and those dissatisfactions survive in *The Town*. Finally, however, they are forced into formulas that are too familiar and simple. What *The Town* constitutes is a revision of Yoknapatawpha as well as a return to it, primarily because it lacks the energizing complications Faulkner's imagination had always needed. As a fictionist, Faulkner had thrived on division. In his need to go in and out, up and down, from engagement to detachment, immersion to flight, and in his imaginative dependence on mutually supportive oppositions (Yoknapatawpha and Lafayette, Jefferson and Oxford, imaginary kingdom and actual land), we locate his dependence on contraries. In this dependence, moreover, his needs as a man and his needs as an artist met and measured one another. Early in his life he had begun to search for a frame that could contain the chaos of consciousness and disclose the inexplicable balancings he felt within himself. As a novelist he had learned to experiment so successfully with frames that in his great fiction it is impossible to say where technique begins and ends. In *The Town*'s most obvious predecessor, *The Hamlet*, he had demonstrated imaginative mastery of economic, social, and demographic shifts that implied radical upheaval. Confident of his power to master drastic changes, he had felt no need to simplify or reduce them in advance. In *The Town*, on the other hand, the balancing of oppositions, the matching of contrary needs, desires, and intentions, gives way to simplifications and reductions, particularly where Gavin Stevens and Linda Snopes are concerned.

With revision of *The Town* completed, Faulkner began moving back and forth between Oxford and New York. In Oxford he tried to help Adlai

Stevenson defeat Dwight Eisenhower. Knowing that his candidate "had three strikes against him: wit, urbanity, and erudition," he found the result disappointing but not surprising.[67] In New York he tried to hold on to Jean Stein, with results that he found painful. Through most of December he stayed in Oxford, reading proof, celebrating Christmas, and riding a dangerous young horse called Tempy. When he returned to New York in January 1957, Jean made clear her desire to be free. The news came after a series of warnings. A year earlier he had wondered whether knowing that he needed her made her feel nervous or vain. Through the writing of *The Town* she had remained supportive, despite apparent nervousness. Still, when the end came, it left him feeling spent and bitter.[68]

After several weeks of drinking and one of hospital care, he left New York for Charlottesville to become writer-in-residence at the University of Virginia. By the time he arrived, in mid-February, classes were underway, and his assigned tasks were waiting. In addition to public appearances, he was expected to meet students in scheduled sessions and keep regular office hours. Although some professors made him feel unlettered and uneasy, his relations were generally cordial. With one or two younger faculty, Frederick Gwynn and especially Joseph Blotner, he became friendly.[69] Around students, he seemed comfortable and forthcoming. Wearing tweed coats, holding his pipe, he looked professorial. Most of the classroom sessions followed an informal question-and-answer format that sooner or later gave him an opportunity to talk about all of his novels and many of his stories. Frequently he fell back on familiar formulas, some of them dating from his days in New Orleans: fiction, he several times remarked, was a compound of "imagination, observation, and experience." Occasionally he forgot or misremembered stories, or recalled versions of them that he had considered and discarded. To him his kingdom was still in motion and inexhaustible. There were many episodes, adventures, even characters that he had yet to write, and a few that he had yet to discover.[70]

In these sessions, as in several interviews, Faulkner's favorite picture of the artist emerged as a somewhat lush fin de siècle version of Romanticism's. The artist, he said, was a demon-driven creature, haunted by a foreknowledge of death and determined to leave a scratch on the wall of oblivion. His needs were simple (solitude, pencil, and paper; tobacco, food, and whiskey), and his only responsibility was to his art. He was completely ruthless, completely amoral; to get his book written, he would do anything. When imagination came into conflict with pattern, "it was the pattern that bulged." But the aim was "to make imagination and the pattern conform, meet, be amicable." For what the artist sought was "not the sum of a lot of scribbling, it's one perfect book. . . . It's one single urn or shape."[71]

Sketched during the fifties, this portrait bears a more obvious resemblance to the man Faulkner had been than to the man he had become. His life was more comfortable now, his finances more secure, his fame more widely established. As late as 1950 his own country had continued to spurn him. The sentiments southerners began expressing soon after publication of *Sanctuary* (1931)—that the depravity of Faulkner's characters had nothing to do with them—the *New York Times* had articulated for all Americans in 1950, after announcement of the Nobel Prize. His world was "too often vicious, depraved, decadent, corrupt." Incest and rape might be common pastimes in Jefferson, but they were "not elsewhere in the United States." "Americans most fervently hope," the *Times* continued, that neither the award given by Sweden nor the "enormous vogue of Faulkner's works" among foreigners meant that they associated American life with his fiction. A few years later, however, even Mississippi and Clifton Fadiman had capitulated. Having earlier refused a free copy of *Soldiers' Pay*, the University of Mississippi had begun a Faulkner collection. Having written a fatuous and ignorant review of *Absalom, Absalom!*, Fadiman had overpraised *A Fable*.[72]

Yet, despite comfort, money, and fame, Faulkner's life was far from placid. Clearly less driven by art, he remained self-driven—as his writing, drinking, and riding show. He and Estelle liked living in Charlottesville, where they could be closer to Jill and her family and farther from threatening calls and obscene letters. They enjoyed spending time at the university and especially at the Keswick and Farmington Hunt clubs. One of the members at Keswick was Linton R. Massey, an intelligent and wealthy man who had been collecting Faulkner's books for nearly thirty years.[73] Other people at both clubs proved kind and friendly. Faulkner's interest in tennis, golf, and flying had faded over the years. Only sailing and riding remained as diversions, and only riding remained a passion. For years he had hunted fox, coon, and deer with Red Brite and Ike Roberts in the river bottoms of Mississippi, where he dined on collards and coon. But he had always enjoyed the hunt more than the kill, and several years before, he had decided to concentrate on the chase: "Because every time I see anything tameless and passionate with motion, speed, life, being alive, I see a young passionate beautiful living shape."[74] In Charlottesville, where the ceremony and pageantry of the hunt counted for so much, he found exactly what he wanted and needed: the sense of ancient rite and ritual; the beauty of animals alive with motion; and the danger of putting large, powerful mounts over high fences.

A month after his arrival in Charlottesville, he left for Greece on another State Department assignment. In Athens he attended the premiere of Dimitri Myrat's production of *Requiem*, received the Silver Medal of the Athens Academy, and delivered another acceptance speech. In between official appearances, he sailed among the islands of the Aegean.

Queried about his current writing, he discussed *The Town*, which had just been published, and *The Mansion*, which he said he intended to write. Back in Charlottesville, he found himself more and more troubled by the fate of the Snopes chronicle—his sense that he had let "so many other things" get "in the way of it," and his sense that "you shouldn't put off too long writing something which you think is worth writing." In May Random House announced a sequel to *The Town*, and Faulkner announced his intention "to keep on writing about" the Snopes family until he had "got it all told."[75]

In June, when he started for home, he had several things in mind. He wanted to reclaim Greenhill Farm from neglect; he wanted to sail and ride; and he wanted to begin *The Mansion*. Since he was serious about fox hunts and hunt clubs, riding had become a task as well as a passion. At times he spoke of it as though he were engaged in serious training. As he soon discovered, simply living in Mississippi in 1957 made race an inescapable preoccupation. Still, despite distractions and interruptions, after some things and in addition to others, he continued trying to put words together. In December he wrote Else Jonsson in terms that echoed letters written two years earlier to Jean Stein. He was working on the third volume of the Snopes trilogy, "which will finish it," he said, "and maybe then my talent will have burnt out and I can break the pencil and throw away the paper and rest, for I feel very tired."[76]

Early in 1958 Faulkner returned to the University of Virginia to begin his second term as writer-in-residence. Hoping to keep his farm from going to pot again, he had made arrangements to return to Oxford for spring planting. Hoping to maintain the momentum he had built up, he had brought his manuscript with him to Charlottesville.[77] Neither the scheduled sessions with students, the occasional public appearances, nor the regular office hours seemed bothersome to him. He liked the university as well as Charlottesville. After his second and last term as writer-in-residence, he maintained a tie with the university by serving as consultant to the Alderman Library in 1959, and as Balch Lecturer on American Literature in 1960. For the rest of his life, Charlottesville seemed almost as much his home as Oxford.

Through it all, however—the students and the office hours, the riding and the drinking—he wrote. At times it seemed like fun again; more often it was all will. Still he continued, first in Virginia and then through a long summer in Oxford. By August, with tourists in the front yard rubbernecking at the house, he was thinking of buying a place in Virginia. Over Christmas he joined his family in Charlottesville, where he also had "good runs with both Keswick and Farmington." Soon after his return to Oxford, his pace quickened. By late January he had a completed draft. It would require "about a month's cleaning up," he wrote

Random House, before he would have a copy to bring or send them.[78]

The last two stages took longer than Faulkner anticipated. It was 9 March before he had finished his long typescript, and July before galleys were ready. Since Saxe Commins had died, on 17 July 1958, Faulkner worked now with Albert Erskine; and since *The Mansion* was the third volume in a trilogy, editing it proved unusually complicated and time-consuming, even after James Meriwether was brought in to help. For a time Faulkner thought of making minor adjustments in his new book, and then reconciling *The Hamlet* and *The Town* to it in later editions. With some prompting, however, he agreed to follow the obvious course of adjusting *The Mansion* to *The Hamlet* and *The Town*. Minor discrepancies he chose to ignore, on grounds "that 'fact' had almost no connection with 'truth'"; where discrepancies could not be ignored, he changed *The Mansion.*[79]

Moving from book to book, Faulkner had always needed to believe that his latest was his best—that with it he had come yet a little nearer his dream of success, the "one single urn or shape." In art as in so much else, he felt respect, even awe, for ancestors, and secret sympathy for the inheritor, which in this case meant *The Mansion*. But there was a special reason, in addition to this confluence, behind his need to insist on *The Mansion*'s priority. Ending books had never been easy for him: the sense of emptiness, lost purpose, and new failure had always come too soon, pushing out the sense of relief, exhilaration, and fulfillment. Over the last several years, with *A Fable* and *The Town*, each ending had seemed more final; with *The Mansion* he had come to the end of his "planned labors." He wanted and needed to feel that it, the part of him now about to be lost, was worth losing, that he had not merely worn it out and so lost it shabbily.[80] But he knew that *The Hamlet* was closer to the vision that had made the trilogy possible, and he knew that it was a finer novel. In the end he found the courage to follow the appropriate as well as practical course of acknowledging its priority.

Like *The Town*, *The Mansion* is uneven. It too was damaged by long deferral and mounting weariness; and it too betrays signs of conflict between the intention of the man who conceived it and the intention of the man who wrote it. The farther Faulkner got into it, however, the more he made it not only a culmination of the Snopes saga but a revision of his kingdom. It brings many scenes and characters together. With Montgomery Ward Snopes we revisit Miss Reba's, a crucial setting in *Sanctuary*. Through one of Flem's deals, we learn more about Benjy Compson's death and Jason Compson's ventures. Like *The Hamlet* and *The Town*, *The Mansion* is part progress and part chronicle. And like them it is insistently commodious: it uses different narrative voices and shifts perspective frequently; it uses old material, including published stories like "By the

People" and "Shingles for the Lord" and unpublished pieces like "Hog Pawn"; and its large cast includes a host of figures that are familiar and several that are new.

Early in the novel we review Mink Snopes's murder of Houston, a crucial event in *The Hamlet*. Later we see Mink sitting in Parchman Prison, an important setting in *The Wild Palms*. There Mink plots the revenge he will take when he is finally free. Convinced that Flem has betrayed him, Mink lives for the day when he will kill his kinsman. Near the end of the novel we see him carry out his plan. Since by then we have come to associate Mink's revenge with the same inexorability that we have observed in Flem's rise, we anticipate the murder itself and so find it almost anticlimactic. What we do not anticipate are the roles Ratliff, Linda Snopes, and Gavin Stevens play in the crime, nor, for that matter, other developments that come between the plan and the deed, including the sympathy Faulkner creates for Mink.

Although Ratliff, Charles Mallison, and the various Snopeses play major roles in *The Mansion*, Gavin Stevens and especially Linda Snopes emerge as the principal figures. Having left the provinces for New York and Greenwich Village, Linda has acquired an interest in politics to match her interest in art. At times she seems to resemble both Jean Stein and Joan Williams. After she marries a sculptor named Barton Kohl, she goes to Spain to fight for the Loyalists. Having returned to Jefferson, wounded and widowed, she serves a cause Faulkner had served and suffers a fate he had suffered: arousing some "ancient subterrene atavistic ethnic fear" in the people around her, she is branded a "Nigger Lover." Although she and Stevens never sleep together, they do become lovers: "because we are the 2 in all the world who can love each other without having to." Later she helps Mink Snopes work his revenge on Flem—in part out of sympathy for Mink and in part out of a desire to avenge her mother. At the end of the novel Mink flees with money sent by Linda and delivered by Ratliff and Stevens.

Earlier we come to see Mink as one of the earth's dispossessed—a man with body worn out and dream dulled. Through him Faulkner expressed for the last time the sympathy he had always felt for almost defeated humanity. Watching him as he flees, Ratliff and Stevens term him one of the earth's "poor sons of bitches," a phrase that becomes *The Mansion*'s equivalent to Gail Hightower's "Poor man. Poor mankind." Having stressed the representativeness of Mink's ordeal and the solidarity of his agony, Faulkner exalts him. Echoing words he had first used in 1922, he sees Mink "equal to any, good as any, brave as any, being inextricable from, anonymous with all of them: the beautiful, the splendid, the proud and the brave, right on up to the very top itself among the shining phantoms and dreams which are the milestones of the long human recording—Helen and the bishops, the kings and the unhomed angels, the scornful and graceless seraphim."[81]

With these lines, which must surely be viewed not simply in relation to Mink's reclamation but as a kind of summation, Faulkner brought the last of his planned efforts to an end. Both relieved and very tired, he tried to recover his talent for idleness. Talking to old friends about the old times, he seemed mellow as well as nostalgic. All his life he had enjoyed teaching children games and telling them stories. In his grandchildren and their playmates he found another version of one of his first audiences. By the time he finished *The Mansion*, Jill's second child, a boy named for him, was more than a year old. Since Cuthbert was a name Faulkner had finally come to accept as his own, it was a name he wanted perpetuated. His second grandson, William Cuthbert Faulkner Summers, was another small boy with a big name. Not long after he learned to talk, his grandfather taught him to stand up straight and call himself "Will Faulkner."[82]

Yet it was for danger more than leisure that Faulkner had acquired talent. He still visited New York occasionally, and he continued making trips for the State Department—to Denver in the fall of 1959 and Venezuela in the spring of 1961. But he spent most of his time now in Oxford and Charlottesville, where he and Estelle had bought a large, comfortable house on Rugby Road. And in both places he continued to ride. It's "been two years now," he said in February 1961, "since I've done anything much but ride and hunt foxes."[83] As a young man his daring had occasionally exceeded his skill; as an experienced horseman his mounting need of danger regularly exceeded it. Over the years he had taken many falls, several of them serious; in the late fifties, as he rode more recklessly, the falls came more frequently and did more damage, repeatedly to his back, occasionally to arms, shoulders, collarbones. In Oxford he rode Tempy, in Charlottesville, Powerhouse, and in both places he not only accepted but courted danger. "There is something about jumping a horse over a fence," he said, "something that makes you feel good. Perhaps it's the risk, the gamble. In any event it's something I need."[84]

One part of what he sought was a sense of mastery, of "physical supremacy, victory," not only over the large, powerful hunters he liked to ride, but over his own weariness and fear. "It is very fine, very exciting," he wrote Joan Williams in 1959. "Even at 62, I can still go harder and further and longer than some of the others." What he demanded of himself, however, beyond skill and endurance, was total disregard of physical injury, a continuing readiness "to risk . . . my bones."[85] It was as though facing danger was the only way he had of showing contempt for destruction; it was as though he needed to walk to the edge of disaster in order to prove again and again that he neither feared nor desired it.

For a time the pleasures of idleness and danger seemed almost to suffice; "since I ran dry three years ago," he wrote in 1961, "I am not even interested in writing anymore."[86] But his larger need, like his greater talent, was for work: he had never known a home that he did not feel required to earn. Having begun early to feel that he was being tested, he had learned early to test himself repeatedly. A nephew named Jim, he remarked, was "the only person" who liked him for what he was. In part a. way of justifying himself, writing was another, older, way of saying *no* to destruction. During his last several years, reminders of mortality came with disturbing regularity: in July 1958, Saxe Commins; in October 1959, Harold Ober; in January 1960, Albert Camus; in July 1961, Ernest Hemingway. On 16 October 1960, at age eighty-nine, Maud Butler Falkner died, a few days after expressing hope of finding a heaven where she would not have to see the husband she had never liked.[87]

Shortly after Camus's death, Faulkner described Camus as a man who had gone on seeking "answers which only God could know," carrying with him through life "that one same foreknowledge and hatred of death" that moved all artists.[88] By the time Hemingway died, Faulkner had begun his nineteenth and last novel. He wrote now in a voice like his own—that of a sixty-five-year-old grandfather reminiscing about his childhood. Called *The Reivers*, Lucius Priest's "Reminiscence" is distinctly ruminative; it comes to us in a November voice. Through its nostalgic recapitulation, it reflects both the reconciliation Faulkner had finally achieved with the memory of his father and the ease he felt with his grandsons. It takes us out to Yoknapatawpha and back to 1905, when Lucius was a boy of ten, working for his father, Maury, in a livery stable. In the course of his remembered adventures, Lucius introduces us to his mother and three younger brothers; to a servant named Aunt Callie and a chauffeur named Ned McCaslin; and to other familiar figures, including Boon Hogganbeck. Twenty years earlier Faulkner had outlined, as "a sort of Huck Finn" story, a novel about a boy's involvement with three adults: a big, warm, courageous man with the mentality of a child; a shrewd, unscrupulous servant; and an aging, generous, wise prostitute. Exposed to "debauchery and degeneracy and actual criminality," Faulkner said, the boy would learn "courage and honor and generosity and pride and pity," "mostly because of the influence of the whore."[89]

In early August 1961 Faulkner described his new novel as "going well, possibly 1/3 done." Convinced that it was humorous, he was writing easily and having fun. Years before he had designed a cover for *Flags in the Dust*. For his new book he already had a jacket blurb:

> "An extremely important message. . . . eminently qualified to become the Western World's bible of free will and private enterprise."

> *Ernest V. Trueblood*
> Literary & Dramatic Critic,
> Oxford, (Miss.) *Eagle*.

A few weeks later he wrote his editor again, saying that he had "suddenly got hot and finished the first draft" a week ago. "I should have a clean copy to you in a month." Three weeks later he had a revised typescript and a title: *The Reivers: A Reminiscence.*[90]

Much of Faulkner's fiction, particularly his great fiction, had been experimental and innovative. Several of his social pronouncements had seemed iconoclastic. But much of his fiction, complexly in *Absalom, Absalom!*, simply in *The Reivers*, had been given to recapturing the past, to locating there "man in conflict with himself, with his fellow man, or with his time and place." Each of these conflicts had been Faulkner's own, and of each of them he had made his kind of poetry.[91] Often it had seemed to him that he stood in a twilight world, at the end of a culture that had been disrupted in the South by the Civil War and in the West by the Great War. From early on he had felt drawn toward the past yet committed to the present. "Life is motion," he said repeatedly. "What the writer's asking is compassion, understanding, that . . . no matter how fine anything seems, it can't endure, because once it stops, abandons motion, it is dead." What the writer seeks, he said, is "not to choose sides at all," but to express and evoke compassion for what is lost. In response to this double commitment, he created not merely roles, masks, and personae, but a set of relations that implied a set of voices, ranging from "back-looking ghosts" like Quentin, who speaks in outrage and bafflement, to Ratliff, who accepts "a change in culture" without anguish, grief, or even nostalgia.[92] In one of these voices Faulkner discovered the element crucial to all tragedy: recognition that man, caught in the ineluctability of time, can never avenge himself on time. In the other, he discovered the element crucial to all comedy: recognition that man, caught in the ineluctability of time, may enjoy it. More deeply divided than either Quentin or Ratliff, Faulkner created both of them, making his art an exploration of the large land that held them. Naming that land Yoknapatawpha, he conceived it both as an imaginative locality and as a place with a history and processes of its own.

For one part of Faulkner, such exploration was the only thing: "Writing, to him," as Shelby Foote said, "was what living was all about."[93] Sitting alone, silently looking out the window of his workroom, he remained a shy and troubled man. Doubts, fears, anxieties, and, above all, the sense of loss and impending darkness, continued to haunt him. Yet he found in the making of narrative fiction a way of moving beyond perplexity and even impasse to momentary peace. Given solitude, a pen, and "unmarred sheets . . . inviolate and unfailing," he could take the most terrible of realities—"hackneyed accidents," even "madness and hatred"—and turn them into "a kind of splendid and timeless beauty."[94] Still, though Faulkner knew that the finer part of him could not do anything but use words, he could not give up his desire to be a living force of a different sort, and so he wanted and tried for everything. Having devoted his genius to art, he saved some of his talent for life, as we see in his imitation of his great-grandfather; in his imitations of the dandy and the bohemian; in his several explorations of the fate of the scorned lover; in his careers as pilot, farmer, and horseman; and in his roles as son, brother, husband, father, and lover. At times, especially early and late, he recited lines that he had already written; at others, he spoke lines that he later wrote, including some he liked well enough to repeat. Through the remarkable oscillations and reciprocities that he lived, he made life a trying out of art and art a trying out of life. Like his concoctions and fabrications, however, his roles, guises, and careers were more protective than expressive. Only in his fiction did the crucial balance shift: it was in his stories and novels that he took great chances, and it was in them that his deeper self found expression.[95]

His novel finished, Faulkner went back to Charlottesville, ready to relax with his family and keep "busy with horses, fox hunting." *The Reivers* had left him feeling almost like his old self, mainly because it had come easily. "I will wait," he said, "until the stuff is ready, until I can follow instead of trying to drive it." He hunted four days a week now, from daylight well into the morning.[96] Near the end of the year, however, he entered a cycle he could not break. The accumulated damage suffered from falls, particularly to his lower back, made minor mishaps painful. By December he was drinking heavily, in part to relieve pain. In late December and early January he was in and out of hospitals in Charlottesville and Richmond. In mid-January, released from a hospital for the third time in little more than a month, he left for Oxford. For several days he rested, waiting for the wet weather and his poor health to improve. In late January, when the string of cloudy days ended, he began hunting quail and riding again. In April he returned to Virginia. Later that month he spent several days at West Point and several in New York. In April and again in May, he and Estelle thought seriously about buying a large Albemarle County estate. By June their attention centered on Red Acres. Thirty years earlier they had bought a dilapidated mansion and 4 acres of land in depression-ridden Mississippi. Red Acres was an impeccable estate in one of the wealthiest sections of America. Consisting of 250 acres, it included a fine brick home, a stable with nine box stalls, a groom's house, a manager's house, a tenant house, an implement house, two barns, a silo, and a smokehouse. Earlier Faulkner had written, with deep ambivalence, in novels as different as *Absalom, Absalom!* and *The Hamlet*, about men who dreamed of owning great mansions. "I like to sit here," Will Varner says to Ratliff early in *The Hamlet* as he contemplates the columned ruins of the Old Frenchman's place with its stables, slave quarters, terraces, and promenades. "I'm trying to find out what it must have felt like to be the fool that would need all this just to eat and sleep in." But Faulkner was also drawn to splendor. Possessions were for him signs of success, a means of silencing people who had called him "a bum"; and like most ambitious people, he enjoyed the personal and the social pleasures of wealth. If Rowan Oak recalled the Old Colonel's grandeur, Red Acres clearly surpassed it. He was weary, but he was willing to do anything, "to write a book or books . . . or lecture," in order "to own Red Acres."[97]

In fact, however, it was not so much toward the future as the past that he was looking now. In March he sat for a portrait; in May he visited Jean in New York; in June he journeyed to Memphis to see Joan. Several times he spoke of premonitions of death. A few months earlier he had believed that he might go on forever, riding, drinking, and writing. In New York in May, as he spoke of the past, Malcolm Cowley detected a tone "that was not exactly new for him, but that seemed to have a new resonance."[98] Passing through Charlottesville, he returned to Oxford for the last time. There on 17 June, he suffered a bad fall. Weary and hurt, he remounted. "I had to conquer him," he said. And, later, "I don't want to die." But the cycle of suffering and drinking had begun for the last time. On 4 July he announced that he was ready to go to the kind of hospital he had always associated with jails and ovens.[99] On 5 July he entered Wright's Sanitarium in Byhalia; there, early on 6 July, the Old Colonel's birthday, he died of a coronary occlusion.

In "A Note on Sherwood Anderson" Faulkner locates Anderson's "whole biography" in a purported dream that he describes as really "an anecdote or perhaps a parable," and in which we see Anderson "walking for miles along country roads, leading a horse which he was trying to swap for a night's sleep."[100] In this dream-anecdote-parable, Faulkner discerns the logic of Anderson's life: his desire to swap the world given him, "his own America," for a world born of the imagination. Although Faulkner goes on immediately to associate the imaginative process with hard, unremitting work, he is less direct in depicting its secret motivation. He suggests that it derives in part from a love of purity and truth, in part from a love of power, and in part from a "consuming unsleeping appeaseless thirst for glory." But he also suggests that it represents an effort to transmute the self and achieve some final apotheosis; only thus, he implies, can one find peace that lies beyond "the consuming unsleeping" struggle.

As James B. Meriwether has suggested, this piece on Anderson "invites comparison with other" pieces Faulkner wrote, particularly "Carcassonne," which is also a parable about the artist's plight and the imagination's power.[101] In "Carcassonne" the artist is the rider of a horse that gallops with "rhythmic and unflagging fury and without progression" toward some ultimate doom-fulfillment that is ever-more-about-to-be. Aside from

associating the artist with pursuit of the unattainable, however, "Carcassonne" is crucial in several ways. First, it associates women not only with
the power of "the Standard Oil Company" but with inferior wisdom:
"They have learned how to live unconfused by reality, impervious to it."
By contrast the male artist is both confused and vulnerable. Haunted by a
desire *"to perform something bold and tragical and austere,"* he gallops
through his world soaring and thundering, all the while knowing that he is
born to fail and die. What finally reconciles him to such a fate—enabling
him to imagine without alarm his body lying on the rippled floor of the
sea, "tumbling peacefully to the wavering echoes of the tides"—is his sense
of what he can make of it. Although one part of him knows "that the end
of life is lying still," another part refuses to "believe it's true." Out of this
division he creates a style of power. As he lies alone in darkness he listens
to the small feet of rats scurrying above him, stealthy and intent. Yet,
from within this darkness, in anticipation of the moment when the rats
will descend to devour him, he assumes "the office of vision." To his
mind's clairvoyant "eye his motionless body" becomes a thousand things
and so exists no more. Sensing the "steady decay which had set up within
his body on the day of his birth," he turns his dis-ease with living and dying into a principle of creation. His glory consists, then, not only in his
ability to transform dark and tragic figures into figures of delicacy and desire, but also in his ability to make wounding discontent serve the purposes
of life. Imaginatively he is able to open closed doors, approach forbidden
figures, and commit dangerous acts as well as make life a prolonged and
inspired defiance of death by turning it into art. In the second half of
what is surely one of the strangest sentences he ever wrote, Faulkner pictures a "lusty, lean" worm as the proper devourer of men; and, later, a
"suavely shaped" worm as the proper devourer of "women, of delicate
girls." In "Carcassonne," however, these images, like that of the stealthy,
intent rats, become "as a seething of new milk" to the artist. What sin
and death were to Christ—namely, his occasion—the image of the devour-
ing worm is to the artist. Similarly, what Christ was to sin and death—their
only possible antidote—art is to man's sense of failure, imperfection, and
impending death. Art becomes, in these terms, man's subtlest strategy, as
we see in the first half of Faulkner's strange sentence, where, among other
things, he explicitly evokes the Christ analogy. Lying alone in darkness,
Faulkner's artist recalls the long decay that is his life and then leaps to a
strategy that is too direct to be called escapist and too aggressive to be
called compensatory: *"The flesh is dead living on itself subsisting consuming itself thriftily in its own renewal will never die for I am the Resurrection
and the Life."*

Early in his life as an artist Faulkner had begun to dread the moment
"when not only the ecstasy of writing would be gone, but the unreluctance

and the something worth saying too."[102] In part because the division within him ran deep, in part because work was what he did best, and in part because his relation to his art was so intense and satisfying, he came to that moment slowly. Gradually, however, as his confidence in what he had done increased and his confidence in what he was doing slipped away, he began identifying himself with the work he had finished, the selves he had become, as though he knew that what was valuable was what he had already created and so had lost not shabbily. Repeatedly testing the self that remained, he went on waiting for "the moment, instant, night: dark: sleep: when I would put it all away forever that I anguished and sweated over, and it would never trouble me anymore."[103] Having looked at that moment many times, with mixed fear and desire but with defiance, too, he came to it, as he thought Albert Camus had, knowing that he had done all things in his life that he could.

APPENDIX A: *Genealogy*

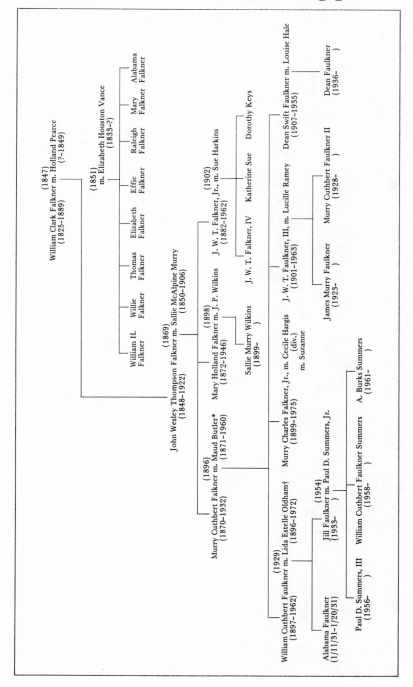

William Clark Falkner m. Holland Pearce (1847)
(1825–1889)   (?–1849)

m. Elizabeth Houston Vance (1851)
(1833–?)

William H. Falkner | Willie Falkner | Thomas Falkner | Elizabeth Falkner | Effie Falkner | Raleigh Falkner | Mary Falkner | Alabama Falkner

John Wesley Thompson Falkner m. Sallie McAlpine Murry (1869)
(1848–1922)   (1850–1906)

Mary Holland Falkner m. J. P. Wilkins (1898)
(1872–1946)

J. W. T. Falkner, Jr., m. Sue Harkins (1902)
(1882–1962)

Sallie Murry Wilkins
(1899–   )

J. W. T. Falkner, IV

Katherine Sue

Dorothy Keys

J. W. T. Falkner, III, m. Lucille Ramey
(1901–1963)

Dean Swift Faulkner m. Louise Hale
(1907–1935)

Murry Cuthbert Faulkner II
(1928–   )

Dean Faulkner
(1936–   )

Murry Cuthbert Falkner m. Maud Butler* (1896)
(1870–1932)   (1871–1960)

Murry Charles Falkner, Jr., m. Cecile Hargis (div.)
(1899–1975)   m. Suzanne

James Murry Faulkner
(1923–   )

William Cuthbert Faulkner m. Lida Estelle Oldham† (1929)
(1897–1962)   (1896–1972)

Jill Faulkner m. Paul D. Summers, Jr. (1954)
(1933–   )

William Cuthbert Faulkner Summers
(1958–   )

A. Burks Summers
(1961–   )

Alabama Faulkner
(1/11/31–1/20/31)

Paul D. Summers, III
(1956–   )

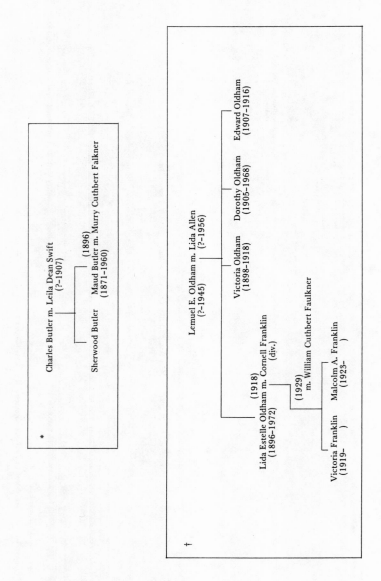

*

Charles Butler m. Leila Dean Swift
(?–1907)

(1896)
Sherwood Butler   Maud Butler m. Murry Cuthbert Falkner
(1871–1960)

†

Lemuel E. Oldham m. Lida Allen
(?–1945)   (?–1956)

Victoria Oldham   Dorothy Oldham   Edward Oldham
(1898–1918)   (1905–1968)   (1907–1916)

Lida Estelle Oldham m. Cornell Franklin
(1896–1972)   (1918)
                   (div.)
                   (1929)
                   m. William Cuthbert Faulkner

Victoria Franklin   Malcolm A. Franklin
(1919–   )   (1923–   )

APPENDIX B: *Chronology*

1825	6 July: William Clark Falkner, later "The Old Colonel," is born in Knox County, Tennessee.
1842	He arrives in Mississippi.
1843–1845	He settles in Ripley, Mississippi.
1846–1847	He serves in the Mexican War.
1847	9 July: he marries Holland Pearce.
1848	2 Sept.: John Wesley Thompson Falkner, later "The Young Colonel," is born.
1849	W. C. Falkner kills Robert Hindman, is tried and acquitted. 31 May: Holland Pearce Falkner dies.
1851	W. C. Falkner kills Erasmus W. Morris, is tried and acquitted. He publishes *The Siege of Monterrey* (an autobiographical poem) and *The Spanish Heroine* (a novel). 12 Oct.: he marries Elizabeth Houston Vance.
1861	9 Jan.: Mississippi secedes. W. C. Falkner and the Magnolia Rifles enter the Civil War.
1862	Replaced as regiment commander by John M. Stone, W. C. Falkner returns to Ripley.
1863	He forms the Partisan Rangers and reenters the war.

1869	2 Sept.: John Wesley Thompson Falkner marries Sallie McAlpine Murry, and they settle in Ripley.
1870	17 Aug.: Murry Cuthbert Falkner is born.
1871	27 Nov.: Maud Butler, daughter of Leila Dean Swift and Charles Butler, is born.
1871-1872	W. C. Falkner, Richard Thurmond, and others organize a company to build a railroad.
1881-1884	W. C. Falkner writes *The White Rose of Memphis*, tours Europe, and writes *Rapid Ramblings in Europe*.
1885	J. W. T. Falkner moves his family to Oxford, Mississippi.
1889	5 Nov.: after being elected to the state legislature, W. C. Falkner is shot by Richard Thurmond. 6 Nov.: he dies.
ca. 1890	Charles Butler deserts Leila Butler, who is forced to forfeit a scholarship for studying sculpture in Rome. Murry Falkner quits the University of Mississippi to work on the family railroad.
1896	19 Feb.: Lida Estelle Oldham is born in Bonham, Texas. 9 Nov.: Murry Falkner marries Maud Butler, and they settle in New Albany, Mississippi.
1897	25 Sept.: William Cuthbert Falkner is born.
1898	Murry Falkner is appointed treasurer of the railroad, and the family moves to Ripley.
1899	26 June: Murry C. Falkner, Jr., is born.
1901	24 Sept.: John Wesley Thompson Falkner, III, is born.
1902	J. W. T. Falkner sells the railroad. Murry Falkner moves his family to Oxford and begins shifting from job to job.
1903	Lemuel E. Oldham, his wife, Lida, and their daughters, Lida Estelle and Victoria, move from Kosciusko, Mississippi, to Oxford.
1905	William Falkner enters the first grade.
1907	1 June: Leila Swift Butler (Damuddy) dies. 15 Aug.: Dean Swift Falkner is born.
1909	William Falkner's decline in attendance and performance at school begins.
1914	He quits school after several years of increasing resistance. His long friendship with Phil Stone begins.
1915	He again begins the eleventh grade and again quits.
1916	He works briefly in his grandfather's bank but gravitates toward student activities at the University of Mississippi.
1917	His first published work, a drawing, appears in the yearbook *Ole Miss*.
1918	Estelle Oldham's parents announce her engagement to Cornell Franklin. William Falkner tries to enlist, is rejected, and leaves for New Haven, Connecticut, where he lives with Phil Stone and works for the Winchester Repeating Arms Company. June: he changes the spelling of his name from *Falkner* to *Faulkner* and enlists in the R.A.F. (Canada). 11 Nov.: World War One ends while he is still in training. Dec.: he returns to Oxford.
1919	8 Feb.: Victoria Franklin is born. Estelle Franklin visits her parents in Oxford. Faulkner works on the poems that become *The Marble Faun*. 6 Aug.: his first published poem, "L'Apres-Midi d'un Faune," appears in the *New Republic*. He enrolls at the university, where he publishes poems and drawings in student publications.
1920	He resigns from the university but continues to work with a student drama group, for which he writes *The Marionettes*.

1921   Spring: Estelle Franklin visits her parents, and Faulkner writes "Vision
            in Spring." Fall: he moves to New York and works in a bookstore.
            Dec.: he returns to Oxford as postmaster of the university post office.
1922   He serves as scoutmaster and postmaster, writes for university publica-
            tions. June: he publishes "Portrait" (a poem) in the *Double Dealer*.
1923   3 Dec.: Malcolm A. Franklin is born.
1924   Faulkner is removed as scoutmaster and resigns as postmaster. 15 Dec.:
            Four Seas publishes *The Marble Faun*.
1925   Faulkner moves to New Orleans, writes for the *Double Dealer* and New
            Orleans *Times-Picayune*, becomes friends with several artists and
            writers, writes *Soldiers' Pay*, and falls in love with Helen Baird. 7 July:
            he sails for Europe where he travels in Italy, Switzerland, France, and
            England, lives in Paris, and writes "Elmer." Dec.: he returns to Oxford.
1926   25 Feb.: *Soldiers' Pay* is published. Splitting time between Oxford,
            New Orleans, and Pascagoula, Faulkner courts Helen Baird, writes
            Mosquitoes, and collaborates on *Sherwood Anderson & Other Famous
            Creoles*.
1927   30 Apr.: *Mosquitoes* is published. Faulkner works on "Father Abra-
            ham" and *Flags in the Dust*, then concentrates on *Flags in the Dust*.
            Nov.: Horace Liveright rejects *Flags in the Dust*.
1928   Faulkner writes *The Sound and the Fury* in Oxford and revises it in
            New York.
1929   31 Jan.: *Sartoris*, a cut version of *Flags in the Dust*, is published. 29
            Apr.: Estelle Franklin's divorce is granted. May: Faulkner finishes
            Sanctuary. 20 June: he and Estelle are married. 7 Oct.: *The Sound and
            the Fury* is published. 29 Oct.: Faulkner begins *As I Lay Dying*.
1930   12 Jan.: he completes revised typescript of *As I Lay Dying*. Prominent
            magazines begin buying his stories. He and Estelle buy an antebellum
            house and name it "Rowan Oak." 6 Oct.: *As I Lay Dying* is published.
            Faulkner revises *Sanctuary*.
1931   Jan.: Alabama Faulkner is born and dies. 9 Feb.: *Sanctuary* is pub-
            lished. Faulkner begins *Light in August*. 21 Sept.: *These 13* is pub-
            lished. Oct.: Faulkner attends a writers' conference in Charlottesville,
            Virginia, then spends seven weeks in New York.
1932   Feb.: he finishes *Light in August*. May: he begins his first job in Holly-
            wood. 7 Aug.: Murry Falkner dies. Oct.: Faulkner returns to Holly-
            wood; *Light in August* is published.
1933   Feb.: Faulkner begins flying lessons. 20 Apr.: *A Green Bough* is pub-
            lished. 24 June: Jill Faulkner is born. Faulkner buys an airplane.
1934   He begins the work that becomes *Absalom, Absalom!*, then writes
            several stories that become *The Unvanquished*. 16 Apr.: *Doctor
            Martino and Other Stories* is published. July: Faulkner goes to Holly-
            wood for several weeks. Back in Oxford, he writes *Pylon*.
1935   He works on *Absalom, Absalom!* 25 Mar.: *Pylon* is published. 10 Nov.:
            Dean Faulkner dies. Dec.: Faulkner leaves for several weeks in Holly-
            wood.
1936   Finishes *Absalom, Absalom!* Feb.–May: he works in Hollywood. His
            affair with Meta Doherty, begun in 1935, deepens. June: he returns
            to Oxford. Late July: he returns to Hollywood with Estelle and Jill,
            expecting to stay a year. 26 Oct.: *Absalom, Absalom!* is published.
1937   Late Mar. or early Apr.: Meta Doherty marries Wolfgang Rebner. May:

Estelle and Jill return to Oxford. Late Aug.: Faulkner follows. Oct.: he goes to New York, where he sees Meta Rebner.

1938 15 Feb.: *The Unvanquished* is published. Faulkner buys "Greenfield Farm," writes *The Wild Palms*, and begins the Snopes trilogy.

1939 19 Jan.: *The Wild Palms* is published. Faulkner is elected to the National Institute of Arts and Letters.

1940 27 Jan.: Mammy Caroline Barr dies. 1 Apr.: *The Hamlet* is published. Faulkner writes stories that become *Go Down, Moses*.

1941 He works on *Go Down, Moses*.

1942 11 May: *Go Down, Moses* is published. Late July: Faulkner begins five-month stint in Hollywood and resumes affair with Meta Doherty.

1943 16 Jan.: he returns to Hollywood for seven months. Oct.: he begins work that becomes *A Fable*.

1944 Feb.: he returns to Hollywood for extended stay. May: he begins correspondence with Malcolm Cowley. Summer: Estelle and Jill join him for two months. Dec.: he returns to Oxford.

1945 He resumes work on his fable. June–Sept.: he works in Hollywood.

1946 Mar.: Robert Haas and Harold Ober secure his release from Warner Brothers. 29 Apr.: *The Portable Faulkner* is published.

1947 Oct.: Faulkner submits a portion of his fable, "Notes on a Horsethief," to the *Partisan Review*, which rejects it.

1948 He puts his fable aside and writes *Intruder in the Dust*. 27 Sept.: *Intruder in the Dust* is published. 23 Nov.: Faulkner is elected to the American Academy of Arts and Letters.

1949 Aug.: he meets Joan Williams. 27 Nov.: *Knight's Gambit* is published.

1950 Jan.: he begins collaboration with Joan Williams on *Requiem for a Nun*. 2 Aug.: *Collected Stories* is published. 10 Nov.: Faulkner learns that he has won the Nobel Prize. Dec.: he and Jill go to Stockholm.

1951 Feb.: *Notes on a Horsethief* is published, and Faulkner goes to Hollywood for five weeks. Mid–Apr.: he leaves for Europe. 27 Sept.: *Requiem for a Nun* is published.

1952 Faulkner moves between Oxford and New York. May: he goes to Europe. Summer: he and Joan Williams become lovers. Nov.: he undergoes a series of electroshock treatments.

1953 He continues to move between Oxford and New York. Nov.: he finishes *A Fable*, dedicates it to Jill, and leaves for Europe.

1954 He remains in Europe for several months, working with Howard Hawks. In St. Moritz, he meets Jean Stein. Mar.: he learns that Joan Williams has married Ezra Bowen and that Jill wants to marry Paul Summers. Apr.: he returns to Oxford. 2 Aug.: *A Fable* is published. 6–16 Aug.: he makes his first trip for the State Department. 21 Aug.: Jill marries Paul Summers. Sept.: Faulkner goes to New York to see Jean Stein.

1955 His involvement in integration controversies intensifies. 29 July: he begins a trip for the State Department that takes him from Japan through Europe to Iceland. 14 Oct.: *Big Woods* is published. Dec.: he takes Jean Stein to Pascagoula and New Orleans.

1956 Faulkner splits time between New York and Oxford, works on *The Town*, and writes articles on integration.

1957 He becomes writer-in-residence at the University of Virginia, Charlottesville, and visits Greece for the State Department. 1 May: *The Town* is published.

1958   Jan.: Faulkner returns to the University of Virginia as writer-in-resi-
            dence. Splitting time between Oxford and Charlottesville, he works
            on *The Mansion.*
1959   He and Estelle buy a house in Charlottesville. He attends UNESCO
            conference in Denver. 13 Nov.: *The Mansion* is published.
1960   16 Oct.: Maud Butler Falkner dies. Dec.: Faulkner wills his manuscripts
            to the William Faulkner Foundation.
1961   Apr.: he goes to Venezuela for the State Department. Summer: he
            makes rapid progress on *The Reivers.*
1962   4 June: *The Reivers* is published. 5 July: Faulkner enters Wright's
            Sanitarium in Byhalia, Mississippi. 6 July: he dies.

APPENDIX C:
Map of
Yoknapatawpha County

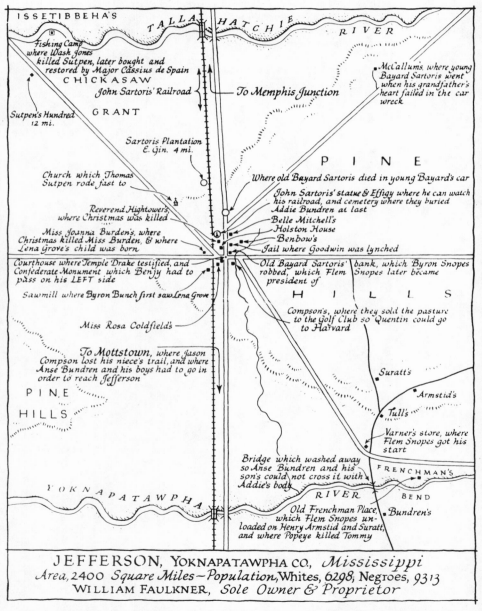

From *Absalom, Absalom!*, New York, Modern Library, Random House, 1936, 1964.
By permission of the publisher.

Bibliographical Note

Several of Faulkner's works and many of his letters have been published since I began this study. Where reliable texts are now available, I have changed my citations from manuscripts to them in order to make my notes more useful to inquisitive readers. To the several research centers that allowed me to examine unpublished materials, however, I remain deeply grateful, as I try to acknowledge elsewhere. In addition, all references to works not yet published are fully acknowledged in appropriate notes. For permission to quote from them, I am indebted to Jill Faulkner Summers. In other matters, too, I have tried to follow familiar conventions. As an additional aid to readers, I preface the notes to each chapter with a general note about the chapter's major sources.

The following bibliographical studies, which I cite as separately noted, have been particularly helpful:

Blotner, Joseph. *William Faulkner's Library: A Catalogue.* Charlottesville: The University Press of Virginia, 1964. Cited as Blotner, *Faulkner's Library*.

Butterworth, Keen. "A Census of Manuscripts and Typescripts of William Faulkner's Poetry." *Mississippi Quarterly*, 26 (Summer 1973), 333–60. Cited as Butterworth, "A Census."

Hayhoe, George F. "Faulkner in Hollywood: A Checklist of His Film Scripts at the University of Virginia." *Mississippi Quarterly*, 31 (Summer 1978), 407-19. Cited as Hayhoe, "Faulkner in Hollywood."

Massey, Linton R. *"Man Working," 1919-1962, William Faulkner: A Catalogue of the William Faulkner Collections at the University of Virginia*. Charlottesville: Bibliographical Society of the University of Virginia, 1968.

Meriwether, James B. "The Books of William Faulkner: A Guide for Students and Scholars." *Mississippi Quarterly*, 30 (Summer 1970), 417-28.

Meriwether, James B. *The Literary Career of William Faulkner: A Bibliographical Study*. Princeton, N.J.: Princeton University Library, 1961. Cited as Meriwether, *Literary Career*.

Meriwether, James B. "The Short Fiction of William Faulkner: A Bibliography." *Proof*, 1 (1971), 293-329.

Meriwether, James B. "William Faulkner: A Check List." *The Princeton University Library Chronicle*, 18 (Spring 1957), 136-58.

Meriwether, James B. *William Faulkner: An Exhibit of Manuscripts*. Austin: The University of Texas Research Center, 1959.

References to Faulkner's published poetry, which I cite by title, are to the following editions:

A Green Bough. New York: Harrison Smith and Robert Haas, 1933. This edition was reissued in 1965 by Random House with *The Marble Faun*, retaining the original pagination.

The Marble Faun. Boston: The Four Seas Company, 1924. This edition was reissued in 1965 by Random House with *A Green Bough*, retaining both the original pagination and Phil Stone's "Preface."

References to collections of Faulkner's early writings, which I cite as separately noted, are to the following editions:

Collins, Carvel, ed. *William Faulkner: Early Prose and Poetry*. Boston: Little Brown and Company, 1962. Cited as *Early Prose and Poetry*.

Collins, Carvel, ed. *William Faulkner: New Orleans Sketches*. New York: Random House, 1968. Cited as *New Orleans Sketches*.

References to works published posthumously, which I cite by title, are to the following editions:

The Marionettes: A Play in One Act. Ed. Noel Polk. Charlottesville: The University Press of Virginia, 1977.

Mayday. Ed. Carvel Collins. South Bend, Ind.: University of Notre Dame Press, 1977.

The Wishing Tree. New York: Random House, 1966.

Several shorter pieces have also been published posthumously. I cite them either by title or as separately noted:

"And Now What's To Do," ed. James B. Meriwether, *Mississippi Quarterly*, 26 (Summer 1973), 399-402.

"A Fourth Book Review by Faulkner," ed. Carvel Collins, *Mississippi Quarterly*, 28 (Summer 1975), 399-42.

"An Introduction to *The Sound and the Fury*," ed. James B. Meriwether, *Southern Review*, 8 (Autumn 1972), 705-10. Cited as "An Introduction to *The Sound and the Fury*" [1972].

"An Introduction to *The Sound and the Fury*," ed. James B. Meriwether,

Mississippi Quarterly, 26 (Summer 1973), 410-15. Cited as "An Introduction to *The Sound and the Fury*" [1973].

"A Note on *A Fable*," ed. James B. Meriwether, *Mississippi Quarterly*, 26 (Summer 1973), 416-20.

"Music—Sweeter Than the Angels Sing," ed. Dean Faulkner Wells and Lawrence Wells, *Southern Review*, 12 (Autumn 1976), 864-71.

"Nympholepsy," ed. James B. Meriwether, *Mississippi Quarterly*, 26 (Summer 1973), 403-9.

"The Priest," ed. James B. Meriwether, *Mississippi Quarterly*, 29 (Summer 1976), 445-50.

References to Faulkner's novels, which I cite by title or shortened title, are to the following editions:

Absalom, Absalom! New York: Random House, 1936.
As I Lay Dying. [1930] New York: Random House, 1964.
A Fable. New York: Random House, 1954.
Flags in the Dust. New York: Random House, 1973.
Go Down, Moses. New York: Random House, 1942.
The Hamlet. [1940] New York: Random House, 1964.
Intruder in the Dust. New York: Random House, 1948.
Light in August. New York: Harrison Smith and Robert Haas, 1932.
The Mansion. New York: Random House, 1959.
Mosquitoes. New York: Boni & Liveright, 1927.
Pylon. New York: Harrison Smith and Robert Haas, 1935.
The Reivers. New York: Random House, 1962.
Requiem for a Nun. New York: Random House, 1951.
Sanctuary. New York: Jonathan Cape & Harrison Smith, 1931.
Sartoris. New York: Harcourt, Brace and Company, 1929.
Soldiers' Pay. New York: Boni & Liveright, 1926.
The Sound and the Fury. [1929] New York: Vintage Books, 1963.
The Town. New York: Random House, 1957.
The Unvanquished. New York: Random House, 1938.
The Wild Palms. New York: Random House, 1939.

References to Faulkner's short fiction, which I cite by title of story and title or shortened title of book, are to the following editions:

Big Woods. New York: Random House, 1955.
Collected Stories. New York: Random House, 1950.
Doctor Martino and Other Stories. New York: Harrison Smith and Robert Haas, 1934.
The Faulkner Reader. New York: Random House, 1954.
Idyll in the Desert. New York: Random House, 1931.
Knight's Gambit. New York: Random House, 1949.
Miss Zilphia Gant. [Dallas:] The Book Club of Texas, 1932.
Notes on a Horsethief. Greenville, Miss.: Levee Press, 1950 [1951].
These 13. New York: Jonathan Cape & Harrison Smith, 1931.

References to published correspondence, which I cite as separately noted, are to the following editions:

Beck, Warren. "Faulkner: A Preface and a Letter." *Yale Review*, 52 (October 1962), 157-60. Cited as Beck, "A Preface and a Letter."

Blotner, Joseph, ed. *Selected Letters of William Faulkner.* New York: Random House, 1977. Cited as *Selected Letters.*

Cowley, Malcolm, ed. *The Faulkner-Cowley File: Letters and Memories, 1944–1962.* New York: Viking Press, 1966. Cited as *Faulkner-Cowley File.*

Meriwether, James B., ed. "Faulkner's Correspondence with the *Saturday Evening Post.*" *Mississippi Quarterly,* 30 (Summer 1977), 461–75. Cited by title.

Meriwether, James B., ed. "Faulkner's Correspondence with *Scribner's Magazine.*" *Proof,* 3 (1973), 253–82. Cited by title.

References to interviews, public letters, speeches, and other miscellaneous writings, which I cite by title or shortened title, are to the following editions:

Fant, Joseph L., and Robert Ashley, eds. *Faulkner at West Point.* New York: Random House, 1964.

Gwynn, Frederick L., and Joseph Blotner, eds. *Faulkner in the University: Class Conferences at the University of Virginia, 1957–1958.* Charlottesville: University of Virginia Press, 1959.

Jelliffe, Robert A., ed. *Faulkner at Nagano.* Tokyo: Kenkyusha Ltd., 1956.

Meriwether, James B., ed. *Essays, Speeches & Public Letters.* New York: Random House, 1966.

Meriwether, James B., and Michael Millgate, eds. *Lion in the Garden: Interviews with William Faulkner, 1926–1962.* New York: Random House, 1968.

References to memoirs written by members of the Faulkner family or by friends and acquaintances, which I cite as separately noted, are to the following editions:

Cantwell, Robert. "The Faulkners: Recollections of a Gifted Family." *New World Writing,* 2 (Nov. 1952), 300–315. Reprinted in F. J. Hoffman and Olga Vickery, eds., *William Faulkner: Three Decades of Criticism.* New York: Harcourt, Brace & World, 1963, pp. 51–66. Cited as Cantwell, "The Faulkners."

Cochran, Louis. "William Faulkner: A Personal Sketch." Memphis *Commercial Appeal,* 6 Nov. 1932. Reprinted in James B. Meriwether, "Early Notices of Faulkner by Phil Stone and Louis Cochran." *Mississippi Quarterly,* 17 (Summer 1964), 136–64. Cited as Cochran, "Faulkner."

Cullen, John B., with Floyd C. Watkins. *Old Times in the Faulkner Country.* Chapel Hill: University of North Carolina Press, 1961. Cited as Cullen, *Old Times.*

Falkner, Murry C. *The Falkners of Mississippi: A Memoir.* Baton Rouge: Louisiana State University Press, 1967. Cited as *Falkners of Mississippi.*

Faulkner, Jim. "Auntee Owned Two," *Southern Review,* 8 (Oct. 1972), 836–44. Cited as "Auntee Owned Two."

Faulkner, John. *My Brother Bill: An Affectionate Reminiscence.* New York: Trident, 1963. Cited as *My Brother Bill.*

Franklin, Malcolm A. "A Christmas in Columbus." *Mississippi Quarterly,* 27 (Summer 1974), 319–22.

Franklin, Malcolm A. *Bitterweeds: Life with William Faulkner at Rowan Oak.* Irving, Tex.: The Society for the Study of Traditional Culture, 1977. Cited as Franklin, *Bitterweeds.*

Green, A. Wigfall. "William Faulkner at Home." *Sewanee Review,* 40 (Summer 1932), 294–306. Cited as Green, "Faulkner."

Stone, Phil. "William Faulkner: The Man and His Work." *Oxford Magazine,* 1 (1934). Reprinted in James B. Meriwether, "Early Notices of Faulkner by Phil Stone and Louis Cochran." *Mississippi Quarterly,* 17 (Summer 1964), 136–64. Cited as Stone, "Faulkner."

Webb, James W., and A. Wigfall Green, eds. *William Faulkner of Oxford*. Baton Rouge: Louisiana State University Press, 1965. Cited as *Faulkner of Oxford*.

Wells, Dean Faulkner, and Lawrence Wells. "The Trains Belonged to Everybody: Faulkner as Ghost Writer." *Southern Review*, 12 (Autumn 1976), 864–71. Cited as Wells, "The Trains."

Wilde, Meta Carpenter, and Orin Borsten. *A Loving Gentleman: The Love Story of William Faulkner and Meta Carpenter*. New York: Simon and Schuster, 1976. Cited as Wilde and Borsten, *A Loving Gentleman*.

The following biographical studies, which I cite as separately noted, have proved especially helpful:

Blotner, Joseph. *Faulkner: A Biography*. New York: Random House, 1974. Cited as Blotner, *Faulkner*.

Collins, Carvel. "Faulkner at the University of Mississippi," which serves as an introduction to *William Faulkner: Early Prose and Poetry*. Boston: Little Brown and Company, 1962, pp. 3–33. Cited as Collins, "Faulkner at the University of Mississippi."

Collins, Carvel. "Introduction," *William Faulkner: New Orleans Sketches*. New York: Random House, 1968, pp. xi–xxxiv. Cited as Collins, "Introduction," *New Orleans Sketches*.

Coughlan, Robert. *The Private World of William Faulkner*. New York: Harper and Brothers, 1954. Cited as Coughlan, *Private World*.

Gidley, M. "One Continuous Force: Notes on Faulkner's Extra-Literary Reading." *Mississippi Quarterly*, 23 (Summer 1970), 299–314. Cited as Gidley, "Faulkner's Extra-Literary Reading."

Millgate, Michael. "The Career," in *The Achievement of William Faulkner*. New York: Random House, 1965, pp. 1–57. Cited as Millgate, "The Career."

Among the large number of critical studies of Faulkner's fiction, the following, which I cite as separately noted, have proved especially valuable:

Beck, Warren. *Man in Motion*. Madison: University of Wisconsin Press, 1961. Cited as Beck, *Man in Motion*.

Brooks, Cleanth. *William Faulkner: The Yoknapatawpha Country*. New Haven, Conn.: Yale University Press, 1963. Cited as Brooks, *Yoknapatawpha Country*.

Brooks, Cleanth. *William Faulkner: Toward Yoknapatawpha and Beyond*. New Haven, Conn.: Yale University Press, 1978. Cited as Brooks, *Toward Yoknapatawpha*.

Guerard, Albert J. *The Triumph of the Novel: Dickens, Dostoevsky, Faulkner*. New York: Oxford Universtiy Press, 1976. Cited as Guerard, *Triumph of the Novel*.

Howe, Irving, *William Faulkner: A Critical Study*. New York: Random House, 1952.

Irwin, John T. *Doubling & Incest/Repetition & Revenge: A Speculative Reading of Faulkner*. Baltimore, Md.: The Johns Hopkins University Press, 1975. Cited as Irwin, *Doubling & Incest*.

Millgate, Michael. *The Achievement of William Faulkner*. New York: Random House, 1966. Cited as Millgate, *Achievement*.

Morris, Wesley A. *Friday's Footprint: Structuralism and the Articulated Text*. Columbus: Ohio State University Press, 1979. Cited as Morris, *Friday's Footprint*.

Reed, Joseph W., Jr. *Faulkner's Narrative*. New Haven, Conn.: Yale University Press, 1973. Cited as Reed, *Faulkner's Narrative*.

Richardson, H. Edward. *William Faulkner: The Journey to Self-Discovery*. Columbia, Mo.: University of Missouri Press, 1969. Cited as Richardson, *Faulkner*.

Notes

PREFACE

1. See Mallarmé as quoted in Richard Ellmann, *Golden Codgers* (New York, 1973), p. x; see also pp. ix, 42.

2. These statements are from a manuscript fragment in the Beinecke Library, Yale University, New Haven, Conn. Quoted by permission of Jill Faulkner Sumner. See also Blotner, "William Faulkner's Essay on the Composition of *Sartoris*," cited on p. 279.

3. To Joan Williams, Wednesday [29 Apr. 1953], *Selected Letters*, p. 348.

4. *Mosquitoes*, p. 251. See *Faulkner in the University*, p. 275. See also Ellmann, *Golden Codgers*, pp. ix–x, 42.

5. For the quotation, see *Early Prose and Poetry*, p. 101. See also James B. Meriwether's excellent review-essay, "Blotner's *Faulkner*," *Mississippi Quarterly*, 28 (Summer 1975), 351–69. On Faulkner's shifting moods, see the works cited in note 3 to chapter 7.

6. See the works cited in note 3 to chapter 7.

7. See Franklin, *Bitterweeds*. In this memoir by Faulkner's stepson, we see Faulkner not only as a man who preferred a traditional, highly stylized life, but also as a man who imposed, sometimes ruthlessly, such a life on everyone around him. Ceremony, formality, tradition, touched everything and everyone at Rowan Oak. See also the description of Faulkner quoted in note 60 to chapter 1.

8. See, for example, the fragment ". . . I should have lived my life in candle light," Humanities Research Center, University of Texas, Austin, where Faulkner's poet lifts his head and stares and imagines "strange impossible tales," including tales of power and passionate adventure with "sensuous women" that "take form and grow." Quoted by permission of Jill Faulkner Summers.

CHAPTER ONE

GENERAL NOTE: Blotner discusses Faulkner's ancestors and heritage in *Faulkner*, chaps. 1–8, and his childhood and youth in chaps. 9–14. See also Millgate, "The Career," pp. 1–6. On this period see Wells, "The Trains," as well as "Auntee Owned Two," *My Brother Bill, Falkners of Mississippi*, and *Faulkner of Oxford*, all of which are helpful. See also Cantwell, "The Faulkners"; Cullen, *Old Times*; and Coughlan, *Private World*. Thomas L. McHaney, "The Falkners and the Origin of Yoknapatawpha County: Some Corrections," *Mississippi Quarterly*, 25 (Summer 1972), 249–64, is of great value in sorting out crucial facts. On the Old Colonel, in addition to Cantwell, Coughlan, and McHaney, as well as the works cited in note 9 to this chapter, see Wilmuth S. Rutledge, "How Colonel Falkner Built His Railroad," *Mississippi Quarterly*, 20 (Summer 1967), 166–70. On Faulkner's early career, see Stone, "Faulkner"; the several works cited in the general notes to chapters 2 and 3; Brooks, *Toward Yoknapatawpha*, pp. 1–31; and Richardson, *Faulkner*, pp. 1–37.

1. William Faulkner changed the spelling of his name when he was still a young man. Although several members of his family adopted his spelling, neither of his parents did. See note 57 to this chapter.

2. See *Faulkner in the University*, pp. 37, 43–44, 131; *Early Prose and Poetry*, p. 116; and especially "Mississippi" in *Essays, Speeches & Public Letters*, pp. 11–43.

3. See *Faulkner's Library*, pp. 25, 46, 113, 115–16. See also John Pilkington, "Nature's Legacy to Faulkner," in Evans Harrington and Ann J. Abadie, eds., *The South and Faulkner's Yoknapatawpha* (Jackson, Miss., 1977), pp. 104–27.

4. *Go Down, Moses*, p. 186; and to Malcolm Cowley [early Jan. 1946], *Selected Letters*, p. 216.

5. See *Faulkner in the University*, pp. 253–55; and C. Vann Woodward, *The Burden of Southern History* (Baton Rouge, La., 1968), pp. 24, 32. See also Daniel Aaron, "The South in American History," in Harrington and Abadie, eds., *The South and Faulkner's Yoknapatawpha*, pp. 3–21; and Michael Millgate, "Faulkner and the South: Some Reflections," in Harrington and Abadie, eds., *The South and Faulkner's Yoknapatawpha*, pp. 195–210.

6. Ezra Pound, Review of Jean Cocteau's *Poesies, 1917–1920, The Dial*, 70 (Jan. 1921), 110.

7. Thornton Wilder quoted in Woodward, *Burden of Southern History*, pp. 22–23.

8. See McHaney, "Falkners and the Origin of Yoknapatawpha County," as cited in the general note to this chapter. See also Coughlan, *Private World*, pp. 39–40, 44–45. On the unvanquished aunts, see "Auntee Owned Two," and *Faulkner in the University*, pp. 253–54.

9. On the Old Colonel, see McHaney, "Falkners and the Origin of Yoknapatawpha County"; and Donald P. Duclos, "Son of Sorrow: The Life, Works, and Influences of Colonel William C. Falkner, 1825–1889" (Ann Arbor, Mich., University Microfilms, 1962). Also helpful are Thomas F. Hickerson, *The Falkner Feuds* (Chapel Hill, N.C., 1964); and Victor Hoar, "Colonel William C. Falkner in the Civil War," *The Journal of Mississippi History*, 27 (Feb. 1965), 42–62.

10. *Flags in the Dust*, p. 12.

11. See Coughlan, *Private World*, p. 27; and Alexander L. Bondurant, "William C. Falkner, Novelist," *Publications of the Mississippi Historical Society*, 3 (1900), 114-15.

12. See the works cited in note 9 to this chapter. See also Orbrey Street to Phil Stone, 7 Oct. and 12 Oct. 1927, in the Humanities Research Center, University of Texas, Austin.

13. See Wells, "The Trains"; and Thomas L. McHaney, "The Image of the Railroad in the Novels of William Faulkner, 1926-1942" (Master's thesis, University of North Carolina, 1962). See also *My Brother Bill*, p. 11.

14. On Murry Falkner see *Falkners of Mississippi*, pp. 10-12; *My Brother Bill*, pp. 10-11, 13-16; Blotner, *Faulkner*, especially pp. 65-67, 79-81; and McHaney, "Falkners and the Origin of Yoknapatawpha County."

15. *My Brother Bill*, p. 11.

16. On Murry Falkner's attempt to buy the railroad, see especially *My Brother Bill*, p. 14.

17. See Blotner, *Faulkner*, pp. 53, 68.

18. Ibid., pp. 79-80, 1761-62.

19. See McHaney, "Falkners and the Origin of Yoknapatawpha County"; *My Brother Bill*, pp. 14-19, 90-91; and *Falkners of Mississippi*, pp. 3-4, 10-11. On the term *Yoknapatawpha*, see *Faulkner in the University*, p. 74.

20. Quoted in Blotner, *Faulkner*, p. 782. See also McHaney, "Falkners and the Origin of Yoknapatawpha County"; Cullen, *Old Times*, p. 5; Coughlan, *Private World*, pp. 44-45; and *Falkners of Mississippi*, pp. 10-12.

21. *Falkners of Mississippi*, pp. 11-12, 25-27; and *My Brother Bill*, pp. 90-92.

22. Quoted in Blotner, *Faulkner*, p. 118. See *My Brother Bill*, pp. 17-18, 128-30; and *Falkners of Mississippi*, pp. 18-20, 81-83, 115-17.

23. Quoted in Blotner, *Faulkner*, p. 187; see also pp. 177-79.

24. *Faulkner in the University*, pp. 259-60.

25. Quoted in Blotner, *Faulkner*, p. 658. Compare Faulkner to Joan Williams, quoted in Blotner, *Faulkner*, pp. 1441-42, when asked why he had worked so hard at writing: "Maybe because I wasn't as tall or as strong as I wanted to be."

26. See Blotner, *Faulkner*, p. 631. On Faulkner as a misogynist, see Guerard, *Triumph of the Novel*, pp. 109-35. See also Linda W. Wagner, "Faulkner and (Southern) Women," in Harrington and Abadie, eds., *The South and Faulkner's Yoknapatawpha*, pp. 128-46.

27. *Falkners of Mississippi*, pp. 9-10, 17-18; and *My Brother Bill*, pp. 38, 122.

28. See Blotner, *Faulkner*, pp. 118-19; *My Brother Bill*, pp. 54-56, 81, 97-100; and *Falkners of Mississippi*, pp. 31-33, 35-43.

29. Rose Rowland in *Faulkner of Oxford*, p. 25. For more general accounts of Damuddy's influence, see *My Brother Bill*, pp. 68-70, 123-25; *Falkners of Mississippi*, pp. 8-9; and Blotner, *Faulkner*, pp. 57-58, 75-76.

30. For different versions of this change in Faulkner, see Cullen, *Old Times*, pp. 3-4; John Markette in *Faulkner of Oxford*, p. 29; *My Brother Bill*, p. 122; and Blotner, *Faulkner*, pp. 120, 122-25, 154-55. See also note 60 to this chapter.

31. Cullen, *Old Times*, pp. 3-4. See Blotner, *Faulkner*, p. 120.

32. See *My Brother Bill*, pp. 54-57, 98-100.

33. Quoted in Coughlan, *Private World*, p. 43. On the Fritz McElroy episode, see *My Brother Bill*, pp. 78-80, 121-22.

34. See *My Brother Bill*, pp. 47-52, 70; and *Falkners of Mississippi*, pp. 13-15, 26-27. Compare Blotner, *Faulkner*, pp. 1159-60.

35. Quoted in Blotner, *Faulkner*, p. 125. See McHaney, "Falkners and the Origin of Yoknapatawpha County."

36. Cullen, *Old Times*, pp. 12–17, 28–48.

37. The quoted phrase is from *Absalom, Absalom!* For examples of it, see Cullen, *Old Times*, pp. 12–17, 25–48; *Falkners of Mississippi*, p. 10; and *My Brother Bill*, pp. 90–92.

38. See *Lion in the Garden*, p. 280.

39. See Blotner, *Faulkner*, pp. 160, 175–79.

40. *Lion in the Garden*, pp. 7, 13. Compare *Selected Letters*, p. 47.

41. See *My Brother Bill*, p. 130; Blotner, *Faulkner*, p. 179; and *Faulkner-Cowley File*, p. 67.

42. See *My Brother Bill*, pp. 81–82, 122; and Blotner, *Faulkner*, pp. 140, 153, 494.

43. Blotner, *Faulkner*, p. 157.

44. See *Falkners of Mississippi*, pp. 44–48. Compare Blotner, *Faulkner*, pp. 56–57, 99–100.

45. To Mrs. Walter B. McLean [Sept. 1925], *Selected Letters*, pp. 19–20.

46. See Blotner, *Faulkner*, pp. 1451, 1487; and *Mosquitoes*, p. 339. See also *My Brother Bill*, pp. 123–24, 138–57; and *Falkners of Mississippi*, pp. 84–86, 89–90.

47. Blotner, *Faulkner*, p. 1442.

48. See Richardson, *Faulkner*, p. 34.

49. Quoted in Blotner, *Faulkner*, pp. 178–79.

50. See *Faulkner in the University*, p. 251.

51. Quoted in Blotner, *Faulkner*, p. 1762. Regarding Faulkner's daily visits, see Victoria Fielden Black, Faulkner's stepdaughter's daughter, quoted in Harrington and Abadie, eds., *The South and Faulkner's Yoknapatawpha*, p. 151. See also Guerard, *Triumph of the Novel*, pp. 109–35.

52. See Victoria Fielden Black as cited in note 51 to this chapter; and *Mosquitoes*, p. 319.

53. See *Absalom, Absalom!*, pp. 308, 320–21.

54. It is interesting that Faulkner clearly wanted daughters rather than sons.

55. See Coughlan, *Private World*, p. 43; and *Falkners of Mississippi*, p. 6.

56. This sketch is in the William Faulkner Collections, Alderman Library, University of Virginia, Charlottesville, and is quoted in *Selected Letters*, p. 7.

57. See Coughlan, *Private World*, pp. 23, 34–35. Faulkner offered several interesting explanations of why he added the *u* to his name, each of which was useful to him.

58. *Falkners of Mississippi*, p. 6.

59. *Lion in the Garden*, p. 238. *Early Prose and Poetry*, p. 115.

60. See *My Brother Bill*, pp. 122, 125, 130–33; and *Falkners of Mississippi*, p. 83. See also Simon Claxton's description of Faulkner, based on an interview, 23 March 1963: "Faulkner is a short, small man, with, for instance, tiny feet. . . . He rarely smiles. His whole person is centered on the face, and especially on the eyes. . . . The whole body is very still. He rarely moves. . . . Everything about the way he holds himself is stately and sedate, composed and motionless—almost to an inhuman extent" (*Lion in the Garden*, p. 273). For another interesting discussion of Faulkner's lasting talent for stillness and silence, and his practice of them, see Maurice Coindreau, "The Faulkner I Knew," as cited in the general note to chapter 5.

61. Sigmund Freud, quoted in Ernest Jones, *The Life and Work of Sigmund Freud*, ed. and abridged by Lionel Trilling and Steven Marcus (New York, 1961), p. 6.

62. See Leslie Brisman, "Swinburne's Semiotics," *Georgia Review*, 31 (Fall 1977), 578–81.

63. See Brooks, *Toward Yoknapatawpha*, pp. 2, 17–18.

64. *Early Prose and Poetry*, p. 101.

65. See Eugene Goodheart, *The Failure of Criticism* (Cambridge, Mass., 1978), pp. 135-57; and Robert Alter, "History and Imagination in the Nineteenth-Century Novel," *Georgia Review*, 29 (Spring 1975), 42-60.

66. See especially "Sweet will it be to us who sleep" and "Where I am dead the clover loved of bees" in the William Faulkner Collection, University of Virginia Library, Charlottesville; "Above the earth, whose tireless cold," in the Humanities Research Center, University of Texas, Austin; and "But now I'm dead: no wine is sweet to me" in the Berg Collection, New York Public Library. Quoted by permission of Jill Faulkner Summers. The items are listed in Butterworth, "A Census," as items 32, 41, 1, and 6, respectively. For discussions of Faulkner's poetry, see George P. Garrett, Jr., "An Examination of the Poetry of William Faulkner," *Princeton University Library Chronicle*, 18 (Spring 1957), 124-35; and Brooks, *Toward Yoknapatawpha*, pp. 1-31. See also the lines quoted in note 8 to the Preface.

67. *Absalom, Absalom!*, p. 230.

68. I am indebted here to an unpublished essay by one of my students, Dawn Trouard.

69. See both versions of the introduction Faulkner wrote to *The Sound and the Fury*.

70. *Absalom, Absalom!*, pp. 234-38, especially p. 238; and pp. 140, 145.

71. *Light in August*, p. 452.

72. Ben Wasson, "The Time Has Come," *Greenville Delta Democrat-Times*, 15 July 1962. See Coughlan, *Private World*, p. 43; and *Falkners of Mississippi*, p. 6.

73. Quoted in Cantwell, "The Faulkners," p. 56.

CHAPTER TWO

GENERAL NOTE: Blotner discusses the war and its aftermath in *Faulkner*, chaps. 15-22. See also Millgate, "The Career," pp. 5-12; and Meriwether, *Literary Career*, pp. 7-10. For the few letters dating from this period, see *Selected Letters*, pp. 3-7. *My Brother Bill* and *Falkners of Mississippi* are helpful on Faulkner's relations with Phil Stone and Estelle Oldham; and Stone's "Faulkner" is helpful on the whole of this period. See also Richardson, *Faulkner*, pp. 38-60. On Faulkner's career as a cadet, see Gordon Price-Stephens, "Faulkner and the Royal Air Force," *Mississippi Quarterly*, 17 (Summer 1964), 123-28; Michael Millgate, "William Faulkner, Cadet," *University of Toronto Quarterly*, 35 (January 1966), 117-29; and Michael Millgate, "Faulkner in Toronto: A Further Note," *University of Toronto Quarterly*, 37 (January 1968), 197-202. On the period just after the war, see Cochran, "Faulkner"; Collins, "Faulkner at the University of Mississippi"; Green, "Faulkner"; Ben Wasson, "The Time Has Come," *Greenville Delta Democrat-Times*, 15 July 1962; Lucy Somerville Howarth, "The Bill Faulkner I Knew," *Delta Review*, 2 (July–Aug. 1965); and Calvin S. Brown, Jr., in *Faulkner of Oxford*, pp. 45-46.

On Faulkner's literary development, see Coughlan, *Private World*, chap. 4; Brooks, *Toward Yoknapatawpha*, pp. 1-66; Richard P. Adams, "The Apprenticeship of William Faulkner," *Tulane Studies in English*, 12 (1962), 113-56; George P. Garrett, Jr., "An Examination of the Poetry of William Faulkner," *Princeton University Library Chronicle*, 18 (Spring 1957), 124-35; George P. Garrett, Jr., "Faulkner's Early Literary Criticism," *Texas Studies in Literature and Language*, 1 (Spring 1959), 3-10; Noel Polk, "William Faulkner's *Marionettes*," *Mississippi Quarterly*, 26 (Summer 1973), 247-80; and Noel Polk, "Introduction," *Marionettes*. The indispensable guide to Faulkner's poetry is Butterworth, "A Census." On Faulkner's work as a translator, see Martin Kreisworth, "Faulkner as Translator: His Versions of Verlaine," *Mississippi Quarterly*, 30 (Summer 1977), 429–32.

1. Quoted in Coughlan, *Private World*, p. 48. On Stone's extended sponsorship of Faulkner, see his correspondence, Humanities Research Center, University of Texas, Austin.
2. To Malcolm Cowley [early Jan. 1946], *Selected Letters*, pp. 215–16.
3. See Blotner, *Faulkner*, p. 163.
4. Stone, "Faulkner," p. 162.
5. *Falkners of Mississippi*, p. 10.
6. Stone, "Faulkner," pp. 162–63.
7. *My Brother Bill*, p. 122.
8. See Blotner, *Faulkner*, p. 378.
9. *Falkners of Mississippi*, p. 83; and Blotner, *Faulkner*, pp. 155, 175–76.
10. See *My Brother Bill*, p. 122; and *Falkners of Mississippi*, pp. 124–25.
11. *The Marble Faun*, p. 12.
12. See *Mosquitoes*, p. 346.
13. *My Brother Bill*, p. 133.
14. Foreword to *The Faulkner Reader*, p. 8.
15. Compare Henry James as quoted in Paul Fussell, *The Great War and Modern Memory* (New York, 1975), p. 8.
16. See W. B. Yeats, "September 1913."
17. On Faulkner and the Great War, see Price-Stephens and Millgate as cited in the general note to this chapter; and Blotner, *Faulkner*, pp. 201–30.
18. See Blotner, *Faulkner*, pp. 210–11.
19. See to Mrs. Murry C. Falkner, Friday [probably 6 Sept. 1918], *Selected Letters*, p. 3.
20. See *Soldiers' Pay*, pp. 7–8, 29–30.
21. *My Brother Bill*, p. 138.
22. Ibid., p. 148.
23. Fussell, *The Great War*, p. 21; compare pp. 29–33, 51, 311–12. See also Michael Millgate, "Faulkner on the Literature of the First World War," *Mississippi Quarterly*, 26 (Summer 1973), 387–93; and Shelby Foote, "Faulkner and War," in Evans Harrington and Ann J. Abadie, eds., *The South and Faulkner's Yoknapatawpha* (Jackson, Miss., 1977), pp. 152–67.
24. To Malcolm Cowley [24 Dec. 1945], *Faulkner-Cowley File*, p. 74.
25. "Verse Old and Nascent: A Pilgrimage," in *Early Prose and Poetry*, p. 116.
26. See Cochran, "Faulkner," p. 143.
27. See *Selected Letters*, p. 3.
28. See Lee Brown to Phil Stone, 3 Feb. and 19 Feb. 1922; and [Phil Stone] to Lee Brown, 28 Feb. 1922, in the Humanities Research Center, University of Texas, Austin.
29. See Coughlan, *Private World*, pp. 104–5; Cochran "Faulkner"; and Howarth and Wasson as cited in the general note to this chapter.
30. See *Faulkner in the University*, pp. 67, 275. On Faulkner's title as "the poet," see the correspondence cited in note 28 to this chapter.
31. See Blotner, *Faulkner*, p. 247.
32. Phil Stone to Louis Cochran, 28 Dec. 1931, in James B. Meriwether, "Early Notices of Faulkner by Phil Stone and Louis Cochran," *Mississippi Quarterly*, 17 (Summer 1964), 139.
33. "Verse Old and Nascent," *Early Prose and Poetry*, p. 115.

34. "L'Apres-Midi d'un Faune," in *Early Prose and Poetry*, pp. 39-40.

35. See *The Marble Faun*, especially pp. 12 and 30.

36. On Faulkner's reading, see Gidley, "Faulkner's Extra-Literary Reading"; Collins, "Faulkner at the University of Mississippi"; Collins, "Introduction," *New Orleans Sketches*; Blotner, *Faulkner*, chaps. 16-21; and Adams, Brooks, and Polk as cited in the general note to this chapter.

37. Polk, "William Faulkner's *Marionettes*," as cited in the general note to this chapter, pp. 247-250. See also Adams and Brooks as cited in the general note to this chapter.

38. See "An Introduction to *The Sound and the Fury*" [1972], p. 708.

39. Lewis Simpson, "Faulkner and the Southern Symbolism of Pastoral," *Mississippi Quarterly*, 28 (Fall 1975), 401-15. See also Brooks, *Toward Yoknapatawpha*, pp. 4-7.

40. *Absalom, Absalom!*, pp. 127-128.

41. Quoted in Phil Stone's preface to *The Marble Faun*, p. 8.

42. Collins, "Faulkner at the University of Mississippi," p. 3.

43. Louis Cochran in *Faulkner of Oxford*, pp. 102-3.

44. Quoted in Millgate, *Achievement*, p. 5.

45. Quoted in Blotner, *Faulkner*, pp. 269, 268.

46. Calvin S. Brown, Jr., in *Faulkner of Oxford*, p. 45.

47. Malcolm Cowley, *Exile's Return* (New York, 1951), p. 5.

48. Calvin S. Brown, Jr., in *Faulkner of Oxford*, pp. 45-46.

49. See Howarth and Wasson as cited in the general note to this chapter; and Polk, "William Faulkner's *Marionettes*," pp. 247, 250.

50. Polk, "William Faulkner's *Marionettes*," pp. 250-51.

51. *Marionettes*, p. 23.

52. Polk, "William Faulkner's *Marionettes*," p. 277. See Blotner, *Faulkner*, pp. 410-13, and compare pp. 367-69, 388-97, 427-28.

53. See Henry James's preface to *The Spoils of Poynton*, in R. P. Blackmur, ed., *The Art of the Novel* (New York, 1934), pp. 120-21.

54. See Elizabeth Anderson and Gerald R. Kelly, *Miss Elizabeth: A Memoir* (Boston, 1969), pp. 26-42.

55. Stone, Letter to Louis Cochran, 28 Dec. 1931, in Meriwether, "Early Notices of Faulkner," p. 139; and *Falkners of Mississippi*, pp. 11-12.

56. See Blotner, *Faulkner*, pp. 338-40.

57. Quoted in Blotner, *Faulkner*, p. 337.

58. See Brooks, *Toward Yoknapatawpha*, pp. 1-66, and especially Butterworth, "A Census."

59. Compare "Books and Things: American Drama: Eugene O'Neill," in *Early Prose and Poetry*, p. 88; *The Hamlet*, p. 186; and *The Mansion*, pp. 435-36. See the same piece on O'Neill, pp. 86-89; and "Books and Things: American Drama: Inhibitions," in *Early Prose and Poetry*, pp. 94-95.

60. See "Books and Things: Joseph Hergesheimer," in *Early Prose and Poetry*, p. 101.

61. See ibid., pp. 101-2; *The Sound and the Fury*, pp. 167, 220-21; "An Introduction to *The Sound and the Fury*" [1973], p. 415; and *Light in August*, p. 453.

62. *Soldiers' Pay*, p. 31. See Brooks, *Toward Yoknapatawpha*, p. 39.

63. Quoted in Blotner, *Faulkner*, p. 350.

64. See Calvin S. Brown, Jr., and George Healey, Jr., in *Faulkner of Oxford*, pp. 47, 57-58. The letter of charges against Faulkner, dated 2 Sept. 1924, was printed in the *New Yorker*, 21 Nov. 1970. On the resolution of the affair, see the correspon-

dence of March 1926 between Phil Stone and B. G. Lowrey, in the Humanities Research Center, University of Texas, Austin.

65. *Faulkner in the University*, p. 231.

CHAPTER THREE

GENERAL NOTE: Blotner discusses this period in *Faulkner*, chaps. 23–27. See also Millgate, "The Career," pp. 12–24; Richardson, *Faulkner*, pp. 61–103; and Meriwether, *Literary Career*, pp. 10–13, 63–64. For the correspondence dating from this period, including the letters Faulkner wrote his mother from Europe, see *Selected Letters*, pp. 8–34. Every student of Faulkner's apprenticeship, and especially of his activities in New Orleans, owes a large debt to Carvel Collins. See his "Faulkner at the University of Mississippi" and "Introduction," *New Orleans Sketches*. His brief introduction to "A Fourth Book Review by Faulkner" is also helpful, particularly on John McClure's support of Faulkner.

On New Orleans during this period, see James K. Feibleman, "Literary New Orleans between World Wars," *Southern Review*, 1 (Summer 1965), 702–19. On the *Double Dealer*, see Frances J. Bowen, "The New Orleans *Double Dealer*, 1921–1926," *Louisiana Historical Quarterly*, 39 (Oct. 1956), 443–56. For important recollections of Faulkner during this period, see Hamilton Basso, "William Faulkner: Man and Writer," *Saturday Review*, 45 (July 1962), 11–12; William Spratling, "Chronicle of a Friendship: William Faulkner in New Orleans," *Texas Quarterly*, 9 (Spring 1966), 34–40; and Elizabeth Anderson and Gerald R. Kelly, *Miss Elizabeth: A Memoir* (Boston, 1969), pp. 80–117.

For Sherwood Anderson's account of his relations with Faulkner, see especially his *Memoirs* (New York, 1942), pp. 351–55, 356–57, 473–77. For Faulkner on Anderson, see *Lion in the Garden*, pp. 117–19, 249–50; *Faulkner in the University*, pp. 229–34, 259–60; "A Note on Sherwood Anderson," in *Essays, Speeches & Public Letters*, pp. 3–10; Foreword, *Sherwood Anderson and Other Famous Creoles* (New Orleans, 1926); and "Sherwood Anderson" in *New Orleans Sketches*, pp. 132–39. See also Walter Rideout and James B. Meriwether, "On the Collaboration of Faulkner and Anderson," *American Literature*, 35 (Mar. 1963), pp. 85–87, together with the two articles of H. E. Richardson that they discuss and correct; and James B. Meriwether, "Faulkner's Essays on Anderson," in G. H. Wolfe, ed., *Faulkner: Fifty Years After "The Marble Faun"* (University, Ala., 1976), pp. 159–81.

On Faulkner's literary development, see Adams, Garrett, and Polk as cited in the general note to chapter 2. On Faulkner's readings in psychology, physiology, aesthetics, and philosophy, see Gidley, "Faulkner's Extra-Literary Reading." See also Richard P. Adams, "Faulkner: The European Roots," Louis D. Rubin, Jr., "The Discovery of a Man's Vocation," and Lewis P. Simpson, "Faulkner and the Legend of the Artist," all in G. H. Wolfe, ed., *Faulkner: Fifty Years After "The Marble Faun,"* pp. 21–41, 43–68, 69–100. In *Toward Yoknapatawpha*, Brooks discusses Faulkner's development with deep insight. See especially pp. 32–66 on the early prose; pp. 67–99 on *Soldiers' Pay*; pp. 101–28 on "Elmer" and scattered prose pieces; and pp. 129–51 on *Mosquitoes*. Also very important are Thomas L. McHaney, "The Elmer Papers: Faulkner's Comic Portraits of the Artist," *Mississippi Quarterly*, 26 (Summer 1973), 281–311; and, on *Mosquitoes*, Irwin, *Doubling & Incest*, pp. 160–66.

1. Faulkner enclosed this sketch in a letter to Four Seas dated 9 Sept. 1924. It is in the William Faulkner Collections, Alderman Library, University of Virginia, Charlottesville, and is quoted in *Selected Letters*, p. 7.

2. See Blotner, *Faulkner*, p. 456.

3. See Collins, "Introduction," *New Orleans Sketches*, pp. xi–xii.

4. See especially Meriwether, "Faulkner's Essays on Anderson," and Anderson and Kelly, *Miss Elizabeth*, as cited in the general note to this chapter.

5. See "Notes on Contributors," *Double Dealer*, 7 (Jan.–Feb. 1925), iii; and Anderson and Kelly, *Miss Elizabeth*, pp. 100–101.

6. Foreword, *Sherwood Anderson and Other Famous Creoles*. Compare R. D. Laing, *The Divided Self* (New York, 1970), p. 90. See also Spratling, "Chronicle of a Friendship," as cited in the general note to this chapter.

7. See Spratling, "Chronicle of a Friendship," especially p. 35.

8. Spratling quoted in Blotner, *Faulkner*, p. 418; and Anderson and Kelly, *Miss Elizabeth*, pp. 80–88.

9. See especially the works of Collins cited in the general note to this chapter.

10. See Adams and Gidley as cited in the general note. See also Blotner, *Faulkner*, pp. 393, 505. Compare Faulkner's reference to Conrad in "Books and Things: Joseph Hergesheimer," *Early Prose and Poetry*, pp. 102–3.

11. "The Longshoreman," *New Orleans Sketches*, p. 9.

12. See *Faulkner in the University*, p. 21; and Faulkner on Anderson in the general note to this chapter. For Anderson's sense that Faulkner had injured him, see Anderson to Horace Liveright, New Orleans, 19 Apr. 1926, in Howard Mumford Jones and Walter Rideout, eds., *Letters of Sherwood Anderson* (Boston, 1953), p. 155.

13. Quoted in "A Note on Sherwood Anderson," *Essays, Speeches & Public Letters*, p. 7. On the collaboration, see Rideout and Meriwether as cited in the general note and Anderson to Faulkner [1927], in *Letters of Sherwood Anderson*, pp. 162–64. This undated letter almost certainly dates from 1925 rather than 1927, the date ascribed to it.

14. "A Note on Sherwood Anderson," *Essays, Speeches & Public Letters*, p. 5; see also pp. 9–10. For James Dickey on Williams, see *Babel to Byzantium* (New York, 1968), p. 191.

15. Compare Lionel Trilling, *The Opposing Self* (New York, 1955), p. 5; and Faulkner, "Sherwood Anderson," *New Orleans Sketches*, p. 133.

16. "A Note on Sherwood Anderson," *Essays, Speeches & Public Letters*, pp. 9–10; and *Faulkner in the University*, pp. 21–22.

17. Spratling, "Chronicle of a Friendship," p. 35. See also Blotner, *Faulkner*, p. 497; and Sherwood Anderson, *We Moderns: Gotham Book Mart, 1920–1940* (New York, 1940), p. 29.

18. See Faulkner, "Literature and War," in Michael Millgate, "Faulkner on the Literature of the First World War," *Mississippi Quarterly*, 26 (Summer 1973), 388.

19. *Soldiers' Pay*, pp. 7, 29–32. Unless otherwise indicated, all quotations in my discussion of *Soldiers' Pay* are from the novel. See Cleanth Brooks, "Faulkner's First Novel," *Southern Review*, 6 (Autumn 1970), 1056–74; Margaret J. Yance, "*Soldiers' Pay*: A Critical Study of William Faulkner's First Novel" (Ann Arbor, Mich.: University Microfilms, 1971); and Millgate, *Achievement*, pp. 61–67. See also Faulkner's "Landing in Luck," in *Early Prose and Poetry*, pp. 42–50. "The Lilacs" became poem I and "An Armistice Day Poem" poem XXX of *A Green Bough*, pp. 7–11 and p. 53.

20. Millgate, *Achievement*, p. 66.

21. See Blotner, *Faulkner*, p. 430.

22. On Helen Baird, see Cleanth Brooks, "The Image of Helen Baird in Faulkner's Early Poetry and Fiction," *Sewanee Review*, 85 (Spring 1977), 220; Brooks, *Toward Yoknapatawpha*, pp. 52–55, 57–60; and Blotner, *Faulkner*, especially pp. 438–39. Although some of "Helen: A Courtship" was written in the summer of 1925, the

manuscript is dated 1926. Several of the documents having to do with Faulkner's relation to Helen Baird are in the Wisdom Collection, Special Collections Division, Howard-Tilton Library, Tulane University, New Orleans.

23. Spratling, "Chronicle of a Friendship," p. 37.

24. See *Selected Letters*, pp. 8-31. Taken together these letters convey a clear sense of Faulkner's habits and travels while he was in Europe.

25. Millgate, *Achievement*, p. 22. See also Brooks, *Toward Yoknapatawpha*, pp. 115-20; and especially McHaney, "The Elmer Papers," as cited in the general note to this chapter. There are two longer fragments and several shorter versions of this story in the William Faulkner Collections, Alderman Library, University of Virginia, Charlottesville. With one exception, described in note 31 to this chapter, I have quoted from an earlier, longer version (about 120 pages of typescript) called "Elmer" rather than from the later, shorter, "A Portrait of Elmer." Unless otherwise noted, all quotations in my discussion of "Elmer" are from these manuscripts and are quoted with permission of Jill Faulkner Summers.

26. The quoted phrases appear early in "Elmer," William Faulkner Collections, Alderman Library, University of Virginia, Charlottesville. There are several flashbacks in "Elmer," and there is much overt self-examination and reflection. Compare Faulkner's late disclaimer about Freud (*Faulkner in the University*, p. 268) with his early reference to him in "Books and Things: American Drama: Inhibitions," *Early Prose and Poetry*, p. 93. See also the discussion in Brooks, *Toward Yoknapatawpha*, pp. 376-77; and McHaney, "The Elmer Papers." Whether or not Faulkner had read much of Freud's work, he was clearly familiar with ideas we now think of as Freudian.

27. See Anderson and Kelly, *Miss Elizabeth*, pp. 41-42, where Anderson recalls Faulkner's telling a story about a girlfriend who married someone else after she was pregnant by him.

28. To Mrs. M. C. Falkner [postmarked 22 Sept. 1925], *Selected Letters*, pp. 23-25.

29. See "The Artist" and "Out of Nazareth" in *New Orleans Sketches*, pp. 12, 46-54. Compare the language in Faulkner's letters to Mrs. Murry C. Falkner [postmarked 6 Sept. 1925], and to Mrs. Walter B. McLean [postmarked 10 Sept. 1925], in *Selected Letters*, pp. 17 and 20.

30. See Ezra Pound, Canto 95. Compare Marietta in *Marionettes*, p. 49: "nothing save death is as beautiful as I."

31. These lines are from "A Portrait of Elmer," William Faulkner Collections, Alderman Library, University of Virginia, Charlottesville. Quoted with permission of Jill Faulkner Summers.

32. To Mrs. Murry C. Falkner [postmarked 22 Sept. 1925], *Selected Letters*, pp. 23-25. See Blotner, *Faulkner*, pp. 460-61, 466-67.

33. See Blotner, *Faulkner*, pp. 481, 483.

34. Ibid., p. 494.

35. Faulkner apparently made only one copy of each of these books. Both are in the Wisdom Collection, Special Collections Division, Howard-Tilton Library, Tulane University, New Orleans. A facsimile of *Mayday*, edited by Carvel Collins, is available. For discussions of these books, see Brooks, *Toward Yoknapatawpha*, pp. 47-59. Not long after he finished writing and revising *Mosquitoes* (1 Sept. 1926), Faulkner hand-lettered a copy of some of the New Orleans sketches for Estelle. Called "Royal Street" and dated 29 October 1926, the book is in the Humanities Research Center, University of Texas, Austin. Its dedication reads: "To Estelle, a/ Lady, with/ Respectful Admiration: / This." Quoted with permission of Jill Faulkner Summers. For discussions of Faulkner and Helen Baird, see the works cited in note 22 to this chapter.

36. This letter is in the Widsom Collection, Special Collections Division, Howard-Tilton Library, Tulane University, New Orleans. Quoted with permission of Jill Faulkner Summers.

37. Quoted in Blotner, *Faulkner*, pp. 438, 549, 510, 512. Compare *Mosquitoes*, p. 320.

38. See the discussion of "Elmer" in this chapter. See also the works cited in note 45 to this chapter.

39. See "Carcassonne" in *These 13*, p. 358.

40. "Nympholepsy" is in the Berg Collection of the New York Public Library. It is now available, edited by James B. Meriwether, in *Mississippi Quarterly*, 26 (Summer 1973), 403-9. See also ". . . I should have lived my life in candle light," Humanities Research Center, University of Texas, Austin. Quoted with permission of Jill Faulkner Summers.

41. Brooks, *Toward Yoknapatawpha*, p. 61.

42. *Mayday*, pp. 38-41.

43. *Mayday*, p. 43.

44. *Mayday*, p. 21.

45. Compare "Helen: A Courtship," especially sonnets II, V, VI, and IX, with "Elmer" as discussed earlier in this chapter. Quoted by permission of Jill Faulkner Summers. See also the works by Faulkner cited in note 40 to this chapter and the following discussions: Mary M. Dunlap, "Sex and the Artist in *Mosquitoes*." *Mississippi Quarterly*, 22 (Summer 1969), 190-206; Phyllis Franklin, "The Influence of Joseph Hergesheimer upon *Mosquitoes*," *Mississippi Quarterly*, 22 (Summer 1969), 207-13; and Irwin, *Doubling & Incest*, pp. 160-66.

46. See "Helen," sonnet V. Quoted by permission of Jill Faulkner Summers. Compare poem XLIII in *A Green Bough*.

47. See the letter that appears on the verso of p. 269 of the typescript of *Mosquitoes*, which is in the William Faulkner Collections, Alderman Library, University of Virginia, Charlottesville. A brief excerpt is in *Selected Letters*, p. 33. Compare *Mosquitoes*, pp. 267-68, 274. See also my discussion of *The Wild Palms* in chapter 7.

48. For discussions of *Mosquitoes*, see Millgate, *Achievement*, pp. 68-75; the works cited in note 45 to this chapter; and especially Brooks and Irwin as cited in the general note to this chapter. Unless otherwise noted all quotations in my discussion of *Mosquitoes* are from the novel.

49. See notes 45 and 46 to this chapter.

50. See Anderson and Kelly, *Miss Elizabeth*, p. 117.

51. The poem Fairchild reads became poem XXXVIII in *A Golden Bough*.

52. See the works cited in note 26 to this chapter.

53. *Mosquitoes*, p. 320. Compare Helen Baird as quoted in Blotner, *Faulkner*, pp. 510, 512.

54. On Helen Baird and *Mosquitoes*, see the works cited in note 22 to this chapter. In revising *Mosquitoes*, Faulkner sharpened stress on sublimation as a theme. See, for example, the lines added to the typescript of *Mosquitoes*, William Faulkner Collections, Alderman Library, University of Virginia, Charlottesville, p. 306. Compare *Soldiers' Pay*, p. 295: "Sex and death: the front door and the back door of the world. How indissolubly are they associated in us!"

55. See the letter cited in note 47 to this chapter. Quoted by permission of Jill Faulkner Summers. Compare *Mosquitoes*, pp. 267-68, 274.

56. See Dunlap, "Sex and the Artist in *Mosquitoes*," and Brooks as cited in the general note to this chapter.

57. The quoted phrases are from *Mosquitoes*, p. 250. Compare Faulkner's descrip-

tion of Keats as "trying to seduce Fanny Brawne with words," quoted in Blotner, *Faulkner*, notes to vol. 1, p. 70. On the idea of Renaissance artists not signing their works, see *Faulkner-Cowley File*, p. 126.

58. See, for example, *Mosquitoes*, p. 46. See also Irwin, *Doubling & Incest*, pp. 160-66. The quoted phrases are from Robert Frost, "The Most of It."

59. *Mosquitoes* manifests clear interest in the relation of literature not only to painting and sculpture but also to music. Julius Wiseman is Faulkner's version of the radical symbolist. See, for example, *Mosquitoes*, p. 130, where he says "the Thing is merely the symbol for the Word." For the lines quoted, see p. 339.

60. See "Verse Old and Nascent: A Pilgrimage," and "Books and Things: Joseph Hergesheimer," in *Early Prose and Poetry*, pp. 115, 101-3; and *Light in August*, p. 453. Frost's line is from "Directive."

61. Faulkner wrote "l'amorsa l'idea" for "l'amorosa idea." See Franklin, "Influence of Joseph Hergesheimer," where she discusses Hergesheimer's association of this idea with "the woman in whom a man sees God."

62. Albert Camus, *The Rebel* (New York, 1969), pp. 268-72.

63. On the relation of "Elmer" to *Mosquitoes*, see McHaney, "The Elmer Papers." The italicized passages in section 9 of the epilogue to *Mosquitoes* (pp. 335-40) represent reworking of a kind of fantasy that first appeared in "Elmer." Faulkner borrowed from several other earlier works in writing *Mosquitoes*. In particular, "Little Sister Death" had turned up in "Mayday" and in "The Kid Learns," *New Orleans Sketches*, p. 91. But more than other borrowings, those in the epilogue suggest how much *Mosquitoes* was for Faulkner a covert examination of art as a vocation.

64. See *Selected Letters*, p. 34.

65. "A Note on Sherwood Anderson," *Essays, Speeches & Public Letters*, p. 10. See also to Horace Liveright, 18 Feb. 1927, *Selected Letters*, pp. 34-35.

CHAPTER FOUR

GENERAL NOTE: Blotner discusses this period in *Faulkner*, chaps. 28-29. See also Millgate, "The Career," pp. 24-26; and Meriwether, *Literary Career*, pp. 13-16, 40-41, 64-65. Faulkner's letters, particularly those to Horace Liveright, are very important. See *Selected Letters*, pp. 33-41. Of considerable help are McHaney, "The Falkners and the Origin of Yoknapatawpha County," as cited in the general note to chapter 1; Cantwell, "The Faulkners"; and Stone, "Faulkner." See O. B. Emerson, "William Faulkner's Literary Reputation in America" (Ph.D. diss., Vanderbilt University, 1962), p. 649, where Stone is quoted as saying that he "invented some few parts" of *Flags in the Dust*. Faulkner's essay "Mississippi," in *Essays, Speeches & Public Letters*, pp. 11-43, is important both for the sense of place it conveys and for the autobiographical information it contains. On it see James B. Meriwether, "Faulkner's 'Mississippi,' " *Mississippi Quarterly*, 25 Supplement (Spring 1972), 15-23. On Faulkner as a regionalist, see Warren Beck, "Faulkner and the South," *Antioch Review*, 1 (Mar. 1941), 82-94; Brooks, *Yoknapatawpha Country*, pp. 1-9; and *Toward Yoknapatawpha*, pp. 152-77; Richardson, *Faulkner*, pp. 164-84; Arlin Turner, "William Faulkner, Southern Novelist," *Mississippi Quarterly*, 14 (Summer 1961), 117-30; Robert Penn Warren, "William Faulkner and His South," a paper delivered at the Peters Rushton Seminar in Contemporary Prose and Poetry, University of Virginia, Charlottesville, 13 Mar. 1951, and available in mimeograph copy at the Humanities Research Center, University of Texas, Austin; and Robert Penn Warren, "Faulkner: The South and the Negro," *Southern Review*, 1 (Summer 1965), 501-29. On the influence of Willard Huntington Wright, see Blotner, *Faulkner*, pp. 320-22; and especially Frances B. O'Brien, "Faulkner and Wright, Alias S. S. Van Dine," *Mississippi Quarterly*, 14 (Spring 1961), 101-7. On the revision of *Flags in the Dust*, see Joseph Blotner, ed., "William Faulkner's Essay on the Composition of *Sartoris*," *Yale University Library Gazette*, 47 (Jan. 1973), 123-24. For an important critique of Douglas Day's editing of *Flags in the Dust*, see George F. Hayhoe, "William Faulkner's *Flags in the Dust*," *Mississippi Quarterly*, 28 (Summer 1975), 370-86.

Several writers have influenced this chapter in more general ways: Eudora Welty, *Place in Fiction* (New York, 1957); Albert Camus, *The Rebel* (New York, 1969), especially pp. 260-62, 268-72; and Robert Alter, "History and Imagination in the Nineteenth-Century Novel," *Georgia Review*, 29 (Spring 1975), 42-60. I have also drawn on Harold Bloom, *The Anxiety of Influence* (New York, 1973); Jacques Derrida, *Of Grammatology* (Baltimore, Md., 1976); and Geoffrey Hartman, *Beyond Formalism* (New Haven, Conn., 1970). In addition I have benefited from several conversations with Herbert Schneidau as well as from his book, *Sacred Discontent* (Baton Rouge, La., 1976), which proved particularly helpful in my discussion of Faulkner's relation to oral traditions. Another large debt is to Morris, *Friday's Footprint*.

1. Foreword, *Faulkner Reader*, p. x; and "The Artist" in *New Orleans Sketches*, p. 12.

2. *Mosquitoes*, p. 210. Compare Addie in *As I Lay Dying*, pp. 165-66.

3. T. S. Eliot, "A Brief Introduction to the Method of Paul Valery," in Paul Valery, *Le Serpent*, trans. Mark Wardel (London, 1924), p. 14; and Camus, *The Rebel*, p. 46.

4. *Mosquitoes*, p. 210; compare pp. 130, 399. See also Weddel's speech in "A Mountain Victory," *Doctor Martino and Other Stories*, pp. 340-41.

5. Northrop Frye, *The Anatomy of Criticism*, (Princeton, N.J., 1957), p. 88.

6. To Warren Beck, 6 July 1941, *Selected Letters*, p. 142. See also Alter, "History and Imagination," as cited in the general note to this chapter.

7. See Alter, "History and Imagination," p. 53.

8. "A Note on Sherwood Anderson," in *Essays, Speeches & Public Letters*, pp. 3-5.

9. "Interviews in Japan" [1955] in *Lion in the Garden*, p. 96.

10. See to Warren Beck, 6 July 1941, *Selected Letters*, p. 142.

11. "Mississippi," in *Essays, Speeches & Public Letters*, p. 21. On this idea as American, see C. Vann Woodward, *The Burden of Southern History* (Baton Rouge, La., 1968), pp. 22-24, 31, 36-37.

12. "Wild Geese" became poem XXVIII in *A Green Bough*. Compare *As I Lay Dying*, pp. 162, 164. "And Now What's To Do" is interesting in several ways, including the fact that parts of it are clearly autobiographical. A two-page manuscript, it was found at Rowan Oak in 1970 and is now available in *Mississippi Quarterly*, 26 (Summer 1973), 399-402.

13. "Verse Old and Nascent: A Pilgrimage," *Early Prose and Poetry*, p. 116. For discussions of anticipations, see Cleanth Brooks, "Faulkner's First Novel," *Southern Review*, 6 (Autumn 1970), 1066-67; Collins, "Faulkner at the University of Mississippi"; and especially Blotner, *Faulkner*: p. 404 (on Caddy); p. 412 (on the Old Colonel and Mr. Compson); pp. 413-14 (on Benjy); pp. 381, 413 (on Addie); p. 491 (on Thomas Sutpen); p. 493 (on Popeye); and p. 502 (on Hightower).

14. Quoted in "A Note on Sherwood Anderson," *Essays, Speeches & Public Letters*, p. 8.

15. Quoted in Collins, "Introduction," *New Orleans Sketches*, p. xvii.

16. See "Books and Things: American Drama: Inhibitions," in *Early Prose and Poetry*, p. 93.

17. *Faulkner in the University*, p. 268. Compare James Dickey regarding Theodore Roethke, in *Babel to Byzantium* (New York, 1968), p. 150.

18. *My Brother Bill*, p. 149. Compare *Faulkner in the University*, pp. 231-32.

19. See *Faulkner in the University*, p. 136; Wallace Stevens, "Notes Toward a Supreme Fiction"; and to Malcolm Cowley, Monday [24 Dec. 1945], *Faulkner-Cowley File*, p. 74.

20. See *Faulkner in the University*, p. 111; and compare Wallace Stevens to Bernard Heringman, 20 Mar. 1951, in Holly Stevens, ed., *Letters of Wallace Stevens* (New York, 1966), p. 710. See also Eudora Welty, *Place in Fiction*, as cited in the general note to this chapter.

21. See F. W. Dupee, *Henry James* (New York, 1951), p. 67; compare *Faulkner in the University*, p. 268.

22. See *Faulkner in the University*, p. 104, for example.

23. See S. N. Dennis, "The Making of *Sartoris*" (Ph.D. diss., Cornell University, Ann Arbor, Mich., University Microfilms, 1969), pp. 10-11. See also the works cited in note 13 to this chapter.

24. See Robert Frost, "Birches."

25. To Horace Liveright, 18 Feb. 1927, *Selected Letters*, pp. 34-35. In a note on p. 35 of *Selected Letters* Blotner identifies the "collection of short stories of my townspeople" as *A Rose for Emily and Other Stories*, which became *These 13*. But Stone's statement, available in James B. Meriwether, "Sartoris and Snopes: An Early Notice," *Library Chronicle of the University of Texas*, 7 (Summer 1962), 36-37, makes it clear that Faulkner was also writing about the Snopeses at this time.

26. The quoted phrases are from a manuscript in the Beinecke Library, Yale University, New Haven, Conn. Quoted by permission of Jill Faulkner Summers.

27. *Lion in the Garden*, p. 253; and *Faulkner in the University*, pp. 59-60. See Richard P. Adams, *Faulkner: Myth and Motion* (Princeton, N.J., 1968); and Karl E. Zink, "Flux and the Frozen Moment: The Imagery of Stasis in Faulkner's Prose," *PMLA*, 71 (June 1956), 285-301.

28. Wright wrote fiction as S. S. Van Dine. Regarding Wright's influence on Faulkner, see Phil Stone to Louis Cochran, 28 Dec. 1931, in Meriwether, "Early Notices of Faulkner by Phil Stone and Louis Cochran," *Mississippi Quarterly*, 17 (Summer 1964), p. 141; Phil Stone in *Faulkner of Oxford*, p. 228; and the article by O'Brien cited in the general note to this chapter.

29. See Camus, *The Rebel*, pp. 262-63; and compare *Lion in the Garden*, p. 255.

30. Compare Robert Frost, "Directive," and *Faulkner in the University*, p. 67. See also the manuscript cited in note 26 to this chapter.

31. See *Essays, Speeches & Public Letters*, p. 8. Compare the piece called "Mississippi" in the same volume; and see Meriwether's discussion of it, cited in the general note to this chapter.

32. The manuscript of "Father Abraham" is in the Arents Collection, New York Public Library. Two partial typescripts are available in the William Faulkner Collections, Alderman Library, University of Virginia, Charlottesville. One of these consists of fifty-four pages (numbered 1-39 and 41-55); the other of fifty-one pages (numbered 1-51). I have quoted from the first of the typescripts. See also "Abraham's Children," William Faulkner Collections, Alderman Library, University of Virginia, Charlottesville. Quoted by permission of Jill Faulkner Summers. For discussions, see Meriwether, *Literary Career*, pp. 40-44, 69-73; Millgate, *Achievement*, pp. 24, 180-83; and Blotner, *Faulkner*, pp. 526-31.

33. See Alter, "History and Imagination," pp. 42-43, 45.

34. *Faulkner in the University*, p. 277; compare p. 253.

35. Ibid., pp. 97, 33; compare p. 197.

36. See *Lion in the Garden*, p. 255; and the map of Yoknapatawpha that Faulkner drew for *Absalom, Absalom!*.

37. *Lion in the Garden*, p. 255.

38. See *Faulkner in the University*, pp. 47, 78, 96, 108; and compare Mark Schorer, *The World We Imagine* (New York, 1968), p. 395.

39. To Mrs. Walter B. McLean, Wednesday [late Sept. 1927], *Selected Letters*, p. 38; and to Horace Liveright, sunday, —october [16 Oct. 1927], in the William Faulkner Collections, Alderman Library, University of Virginia, Charlottesville. Quoted by permission of Jill Faulkner Summers.

40. *Faulkner in the University*, p. 285. On the text of *Flags in the Dust* as it is now available to us, see the article by Hayhoe, "William Faulkner's *Flags in the Dust*," cited in the general note to this chapter.

41. *Flags in the Dust*, p. 12. See my discussion of Faulkner's family in chapter 1.

42. Malcolm Cowley, *The Portable Faulkner* (New York, 1946), p. 19.

43. *Flags in the Dust*, p. 5. Compare Faulkner's remarks regarding the Old Colonel in Cantwell, "The Faulkners."

44. Murry Falkner and his family moved from Ripley to Oxford in 1902.

45. See *Faulkner in the University*, p. 251; and Brooks, *Toward Yoknapatawpha*, pp. 393-95.

46. See *Sartoris*, p. 245. Compare *Flags in the Dust*, pp. 229-41.

47. See W. H. Auden, *The Enchaféd Flood* (London, 1951), pp. 20-24.

48. See *Flags in the Dust*, pp. 190-91. Compare my discussion of *Mosquitoes* in chapter 3 and of *The Sound and the Fury* in chapter 5.

49. To Malcolm Cowley, Thursday [16 Aug. 1945], *Faulkner-Cowley File*, p. 25.

50. Woodward, *Burden of Southern History*, p. 34.

51. See Camus, *The Rebel*," pp. 260-62; Welty, *Place in Fiction*; and Alter, "History and Imagination."

52. Quoted in Collins, "Introduction," *New Orleans Sketches*, p. xvii. See McHaney, "Falkners and the Origin of Yoknapatawpha County."

53. I am indebted here to several works cited in the general note to this chapter, especially Morris, *Friday's Footprint*.

54. See Blotner, *Faulkner*, pp. 101, 97; and to Bennett Cerf and Robert K. Haas [10 Jan. 1945], *Selected Letters*, p. 188. Compare *Selected Letters*, pp. 216, 296.

55. Quoted in Cantwell, "The Faulkners," p. 56.

56. See Friedrich Nietzsche, *On the Genealogy of Morals*, in Walter Kaufman, ed., *The Basic Writings of Nietzsche* (New York, 1966), p. 497.

57. *Faulkner in the University*, p. 251; Sigmund Freud, *Moses and Monotheism*, in James Strachey and others, ed. and trans., *Standard Edition of the Complete Psychological Works of Sigmund Freud* (London, 1953), 23:135. See Bloom, *Anxiety of Influence*, as cited in the general note to this chapter.

58. Liveright to Faulkner, 25 Nov. 1927, in the William Faulkner Collections, Alderman Library, University of Virginia, Charlottesville, and quoted in Blotner, *Faulkner*, pp. 559-60.

59. To Horace Liveright, 30 Nov. [1927], *Selected Letters*, p. 39.

60. See *Selected Letters*, pp. 38-41; and *My Brother Bill*, p. 156. See also the discussion in Blotner, *Faulkner*, p. 561. One sending schedule, dating from the early 1930s, is in the William Faulkner Collections, Alderman Library, University of Virginia, Charlottesville. But as Blotner points out, the one described in *My Brother Bill* probably dates from an earlier period and has been lost.

61. To Horace Liveright [mid-or late Feb. 1928], *Selected Letters*, p. 39.

62. To Mrs. Walter B. McLean, Thursday [probably Spring 1928], *Selected Letters*, pp. 40–41.

63. See Hayhoe, "William Faulkner's *Flags in the Dust*," which is the most reliable account we have of what happened to *Flags in the Dust* after Liveright rejected it.

64. For Faulkner's account of this process, see the essay written about two years after *Sartoris* was published, as edited by Blotner and as cited in the general note to this chapter.

65. To Ben Wasson [early summer 1929], *Selected Letters*, pp. 45–46.

CHAPTER FIVE

GENERAL NOTE: Blotner discusses this period in *Faulkner*, chaps. 29–31. See also Meriwether, *Literary Career*, pp. 16–17, 18–20, 59–60, 65; Millgate, "The Career," pp. 26–29; and especially *Selected Letters*, pp. 39–46. The best discussion of the early Compson stories is in Norman Holmes Pearson, "Faulkner's Three Evening Suns," *Yale University Library Gazette* (29 Oct. 1954), pp. 61–70. On the dating of these stories, see Millgate, *Achievement*, p. 90; and Blotner, *Faulkner*, pp. 565–67 and notes to vol. 1, p. 82. See also the discussion in note 6 to this chapter. On the writing of *The Sound and the Fury*, see Maurice Coindreau's preface to *Le bruit et la fureur* (Paris, 1938), which is available, translated by George M. Reeves, in "Preface to *The Sound and the Fury*," *Mississippi Quarterly*, 19 (Summer 1966), 107–15. Also helpful is Coindreau's "The Faulkner I Knew," *Shenandoah*, 16 (Winter 1965), 26–35, which makes clear not only the very special place *The Sound and the Fury* occupied in Faulkner's life but also the exactness of his memory of it. Describing a conversation that took place in June 1937, Coindreau remarks that Faulkner "seemed to know *The Sound and the Fury* by heart, referring me to such and such a paragraph, to such and such a page, to find the key to some highly enigmatic obscurity" (p. 29). Also valuable is James B. Meriwether, "Notes on the Textual History of *The Sound and the Fury*," *Papers of the Bibliographical Society of America*, 56 (1962), 285–316. Both the shorter (1972) and longer (1973) versions of Faulkner's "An Introduction to *The Sound and the Fury*" are of deep interest.

On the origins of *Sanctuary*, see especially Carvel Collins, "A Note on *Sanctuary*," *Harvard Advocate*, 135 (Nov. 1951), 16. The most interesting discussion of *The Sound and the Fury* in relation to Faulkner's preoccupations as a writer is in Irwin, *Doubling & Incest*. In addition, Otto Rank, *The Double*, trans. and ed. Harry Tucker, Jr. (Chapel Hill, N.C., 1971), and Søren Kierkegaard, *Repetition*, trans. Walter Lowrie (New York, 1964), have been very useful to me. On Faulkner as misogynist and on *Sanctuary*, see Guerard, *Triumph of the Novel*, especially pp. 109–35. See also Sharon Smith Hult, "William Faulkner's 'The Brooch': The Journey to the Riolama," *Mississippi Quarterly*, 27 (Summer 1974), 291–305, for an interesting discussion of Faulkner's male protagonists as crippled by some "fantasy of an ideal female." In relation to this theme, see especially Faulkner's "Nympholepsy." On Faulkner's efforts to place his short fiction see James B. Meriwether, ed., "Faulkner's Correspondence with *Scribner's Magazine*" and "Faulkner's Correspondence with the *Saturday Evening Post*."

1. To Harold Ober, 4 Feb. 1959, *Selected Letters*, p. 421.

2. Introduction to *Sanctuary*, in *Essays, Speeches & Public Letters*, p. 176.

3. See Blotner, *Faulkner*, pp. 555–56; and [Phil Stone] to H. V. Kincannon, 29 Oct. 1927, in the Humanities Research Center, University of Texas, Austin.

4. This letter was probably written in the first half of 1928. It is in the William

Faulkner Collections, Alderman Library, University of Virginia, Charlottesville, and is quoted with permission of Jill Faulkner Summers.

5. J. W. Harmon in *Faulkner of Oxford*, pp. 93–94.

6. On the dating of these stories see Pearson, Millgate, and Blotner as cited in the general note. "That Evening Sun Go Down" was first published in *The American Mercury* (Mar. 1931). It later appeared, slightly revised, as "That Evening Sun" in *These 13* (1931). For an earlier version, see "Never Done No Weeping When You Wanted to Laugh," a manuscript in the Beinecke Library, Yale University, New Haven, Conn. Although there is no conclusive evidence for dating the stories earlier than *The Sound and the Fury*, there is good circumstantial evidence—that Quentin is older in "That Evening Sun" than he lives to be in *The Sound and the Fury*; and that Benjy does not appear in the stories. On anticipations of the Compsons in earlier writings, see note 13 to chapter 4.

7. "A Justice," in *These 13*, p. 207.

8. See *Mosquitoes*, p. 319; and Faulkner as quoted in Blotner, *Faulkner*, p. 1169.

9. See *Lion in the Garden*, p. 276.

10. To Horace Liveright [mid- or late Feb. 1928], *Selected Letters*, pp. 39–40.

11. See both versions of Faulkner's "An Introduction to *The Sound and the Fury*."

12. Maurice Coindreau, "Preface," *Le bruit et la fureur*, (1938), p. 14. See Meriwether, "Notes on the Textual History of *The Sound and the Fury*," especially p. 288; and the translation of Coindreau's preface, p. 114, as cited in the general note to this chapter.

13. See Meriwether, "Notes on the Textual History of *The Sound and the Fury*," p. 289; and Blotner, *Faulkner*, pp. 579–80.

14. Faulkner had three brothers, of course, but during the crucial years to which his memory turned in *The Sound and the Fury*, he had two. Leila Dean Swift, the grandmother Faulkner called Damuddy, died on 1 June 1907. Dean Swift Faulkner was born on 15 August 1907.

15. See Conrad Aiken, "William Faulkner: The Novel as Form," *Harvard Advocate*, 135 (Nov. 1951), 13, 24–26; Donald M. Kartiganer, "*The Sound and the Fury* and Faulkner's Quest for Form," *ELH* 37 (Dec. 1970), 613–39; and Isadore Traschen, "The Tragic Form of *The Sound and the Fury*," *Southern Review*, 12 (Autumn 1976), 798–813.

16. See Faulkner on Hergesheimer in *Early Prose and Poetry*, p. 102; *Faulkner in the University*, p. 6; and the translation of Coindreau's preface, p. 109.

17. *Faulkner at Nagano*, pp. 103–5.

18. See F. H. Bradley, *Appearance and Reality* (New York, 1908), p. 346; and compare T. S. Eliot's note to line 412 of *The Waste Land*.

19. *Faulkner at Nagano*, pp. 103–5.

20. See "An Introduction to *The Sound and the Fury*" [1973].

21. *Faulkner at Nagano*, p. 72. See *Lion in the Garden*, p. 128. Note the relation between Faulkner's defense of indirection and Mallarmé's assertion: "*Nommer* un object, c'est supprimer les trois-quarts de la jouissance du poeme." See also A. G. Lehmann, *The Symbolist Aesthetic in France, 1885–1895* (Oxford, 1950), particularly chaps. 1, 2, 6.

22. *Lion in the Garden*, p. 146. For an earlier version of Benjy, see "The Kingdom of God," *New Orleans Sketches*, pp. 55–60.

23. See Faulkner's "An Introduction to *The Sound and the Fury*" [1972].

24. *Lion in the Garden*, p. 146.

25. See Guerard, *Triumph of the Novel*, pp. 109-35.

26. See Faulkner's "An Introduction to *The Sound and the Fury*" [1973].

27. Ibid.

28. See Allen Tate, "The Angelic Imagination" in *The Man of Letters in the Modern World* (New York, 1955), pp. 113-31; and Robert M. Slabey, "The 'Romanticism' of *The Sound and the Fury*," *Mississippi Quarterly*, 16 (Summer 1963), 152-57.

29. See the piece on Hergesheimer in *Early Prose and Poetry*, p. 102.

30. See Faulkner's "An Introduction to *The Sound and the Fury*" [1972].

31. See my discussion of *Mosquitoes* in chapter 3.

32. See Faulkner's "An Introduction to *The Sound and the Fury*" [1973]. Compare my discussion of Donald Mahon and *Soldiers' Pay* in chapter 3.

33. See "The Kid Learns," *New Orleans Sketches*, p. 91; and *Mayday*, as discussed in chapter 3. See also the discussion in Collins, "Introduction," *New Orleans Sketches*, pp. xxix-xxx.

34. *Soldiers' Pay*, p. 318. Compare Marietta in *Marionettes*: "nothing save death is as beautiful as I am."

35. See Faulkner's "An Introduction to *The Sound and the Fury*" [1973].

36. *Mosquitoes*, p. 210.

37. Compare *Flags in the Dust*, pp. 162-63; and *Faulkner in the University*, p. 6.

38. *Mosquitoes*, p. 250.

39. See Irwin, *Doubling & Incest*, pp. 160-61.

40. William Spratling, "Chronicle of a Friendship: William Faulkner in New Orleans," *Texas Quarterly*, 9 (Spring 1966), 38.

41. See "An Introduction to *The Sound and the Fury*" [1973].

42. See Irwin, *Doubling & Incest*, pp. 162-63.

43. *Lion in the Garden*, p. 147; *Faulkner in the University*, p. 67.

44. See "An Introduction to *The Sound and the Fury*" [1973].

45. Quoted in Coindreau, preface to *The Sound and the Fury*, p. 109.

46. *Mosquitoes*, p. 339. Compare Faulkner to Mrs. M. C. Falkner [postmarked 6 Sept. 1925], *Selected Letters*, pp. 17-18, for an early description of his response to the sense of having written something beautiful and perfect.

47. *Faulkner in the University*, p. 65. Compare *Soldiers' Pay*, p. 283. For a sense of how far back Faulkner's preoccupation with imperfect success went, see the fragment ". . . [Th]is life you bear like an invulnerable shield. . . .": "Would you possess a thing/You had not striven for, and failed, and striven again?" And later: "Know you not that when once you have wrought/The absolute, then you can only die?" Humanities Research Center, University of Texas, Austin. Quoted by permission of Jill Faulkner Summers.

48. To Malcolm Cowley, Friday [11 Feb. 1949], *Faulkner-Cowley File*, p. 126. Compare Irwin, *Doubling & Incest*, pp. 171-72.

49. *My Brother Bill*, p. 275.

50. This quote is from a manuscript fragment in the Beinecke Library, Yale University, New Haven, Conn. Quoted by permission of Jill Faulkner Summers.

51. See to Alfred Harcourt, 18 Feb. 1929, *Selected Letters*, pp. 42-43; and the introduction to *Sanctuary*, in *Essays, Speeches & Public Letters*, p. 177.

52. This statement is from an unpublished portion of one of the sessions at the University of Virginia, 5 June 1957. Quoted by permission of Jill Faulkner Summers. A portion of this session is in *Faulkner in the University*, pp. 201-8. The full text of the session is available in the William Faulkner Collections, Alderman Library, University of Virginia, Charlottesville.

53. To Mrs. Walter B. McLean, Wednesday [probably Oct. 1928], *Selected Letters*,

p. 41. On Faulkner's revision of *The Sound and the Fury*, see Meriwether as cited in the general note, pp. 293–94.

54. See Faulkner's introduction to *Sanctuary*, in *Essays, Speeches & Public Letters*, pp. 176, 177.

55. Quoted in Meriwether, "Notes on the Textual History of *The Sound and the Fury*," p. 289.

56. To Mrs. Murry C. Falkner [postmarked 6 Sept. 1925], *Selected Letters*, pp. 17–18.

57. See W. H. Auden, sonnet XXIII, in "In Time of War," in W. H. Auden and Christopher Isherwood, *Journey to a War* (New York, 1944). Compare Auden, sonnet XIX, in "Sonnets from China," in *Collected Shorter Poems, 1927–1957* (New York, 1966). See also *Absalom, Absalom!*, pp. 373–74.

58. Blotner, *Faulkner*, pp. 590–92.

59. *Mosquitoes*, p. 339.

60. See Blotner, *Faulkner*, pp. 591–98. See Faulkner to Alfred Dashiell [answered 22 Dec. 1928], *Selected Letters*, 41–42.

61. See Blotner, *Faulkner*, p. 603; and *Selected Letters*, pp. 42–45.

62. To Ben Wasson [early summer 1929], *Selected Letters*, pp. 44–45.

63. See "An Introduction to *The Sound and the Fury*" [1972].

64. Introduction to *Sanctuary*, in *Essays, Speeches & Public Letters*, p. 177.

65. Compare, for example, ibid; "Speech of Acceptance upon the Award of the Nobel Prize for Literature," in *Essays, Speeches & Public Letters*, pp. 119–21; and *Faulkner in the University*, pp. 90–91.

66. See the typescript of *Sanctuary* in the William Faulkner Collections, Alderman Library, University of Virginia, Charlottesville.

67. *Faulkner in the University*, pp. 90–91. Compare his introduction to *Sanctuary*, in *Essays, Speeches & Public Letters*, p. 177.

68. See the title page and p. 358 of the typescript of *Sanctuary*, William Faulkner Collections, Alderman Library, University of Virginia, Charlottesville. Faulkner began the manuscript in January and finished the typescript on 25 May 1929.

69. See Beatrice Lang, "An Unpublished Faulkner Story: 'The Big Shot,'" *Mississippi Quarterly*, 26 (Summer 1973), 312–24; Robert Cantwell, "Faulkner's Popeye," *Nation*, 186 (1958), 140–41; Collins, "A Note on *Sanctuary*," as cited in the general note to this chapter; and L. S. Kubie, "William Faulkner's *Sanctuary*," *Saturday Review of Literature*, 11 (1934), 218, 224–26. See also Phil Stone to Louis Cochran, 28 Dec. 1931, Faulkner Collections, Humanities Research Center, University of Texas, Austin.

70. Guerard, *Triumph of the Novel*, p. 8.

71. See Victoria Fielden Black, quoted in Evans Harrington and Ann J. Abadie, eds., *The South and Faulkner's Yoknapatawpha* (Jackson, Miss., 1977), p. 151.

72. Quoted in Blotner, *Faulkner*, p. 1169.

73. Ibid., p. 613.

74. See the discussion in Brooks, *Yoknapatawpha Country*, pp. 121–27, 392.

75. Emily W. Stone, "Faulkner Gets Started," *Texas Quarterly*, 8 (Winter 1965), 144.

76. Quoted in Faulkner's introduction to *Sanctuary*, in *Essays, Speeches & Public Letters*, p. 177. Compare *Faulkner in the University*, pp. 90–91.

77. Introduction to *Sanctuary*, in *Essays, Speeches & Public Letters*, p. 177.

78. See Blotner, *Faulkner*, pp. 618–20.

79. Ibid., pp. 10, 85.

CHAPTER SIX

GENERAL NOTE: Blotner discusses this period in *Faulkner*, chaps. 32-35. See also Meriwether, *Literary Career*, pp. 16-21, 65-66; and Millgate, "The Career," pp. 27-34; and especially *Selected Letters*, pp. 42-55. On the revision of *The Sound and the Fury*, see *Selected Letters*, pp. 44-46; and James B. Meriwether, "Notes on the Textual History of *The Sound and the Fury*," as cited in the general note to chapter 5. On the revision of *Sanctuary*, see Linton Massey, "Notes on the Unrevised Galleys of Faulkner's *Sanctuary*," *Studies in Bibliography*, 8 (1956), 195-208; and James B. Meriwether, "Some Notes on the Text of Faulkner's *Sanctuary*," *Papers of the Bibliographical Society of America*, 55 (1961), 192-206. Galley proofs of the unrevised version of *Sanctuary* are in the Humanities Research Center, University of Texas, Austin. See Gerald Langford, *Faulkner's Revision of "Sanctuary": A Collation of the Unrevised Galleys and the Published Book* (Austin, Tex., 1972).

For a sense of Faulkner's early fame, see Emily Clark, "A Week-end at Mr. Jefferson's University," *New York Herald Tribune Books*, 8 Nov. 1931; Gordon Price-Stephens, "The British Reception of William Faulkner—1929-1962," *Mississippi Quarterly*, 18 (Summer 1965), 119-200; Maurice Coindreau, "The Faulkner I Knew," as cited in the general note to chapter 5; Anthony Buttitta, "William Faulkner: That Writin' Man of Oxford," *Saturday Review*, 18 (21 May 1938), 7-9; Anthony Buttitta, "A Memoir of Faulkner in the Early Days of His Fame," *San Francisco Sunday Chronicle*, 15 July 1962; and especially O. B. Emerson, "William Faulkner's Literary Reputation in America," as cited in the general note to chapter 4. On Faulkner's efforts to place his short fiction, see the collections of correspondence cited at the end of the general note to chapter 5. For a sense of life at Rowan Oak, see Franklin, *Bitterweeds*, where we see Faulkner's determination to restore and enlarge his home and his determination to shape its life strictly along traditional, ceremonial lines.

1. See Blotner, *Faulkner*, pp. 618-20. Stone's attitude did not change quickly. See his letter to Hubert Starr, 27 June 1930, Faulkner Collections, Humanities Research Center, University of Texas, Austin, where he expresses surprise that Faulkner had ever married and surprise that he was still married.

2. Blotner, *Faulkner*, p. 631.

3. For a more detailed account of the wedding trip, see ibid., pp. 624-30.

4. See *My Brother Bill*, pp. 85, 122.

5. Ben Wasson [early summer 1929], *Selected Letters*, pp. 44-45. See the subsequent letter to Wasson, pp. 45-46.

6. Compare Faulkner as quoted in note 72 to this chapter.

7. See Blotner, *Faulkner*, p. 630.

8. See *My Brother Bill*, pp. 133-34.

9. To Joan Williams, Thursday [6 Nov. 1952], William Faulkner Collections, Alderman Library, University of Virginia, Charlottesville, quoted in Blotner, *Faulkner*, p. 1437. For a heavily edited version, see *Selected Letters*, p. 343.

10. Compare Faulkner to Mrs. Walter B. McLean as cited in note 4 to chapter 5, with Estelle (quoted, Blotner, *Faulkner*, p. 564) and with Estelle's sister, Dorothy Oldham (paraphrased, ibid., p. 619). See the letter to Joan Williams cited in note 9 to this chapter.

11. *Mosquitoes*, p. 339.

12. Ibid., p. 270.

13. See Meriwether, ed., "Faulkner's Correspondence with *Scribner's Magazine*."

14. See, for example, the introduction to *Sanctuary*, in *Essays, Speeches & Public Letters*, pp. 177-78.

15. See *Lion in the Garden*, p. 13.

16. To Horace Liveright [mid- or late Feb. 1928], *Selected Letters*, pp. 39–40.

17. See *My Brother Bill*, p. 207; and Victoria Fielden Black, quoted in Evans Harrington and Ann J. Abadie, eds., *The South and Faulkner's Yoknapatawpha* (Jackson, Miss., 1977), p. 151. See also Blotner, *Faulkner*, p. 631, for a discussion of Stone's sense that Faulkner and his brothers "were tied to their mother and resented it" and that this was partly responsible for "an animosity toward women that he saw in" Faulkner. See also Guerard, *Triumph of the Novel*, pp. 109–35; and Hult, "William Faulkner's 'The Brooch,'" cited in the general note to chapter 5.

18. "An Introduction to *The Sound and the Fury*" [1972].

19. See Conrad Aiken, "William Faulkner: The Novel as Form," *Harvard Advocate*, 135 (Nov. 1951), 13, 24–26.

20. In several respects, Addie resembles Mr. Compson while Anse resembles Mrs. Compson—an interesting reversal of roles.

21. See the introduction to *Sanctuary*, in *Essays, Speeches & Public Letters*, pp. 177–78. Faulkner wrote this piece in late 1931.

22. See *Lion in the Garden*, pp. 13, 32, 180, 222. Compare *Faulkner in the University*, pp. 87, 207.

23. *Lion in the Garden*, p. 255.

24. See Gordon Price-Stephens, "British Reception of William Faulkner," as cited in the general note to this chapter. See also Blotner, *Faulkner*, p. 642; and Meriwether, *Literary Career*, pp. 101–2.

25. Faulkner's "short story sending schedule" is in the William Faulkner Collections, Alderman Library, University of Virginia, Charlottesville. For discussions of it, see Meriwether, *Literary Career*, pp. 167–80; and Blotner, *Faulkner*, p. 643.

26. For additional details, see Meriwether, *Literary Career*, pp. 167–69. See also the two collections of correspondence cited in the general note to chapter 5.

27. *Lion in the Garden*, pp. 20, 181–82.

28. See Blotner, *Faulkner*, pp. 647–48, 664–65.

29. See Faulkner to Ben Wasson [1930], William Faulkner Collections, Alderman Library, University of Virginia, Charlottesville: "I have bought the old Bailey place, the one on the edge of town, with all the cedars." Quoted by permission of Jill Faulkner Summers. For details regarding the purchase and renovation, see *My Brother Bill*, pp. 145–46; Blotner, *Faulkner*, pp. 650–62; and see especially Franklin, *Bitterweeds*.

30. Having lost his position at the University of Mississippi in a political shuffle, Murry Falkner had to move out of his house on campus. See Blotner, *Faulkner*, p. 662; and Thomas L. McHaney, "The Falkners and the Origin of Yoknapatawpha County: Some Corrections," *Mississippi Quarterly*, 25 (Summer 1972), 260.

31. See Blotner, *Faulkner*, pp. 647–48, 664–65.

32. On the production and cast of *Corporal Eagen*, see Blotner, *Faulkner*, pp. 665–66. On Faulkner's interest in drama, see James E. Kibler, Jr., "William Faulkner and Provincetown Drama, 1920–1922," *Mississippi Quarterly*, 22 (Summer 1969), 226–36.

33. *Lion in the Garden*, p. 123. On the writing and revision of *Sanctuary*, see Massey, Meriwether, and Langford as cited in the general note to this chapter.

34. Introduction to *Sanctuary*, in *Essays, Speeches & Public Letters*, p. 178.

35. Massey, "Notes on the Unrevised Galleys of Faulkner's *Sanctuary*," p. 202.

36. Ibid., p. 204.

37. Introduction to *Sanctuary*, in *Essays, Speeches & Public Letters*, p. 178.

38. *Lion in the Garden*, pp. 123–24.

39. *As I Lay Dying*, pp. 165-66. See to Dayton Kohler, 10 Jan. 1950, *Selected Letters*, pp. 296-97.

40. "Mountain Victory," *Doctor Martino and Other Stories*, pp. 340-41.

41. Quoted in Blotner, *Faulkner*, p. 682.

42. Ibid., pp. 681-83.

43. Ibid., pp. 683, 721, 744.

44. Ibid., p. 685.

45. *My Brother Bill*, p. 171.

46. See Meriwether, *Literary Career*, pp. 20-21; and Blotner, *Faulkner*, pp. 692-93, 708, 716.

47. See Meriwether, *Literary Career*, pp. 123-27, 133-35; the works of Emerson, Price-Stephens, and Coindreau, cited in the general note to this chapter; and Blotner, *Faulkner*, p. 693.

48. See "An Introduction to *The Sound and the Fury*" [1972].

49. *Light in August*, p. 465. Regarding the title, see *Faulkner in the University*, pp. 74, 199.

50. The *Post* and *Woman's Home Companion* also turned it down. See Meriwether, *Literary Career*, p. 175; and Blotner, *Faulkner*, pp. 700-701. The story remains unpublished but exists in manuscript form in the William Faulkner Collections, Alderman Library, University of Virginia, Charlottesville.

51. "Carcassonne" in *These 13*, p. 358. Italics deleted.

52. *Faulkner in the University*, p. 45.

53. *Lion in the Garden*, p. 253.

54. *Faulkner in the University*, p. 72. Compare *Faulkner in the University*, pp. 96-97, 118, and *Faulkner at West Point*, p. 83.

55. See To James Southall Wilson, 24 Sept. 1931; and to Estelle Faulkner, Thursday [22 Oct. 1931], in *Selected Letters*, pp. 51, 52.

56. To Laura Lou Copenhaver [Baltimore, Md., 24 Oct. 1931], in Howard Mumford Jones and Walter Rideout, eds., *Letters of Sherwood Anderson* (Boston, 1953), p. 252. For a fine account of the conference, see this long, detailed letter, pp. 251-54. See also the piece by Emily Clark, "A Week-end," cited in the general note to this chapter. For discussions of Faulkner's drinking, see Robert N. Linscott, "Faulkner without Fanfare," *Esquire*, 60 (July 1963), pp. 36-38; Millgate, *Achievement*, pp. 30-33; Blotner, *Faulkner*, pp. 707-21; and Cowley, *Faulkner-Cowley File*, pp. 103-14.

57. *Mosquitoes*, p. 186. See to Ben Wasson [mid-Jan. 1932], *Selected Letters*, pp. 56-57, where Faulkner describes the "state I seem to get into when . . . I begin to visualize a kind of jail corridor of literary talk."

58. See Linscott, "Faulkner without Fanfare," p. 36. See the letter to Wilson cited in note 55 to this chapter.

59. Ibid. See Millgate, Blotner, and Cowley as cited in note 56 to this chapter.

60. See Blotner, *Faulkner*, pp. 721, 724-25; compare p. 744.

61. See Blotner, *Faulkner*, pp. 714-15. Faulkner also embarrassed himself at the home of Princess Troubetzkoy. See Millgate, "The Career," p. 30; and Blotner, *Faulkner*, pp. 712-13.

62. Clark, "A Week-end," p. 1.

63. To Estelle Faulkner [13 Nov. 1931], *Selected Letters*, pp. 53-54.

64. Quoted in Blotner, *Faulkner*, p. 731.

65. Ibid., pp. 735-36.

66. Ibid., pp. 741-43.

67. See to Estelle Faulkner [13 Nov. 1931], *Selected Letters*, pp. 53-54.

68. To Estelle Faulkner [4 Nov. 1931], *Selected Letters*, pp. 52-53.

69. To Hal Smith [July 1933], *Selected Letters*, p. 72. Compare to Robert K. Haas, Friday [7 June 1940], *Selected Letters*, pp. 127-29.

70. To Estelle Faulkner [4 Nov. 1931], *Selected Letters*, pp. 52-53.

71. Quoted in Blotner, *Faulkner*, p. 726. *As I Lay Dying* is dedicated to Hal Smith. The new firm was Harrison Smith and Robert K. Haas.

72. See Millgate, *Achievement*, p. 32; and Blotner, *Faulkner*, pp. 745-49. Compare to Estelle [4 Nov. 1931], *Selected Letters*, pp. 52-53, regarding a possible job in Hollywood: "We could live like counts at least on that, and you could dance and go about."

CHAPTER SEVEN

GENERAL NOTE: Blotner discusses this period in *Faulkner*, chaps. 36-43. See also Meriwether, *Literary Career*, pp. 22-27, 66-68; and Millgate, "The Career," pp. 34-40; and especially *Selected Letters*, pp. 54-96. For helpful impressions of Faulkner at this time, see the two articles by Anthony Buttitta cited in the general note to chapter 6 and the article by Maurice Coindreau cited in the general note to chapter 5. On Faulkner's work in Hollywood, see Hayhoe, "Faulkner in Hollywood"; Bruce Kawin, *Faulkner and Film* (New York, 1977); and George R. Sidney, "Faulkner in Hollywood: A Study of His Career as Scenarist" (Ph.D. diss., University of New Mexico, 1959). See also Meriwether, *Literary Career*, pp. 155-62. For a sense of Faulkner's attitude toward Hollywood, see his story "Golden Land," first published in *American Mercury*, 35 (May 1935), 1-14. On his life in Hollywood, see Coindreau as cited in the general note to chapter 5; Stephen Longstreet, "William Faulkner in California," *Orange County Illustrated*, May 1964; Samuel Marx, "Faulkner in Hollywood," *Beverly Hills Courier*, 1 Oct. 1965; Laurence Stallings, "Faulkner in Hollywood," *New York Sun*, 3 Sept. 1932; Lauren Bacall, *By Myself* (New York, 1979), pp. 95-96, 112-13, 121-22, 216; and Meta Carpenter Wilde as cited later in this note.

On *The Unvanquished*, see Carvel Collins, "Foreword," *The Unvanquished* (New York, 1959); and James B. Meriwether, "The Place of *The Unvanquished* in Faulkner's Yoknapatawpha Series" (Ph.D. diss., Princeton University, 1958). On *Pylon*, see Brooks, *Toward Yoknapatawpha*, pp. 178-204, 395-405; and Michael Millgate, "Faulkner and the Air: The Background of *Pylon*," *Michigan Quarterly Review*, 3 (Fall 1964), 271-77.

On *Absalom, Absalom!*, see Gerald Langford, *Faulkner's Revision of "Absalom, Absalom!"* (Austin, Tex., 1971); and especially Noel Polk, "The Manuscript of *Absalom, Absalom!*," *Mississippi Quarterly*, 25 (Summer 1972), 359-67.

Of great value in understanding Faulkner's life and work during these years is Wilde and Borsten, *A Loving Gentleman*; and Meta Doherty Wilde, "An Unpublished Chapter from *A Loving Gentleman*," *Mississippi Quarterly*, 30 (Summer 1977), 449-60. The most interesting discussion of *The Sound and the Fury* in relation to Faulkner's preoccupations as a writer is in Irwin, *Doubling & Incest*. See also Otto Rank, *The Double*, and Søren Kierkegaard, *Repetition*, as cited in the general note to chapter 5; Harold Bloom, *The Anxiety of Influence*; and Morris, *Friday's Footprint*.

1. See *Lion in the Garden*, p. 32.

2. Hal Smith's letter to Phil Stone [16 Apr. 1934], quoted in Blotner, *Faulkner*, p. 841.

3. See *Lion in the Garden*, pp. 31, 267-69; Spratling, "Chronicle of a Friendship," as cited in the general note to chapter 3; and Anderson and Kelly, *Miss Elizabeth*, pp. 100-101, also as cited in the general note to chapter 3.

4. Anthony Buttitta, "William Faulkner: That Writin' Man of Oxford," as cited in

the general note to chapter 6, pp. 6-8. *Contempo*, the little magazine Buttitta edited, published nine of Faulkner's poems and one short story in a special Faulkner issue, Feb. 1932. See *Selected Letters*, pp. 55-58.

5. To Ben Wasson [probably late Sept. 1932], *Selected Letters*, p. 66.

6. Blotner, *Faulkner*, p. 749.

7. To Ben Wasson [received 26 Jan. 1932], *Selected Letters*, p. 59.

8. *Lion in the Garden*, p. 32.

9. To Hal Smith [winter 1932], *Selected Letters*, p. 59.

10. To Ben Wasson [probably late winter 1932] and [spring 1932], *Selected Letters*, pp. 61, 62.

11. See Sidney, "Faulkner in Hollywood," as cited in the general note to this chapter; and Blotner, *Faulkner*, p. 767.

12. See Marx, "Faulkner in Hollywood," as cited in the general note to this chapter; and Blotner, *Faulkner*, p. 772.

13. Quoted in Blotner, *Faulkner*, p. 773.

14. See ibid., pp. 773-74, and Kawin, *Faulkner and Film*, as cited in the general note to this chapter.

15. To Ben Wasson [probably late Sept. 1932], *Selected Letters*, p. 66; compare pp. 64-65. See Blotner, *Faulkner*, p. 776, where he dates Faulkner's meeting Meta Doherty from this trip to Hollywood. According to Meta Doherty, on the other hand, the first meeting came later. See Wilde and Borsten, *A Loving Gentleman*, pp. 15-22. Although Blotner may be correct, I have followed Doherty—primarily because the beginning of the affair is less crucial than its intensity, on which Doherty is more reliable than Blotner.

16. To Ben Wasson [probably late Sept. 1932], *Selected Letters*, p. 66; compare pp. 64-65.

17. Quoted in Blotner, *Faulkner*, p. 780.

18. Ibid. See Sidney, "Faulkner in Hollywood," and Kawin, *Faulkner and Film*, as cited in the general note; and to Estelle Faulkner, Thursday [postmarked 2 June 1932], *Selected Letters*, pp. 64-65.

19. To Ben Wasson [received 25 Sept. 1932] and [probably late Sept. 1932], *Selected Letters*, pp. 65, 66. See *My Brother Bill*, chap. 16.

20. Quoted in Blotner, *Faulkner*, p. 782.

21. *Falkners of Mississippi*, pp. 200-201; *My Brother Bill*, chap. 16; and to Ben Wasson [received 25 Sept. 1932], *Selected Letters*, p. 65.

22. To Ben Wasson [probably late Sept. 1932], *Selected Letters*, p. 66.

23. To Hal Smith [probably late Oct. 1932], *Selected Letters*, pp. 66-67.

24. *Faulkner in the University*, p. 4. See the letter cited in note 23 to this chapter.

25. This chronicle was never published and probably was never finished. A fragment of it, labeled Rowan Oak 1932, is in the William Faulkner Collections, Alderman Library, University of Virginia, Charlottesville. On it, see James B. Meriwether, "The Novel Faulkner Never Wrote: His Golden Book or Doomsday Book," *American Literature*, 42 (Mar. 1970), 93-96. See also Blotner, *Faulkner*, pp. 790-91.

26. See, for example, to Ben Wasson [received 27 June 1933], *Selected Letters*, p. 71.

27. Compare *Lion in the Garden*, p. 24, with two letters to Hal Smith [received 20 July 1933] and something Oct. [1933], *Selected Letters*, pp. 72, 75.

28. *Faulkner in the University*, p. 111. In my discussion of Faulkner's characters as almost hallucinatory voices, I am indebted to conversations with Jerome Charyn.

29. Quoted in Blotner, *Faulkner*, p. 816. See "To the Editor" [early 1930], *Se-*

lected Letters, p. 47, where Faulkner says he had started flying again. The lessons, however, began in 1933.

30. To Ben Wasson [received 27 June 1933], and [summer 1933], *Selected Letters*, p. 71, 73–74.

31. The edition was never published, but the introduction Faulkner wrote for it survives in two forms. See my Bibliographical Note.

32. To Hal Smith, something Oct. [1933], *Selected Letters*, p. 75.

33. When Ben Wasson left New York for California, Morton Goldman became Faulkner's agent. See *Selected Letters*, p. 75.

34. To Hal Smith [probably Feb. 1934], *Selected Letters*, pp. 78–79.

35. To Morton Goldman [probably winter or early spring 1934], *Selected Letters*, p. 79.

36. To Morton Goldman [probably late spring or early summer 1934], *Selected Letters*, pp. 80–81; and to Hal Smith, something Oct. [1933], *Selected Letters*, p. 75.

37. To Estelle Faulkner [postmarked 7 July 1934], and Friday [20 July 1934], *Selected Letters*, pp. 81, 82–83.

38. To Hal Smith, Thursday [Aug. 1934]; and to Morton Goldman [Aug. 1934], *Selected Letters*, pp. 83–84, 84.

39. The stories appeared in the *Post* on 29 Sept. 1934, 13 Oct. 1934, 3 Nov. 1934, 14 Nov. 1936, and 5 Dec. 1936. "Skirmish at Sartoris" appeared in *Scribner's*, Apr. 1935.

40. On *The Unvanquished*, see Collins and Meriwether as cited in the general note to this chapter.

41. To Morton Goldman [Aug. 1934], *Selected Letters*, p. 84.

42. See Brooks, *Yoknapatawpha Country*, p. 76; and Millgate, *Achievement*, p. 170.

43. To Morton Goldman [probably 18 Oct. 1934], *Selected Letters*, p. 85.

44. To Hal Smith [late Dec. 1934], *Selected Letters*, pp. 86–87. In addition to Faulkner's description of parallels, see Millgate, *Achievement*, pp. 138–41; Blotner, *Faulkner*, pp. 862–75; and especially Brooks, *Toward Yoknapatawpha*, and Millgate, "Faulkner and the Air," as cited in the general note to this chapter.

45. See Brooks, *Toward Yoknapatawpha*, and Millgate, "Faulkner and the Air," as cited in the general note. See also Faulkner's "Folklore of the Air," a review of Jimmy Collins, *Test Pilot*, in *Essays, Speeches & Public Letters*, pp. 189–92.

46. See Millgate, *Achievement*, pp. 142–49; D. T. Torchiana, "Faulkner's *Pylon* and the Structure of Modernity," *Modern Fiction Studies*, 3 (Winter 1957–58), 307; Blotner, *Faulkner*, pp. 872–74; and Brooks, *Toward Yoknapatawpha*, as cited in the general note to this chapter.

47. *Faulkner in the University*, p. 36.

48. See the several theoretical works cited at the end of the general note to this chapter.

49. To Hal Smith [probably early Feb. 1935], *Selected Letters*, p. 88.

50. To Morton Goldman [probably Mar. 1935] and [probably Apr. 1935], *Selected Letters*, pp. 90–91.

51. *Faulkner in the University*, pp. 75–76.

52. See Brooks, *Yoknapatawpha Country*, pp. 295–324, and especially pp. 429–36; Blotner, *Faulkner*, pp. 890–92; and Brooks, *Toward Yoknapatawpha*, pp. 301–28.

53. See to Hal Smith [probably Feb. 1934], *Selected Letters*, pp. 78–79; and Irwin, *Doubling & Incest*, especially pp. 35–59, 84–85, 151–53, 158–59. See also my discussion of *Mosquitoes* in chapter 3.

54. To Morton Goldman [probably late July 1935], *Selected Letters*, p. 92. See Blotner, *Faulkner*, p. 898. See also the letter cited in note 55 to this chapter.

55. Estelle Faulkner [5 Oct. 1935], *Selected Letters*, p. 93.

56. See the letter cited in note 55 to this chapter as quoted in Blotner, *Faulkner*, p. 902.

57. On the death of Dean Faulkner, see Blotner, *Faulkner*, pp. 913–17; *Falkners of Mississippi*, pp. 130–33; and *My Brother Bill*, pp. 167–70, 176, 217–19.

58. To Morton Goldman, 4 Dec. [1935], *Selected Letters*, pp. 93–94.

59. See Meriwether, *Literary Career*, p. 157; Blotner, *Faulkner*, pp. 923–26; and especially Hayhoe, "Faulkner in Hollywood," as cited in the general note to this chapter.

60. Quoted in Blotner, *Faulkner*, p. 927; compare pp. 926–29.

61. *Faulkner in the University*, p. 37; compare p. 3.

62. See Brooks, *Toward Yoknapatawpha*, pp. 283–300.

63. *Faulkner in the University*, p. 73. See also Irwin, *Doubling & Incest*, especially pp. 35–59, 84–85, 151–53, 158–59.

64. See Guerard, *Triumph of the Novel*, pp. 313–14.

65. *Faulkner in the University*, p. 198; see pp. 35, 97–98.

66. See the several theoretical works cited at the end of the general note to this chapter.

67. See note 27 to this chapter.

68. See Irwin, *Doubling & Incest*, pp. 35–59, 84–85, 151–53, 158–59.

69. See Guerard, *Triumph of the Novel*, pp. 302–39.

70. To Bennett Cerf and Robert K. Haas, 10 Jan. 1945, *Selected Letters*, p. 188.

71. Meta Doherty's first husband was named Carpenter. After they were divorced, she retained her married name, but Faulkner used both Doherty and Carpenter. She later married Wolfgang Rebner twice and then Arthur Wilde. The story of her love affair with Faulkner is told in the book by Wilde and Borsten, *A Loving Gentleman*. On the issue of this book's reliability, see note 15 to this chapter and note 3 to chapter 8.

72. See Wilde and Borsten, *A Loving Gentleman*, pp. 15–58. On dating the beginning of this affair, see note 15 to this chapter.

73. Compare to Ben Wasson [mid-Aug. 1933], with to Harold Ober [received 20 July 1942], *Selected Letters*, pp. 74, 159. See also *Selected Letters*, pp. 69, 70, 78.

74. Blotner, *Faulkner*, p. 940.

75. *Lion in the Garden*, p. 26.

76. See Blotner, *Faulkner*, pp. 940, 943, 944. See also Joan Williams, *The Wintering* (New York, 1971), which is a fictionalized account of her love affair with Faulkner in the 1950s, especially p. 101.

77. See to Else Jonsson [19 Aug. 1952], *Selected Letters*, p. 339; and Wilde and Borsten, *A Loving Gentleman*, especially pp. 50–54.

78. Wilde and Borsten, *A Loving Gentleman*, pp. 15–58.

79. Ibid., p. 62; see p. 80.

80. Ibid., pp. 75–76.

81. Ibid., pp. 75, 77; compare pp. 76–78.

82. Ibid., pp. 76–77.

83. Ibid., p. 77. See my discussion of "Elmer" in chapter 3 and of *Light in August* in chapter 6.

84. Wilde and Borsten, *A Loving Gentleman*, p. 77.

85. Ibid., p. 279.

86. Ibid., pp. 85, 88–89.

87. These documents are in the William Faulkner Collections, Alderman Library,

University of Virginia, Charlottesville. Quoted by permission of Jill Faulkner Summers. On them see Blotner, *Faulkner*, p. 937. See also Wilde and Borsten, *A Loving Gentleman*, pp. 85–93.

88. To Morton Goldman [probably June 1936], *Selected Letters*, pp. 95–96.

89. Quoted in Blotner, *Faulkner*, p. 938. See Wilde and Borsten, *A Loving Gentleman*, pp. 156–58.

90. See Wilde and Borsten, *A Loving Gentleman*, pp. 101, 103–4, 156–57; and Blotner, *Faulkner*, pp. 938–40.

CHAPTER EIGHT

GENERAL NOTE: Blotner discusses this period in *Faulkner*, chaps. 44–50. See also Meriwether, *Literary Career*, pp. 27–32; Millgate, "The Career," pp. 39–42; and especially *Selected Letters*, pp. 94–160. On Faulkner's life and work in Hollywood, see the story "Golden Land" and the works by Hayhoe, Kawin, Sidney, Longstreet, Marx, and Stallings, all as cited in the general note to chapter 7. The crucial work, however, is Wilde and Borsten, *A Loving Gentleman*; and Wilde, "An Unpublished Chapter from *A Loving Gentleman*," as cited in the general note to chapter 7. On *The Unvanquished*, see Collins, "Foreword to *The Unvanquished*," and Meriwether, "The Place of *The Unvanquished* in Faulkner's Yoknapatawpha Series," as cited in the general note to chapter 7. On *The Wild Palms*, see Brooks, *Toward Yoknapatawpha*, pp. 205–29, 406–13; R. V. Cassill, "Introduction," *The Wild Palms* (New York, 1968); Maurice Coindreau, "Préface aux Palmiers sauvages," *Temps Modernes*, 8 (Jan. 1952), 1187–96; and especially, Thomas L. McHaney, *William Faulkner's "The Wild Palms": A Study* (Jackson, Miss., 1976).

On *The Hamlet* see Joseph J. Arpad, "William Faulkner's Legendary Novels: The Snopes Trilogy," *Mississippi Quarterly*, 22 (Summer 1969), 214–25; Reed, *Faulkner's Narrative*; Robert Alter, "History and Imagination in the Nineteenth-Century Novel," *Georgia Review*, 29 (Spring 1975), 42–60; and especially, Beck, *Man in Motion*.

On *Go Down, Moses* in particular and theoretical issues in general, see Morris, *Friday's Footprint*.

1. See Wilde and Borsten, *A Loving Gentleman*, pp. 167–68; and Blotner, *Faulkner*, pp. 941–42, 953–54. In March 1937 the Faulkners moved into a smaller house in Beverly Hills.

2. See Wilde and Borsten, *A Loving Gentleman*, pp. 183–86, 194–95; and Blotner, *Faulkner*, pp. 944–45, 956.

3. See Wilde and Borsten, *A Loving Gentleman*, pp. 109–49. Compare Blotner, *Faulkner*, pp. 941–47. A reader interested in sorting out the facts of this period needs to examine both of these works, being careful to note discrepancies between them. The first confuses dates, among other things, and even the timing of some of Faulkner's trips. But it is valuable on many counts, particularly since it provides the only record we have of what Faulkner said to Meta Doherty. Given what we know of Faulkner's life at this time, her reports are generally convincing.

4. Wilde and Borsten, *A Loving Gentleman*, p. 129.

5. Ibid., pp. 169–70, 171–74, 177, 182–89.

6. Ibid., pp. 187–95.

7. The inscribed sheet is now in the William Faulkner Collections, Alderman Library, University of Virginia, Charlottesville. Quoted by permission of Jill Faulkner Summers. See Blotner, *Faulkner*, pp. 946–47.

8. Blotner, *Faulkner*, pp. 945-55.

9. Ibid., p. 930; see p. 946.

10. Ibid., p. 960.

11. Ibid., p. 956; see pp. 946-47, 960, 964. Compare Wilde and Borsten, *A Loving Gentleman*, pp. 188-95.

12. See *My Brother Bill*, p. 149; and Cullen, *Old Times*, p. 17.

13. Robert N. Linscott, "Faulkner without Fanfare," *Esquire*, 60 (July 1963), 36.

14. *Faulkners of Mississippi*, pp. 194-97. See Blotner, *Faulkner*, p. 964. See also "Golden Land," as cited in the general note to this chapter, for an interesting tie between Faulkner's drinking and his distaste for Hollywood.

15. See Blotner, *Faulkner*, pp. 942-43, 946-47.

16. To Morton Goldman, 4 Sept. 1936, *Selected Letters*, p. 96. Compare Faulkner's note to Nunnally Johnson, quoted in Blotner, *Faulkner*, pp. 946-47.

17. To Bennett Cerf, 28 Dec. 1936, *Selected Letters*, pp. 97-98.

18. To Estelle Faulkner [28 July 1937], *Selected Letters*, p. 101; and to Mrs. William F. Fielden [n.d.], quoted in Blotner, *Faulkner*, p. 957. See also Blotner, *Faulkner*, p. 964-68.

19. See Blotner, *Faulkner*, p. 968.

20. Ibid., p. 970.

21. See to Robert K. Haas, 19 Nov. [1937], *Selected Letters*, pp. 101-2. Compare follow-up letters to Haas, pp. 102-3.

22. The two most important accounts of the trip are Wilde and Borsten, *A Loving Gentleman*, pp. 218-30, and Blotner, *Faulkner*, pp. 972-77.

23. "A Note on Sherwood Anderson," in *Essays, Speeches & Public Letters*, p. 10. See Blotner, *Faulkner*, p. 974.

24. See Wilde and Borsten, *A Loving Gentleman*, pp. 218-20.

25. To Joan Williams [8 Aug. 1952], *Selected Letters*, p. 338.

26. See Blotner, *Faulkner*, pp. 974-75; and Wilde and Borsten, *A Loving Gentleman*, pp. 223-25.

27. Blotner, *Faulkner*, p. 975.

28. To Robert K. Haas, 19 Nov. [1937], and to Bennett Cerf [received 19 Jan. 1939], *Selected Letters*, pp. 101, 109. On the original title, see Meriwether, *Literary Career*, p. 69; and Brooks, *Toward Yoknapatawpha*, pp. 406-7.

29. To Robert K. Hass, 29 Nov. [1937], 21 Dec. [1937], and 1 Apr. 1938, in *Selected Letters*, pp. 102-3, 105.

30. See Brooks, Cassill, and McHaney as cited in the general note to this chapter.

31. *Lion in the Garden*, pp. 247-48; and *Faulkner in the University*, pp. 171-80.

32. See *Faulkner in the University*, pp. 174-75.

33. Ibid., p. 171.

34. See Millgate, *Achievement*, p. 178; as well as Brooks, Cassill, and McHaney as cited in the general note to this chapter.

35. See *As I Lay Dying*, p. 162.

36. These words are similar to words Faulkner had given to Temple Drake in *Sanctuary* and to Joe Christmas in *Light in August*.

37. See *Absalom, Absalom!*, p. 146.

38. See Cassill, introduction to *The Wild Palms*, and Coindreau, "Préface aux Palmiers sauvages," as cited in the general note; and especially Cassill, pp. xi-xii.

39. See Brooks, *Toward Yoknapatawpha*, pp. 214-16. Brooks notes that his discussion draws heavily on Denis de Rougemont's *Love in the Western World* and *Love Declared*, particularly on Rougemont's notion that "romantic lovers are really in love with death": that they demand a consummation so perfect, a union so absolute,

that it can come only in death. See especially Brooks, *Toward Yoknapatawpha*, p. 215, n. 10. Then compare my discussion of Faulkner's love affair with Meta Doherty, particularly his fascination with the forbidden and the pure, in chapter 7. As Brooks observes, Harry not only "alludes to the 'romance of illicit love' which attracts men," but also ties it to "the passionate idea of two [lovers] damned and doomed and isolated forever against the world and God and the irrevocable" (see p. 215, n. 8). Compare Charlotte's absolutism ("It can't be anything else," she says to Harry. "Either heaven, or hell.") with Quentin's in *The Sound and the Fury*. When the possibility of translation into a timeless, private corner of heaven is lost, Quentin opts for a timeless and private corner of hell, where he and Caddy, in the figure of Little Sister Death, can be alone forever.

40. See Millgate, *Achievement*, p. 179; and Brooks, *Toward Yoknapatawpha*, p. 220.

41. To Robert K. Haas, 1 Apr. 1938 and 8 July 1938, in *Selected Letters*, pp. 105, 106.

42. See the letter cited in note 25 to this chapter.

43. Quoted in Blotner, *Faulkner*, p. 979.

44. See Ibid., p. 981.

45. See *Faulkner in the University*, pp. 231-32; compare pp. 174-75. And see especially the fragment ". . . Him with unflagging hope/I should have been a priest in floorless halls/I should have risen by grey silent walls/And walked my life's length to another wall," Humanities Research Center, University of Texas, Austin. The phrase "I should have been a priest" turns up in several fragments in different contexts. Quoted by permission of Jill Faulkner Summers.

46. See Wilde and Borsten, *A Loving Gentleman*, p. 279; and Franklin, *Bitterweeds*.

47. "Books and Things: Joseph Hergesheimer," *Early Prose and Poetry*, p. 101.

48. See note 39 to this chapter.

49. To Robert K. Haas, 8 July 1938, *Selected Letters*, pp. 106-7.

50. To Morton Goldman, 19 Feb. 1938, *Selected Letters*, pp. 103-4.

51. See *My Brother Bill*, chap. 17; and *Flags in the Dust*, pp. 267-68.

52. On Harold Ober, see Catherine Drinker Bowen, "Harold Ober, Literary Agent," *Atlantic Monthly*, 206 (July 1960), 35-40.

53. See Blotner, *Faulkner*, p. 1001.

54. To Robert K. Haas [received 15 Dec. 1938], *Selected Letters*, pp. 107-9. See also Arpad, "William Faulkner's Legendary Novels," Reed, *Faulkner's Narrative*, and Beck, *Man in Motion*.

55. To Saxe Commins [Oct. 1939]; to Robert K. Haas [received 29 Nov. 1939], and Monday [received 7 Dec. 1939], *Selected Letters*, pp. 115, 115-16, 116.

56. To Robert K. Haas [received 24 Apr. 1939], *Selected Letters*, p. 113.

57. See Blotner, *Faulkner*, pp. 1015-16.

58. Cantwell, "The Faulkners," p. 56.

59. To Bennett Cerf [received 19 Jan. 1939]; and to Robert K. Haas [received 7 Feb. 1939], *Selected Letters*, pp. 109, 109-10.

60. Quoted in Blotner, *Faulkner*, p. 903. See pp. 1019-20.

61. To Robert K. Haas [received 22 Mar. 1939], *Selected Letters*, p. 111.

62. See to Robert K. Haas, 25 March 1939 and Wednesday [29 Mar. 1939], *Selected Letters*, pp. 112, 112-13; and Blotner, *Faulkner*, p. 1020.

63. Wilde and Borsten, *A Loving Gentleman*, pp. 241-44.

64. See to Saxe Commins [Oct. 1939], *Selected Letters*, p. 115.

65. Ibid. For the dates and places of publication of the stories that became

The Hamlet, see Meriwether, *Literary Career*, pp. 29–30, 40–43, 62, 69–73, 170, 173–74. See also the works cited in note 54 to this chapter.

66. See the letter cited in note 56 to this chapter.

67. See, for example, *Faulkner in the University*, p. 197.

68. My discussion of *The Hamlet* is indebted to Arpad, Reed, Beck, and Alter as cited in the general note to this chapter.

69. See to Malcolm Cowley [16 Aug. 1945], *Faulkner-Cowley File*, pp. 24–27.

70. See Alter, "History and Imagination," as cited in the general note to this chapter, pp. 44–45.

71. *Faulkner in the University*, p. 197.

72. Ibid., p. 253.

73. To Robert K. Haas [received 29 Nov. 1939], and [received 7 Dec. 1939], *Selected Letters*, pp. 115–16, 116–17.

74. To Robert K. Haas, 5 Feb. [1940], *Selected Letters*, p. 117.

75. See to Robert K. Haas, Thursday [18 Apr. 1940], and Sunday [28 Apr. 1940], *Selected Letters*, pp. 120–21, 121–22.

76. See to Robert K. Haas, Sunday [28 Apr. 1940], and Friday [3 May 1940], *Selected Letters*, pp. 121–22, 122–24.

77. See Blotner, *Faulkner*, pp. 1048–53; and *Selected Letters*, pp. 121–34.

78. See Blotner, *Faulkner*, p. 1097; and to Robert K. Haas, Saturday [1 June 1940], and to Harold Ober, 16 Aug. 1940, *Selected Letters*, pp. 126–27, 136.

79. See Blotner, *Faulkner*, pp. 1008–13; and *My Brother Bill*, chap. 18.

80. To Robert K. Haas, Friday [3 May 1940], and Friday [7 June 1940], *Selected Letters*, pp. 122–24, 127–29. Compare *Selected Letters*, pp. 90–91.

81. To Robert K. Haas, Sunday [28 Apr. 1940], Friday [3 May 1940], Saturday [1 June 1940], and Friday [7 June 1940], in *Selected Letters*, pp. 121–22, 122–24, 126–27, and 127–29. Compare *Lion in the Garden*, p. 9.

82. To Robert K. Haas, Friday [21 Mar. 1941], *Selected Letters*, p. 139. Compare to Robert K. Haas, Monday [27 May 1940], *Selected Letters*, p. 125.

83. To Robert K. Haas, Thursday [1 May 1941], *Selected Letters*, pp. 139–40.

84. Ibid.

85. To Robert K. Haas, 2 Dec. [1941], *Selected Letters*, p. 146. My discussion of *Go Down, Moses* is indebted principally to Morris, *Friday's Footprint*, as cited in the general note to this chapter.

86. To Robert K. Haas, Wednesday [26 Jan. 1949], *Selected Letters*, pp. 284–85.

87. See *Faulkner in the University*, p. 88; and Reed, *Faulkner's Narrative*, pp. 276–77.

88. See Blotner, *Faulkner*, pp. 1085–86.

89. See Millgate, *Achievement*, pp. 207–9; and Brooks, *Yoknapatawpha Country*, pp. 271–75.

90. *Lion in the Garden*, p. 225. Compare *Faulkner in the University*, p. 246.

91. Blotner, *Faulkner*, p. 1090.

92. To Warren Beck, 6 July 1941, *Selected Letters*, pp. 142–43. See Warren Beck, "Faulkner: A Preface and a Letter," *Yale Review*, 52 (Oct. 1962), 157–60.

93. To Harold Ober, Sunday [28 June 1942], *Selected Letters*, pp. 155–56.

94. See Blotner, *Faulkner*, p. 1073.

95. The basic correspondence on these negotiations is in *Selected Letters*, pp. 155–62. See also Blotner, *Faulkner*, pp. 1109–13.

96. See to William Herndon, 18 July 1942, and to Harold Ober, 19 July 1942, in *Selected Letters*, pp. 157–58, 160; and Blotner, *Faulkner*, pp. 1110–11.

97. To Harold Ober, 1 Aug. 1942, *Selected Letters*, pp. 161–62. Faulkner learned of the long series of options only after he arrived in California.

CHAPTER NINE

GENERAL NOTE: Blotner discusses this period in *Faulkner*, chaps. 51-58. See also Meriwether, *Literary Career*, pp. 32-35, 47-48, 75-78; and Millgate, "The Career," pp. 42-49. Faulkner's correspondence, *Selected Letters*, pp. 156-310, is of major importance, especially regarding his sense of Hollywood and the Herndon contract as a kind of captivity and his anxiety over being blocked as a writer. One crucial part of his correspondence is available in *Faulkner-Cowley File*, the pertinent pages being 3-129. Cowley's portraits and insights make this a valuable book. In addition to reflecting Faulkner's dislike of Hollywood and his mounting anxiety, his letters reflect his resentment over being neglected and his lingering hope of rediscovery. Robert N. Linscott's "Faulkner without Fanfare," *Esquire*, 60 (July 1963), 36, 38, also presents a useful picture of Faulkner during these years. On Faulkner and Hollywood, see the story "Golden Land" and the works by Hayhoe, Kawin, Sidney, Longstreet, Stallings, and Bacall, all as cited in the general note to chapter 7. Of crucial importance is Wilde and Borsten, *A Loving Gentleman*. On Faulkner's move toward more didactic fiction, see Hodding Carter, "Faulkner and His Folk," *Princeton University Library Chronicle*, 18 (Spring 1957), 95-107; and Dayton Kohler, "William Faulkner and the Social Conscience," *College English*, 11 (Dec. 1949), 119-27. Compare *Selected Letters*, pp. 296-97, and *Faulkner-Cowley File*, p. 102.

On Faulkner and Joan Williams, see Blotner, *Faulkner*, beginning in chap. 57; and *Selected Letters*, especially pp. 296-301, 303-4, 305, 306-7, 308. But see also Joan Williams, *The Wintering* (New York, 1971), which is a fictionalized account of their relationship. Judging from the way this novel echoes the language of Faulkner's letters to Joan Williams, I think it probable that it also echoes actual conversations. The picture of Jeff Almoner's wife bears a close resemblance to the picture of Estelle in *A Loving Gentleman*. For other important parallels, see *The Wintering*, pp. 79-80, 101, 106, 115, 120-21, 131-32, 142, 278-80, 292, 297, 306-7, 329, 342. On *A Fable*, see Brooks, *Toward Yoknapatawpha*, pp. 230-50, 414-23. On *Requiem for a Nun*, see the several articles by Noel Polk cited in the general note to chapter 10.

1. To Harold Ober, Saturday [21 Feb. 1942], *Selected Letters*, p. 149. See Blotner, *Faulkner*, p. 1113.

2. To Malcolm Cowley, Hollywood, Sunday, 7 May [1944], *Faulkner-Cowley File*, pp. 6-7.

3. To Harold Ober, Saturday [22 Apr. 1944], *Selected Letters*, pp. 180-81.

4. To Harold Ober, 1 Aug. 1942, Monday [15 Mar. 1943], and Friday [25 May 1945], *Selected Letters*, pp. 161-62, 168-69, 192. See Wilde and Borsten, *A Loving Gentleman*, p. 281; and Blotner, *Faulkner*, pp. 1121-22.

5. Wilde and Borsten, *A Loving Gentleman*, pp. 243-45, 255-56, 263-64, 275-76.

6. Ibid., pp. 277-80, 283.

7. Ibid., pp. 283-85.

8. Quoted in Blotner, *Faulkner*, p. 1265; see also pp. 1125-28.

9. Ibid., pp. 1196-97. See the piece by Longstreet, "William Faulkner in California," cited in the general note to chapter 7.

10. To Mrs. William F. Fielden, Saturday [19 Sept. 1942], *Selected Letters*, pp. 163-64. See Wilde and Borsten, *A Loving Gentleman*, pp. 281, 283, 285-87; and Blotner, *Faulkner*, pp. 1123-24, 1129, 1157.

11. Wilde and Borsten, *A Loving Gentleman*, pp. 278, 281-83, 287.

12. To Mrs. Murry C. Falkner, Sunday [15 Nov. 1942], *Selected Letters*, p. 164. See Wilde and Borsten, *A Loving Gentleman*, pp. 287-88; and Blotner, *Faulkner*, p. 1136.

13. To Harold Ober, Monday [25 Jan. 1943]; and to William F. Fielden, Tuesday [27 Apr. 1943], *Selected Letters*, pp. 167, 172–73.

14. To Mrs. William C. Faulkner, Sunday [1 Aug. 1943], *Selected Letters*, pp. 176–77. See Blotner, *Faulkner*, pp. 1141–44; and Wilde and Borsten, *A Loving Gentleman*, pp. 285–88.

15. Quoted in Blotner, *Faulkner*, p. 1148.

16. Ibid., pp. 1148–50. See *Selected Letters*, pp. 177–78.

17. Wilde and Borsten, *A Loving Gentleman*, pp. 281, 287; and to Harold Ober, Thursday [26 Nov. 1942], *Selected Letters*, pp. 164–65.

18. Quoted in Blotner, *Faulkner*, p. 1132. Italics omitted.

19. See ibid., p. 1152.

20. To Harold Ober [received 17 Nov. 1943], and Saturday [30 Oct. 1943], *Selected Letters*, pp. 178–79, 178.

21. To Saxe Commins [probably early June 1951], *Selected Letters*, p. 316. Similar phrases turn up in letters written throughout the late forties and early fifties.

22. Quoted in Blotner, *Faulkner*, p. 1465. This notion is expressed in several letters to friends and publishers dating from the late forties and early fifties.

23. See Millgate, *Achievement*, pp. 232–33; and Reed, *Faulkner's Narrative*, pp. 176–217.

24. See to Harold Ober, Saturday [22 Apr. 1944]; and to Malcolm A. Franklin, Saturday [5 Dec. 1942], *Selected Letters*, pp. 180–81, 165–66.

25. To James M. Faulkner, Saturday afternoon [3 Apr. 1943]; and to Malcolm A. Franklin, Saturday [5 Dec. 1942], *Selected Letters*, pp. 170–71, 165–66.

26. To Malcolm A. Franklin, 24 May 1943, quoted in Blotner, *Faulkner*, pp. 1143–44, and Sunday [4 July 1943], *Selected Letters*, pp. 175–76.

27. To Malcolm A. Franklin, 24 May 1943, quoted in Blotner, *Faulkner*, pp. 1143–44, and Saturday [5 Dec. 1942], *Selected Letters*, pp. 165–66.

28. To Robert K. Haas, Saturday [15 Jan. 1944], *Selected Letters*, p. 180.

29. To Harold Ober, Saturday [22 Apr. 1944], *Selected Letters*, pp. 180–81. See W. H. Auden, "In Memory of W. B. Yeats": "For poetry makes nothing happen."

30. See to Malcolm Cowley, Saturday [early Nov. 1944], *Faulkner-Cowley File*, pp. 14–17.

31. See Blotner, *Faulkner*, pp. 1158–59; and Kawin, *Faulkner and Film*, as cited in the general note to chapter 7.

32. Quoted in Blotner, *Faulkner*, p. 1156. See Bacall, *By Myself*, as cited in the general note to chapter 7; Wilde and Borsten, *A Loving Gentleman*, pp. 297–300; and *Lion in the Garden*, p. 240.

33. Quoted in Blotner, *Faulkner*, pp. 1159–60; see pp. 1133–35. See also Wilde and Borsten, *A Loving Gentleman*, pp. 284–85, 296, 304–5.

34. Wilde and Borsten, *A Loving Gentleman*, p. 300; and to Harold Ober, Saturday [22 Apr. 1944], *Selected Letters*, pp. 180–81. See Wilde and Borsten, p. 287.

35. Malcolm Cowley to Faulkner [early months of 1944], and Faulkner to Malcolm Cowley, Sunday, 7 May [1944], *Faulkner-Cowley File*, pp. 6–7.

36. To Mrs. William Fielden, Sunday [30 Apr. 1944], *Selected Letters*, p. 181; and Wilde and Borsten, *A Loving Gentleman*, pp. 301–3. See Blotner, *Faulkner*, pp. 1166–68.

37. Quoted in Blotner, *Faulkner*, p. 1169.

38. Quoted in Blotner, *Faulkner*, p. 1171. See Wilde and Borsten, *A Loving Gentleman*, pp. 309–10; and Bacall, *By Myself*, pp. 95–96, 112–13, 121–22, 216.

39. See Blotner, *Faulkner*, p. 1171, where he says Faulkner was living with the

Bezzerides again; and Wilde and Borsten, *A Loving Gentleman*, pp. 305-16, where Meta describes him as living with Henrietta and Frank Martin.

40. Wilde and Borsten, *A Loving Gentleman*, pp. 308-9; and Cowley to Faulkner, 22 July 1944, in *Faulkner-Cowley File*, pp. 9-10. See Malcolm Cowley, "William Faulkner's Human Comedy," *New York Times Book Review*, 29 Oct. 1944, p. 4.

41. Quoted in Blotner, *Faulkner*, p. 1173; see pp. 1173-76. See also Wilde and Borsten, *A Loving Gentleman*, pp. 308-12.

42. To Malcolm Cowley, Saturday [early Nov. 1944], *Faulkner-Cowley File*, pp. 14-17.

43. To Bennett Cerf and Robert K. Haas, 10 Jan. 1945, *Selected Letters*, p. 188.

44. To Malcolm Cowley, Saturday [early Nov. 1944], *Faulkner-Cowley File*, pp. 14-17. Compare the letter cited in note 43 to this chapter.

45. "A Note on Sherwood Anderson," in *Essays, Speeches & Public Letters*, pp. 3-4.

46. Compare the letter cited in note 43 to this chapter with to Warren Beck, 6 July 1941, *Selected Letters*, pp. 142-43; and especially with the essay cited in note 45 to this chapter, p. 5.

47. To Harold Ober, Monday [19 Mar. 1945], *Selected Letters*, pp. 190-91.

48. To Harold Ober, Friday [25 May 1945], *Selected Letters*, p. 192.

49. Longstreet, "William Faulkner in California." See also the letter cited in note 48 to this chapter, and Blotner, *Faulkner*, pp. 1183-84.

50. Cowley to Faulkner, 9 Aug. 1945, and Faulkner to Cowley, Thursday [16 Aug. 1945], *Faulkner-Cowley File*, pp. 21-24, 24-27. On the Renoir movie, called *The Southerner*, see *Faulkner-Cowley File*, p. 106; and Blotner, *Faulkner*, pp. 1184.

51. See Wilde and Borsten, *A Loving Gentleman*, pp. 310-12; and to Harold Ober, Monday [20 Aug. 1945], *Selected Letters*, pp. 199-200.

52. See the several letters to Harold Ober in *Selected Letters*, pp. 190-91, 192, 193-94, 195-96, 199-200; and to William Herndon, in *Selected Letters*, pp. 176, 193. See also Blotner's editorial notes, *Selected Letters*, pp. 195, 199; and to Estelle Faulkner, Sunday [1 Aug. 1943], *Selected Letters*, pp. 176-77.

53. Quoted in Blotner, *Faulkner*, p. 1189.

54. Wilde and Borsten, *A Loving Gentleman*, p. 311; compare pp. 311-12. To Harold Ober, Monday [20 Aug. 1945], *Selected Letters*, pp. 199-200.

55. Wilde and Borsten, *A Loving Gentleman*, pp. 317, 311-12.

56. *Lion in the Garden*, pp. 244-45.

57. See the exchanges in *Faulkner-Cowley File*, pp. 71-85, especially 74-75, 82-83.

58. To J. L. Warner, 15 Oct. 1945, *Selected Letters*, pp. 204-5. See Blotner, *Faulkner*, p. 1197.

59. See to Robert K. Haas, Friday [2 Nov. 1945], *Selected Letters*, pp. 209-10; and to Malcolm Cowley, Thursday [19 Oct. 1945], *Faulkner-Cowley File*, pp. 36-37. See Cowley's discussion of the appendix, pp. 37-40 and 45-47.

60. To Robert K. Haas, Saturday [30 Mar. 1946], *Selected Letters*, pp. 231-32. See Blotner, *Faulkner*, pp. 1209-11; and *Selected Letters*, pp. 226-32.

61. See Blotner, *Faulkner*, pp. 1222-24; and *Selected Letters*, pp. 240-41, 243-45.

62. See to Malcolm Cowley, Tuesday [23 Apr. 1946], *Faulkner-Cowley File*, pp. 90-91; to Harold Ober [18 Apr. 1946]; and to Robert K. Haas, Friday [3 Oct. 1947], *Selected Letters*, pp. 232-33, 255-57.

63. See to Harold Ober, Monday 27 May [1940], and compare to Harold Ober [received 30 Mar. 1942] and to Robert K. Haas, Friday [3 Oct. 1947], *Selected Letters*, pp. 124-25, 150, 255-57.

64. To Malcolm Cowley, Sunday [Dec. 1946], and to Robert K. Haas, Monday [possibly 24 Mar. 1947] and Friday [3 Oct. 1947], in *Selected Letters*, pp. 244–45, 247, 255–57.

65. To Robert K. Haas, Sunday [24 Aug. 1947]; and to Harold Ober [received 14 Nov. 1947], *Selected Letters*, pp. 253–54, 259–60.

66. Ibid. See the correspondence cited in note 65 to this chapter.

67. To Harold Ober, Friday [5 Dec. 1947], and 1 Feb. [1948], *Selected Letters*, pp. 261–62, 262.

68. See to Harold Ober, 1 Feb. [1948], *Selected Letters*, p. 262.

69. *Intruder in the Dust*, p. 206. Compare this and similar passages in the novel with the language of Faulkner's letters of the forties.

70. See Blotner, *Faulkner*, pp. 1257, 1263; and to Bennett Cerf, Tuesday [18 May 1948], and Tuesday [probably 13 July 1948], *Selected Letters*, pp. 269–70.

71. To Malcolm Cowley, Sunday [Dec. 1946], *Faulkner-Cowley File*, pp. 97–98.

72. To Bennett Cerf, Tuesday [28 Sept. 1948], *Selected Letters*, p. 276. See *Faulkner-Cowley File*, pp. 115–16.

73. Quoted in Blotner, *Faulkner*, p. 1265.

74. See Blotner, *Faulkner*, pp. 1264–70; Cowley in *Faulkner-Cowley File*, pp. 103–14; and Millgate, *Achievement*, p. 31.

75. To Saxe Commins, Wednesday [possibly 24 Nov. 1948], *Selected Letters*, p. 280. The filming began in Feb. 1949. See to Saxe Commins, Wednesday [possibly 18 May 1949], and Sunday [mid-June 1949], *Selected Letters*, pp. 291, 291–92.

76. See Millgate, *Achievement*, pp. 268–70; and Blotner, *Faulkner*, pp. 1285–87.

77. See, for example, to Robert K. Haas, 5 July [1949], *Selected Letters*, p. 292.

78. See Blotner, *Faulkner*, pp. 1293–98.

79. See to Saxe Commins, Sunday [31 Oct. 1948], *Selected Letters*, 277; and to Malcolm Cowley, Monday [1 Nov. 1948], *Faulkner-Cowley File*, pp. 114–18.

80. Blotner, *Faulkner*, p. 1311; and to Harold Ober, 19 Dec. 1952, *Selected Letters*, pp. 343–44. For a more general description of the work's double entanglement, see Blotner, *Faulkner*, pp. 1304–13; and *Selected Letters*, pp. 297–301.

81. See Blotner, *Faulkner*, pp. 1292–93, especially Faulkner to Joan Williams, 31 Aug. 1949, quoted by Blotner, pp. 1293, 1299. Compare Joan Williams, *The Wintering* (New York, 1971), especially pp. 41–55, 57–58, 64–65, 68–70.

82. To Joan Williams, 14 Oct. 1949, quoted in Blotner, *Faulkner*, p. 1299. Compare Williams, *The Wintering*, pp. 41–55, 57–58, 64–65, 68–70.

83. See Blotner, *Faulkner*, pp. 1301–3, where it is clear that the initiative was Joan's at this point; and see especially Faulkner to Joan Williams, 7 Jan. 1950, quoted by Blotner, pp. 1302–3. Compare *The Wintering*, pp. 64–65, 68–69, 79, 100–106, 115–16, 142, 342.

84. To Joan Williams, Wednesday night [22 Feb. 1950], *Selected Letters*, pp. 299–300; and as quoted in Blotner, *Faulkner*, p. 1313. Compare *The Wintering*, pp. 102–22.

85. To Joan Williams, Friday night [29 Sept. 1950], *Selected Letters*, p. 307. See Blotner, *Faulkner*, p. 1332. The line quoted is from a story "idea" that Faulkner outlined for Joan about a young college coed who is visited by a famous man, then slowly understands why he came. Compare *The Wintering*, especially pp. 122–24.

86. Quoted in Blotner, *Faulkner*, p. 1319.

87. To Secretary, American Academy, 12 June 1950, in *Faulkner-Cowley File*, p. 141.

88. See Blotner, *Faulkner*, pp. 1326–27. See also to Joan Williams, 31 Aug. 1949, and 23 Feb. 1950, quoted in Blotner, *Faulkner*, pp. 1313, 1293. Compare *The Wintering*, pp. 134–47.

89. Blotner, *Faulkner*, pp. 1337-38.

90. Quoted by Malcolm Cowley to Faulkner, 9 Aug. 1945, *Faulkner-Cowley File*, p. 24.

91. See Blotner, *Faulkner*, pp. 1207, 1270, 1301.

92. See Millgate, *Achievement*, p. 49; and Blotner, *Faulkner*, p. 1349.

93. Quoted in Blotner, *Faulkner*, pp. 1352 and 1362.

94. Ibid., p. 1366. See pp. 1352-68.

95. Compare "Speech of Acceptance upon the Award of the Nobel Prize for Literature," *The Faulkner Reader*, pp. 3-4; with *Selected Letters*, pp. 165-76, 142-43; and with *Faulkner-Cowley File*, pp. 65-68, 77-80, 114-16, 125-26, 141.

96. Quoted in Blotner, *Faulkner*, p. 1369.

97. Compare to Harold Ober, 5 Jan [19]46, *Selected Letters*, pp. 217-18; and "Speech of Acceptance," *The Faulkner Reader*, p. 3.

CHAPTER TEN

GENERAL NOTE: Blotner discusses this period in *Faulkner*, chaps. 60-76. See also Meriwether, *Literary Career*, pp. 36-44, 78-80; Millgate, "The Career," pp. 48-57; and especially Faulkner's correspondence, in *Selected Letters*, pp. 310-463, and in *Faulkner-Cowley File*, pp. 121-75. To make sense of Faulkner's affair with Joan Williams, the reader must work carefully with Blotner's account of it, especially chaps. 57-64; with Faulkner's letters to Joan Williams in *Selected Letters*, especially pp. 296-301, 303-4, 305, 306-7, 308; and with Williams's fictionalized account of the affair in *The Wintering* (New York, 1971). This novel is also useful in trying to understand Faulkner's drinking, as is his story "Golden Land," cited in the general note to chapter 7, and especially his story "Mr. Acarius," which was published posthumously in *Saturday Evening Post*, 9 Oct. 1965. For a discussion of this story, which was written in the 1950s, probably in late 1952 or early 1953, see Michel Gresset, "Weekend, Lost and Revisited," *Mississippi Quarterly*, 21 (Summer 1968), 173-78.

On Faulkner's public career, see Meriwether, *Literary Career*, pp. 49-53, where Meriwether gives the dates and describes the occasions of sixteen of Faulkner's most important speeches, public letters, and essays. See also *Essays, Speeches & Public Letters*. The earliest of the twelve essays in this collection dates from 1953. Of fourteen speeches, thirteen date from 1950 to 1963. Of thirty-one public letters, twenty-six date from 1950 to 1960. See also Dayton Kohler, "William Faulkner and the Social Conscience," and Hodding Carter, "Faulkner and His Folk," as cited in the general note to chapter 9; Charles D. Peavy, *Go Slow Now: Faulkner and the Race Question* (Eugene, Oreg., 1971); and Robert Penn Warren, "Faulkner: The South and the Negro," *Southern Review*, 1 (Summer 1965), 501-29. See also James W. Silver, *Mississippi: The Closed Society* (New York, 1964).

On Faulkner's career as diplomat, see Gay Wilson Allen, "With Faulkner in Japan," *American Scholar*, 31 (Fall 1962), 566-71. On Faulkner's work on *Land of the Pharaohs*, see Bacall, *By Myself*, as cited in the general note to chapter 7, especially pp. 214-17. The most helpful personal impressions for this period are Harvey Breit, "A Sense of Faulkner," *Partisan Review*, 18 (Jan.-Feb. 1951), 88-94; Linscott, "Faulkner without Fanfare," as cited in the general note to chapter 9; and Coughlan, *Private World*. Several of Faulkner's finest interviews date from this period. See especially those with Harvey Breit, Cynthia Grenier, and Jean Stein in *Lion in the Garden*, pp. 80-83, 215-27, and 237-56. On Faulkner's stay at the University of Virginia, see *Faulkner in the University*.

On *A Fable*, see Brooks, *Toward Yoknapatawpha*, pp. 230-50, 414-23. On *Requiem for a Nun*, see Thomas L. McHaney, "Faulkner Borrows from the Mississippi Guide," *Mississippi Quarterly*, 19 (Summer 1966), 116-20; Nancy D. Taylor, "The Dramatic Productions of *Requiem for a Nun*," *Mississippi Quarterly*, 20 (Summer 1967), 127-39; and Noel Polk's four essays: "Alec Holston's Lock and the Founding of Jefferson," *Mississippi Quarterly*, 24 (Summer 1971), 247-70; "The Staging of *Requiem for a Nun*," *Mississippi Quarterly*, 24 (Summer 1971), 299-314; "Faulkner's 'The Jail' and the Meaning of Cecilia Farmer," *Mississippi Quarterly*, 25 (Summer 1972), 305-25; and "The Textual History of Faulkner's *Requiem for a Nun*," in Joseph Katz, ed., *Proof*, 4 (Columbia, S.C., 1975), pp. 109-28.

On *The Town* and *The Mansion*, see Arpad, "William Faulkner's Legendary Novels," cited in the general note to chapter 8; Reed, *Faulkner's Narrative*; and Beck, *Man in Motion*. See also Eileen Gregory, "Faulkner's Typescript of *The Town*," *Mississippi Quarterly*, 26 (Summer 1973), 361-87. On Faulkner's death, see Hughes Rudd, "The Death of William Faulkner," *Saturday Evening Post*, 20 July 1962, pp. 32-34; and especially, William Styron, "As He Lay Dead, a Bitter Grief," *Life*, 53 (20 July 1962), 39-42.

1. See to Joan Williams, Sunday [28 Jan. 1951], *Selected Letters*, p. 312. See *The Wintering*, pp. 116-22.

2. See to Ruth Ford, Monday [probably 18 June 1951], *Selected Letters*, pp. 317-18; and Blotner, *Faulkner*, pp. 1381-84. On his drinking, see especially p. 1383.

3. See *Essays, Speeches & Public Letters*, pp. 122-24.

4. See to Joan Williams, [13 Feb. 1950], and Wednesday [22 Mar. 1950]; to Robert K. Haas, [received 15 May 1952]; to Bennett Cerf, Monday [probably 15 Mar. 1950]; to Saxe Commins, [late Mar. 1951], *Selected Letters*, pp. 298, 300-301, 302-3, 303, 313. But see especially to Joan Williams, Friday [19 May 1950], *Selected Letters*, pp. 303-4: "Am about done with my version of 3rd act. It is not a play, will have to be rewritten as a play. It is now some kind of novel, can be printed as such, rewritten into a play." See also the several works on *Requiem for a Nun* cited in the general note.

5. See the essay by McHaney, "Faulkner Borrows from the Mississippi Guide," cited in the general note to this chapter.

6. *Faulkner in the University*, p. 61. See the third of the articles by Polk, "Faulkner's 'The Jail,'" cited in the general note to this chapter.

7. To Saxe Commins [probably early June 1951], *Selected Letters*, pp. 315-16; and *Faulkner in the University*, p. 122.

8. To Else Jonsson, [4 June 1951], [22 June 1951], [early July 1951], [19 July 1951], [13 Aug. 1951], [30 Sept. 1951], [30 Nov. 1951], *Selected Letters*, pp. 315, 318, 319, 319, 320, 322, 323.

9. On adaptations and productions, see Meriwether, *Literary Career*, pp. 36-37, together with the essay by Taylor and the second of the essays by Polk, "The Staging of *Requiem*," cited in the general note to this chapter. See also to Joan Williams, Monday [18 June 1951]; and to Harold Ober, [Jan. 1952], *Selected Letters*, pp. 317, 324.

10. See to Else Jonsson [2 Mar. 1952], *Selected Letters*, p. 328; to Joan Williams [8 Sept. 1951], quoted in Blotner, *Faulkner*, p. 1395; and to Joan Williams [7 May 1952], *Selected Letters*, pp. 331-32. See *The Wintering*, pp. 106-7, 115-16.

11. See to Saxe Commins, Sunday [8 June 1952]; to Monique and Jean-Jacques Salomon, Monday [16 June 1952]; and to Harold Raymond, 28 June 1952, *Selected Letters*, pp. 332, 332-33, 335.

12. To Joan Williams [19 June 1952], quoted in Blotner, *Faulkner*, p. 1427; see pp. 1426-27. Compare *The Wintering*, pp. 174, 228-29, 239-48.

13. See *Mosquitoes*, p. 346; to Joan Williams [7 Aug. 1952], quoted in Blotner, *Faulkner*, p. 1431; and to Joan Williams, Friday [8 Aug. 1952], *Selected Letters*, p. 338, and as quoted in Blotner, *Faulkner*, pp. 1431-32. See *The Wintering*, pp. 123-24.

14. To Joan Williams, Friday [8 Aug. 1952]; to Harold Ober, 20 Aug. 1952; and to Else Jonsson [19 Aug. 1952], *Selected Letters*, pp. 338, 339, 339. See *The Wintering*, pp. 276-80.

15. To Joan Williams [6 Nov. 1952] and [27 Oct. 1952], quoted in Blotner, *Faulkner*, p. 1437. An excerpt from the first of these letters is in *Selected Letters*, p. 343, but it is heavily edited; the second was withheld. The originals of both are in the William Faulkner Collections, Alderman Library, University of Virginia, Charlottesville. See also *The Wintering*, pp. 121-22.

16. See Blotner, *Faulkner*, pp. 1441-42, where Faulkner is also quoted as attributing his being a writer and laboring so hard to his not being "as tall or as strong as I wanted to be."

17. *Lion in the Garden*, p. 72; and to Joan Williams, Wednesday [31 Dec. 1952], *Selected Letters*, p. 344. Compare the other letters to Joan Williams and the one to Saxe Commins, pp. 344-45.

18. See to Malcolm A. Franklin, Monday [16 Feb. 1953]; and to Else Jonsson [22 Feb. 1953], *Selected Letters*, pp. 346, 346-47. See also the essay by Gresset, "Weekend, Lost and Revisited," cited in the general note to this chapter.

19. See *Essays, Speeches & Public Letters*, pp. 3-10, 11-43. The quote is from p. 21. Compare Faulkner to Else Jonsson [22 Feb. 1953], *Selected Letters*, pp. 346-47.

20. Faulkner to Joan Williams, Wednesday [29 Apr. 1953], *Selected Letters*, p. 348. Faulkner was back in Oxford.

21. Faulkner delivered the commencement address at Pine Manor. See *Essays, Speeches & Public Letters*, pp. 135-42. On Estelle's proposal, see Blotner, *Faulkner*, p. 1430, and the letter to Joan Williams [29 July 1952] quoted there. A brief excerpt from this letter is in *Selected Letters*, p. 337. Compare *The Wintering*, pp. 147-48. See also to Saxe Commins, Friday [Aug. or Sept. 1953], *Selected Letters*, pp. 352-53; and Blotner, *Faulkner*, pp. 1462-63.

22. To Saxe Commins [early Aug. 1953], and Friday [Aug. or Sept. 1953], *Selected Letters*, pp. 352-53.

23. *Lion in the Garden*, p. 72. See also to Malcolm A. Franklin, Tuesday [Oct. 1953], *Selected Letters*, pp. 354-55; and Blotner, *Faulkner*, pp. 1462-66.

24. These pieces became *The Private World of William Faulkner* (New York, 1954). See pp. 25, 138. On the writing of them, see *Faulkner-Cowley File*, pp. 103, 127, and especially 130-37.

25. These are the dates he gives on page 654 of the manuscript, but the first "synopsis" dates from the fall of 1943. See *Selected Letters*, pp. 178-80.

26. See Brooks, *Toward Yoknapatawpha*, pp. 247-48.

27. See Millgate, *Achievement*, pp. 227-28. On this scene as resembling the confrontation between Christ and the Grand Inquisitor in Dostoevsky's *The Brothers Karamazov*, see Brooks, *Toward Yoknapatawpha*, pp. 231-32, 242-47. Brooks also discusses parallels with Conrad's *The Heart of Darkness* and, surprisingly yet convincingly, with James Branch Cabell's *Jurgen*.

28. *Faulkner in the University*, p. 167. Compare *Lion in the Garden*, p. 112; and *Faulkner-Cowley File*, pp. 8-16.

29. *Faulkner at Nagano*, pp. 159-60. Compare *Faulkner-Cowley File*, pp. 8-16, especially pp. 14-16.

30. *A Fable* was published 2 August 1954. He had also finished his work on *The Faulkner Reader*, which includes a brief foreword that was new, fourteen stories, and the fourth section of *The Sound and the Fury*. It was published on 1 April 1954.

31. *Faulkner at Nagano*, p. 130. Compare *Lion in the Garden*, p. 162.

32. He gave the manuscript to her in the summer of 1950. For details, see Blotner, *Faulkner*, pp. 1327-28, 1746-47; and *Selected Letters*, pp. 438-39. Compare *The Wintering*, pp. 278-80, 292, 297.

33. See the letter to Harold Ober cited in n. 14 above; and to Mrs. Murry C. Falkner, Monday [19 Oct. 1953], *Selected Letters*, p. 355. Compare Bacall, *By Myself*, as cited in the general note to this chapter.

34. Quoted in Bacall, *By Myself*, p. 216. See *Selected Letters*, pp. 356-60.

35. See Bacall, *By Myself*, p. 216; and Blotner, *Faulkner*, pp. 1489-90.

36. Quoted in Blotner, *Faulkner*, p. 1484. This letter, which is not in *Selected Letters*, is in the William Faulkner Collections, Alderman Library, University of Virginia, Charlottesville.

37. To Saxe Commins, 4 Feb. 1954, and Friday [18 June 1954], *Selected Letters*, pp. 361-62, 365. See Blotner, *Faulkner*, pp. 1491-92.

38. *The Wintering*, p. 69. See pp. 87, 101, 131-32.

39. Ibid., pp. 329, 353-54, 248. See pp. 79, 124.

40. Ibid., pp. 229-30. See pp. 279-80, 306, 309. See also Brooks, *Toward Yoknapatawpha*, pp. 56-57; and compare *Selected Letters*, p. 338, and *The Wintering*, p. 123.

41. *The Wintering*, pp. 306-7; compare pp. 260-67.

42. Ibid., pp. 244, 329.

43. See Blotner, *Faulkner*, pp. 1492-93.

44. To Jean Stein, Monday, 10 [May 1954], and Saturday [29 May 1954], *Selected Letters*, p. 364.

45. To Saxe Commins, Friday [18 June 1954]; Muna Lee, 29 June 1954; and Saxe Commins, Friday [probably 2 or 9 July 1954], *Selected Letters*, pp. 365, 367, 368. Between 1950, when he went to Stockholm for the Nobel ceremony, and 1961, Faulkner made seven trips abroad, including four for the State Department.

46. See Blotner, *Faulkner*, pp. 1504-6; *Lion in the Garden*, pp. 267-69; and to Harold E. Howland, 15 Aug. 1954, *Selected Letters*, p. 369.

47. See to Joan Williams, Thursday [6 Nov. 1952], *Selected Letters*, p. 343. Compare *The Wintering*, pp. 120, 132, 247.

48. *Intruder in the Dust*, p. 206. Compare "Letter to a Northern Editor" and "On Fear: Deep South in Labor: Mississippi, 1956," in *Essays, Speeches & Public Letters*, pp. 86-91, 92-106.

49. To Harold E. Howland, 13 Aug. 1954; and to Else Jonsson, [19 Feb. 1955], *Selected Letters*, pp. 369, 377-78. See *Selected Letters*, pp. 369-75 and 381-82.

50. See "Sepulture South: Gaslight," *Harper's Bazaar*, 138 (Dec. 1954), 84-85, 140-41. Compare to Else Jonsson, in *Selected Letters*, pp. 381-82.

51. To Else Jonsson [19 Feb. 1955]; to Saxe Commins, Friday [probably 17 and 18 Feb. 1955]; to Else Jonsson [12 June 1955], and [20 Oct. 1955], *Selected Letters*, pp. 377-78, 376-77, 381-82, 387. For the *Sports Illustrated* pieces, the second of which is very interesting, see *Essays, Speeches & Public Letters*, pp. 48-51 and 52-61.

52. See the first and last pages of *Big Woods*.

53. See to Malcolm A. Franklin, Sunday [4 July 1943], *Selected Letters*, pp.

175-76; *Essays, Speeches & Public Letters*, pp. 215-16; and *My Brother Bill*, p. 268. Compare *Falkners of Mississippi*, pp. 190-91.

54. See *My Brother Bill*, p. 268; and to Else Jonsson [12 June 1955], *Selected Letters*, pp. 381-82. Compare the letters to Jean Stein and Bob Flautt, *Selected Letters*, pp. 388, 389-90.

55. See the letter to Else Jonsson cited in note 54 to this chapter and the several letters to Harold Howland in *Selected Letters*, pp. 380-81, 382-83, 384-85. See also *Essays, Speeches & Public Letters*, pp. 218-20; and Blotner, *Faulkner*, pp. 1542-46.

56. See Blotner, *Faulkner*, pp. 1546-66. For a record of the discussions, see *Faulkner at Nagano*. See also Gay Wilson Allen, "With Faulkner in Japan," as cited in the general note to this chapter.

57. See *Essays, Speeches & Public Letters*, pp. 222-23; and to Else Jonsson [20 Oct. 1955], *Selected Letters*, p. 387.

58. Blotner, *Faulkner*, pp. 1579-81, 1583-84, 1585-86.

59. To Saxe Commins [probably Dec. 1955 or Jan. 1956]; and to Jean Stein, Friday [13 Jan. 1956], *Selected Letters*, pp. 390, 391.

60. To Jean Stein, Saturday [28 Jan. 1956], Saturday [possibly 17 Mar. 1956], and Saturday [24 Mar. 1956], *Selected Letters*, pp. 393, 396, 397.

61. See *Essays, Speeches & Public Letters*, pp. 86-91, 92-106; to W. E. B. Dubois, 17 Apr. 1956; and to Jean Stein, [28 or 29 Nov. 1955], *Selected Letters*, pp. 397-98, 388.

62. See "Kentucky: May: Saturday," in *Essays, Speeches & Public Letters*, pp. 52-61.

63. To Jean Stein [12 Aug. 1956], and [22 Aug. 1956]; and to Saxe Commins [25 Aug. 1956] in *Selected Letters*, pp. 402, 403. For details on the pieces that went into *The Town*, see Meriwether, *Literary Career*, pp. 44-45, 80.

64. See to Robert K. Haas [received 15 Dec. 1938], *Selected Letters*, pp. 107-8; and *Faulkner in the University*, pp. 107-8.

65. To Saxe Commins [probably early June 1956], *Selected Letters*, pp. 399-400.

66. Compare this situation with Faulkner's letters to Joan Williams, Saturday 10:00 PM [1 Nov. 1952], and Thursday [6 Nov. 1952], *Selected Letters*, pp. 342, 343; and with the relation between Jeff Almoner and Amy Howard in *The Wintering*.

67. Quoted in Blotner, *Faulkner*, p. 1622.

68. See to Jean Stein, Friday [13 Jan. 1956], in *Selected Letters*, p. 391, and as quoted in Blotner, *Faulkner*, p. 1587; compare pp. 1621-31.

69. See to Floyd Stovall, 18 Oct. 1956, *Selected Letters*, p. 406; "Preface" to *Faulkner in the University*, pp. vii-ix; and Blotner, *Faulkner*, pp. 1636-40.

70. *Faulkner in the University*, pp. 103, 197-98.

71. Ibid., pp. 84, 61, 19-20, 51-52, 65. Compare *Lion in the Garden*, pp. 238-44.

72. The piece from the *Times* is quoted in Robert Penn Warren's introduction to *Faulkner: A Collection of Critical Essays* (Englewood Cliffs, N. J., 1966), p. 9. Fadiman's review appeared in the *New Yorker*, 12 (31 Oct. 1936), 62-64. Regarding Fadiman and *A Fable*, see Blotner, *Faulkner*, pp. 1224-25. Fadiman also overpraised *The Reivers*.

73. On Massey, see him to Adrian H. Goldstone, 26 Nov., 12 Aug., 13 Nov., and 8 Dec. 1959, in the Humanities Research Center, University of Texas, Austin. See also Blotner, *Faulkner*, pp. 1641, 1679, 1699, 1723-24, 1772-73, 1832-33. See pp. 1736-37 on Massey's organizing an important exhibition of Faulkner's work: "William Faulkner: Man Working: 1919-1959." On the hunt clubs of Albemarle County, see Blotner, *Faulkner*, pp. 1641-42, 1703-8, 1722-25, 1748-51, 1770-71,

1898, 1816, 1822–25. Faulkner later became a member of the Farmington Hunt Club.

74. To Jean Stein [possibly mid-Nov. 1954], *Selected Letters*, p. 372.

75. See Blotner, *Faulkner*, pp. 1644–54; and *Faulkner in the University*, pp. 107–8, 193.

76. To Else Jonsson [13 Dec. 1956], *Selected Letters*, p. 407.

77. To Floyd Stovall, 9 Sept. 1957, *Selected Letters*, pp. 411–12; and Blotner, *Faulkner*, pp. 1682–83.

78. To Harold Ober [Aug. 1958]; and to Donald S. Klopfer, [mid-January 1959], *Selected Letters*, pp. 415, 419.

79. For the several letters covering the extended revision process, see Faulkner to Albert Erskine [probably 10 Feb. 1959], [Mar. 1959], 7 Apr. 1959, [mid-Apr. 1959], Wednesday [probably 7 May 1959], and Tuesday [21 July 1959], in *Selected Letters*, pp. 423–24, 425–26, 427, 429, 429–30, 432.

80. Compare *Faulkner in the University*, p. 65; as quoted in Wilde and Borsten, *A Loving Gentleman*, p. 317; and "An Introduction to *The Sound and the Fury*" [1973].

81. See *Light in August*, p. 93, and *The Mansion*, pp. 82, 271, 435–36. Faulkner used some of the phrases with which he ends *The Mansion* off and on for nearly forty years. See *Early Prose and Poetry*, p. 88; poem III in *A Green Bough*; and *The Hamlet*, p. 186. For a fine discussion see Richard P. Adams, *Faulkner: Myth and Motion* (Princeton, N.J., 1968), p. 29.

82. Faulkner's grandson was born on 2 February 1958. See Blotner, *Faulkner*, pp. 1710, 1767–68, on the naming of the child and Faulkner's fondness for him. On Faulkner's nostalgia, see p. 1709 and Cullen, *Old Times*, pp. 46–47.

83. To Ivan von Auw, Jr., 14 Feb. 1961, *Selected Letters*, p. 451.

84. Elliott Chaze, "Visit to a Two-Finger Typist," *Life*, 51 (14 July 1961), pp. 11–12. See *Selected Letters*, pp. 426–27, 438–39.

85. To Joan Williams, Friday [6 Nov. 1959], *Selected Letters*, pp. 438–39. See David Yalden-Thomson, who rode with Faulkner and was obviously perceptive, as quoted in Blotner, *Faulkner*, pp. 1748–49.

86. To Muna Lee, Wednesday [possibly 8 Mar. 1961], *Selected Letters*, p. 452.

87. Quoted in Blotner, *Faulkner*, p. 1775. Jim was the nephew to whom Faulkner gave his R.A.F. pip. Regarding the death of Miss Maud, see p. 1762.

88. "Albert Camus," *Essays, Speeches & Public Letters*, pp. 113–14.

89. To Robert K. Haas, Friday [3 May 1940], *Selected Letters*, pp. 122–24.

90. To Albert Erskine, [Aug. 1961], Monday [28 Aug. 1961], Tuesday [19 Sept. 1961], in *Selected Letters*, pp. 455, 455–56, 456.

91. *Faulkner in the University*, p. 19. Compare Yeats's statement that it is of our quarrel with ourselves that we make poetry and of our quarrel with others that we make rhetoric.

92. *Lion in the Garden*, p. 253; and *Faulkner in the University*, pp. 277, 253.

93. Edwin Howard, "Foote-note on Faulkner," *Delta Review*, 2 (July-Aug. 1965), 37.

94. See chapter 5, notes 44, 45, 46.

95. See Faulkner to Malcolm Cowley, Friday [11 Feb. 1949], *Faulkner-Cowley File*, pp. 125–26.

96. To Bennett Cerf, Friday [3 Nov. 1961]; and to James M. Faulkner, Friday [probably May or June 1961], *Selected Letters*, pp. 458, 454. Compare to Joan Williams, Friday 10:00 PM [2 Jan. 1953], *Selected Letters*, p. 344: "The work, the mss. [*A Fable*] is going again. Not as it should, in a fine ecstatic rush like the orgasm we

spoke of at Hal's [Harrison Smith's] that night. This is done by simple will power."

97. See Blotner, *Faulkner*, pp. 1802-10; and to Linton Massey, Friday [29 June 1962], *Selected Letters*, pp. 461-62.

98. See Blotner, *Faulkner*, pp. 1824, 1827, 1812, and compare pp. 1829-30. See also, *Faulkner-Cowley File*, pp. 148-50.

99. Quoted in Blotner, *Faulkner*, pp. 1828, 1829; see pp. 1834-38, especially p. 1835.

100. In *Essays, Speeches & Public Letters*, pp. 3-10.

101. James B. Meriwether, "Faulkner's Essays on Anderson," in G. H. Wolfe, ed., *Faulkner: Fifty Years After "The Marble Faun"* (University, Ala., 1976), pp. 159-81, especially pp. 167-69. "Carcassonne" in *These 13*, pp. 352-58. See also Brooks, *Yoknapatawpha Country*, 62-64.

102. See "An Introduction to *The Sound and the Fury*" [1973], pp. 410-15.

103. To Secretary, American Academy, 12 June 1950, *Faulkner-Cowley File*, p. 141.

Index